'As discursive and innocent as Chatwin was restrained and omniscient, Green retraces Darwin's route, supposedly on horseback, although he is often horseless. Green is a hopeless hero, and an endearing one, full of heart. He is also a perceptive guide' *Daily Telegraph*

'There is tremendous honesty in Green's style . . . [He] skilfully splices interesting gobbets of Darwinian thought into his travelogue and comments intelligently on contemporary "selfish gene" arguments in evolutionary theory' *Independent*

'Green is an intelligent and observant traveller'
Sunday Times

'Green . . . provides poetic insights, mulls over cultural and sociological issues and vividly captures the people – policemen, peasants, horse traders, army conscripts, drunks – he meets. The resulting book is good-humoured and thoughtful, its pace echoing the manner of the journey' *Traveller Magazine*

'Intriguing . . . part travelogue, partly historical quest, part evolutionary musing' *Guardian*

'Green's account of the people he met on the way is a delight . . . Green's [book] has many charms' *Nature*

'An epic journey and an astonishing tale' W. G. Sebald

Toby Green was born on 12 February 1974, 165 years to the day after the birth of Charles Darwin. He has travelled in thirty countries, working as a teacher in Chile and as a charity fundraiser in Southern Africa. He graduated from Cambridge in 1996 with a first in Philosophy, and was awarded a Heineken Export Travel Bursary to retrace Darwin's route in South America on horseback. He works as a literary agent in London and is travelling extensively in West Africa, researching his next book. *Saddled with Darwin* was nominated for the *Guardian* First Book Award in 1999.

Saddled with Darwin

A Journey through South America on Horseback

TOBY GREEN

PHŒNIX

A PHOENIX PAPERBACK

First published in Great Britain
by Weidenfeld & Nicolson in 1999
This paperback edition published in 2000
by Phoenix,
an imprint of Orion Books Ltd,
Orion House, 5 Upper St Martin's Lane,
London WC2H 9EA

A CIP catalogue record for this book
is available from the British Library.

ISBN: 0 75381 015 8

Printed and bound in Great Britain by
The Guernsey Press Co. Ltd, Guernsey, C.I.

'It is impossible to bear too strong testimony to the kindness, with which travellers are received in almost every part of South America.'

Charles Darwin

'Essential to an experience is that it cannot be exhausted in what can be said of it or grasped as its meaning.'

Hans-Georg Gadamer

AUTHOR'S NOTE

Since this is a non-academic book, I have decided not to mar the narrative thread with the hundred-plus footnotes which would have been necessary to cite all the sources for the quotes from Charles Darwin. Almost all of these come from *The Voyage of the Beagle* and Darwin's letters – references to the appropriate books can be found in the bibliography. Those sources which are given footnotes refer to works which are either in copyright or comparatively obscure.

CONTENTS

ILLUSTRATIONS

Between pages 178 & 179

[1] Down House, Downe, Kent, UK/Bridgeman Art Library, London/New York
[2] British Library, London, UK/Bridgeman Art Library, London/New York

PREFACE

This book tells the stories of three South American journeys. One began as a scientific study and ended in the most revolutionary theory of our times; neither of the others would have been made without it.

The first journey was an adventure undertaken on the threshold of the Victorian age. At the end of 1831, Charles Darwin set off aboard the brig* *Beagle*, an eager young naturalist. He had just finished his divinity studies at Cambridge, and this was the opportunity of a lifetime: an extended period in which to study natural history. The journey took five years, most of which were spent in South America. Although voyaging extensively by boat, he also travelled long distances by horse whenever pursuing collecting expeditions in the interior. These land journeys furnished Darwin with the great wealth of material which he later used to develop his theory of evolution by natural selection – material which today can help us to reconstruct his extraordinary journey.

Darwin could not have made these countless observations on geology and speciation from a vehicle. The discoveries were possible because he took time, travelling slowly whenever he ventured inland. Journeying by horse, he became a part of the areas which he travelled through, and so came to understand them with an acuity that even now seems incredible. These excursions were more than a collection of disparate ventures: they were travels with a purpose. In most cases there was some scientific rationale behind his route, as he attempted to develop a definitive understanding of the forces which shaped the land and organisms that he found.

Darwin's ideas had already been sharpened by his time at Cambridge. Whilst studying there he had met many leading scientific intellectuals and had become the protégé of John Henslow, the Professor of Botany. Nonetheless, at the outset of his journey he had no inklings of the revelations which were to shake the moral and scientific foundations of the world. At Edinburgh, under the wing of the Lamarckian Robert

* This being a square-rigged ship with two masts.

Grant, Darwin had made his first scientific discovery, relating to the fertilization 'dances' of seaweed and other simple organisms. A collector of animal life from a young age, he had continued his scientific interest with serious collecting at Cambridge, becoming fascinated by beetles. But the idea of natural selection supplanting divine creation did not occur to him until long afterwards, and at this early stage in his career Darwin saw himself as fulfilling the traditional role that nineteenth-century naturalists ascribed to themselves: describing and cataloguing the many creations of God.

In fact, until the moment when the opportunity arose to sail with the *Beagle*, Darwin envisaged a religious life for himself. His elder brother Erasmus mocked his dreams of a staid married life in a country vicarage, but Darwin aspired to nothing more. Chided for being a slow learner at Shrewsbury School, he had dropped out of his medical studies at Edinburgh, and so in the conservative climate of the emerging capitalist classes the Church was almost the only field open to him. Until, that is, he set sail for South America, beginning the journey which would change the world.

The second journey grew out of my attempt to piece together Darwin's travels in my imagination. In 1996, 165 years after Darwin set sail from Plymouth, I decided to attempt a horseback journey of several thousand kilometres, retracing his steps in South America. Darwin's journey had fascinated me since my return to Britain after working as an English teacher in Chile. He had spent over a year in that country which I now loved, plying between Tierra del Fuego and the northern deserts, and after reading *The Voyage of the Beagle* I had the idea of following him through South America, travelling as far as possible in the way in which he himself had travelled.

The main drawback was that I could not ride a horse. I tried to forget that the first time I had sat on a horse, aged five, I had been thrown unceremoniously onto a concrete yard – and that on one of the other two occasions my horse had bolted for kilometres along a beach. It was not easy, but through constant self-delusion I convinced myself that I would find riding a horse even easier than falling off.

All I needed was money to realize my dream. On seeing an advertisement for a travel bursary funded by Heineken Export, I posted off my application. Out of the blue, three months later, I was invited to an interview. I rehearsed the rationale behind the journey, and the reasons why it would be likely to succeed: the regions were safe, I did at least speak Spanish, and it was apt to attempt this journey at the end of a century whose development had so much been influenced by Darwin's theory. Ten days later I found myself with a substantial cheque, and the prospect of unlimited saddle-sores.

In undertaking to follow Darwin I hoped to uncover the third journey recounted in this book, that made by South America since the 1830s. Very few people have documented a journey as fully as Darwin did his own. His diary, letters and notebooks are testament to the South America that he found – open invitations to assess the progress of the modern world. Travelling on horseback, like Darwin, I wanted to make a comparison that would not have been possible travelling by bus or car. In this way I hoped that my journey might make some sense of how Darwin's ideas have affected the world. For there is no doubt that his theory of evolution has been one of the most important forces in shaping the twentieth century – affecting in turn those places in which he found inspiration.

Of course, I had my own ideas as to what I would find. But I also knew, from my encyclopaedic but useless knowledge of horse racing, that all predictions regarding this journey were pointless. For if you had put me in front of any horse race I could have suggested many reasons for backing the wrong animal. Similarly, since my knowledge of horses was limited to the betting shop, I could have given you any number of reasons why the journey should have gone wrong. I would be travelling with my girlfriend, Emily, even though neither of us could ride. This journey was the definition of lunacy, and disaster was the short-priced favourite. But I was unreasonably optimistic, because my expensive apprenticeship poring over the form book had taught me that, when it comes to horses, confident predictions generally turn out to be inaccurate.

PART ONE

Urban Latin America: Rio and Montevideo

I

Delight is a weak term to express the feelings of a naturalist who for the first time has wandered by himself in a Brazilian forest ... such a day brings a deeper pleasure than he can ever hope to experience again.

Charles Darwin on the jungles near Rio

We arrived in Rio de Janeiro one September morning, and caught a taxi to Copacabana. The city emerged pastily through the aura of golden dawn sunlight, while the mountains, masked by jungle, beamed in the brilliant light. They fell to earth vertiginously, collapsing in a welter of preposterous shapes; dying abruptly when they met the grey city.

Rio intruded everywhere. In the great bay were tankers and cranes and the lumbering shadows cast by containers being swung out to sea. Across the bay was a brood of skyscrapers, the city of Niterôi. Masses of dirty and chaotic shacks swarmed up hills, uniform and determined as soldier ants: these were the *favelas*. The *favelas* are overseers of Rio's skyscrapers, the glass-fronted office blocks which bang their heads against a yellow ceiling of smog. The taxi driver took us along a flyover that snaked over the city centre, and then careered through two tunnels bored through the mountains in the middle of the city.

There seemed to be only one rule on the flyover, and that was to overtake on the inside at double the legal speed. In the land of Piquet and Senna, they all thought this was an arcade game. Someone needed to tell them, I decided, that this wasn't virtual reality. Every motorized conveyance that you can imagine was vying for its own two square centimetres of inside lane with breathtaking nerve. There was a plethora of Beetles, mopeds, police cars, an old truck carrying a listing load of watermelons; and so on, and worse as well. I soon realized that we were going to be far safer following Darwin's route on a horse than we ever would have been in a car.

We emerged on the far side of the tunnel into the great sweep of Botafogo Bay. Darwin spent over two months in Rio, hiring a cottage in the 'village' of Botafogo as his base. His initial guide was the *Beagle*'s first artist, Augustus Earle, who had visited Rio before. One of Earle's sketches is of the bay, then a tranquil lagoon with a backdrop of untouched jungle and no one in sight. As Darwin said, 'Every one has heard of the beauty of the scenery near Botafogo.'

In 1832 Botafogo was a village, six kilometres from Rio itself. There is no discernible difference between the two any more. Now, in the early morning mist, there was a semblance of order. A portly woman ran her dog along the promenade beside the lagoon. The traffic had cleared a little from the mayhem on the flyover, but my eyes and ears still sensed nothing but pervasive irritants. This was a modern city, and modern cities struggle to please as much as Darwin's delightful forests. We were both exhausted and jetlagged, wondering when we were going to be robbed, since we'd been told that this was virtually guaranteed, and worrying about how, precisely, we were going to ride unimaginable distances on horseback.

The taxi driver dropped us at our hotel, and we went in to register. Recognizing our ghostly faces with the eye of a practised con-man, the receptionist claimed that there was no record of our reservation and asked for details of my credit card, to 'check up'. I was feeling worse than death, and almost fell for it. He mysteriously disappeared as I caught on to his trick, our room mysteriously materialized, and we collapsed.

Charles Darwin's journey was made on board the *Beagle*, a brig belonging to the English navy. Typically, it was only through the nepotism of the English aristocracy that the boat travelled to South America at all. Its captain, Robert FitzRoy, was himself only four years older than Darwin. He had taken the helm following the suicide of Captain Pringle Stokes near Port Famine, on the Magellan Straits, in 1828. On its first voyage in the Americas, the *Beagle* had been commissioned to survey the southern coasts of South America, from the estuary of the River Plate, around Cape Horn and north to the island of Chiloé. This time, FitzRoy was given the task of completing the survey, before studying as much of the Pacific coast as possible.

Yet FitzRoy had needed the intervention of his uncle in the Admiralty, the Duke of Grafton, to win support for a second voyage of the

Beagle. At the time, Britain was vying with other European powers and the newly created American republics for control of trading routes, and a detailed survey of the region's geography would help secure this objective. One of the greatest supporters of this second expedition was the Admiralty's hydrographer, Francis Beaufort. This amounted to Beaufort's biggest project thus far, and he and FitzRoy worked closely together in preparing the voyage.

Beaufort was instrumental in Darwin's journey. He was asked by FitzRoy to find him a 'suitable' gentleman companion with an interest in natural history for the long journey, since the captain was worried that he might be driven to the edge without any company from a man broadly of his type. Perhaps FitzRoy had an inkling that the journey would last far longer than the two years originally anticipated. Or perhaps he was just worried that the loneliness would drive him to insanity, something to which his family was prone. Beaufort asked around among his friends at Cambridge for someone who might be suitable.

He picked the brains of George Peacock, a Fellow of Trinity College and a well-known lecturer in mathematics. At first, Peacock offered the post to Leonard Jenyns, a naturalist and local curate at Bottisham, but Jenyns did not think it right to desert his parishioners, a decision that he was to rue for the rest of his life. Then Peacock asked John Henslow. Henslow would have loved to have gone, but he was married and his wife had recently given birth. And so he, in turn, thought of Darwin.

Darwin and Henslow had only recently cemented their growing friendship. Darwin had taken to dining with the Henslow family, and through his mentor had been introduced to many important scientists. In the past few months, Darwin had developed an obsession with visiting Tenerife, mainly due to reading the travelogue of Alexander von Humboldt, the great scientist and naturalist. He had even begun to learn some Spanish, yearning as he did to travel.

There was nothing to hold him back. An improbable series of coincidences had presented him with his future career. He received the offer in a letter from Henslow on 29 August 1831, on his return from a geological expedition to Wales with Adam Sedgwick. Completely unannounced, Henslow informed Darwin of the *Beagle*'s impending voyage, and of FitzRoy's desire for a gentleman companion.

'I immediately said I would go,' Darwin wrote in his diary. He went to London on 5 September to meet FitzRoy, and although FitzRoy had some initial doubts the two men were quickly on good terms. FitzRoy's reservations appear to have revolved around the fact that he had an interest in phrenology, and Darwin's face – particularly his nose – made him doubt that he was up to the rigours of the voyage. However, during their conversations the two men warmed quickly to each other, and the matter was decided. After three months of preparations and anxious waiting, they sailed from Plymouth on 27 December 1831.

Although their first landfall in Brazil was at Salvador da Bahía in the north, an infection confined Darwin to his hammock for eight days, and he saw little there. He was forced largely to imagine for himself the multicoloured delights of the jungle and the elaborate tangle of its thick canopy, waiting for the time when it could become his own laboratory. We decided to bypass Salvador, since it was only on reaching Rio that Darwin began serious exploration. It was in Rio that he quickly fell in love with the profuse wonders of the wildlife gabbling from above the seams of one of South America's great cities. Later in his journey, stuck in the bleak wildernesses of Patagonia and Tierra del Fuego, he dreamt wistfully of Rio's thick tropical heat and of the jungle in which he could collect more specimens in a week than he might find in Britain in a year.

All bar one of Darwin's rides were in the southern cone countries of Uruguay, Argentina and Chile, and since much of southern Brazil is enveloped by sprawling cities – making horseback travel dangerously impractical – we decided to visit Darwin's haunts in Rio and Botafogo before beginning the journey proper in Uruguay. Ever since I can remember, I had always wanted to visit Rio, dreaming of the jungle rising into the sky, clearing my mind with its exuberance, illuminated by the sharp light of cloudless days and Copacabana beach washed by the endlessly recurring beauty of the sky and the ocean; the natural beauty punctured by the annual chaos of samba schools and Carnival.

With an improbability which was only to be expected, the hotel with the crooked receptionist was not only cheap but just a block from Copacabana beach. Even though we were exhausted by the flight, as soon as we had caught a few hours' sleep we went to the promenade, hurrying to the dream of the sands. My mind buzzed with stories that I'd heard: kids ripping my shirt pocket off me and sprinting off with its contents, transvestites grabbing my balls with one hand and pick-pocketing me with the other, beach volleyball on some of the best sand on earth. We reached the promenade and crossed over to the beach, our feet already hot from the scorching tarmac. It was only now that it quickly became apparent that it was hot to us, but to no one else – September is still winter in southern Brazil, the low season, and hardly anyone was here.

Faraway from my dream we came across a few deserted beach bars, an ageing jogger plodding along the waterfront, and a handful of skate-boarders and rollerbladers trundling around. At the end of the beach, the sugarloaf mountain reared up like a monument into the Atlantic spray, shielded by the distance and the shimmering haze. Then the coast swung into another bay, sweeping past the vague silhouettes of the disembodied skyscrapers, past the city, away to the heat of the north. We walked along for several minutes, and I kept expecting a sudden raid by a sneak thief, or a cavalcade of tourists to descend and join us on the beach. I kept expecting my dream to emerge playfully from my head and dance for me on the sand of Copacabana, but it would not co-operate, and nothing happened in the dreariness of our wintry experience.

Honestly, we weren't even robbed.

On our third day in Rio it began to rain with a remorselessness that I had never seen before. The clouds unleashed two days of cold rain into the chilly air, two days of miserable rain pounding with relentless fury, like an ocean frothing to howling gales. The water tumbled in torrents from the flyovers, spawning thundering waterfalls which ripped up the tarmac below and made the potholes infinitely worse than they had been before. To my nervous imagination, this was a dangerous warning from the incipient journey.

Since Copacabana had refused to play along with my impossible dreams, I could only lose myself in new ones. Emily and I rushed about Rio, trying and failing to feel energetic. We tried to go to the summit of the Corcovado, Rio's great mountain crowned with the famous statue of Christ with his open arms, welcoming migrants and sailors and those cursed by travelling disease to a *cidade maravilhosa* – but when we arrived, the mountain was covered in cloud and we realized that we would see nothing. We wavered at the bottom of the mists, as the rain teemed down.

'*Senhor, Senhora*,' cried a tout when he saw us loitering there. 'A T-shirt? Pele? Garrincha? Bebeto? Romario?'

I looked around, and gathered that we were the only tourists stupid enough to be considering ascending Corcovado in the mist.

'*Senhor.* Romario – *o melhor do Brasil.*'

When he said Romario, it sounded like 'Homahio'. This confused my scatter-tongue attitude to Portuguese, which was that I would speak Spanish in what I imagined sounded like a Portuguese accent. I called it *Portuñol*, although most people would have been happier to know it as gobbledegook.

'Let's go and have something to drink,' Emily suggested.

We fled the football shirts to the nearest café, where we decided to try a cup of *mate*. *Mate* is a bitter green herbal tea found across the southern half of South America. In the rural heartland of Brazil, Uruguay and Argentina, the country people live by its law. A wooden gourd is half filled by the herbs, then infused with boiling water and passed round the group of those present. Each person drinks the tea through a steel pipe, and drains the gourd before passing it back to be filled with water again. The boiling water is replenished for half an hour or more, each time puffing up the herbs so that they froth and swell with the water like a river in spate. And as the gourd traverses the circle of hands and mouths, stories and jokes and arguments ebb and flow along with it, dying only when the bitterness of the tea is washed out by the repeated passage of the boiling water and the herbs are spent and have lost their taste for good, consumed and consigned to uselessness.

Mate seemed like a good idea, a gentle foretaste of the way of life which we would soon be leading. I could see it on the menu, number nine.

'Two cups of *mate*, please.'

'What?'

'*Mate*.'

'What?'

There was clearly something the matter with his hearing – unless it was my *Portuñol*.

'Look,' I said, pointing at the menu. '*Numero novo.*'

'Ah,' he said, all smiles. '*Mazhhhhh.*'

He went off to get the *mazhhhhh*, and we turned to look out of the window, instinctively trying to avoid the hilarity which we had caused.

'*Senhor, senhora,*' our footballing friend cried out to us. 'Look!'

He was staring at us again, grinning, with an axe sticking out of his head. Now he turned around, delightedly showing off the toy, complete with appalling fake blood. We weren't about to start picking up souvenirs when we already had far too much baggage for a horseback journey, and after our *mazhhhhh* we caught a bus and trundled back to Copacabana. Most people looked miserable as we stared at them through misted-up bus windows on our way through the city, because nothing could possibly make Cariocas – inhabitants of Rio – more gloomy than cold wet weather. Faces glowered, mirrors to the skies, picked out by our headlights against the shining signs advertising McDonald's, C & A and Pizza Good-Good.

We spent several more days in Rio, but the clouds and the sense of foreboding we both felt stubbornly refused to lift. As we travelled about the city, it was easily apparent that Brazil was once one of the capitals of the African slave trade. We both noticed how all the poorest and most destitute people we saw in Rio were descendants of the slaves. This could have been the American South or South Africa, judging by the division of labour and wealth. All the rubbish collectors were black, as were the municipal park cleaners, the street cleaners, the beggar fanning a wavering fire of cardboard beneath a flyover, and the old man with his head covered in plastic and only one leg, sleeping awkwardly on the pavement one block from Copacabana beach – ignored by the sunglasses and strutting suits.

When the *Beagle* visited Brazil, slavery was a key issue in the country, and nearly caused a severe rupture between Darwin and FitzRoy. As is only natural for two strangers sharing very confined quarters the men often found themselves struggling to overcome tensions, and the first flashpoint flared over the incidence of slavery in Salvador. On arriving there, Darwin was disgusted to see that the Brazilians were still legally importing slaves from Africa. His grandfathers had taken a strong abolitionist stance in Britain, and the Brazilian slave trade – which was dismantled only in 1858 – enraged him. FitzRoy, however, had willingly accepted the word of a landowner, who reported that he had asked his slaves if they wished to be free, and they had replied that they did not. Darwin asked the captain – probably with more than a hint of superciliousness – if he thought that the slaves' answer should be taken at face value, since it had obviously been given to appease their master. At this, FitzRoy tore out of the cabin in disgust at his word being doubted. The storm cleared, but a cloud was left over their friendship.

When he reached Rio, Darwin embarked on a fifteen-day journey to a coffee plantation owned by an Irishman called Patrick Lennon. Travelling by horse, they stayed at local inns, where they ate scantily, lived in filth – so much so that Darwin did not undress for the first five days – and were treated like dirt: 'The hosts are most ungracious and disagreeable in their manners ... I am sure no cottage or hovel in England could be found in a state so utterly destitute of every comfort.' When they hinted to the innkeepers that they would like to eat soon, the reply was, invariably, 'It will be ready when it is ready.'

But it was witnessing the brutal treatment of slaves which really revolted Darwin on this journey, far more than his own state of personal hygiene. On the way to Lennon's estate they passed a granite cliff from which an old African woman had committed suicide rather than be forced into slavery. Darwin noted that this was seen as a slave's brutal obstinacy, rather than a nobler love of freedom. Then Lennon, whom Darwin liked at first, behaved like a despot when he reached his plantation, threatening out of sheer callousness to take all the female and child slaves away from their men and sell them at Rio's slave market. And on the return journey, a slave shied away from Darwin when the Englishman made an affable gesture towards the man with his hand, certain that he would be struck.

Darwin needed no further evidence of the terror in which the slaves lived, and this relationship between master and slave made a lasting impression. A year after leaving Rio, he wrote to his sister Catherine: 'I was told before leaving England, that after living in slave countries, all my opinions would be altered; the only alteration I am aware of is forming a much higher estimate of the negro character. It is impossible to see a negro and not feel kindly towards him; such cheerful, open, honest expressions.' Race is still a defining feature of Brazil, and the mixture is unique. It is not unknown for a family to have several children, all of different colours. But as we drove through the city, and saw the evidence of racial discrimination in the work still done today, it was difficult not to observe the legacy of the slave trade which so disgusted Darwin. A month after we left Rio, a Uruguayan businessman told us about a time he had visited the north of Brazil:

'I had to go to Maceío state. A friend invited me to visit a sugar plantation there, and I couldn't believe what I saw. The people were slaves – all black, of course, and treated like animals. At dawn, they herded them into the backs of trucks and took them to the plantations. They put one person at the start of each line of canes, with a machete, and they had to cut the canes all day. At the end of their line of canes was a bag with a thick slice of bread, and that was lunch. If they cheated or worked slowly, they were whipped and beaten. After lunch, they had to work back the other way to the beginning of the line. Then they were driven back to the compound at dusk. They all lived under one roof with no toilet, no bathroom – like pigs.'

Tensions like this racial issue trickled through to us, and made us feel edgy. Emily and I had never travelled together, not even in England – far less in South America, with the prospect of a horseback journey of several thousand kilometres in front of us. However much we had trained ourselves for the difficulties which we were bound to face, it was only once we were here that we knew what the experience would be like. We were probably slightly paranoid, but we felt tension everywhere. Our thoughts span round the dangers and possibilities that might lie ahead: accidents, assaults, natural disasters. Darwin had observed all of these, and there was no reason why we should not do so as well. It rained on, and on, and the clouds never parted and the crowds never came to the beach. Instead, people told us how unseasonable the weather was, as if this was some sort of consolation.

'You should have been here in August – we were all on the beach then.'

The obscene extremes of wealth and the feeling that we had an impossible journey in front of us made us retreat from the insistent city beyond the hotel. From the cramped room on the tenth floor of our grey hotel block the idea of the journey seemed fantastic. We found comfort in cable television and takeaways, living as far as possible from the bare realities into which we were soon to be thrown. Neither of us could imagine what travelling on horseback would be like:

'I think it'll be really relaxing,' Emily said, trying to be optimistic. 'As soon as we know what we're doing, we'll find it quite easy.'

'Or easi-*er*,' I said. 'Once we've got used to our horses...'

'That's the most important thing. We have to get horses whom we really trust and get to know well.'

'That can't be very difficult. There must be so many horses in Uruguay. Everyone knows that South America is full of horses.'

The rain continued to pour, and we decided we had to leave Rio before our courage vanished completely. We booked a bus ticket towards Montevideo, and then, on our last day in Rio, we went to the Botanical Gardens. Darwin had loved this quiet retreat from the city, and the gardens were as peaceful as a cemetery after the cacophony beyond them. Birds chirruped their orchestra through the unexpected silence, and squirrels twitched like acrobats along branches high above us, in the huge trees which dispersed into cascades of lianas. We passed a lagoon draped in lilies and shielded by palms, and then came to a small waterfall trickling down through the forest. Next to the waterfall, a model was being filmed for a TV commercial.

We walked past the shoot, into the slight air of dilapidation that seeped through the gardens. Felled trees sprawled unattended over the lawns amid other signs of decay: large weeds, dried-out palm fronds left haphazardly over the pathways, crumbling stonework gone green with moss. The air of entropy and history made the passage of time senseless here. You could imagine Darwin pottering through this whispering haven of a million shades of green, turning over logs in his search for beetles and snakes, staring at the minutiae of the natural world. Perhaps he was still there in a lost corner of the gardens, dancing with the ghosts of history.

We took a bus from Rio to Montevideo, and met Mac Herrera. Mac was an old friend of Emily's uncle, and had offered to help us begin the journey, unaware of what he was letting himself in for. He lived in an attractive apartment fifty metres from the estuary of the River Plate, and invited us round as soon as we arrived in the city.

We were met by Lucia, his wife.

'Welcome,' she cried, flashing her wide eyes at us both. 'So you are the crazy ones!'

Mac soon appeared, grinning impishly at us. His grandfather had been Scottish, and with Mac's shaggy white beard and rubicund face this was easy to believe. His eyes shone whenever he looked at you.

'You know,' he said, 'a lot of people will suggest different ideas to you, but at the end of the day *you* must decide. It's your arses in the saddle!'

Immensely pleased with this idiom, he chuckled at the thought of the agonies in store for us.

He suggested using a relay of horses from farm to farm, with the help of the Uruguayan horsebreeders, and changing horses at the border with Argentina. But we both wanted to keep the same horses if we could.

'It'll be a problem to cross the border with Argentina,' he said. 'The horses will need sanitary certificates, and those are hellish to get hold of.'

But I didn't believe that this could be as complicated as he said. We decided to buy our horses. Each *Criollo* (the native pampas horse) would cost 500 dollars and, Mac told us, would easily cover thirty kilometres in a day.

'What we have to do now,' he said, 'is meet the breeders.'

So that afternoon we met Mac at the Prado.

The Prado is Uruguay's annual agricultural fair, comprising a warren of barns and corrals on the fringes of Montevideo. There were sheds stuffed full of sheep, cows, pigs, cockerels, goats, rabbits and horses. They had been trained up for months for this beauty contest. The pigs were by far the cleanest I had ever seen, and proved the error in the Uruguayan saying that 'a clean pig is never a fat one' by being absolutely enormous. The cows – Friesians, Aberdeen Angus and Hereford – looked as though they had not seen a field since birth. The rabbits were inexplicably all albinos, almost exclusively several times the size of any rabbit that I had come across before.

However, there is not much money in agriculture any more, and so the fair was also squeezed full of various trade missions from around the world. Britain had sent tea and whisky, America chocolate and computers. Most of the families seemed more interested in Johnnie Walker and Microsoft than in the assorted livestock. They walked through the park, eating candyfloss or sweet pastries, riveted by global technology brought before their eyes, before turning to the animal sheds and venturing into the lingering smells of excrement and rotting straw.

Tucked away, as far from the visitors as possible, were the *gauchos* – the country people. This was the only time in the year that they came to the city, and they had come dressed in their smartest get-up: baggy *bombachas* (riding trousers) immaculately pressed and barely ever used, tucked into leather boots laced up to the knee, the boots gleaming even under the gloomy skies; silver belts up to thirty centimetres wide, inlaid with gems and antique silver coins and decorated with intricate etchings, glittering like a pirate's chest, fastened the *bombachas* tight; and silver knives, stretching extravagantly from handle to point were slotted into the belts. They wore neckerchiefs and black felt hats. They spent their time quietly, sipping *mate* with one another, occasionally cracking jokes before plunging into melancholic silence once again. They shared their melancholy with the horses which they looked after, the *Criollos* and the Arab breeds, their friends from the wild country.

It was raining. Mac was waiting for us outside the office of the *Criollo* breeders, splashing about happily in yellow wellington boots and a sou'wester.

'This is the first proper rain we've had in months,' he explained. 'We've had a real drought this winter.'

We went and had coffee with the breeders' committee. We met their president, the secretary, the president-in-waiting, an Argentine breeder who happened to be there and a journalist. They were all convinced that we were mad.

'I am Scottish,' the secretary, 'Willy' Lockhart, said proudly.

'Well. We're not quite sure where he's from,' laughed Mac. 'There's a bit of Irish in there too.'

The president, Esteban Uriarte, was a swarthy man who looked uncomfortable in his suit. He also looked as though he could think of several cocktail parties which would be more entertaining than succouring our madness.

'Well,' said Uriarte, 'we called this meeting so that we could hear your plans, and tell you in turn what we can offer. I mean, why do you want to do this?'

I tried to explain. I said that I was fascinated by Darwin's journey, that I wanted to see what had changed with the years, and that horses were the best way since they were what Darwin himself had largely used.

'But, wouldn't a car be easier?'

People said this every day. It was obvious that none of them would have been seen dead riding these distances, but they tried to help nonetheless. They quickly delved into complex discussions about quarantine regulations, who could sell us the horses, how many we needed, and so on.

'You need four horses,' Uriarte told us.

'I thought we'd use three.'

'No,' said Mac, 'they're all saying that you must have four.'

'The main problem,' said Lockhart, 'is where to find them. Good *Criollos* aren't common, and people don't want to sell them if they have them.'

They plunged into the logistical problems once again, and Uriarte began to look increasingly annoyed.

'But,' he said, turning to me, exasperated, 'how the devil did it occur to you to do this journey by *horse*?'

The journalist was busy making notes and ringing up her producer. Suddenly things seemed clearer, and they all agreed that they could begin to look for the horses. People began to talk at cross-purposes.

'Did you do any training before you came?'

'I worked a little at the Hyde Park riding stables.'

This caused immense hilarity, since horses in Hyde Park and Uruguay are about as similar to one another as tabbies to the pumas which used to patrol Uruguay's plains.

They laughed gleefully, like the puma who knows that nothing can prevent its jaws from swinging shut.

Darwin first saw Montevideo in upheaval. From Rio, the *Beagle* sailed south along the coast of Brazil to harbour at Buenos Aires. However, as they arrived they were greeted by a cannon shot fired from a distinctly unfriendly guard ship. It was a blank, fired in order to enforce quarantine regulations in place against cholera, but FitzRoy was furious none-theless, and ordered the ship to cross back over the River Plate. They were in Montevideo by nightfall.

Here they met with the chief of police, who asked for their help in quelling an insurrection. A group of soldiers were on the verge of rioting and looting. They had seized the central fort, which held the city's ammunition dump, and had started to man cannons in the street. FitzRoy despatched fifty-two men armed with pistols and cutlasses, including Darwin, charging them to occupy the fort and wait for reinforcements. The *Beagle* crew occupied balconies and defended the streets from the rebels. They were soon replaced by Montevideños, and the revolt was quickly brought under control – so much so that the crew were able to relax and even began to prepare an *asado* (barbecue) in the courtyards.

The new American republics were still in the first throes of statehood. Uruguay, always a bone of contention between the Portuguese and the Spanish in colonial times, had only achieved independence in 1828; the British, keen for the shores of the River Plate to be divided, brokered the division from Buenos Aires. Other countries were scarcely more than a decade older, and revolution followed revolution. The champions of independence were themselves brushed aside: Simón Bolivar fell to a solitary death in a boarding house in Santa Marta, Colombia; in Chile, Bernardo O'Higgins only lasted six years before his downfall; in Argentina, José de San Martín was so disillusioned that he retired to France. The continent, understandably, was still in turmoil at the time of the *Beagle*'s visit.

In keeping with the spirit of the past, we were staying in the Hotel Torremolinos, in the heart of the old city which Darwin would have known – light years away from the fireworks of the foiled insurrection.

The entrance to the Torremolinos led up a precipitous flight of stairs with sagging floorboards covered in a threadbare beige carpet. Visitors then swung through a double door dressed in lace curtains, and emerged into an immensely airy hall, with leather settees and a fading mosaic on the marble floor. It seemed just like Paris. Tango music crackled from a venerable gramophone. A rusting stairwell wound up to a skylight, and disappeared into the imagination. Sickly yellow light filtered through the window panes. A Singer, in its declining years, clackety-clacked for most of the day, presided over by assorted members of staff in voluminous aprons. Next to the Singer was a panelled mahogany cabinet full of cracks and tasteless china ornaments. Everything was blue, even the lightbulbs. The electrical fittings could only take twenty-watt bulbs, and the whole building was swathed in gloom even by day.

The hotel smelt of age and poverty, and was thoroughly depressing. What was worse was that we had to spend whole days holed up in it, with nothing but the dimness and the drumming rains of late winter to distract us from the imminent journey. Those who lived in the Torremolinos were either prostitutes or drunkards. At first we didn't care, since it was the cheapest place in the city; but gradually the Torremolinos became unbearable. The man next door ranted and bawled until three in the morning, and the walls were as thin as air. You could feel every sound as if it was yours, the belches and the farts and the desperate groans, the bottles thudding against the floorboards, and the arguments. Worst of all was the music. He was a fan of Venezuelan *cumbia*. I like *cumbia*, but not when it's the same tape played for hours at a time at full volume.

So we moved to the City Hotel – which also received no daylight and also depressed us completely. We had come to get away from city life, but instead we spent weeks in these depressing places trying to get the journey off the ground. This was not a situation calculated to make our relationship easy. After bickering about our difficulties, we often found ourselves strolling grumpily through the city, trying to pretend that we weren't with each other. But at other times we thought about all the places which we would visit, and the stress would be forgotten. We laughed when we went into the same restaurant every day, and the same waiter said the same thing, undeterred, whenever we had completed our order:

'*Bueno.*'

He responded perfunctorily, almost as if any other response would have been impossible. When it was time to have lunch we would say to each other:

'Let's go to "*bueno*".'

'*Bueno*' was just by the Torremolinos, also in the heart of Montevideo's old city. This part of the city is now almost a slum. The buildings – known as *conventillos* – must have seemed tall and elegant in the nineteenth century, but now they are grey homes to families of migrants from the interior, from Salto and Rivera, Artigas and Tacuarembó. There are scores of tiny rooms in each building, and people condense their possessions into these inhuman boxes of darkness, squeeze all their clothes into the wardrobe and all their crockery onto the table, as their lives are filched away by the decay in the heart of Montevideo. They live on top of each other, one family to a room. The lucky ones have a balcony where the clothes are hung out to dry, and when walking through any street in the old city all the balconies look like miniature haberdashery departments. Portable gas stoves are shared by the families, as are the long sinks where they wash their clothes.

Both the Torremolinos and the City were like this. Many of the residents seemed to have lived there for years. In the City, there was a kindly old man who had been living in a minuscule room for eight years with only a cat for company. We met him once in the local café, as we were eating lunch. This place was typical of the old city. The bar was scratched and ancient, and behind it were rows of empty whisky bottles, trophies of drinking wars that had long since passed away. There were faded posters and pennants of Peñarol, Uruguay's most successful football team. Our neighbour was dressed immaculately, in spite of the dreariness amid which he lived. He was wearing a suit and hat, and he walked with a cane. He carried himself impeccably, and if you had seen him in the street, you would have thought him an aristocrat.

He came over to speak a little with us, but told us that he had to hurry to buy a lottery ticket. He soon rushed out into a fine drizzle, and was quickly swallowed up by the winding streets where Darwin arrived, fresh-faced and still eager for foreign travel, in 1832.

In those days, there was nothing more to Montevideo than the city around the port. The Avenida 18 de Julio, one of the main commercial districts in Montevideo today, led up to the triumphal arch at the city's entrance. The arch still stands. The city's port – always the best on the River Plate – still thrives, and the layout of the old city is the same, but everything else has gone. The wealthy classes have moved several kilometres east up the coast to the districts of Carrasco and Pocitos, and the whiff of danger and revolution has evaporated. Only the shell of Darwin's Montevideo remains.

The landmark which has least changed is a natural one. The city gets its name from a hill which rises from the bay. A Portuguese lookout in colonial times, sailing this dreary coast of sand hillocks, was so relieved at spying even a tiny bit of higher land that he cried out: '*Monte vide eu.*' – 'I see a hill.' The hill, it must be said, is a pretty pathetic one. It scarcely rises above a hundred metres. I empathized with the story I heard of a Chilean who, with the image of the towering Andes in his mind, climbed the hill and was heard to say: 'Where is it? Where's the hill?'

The hill looks out across the bay to the city, and the shanties that lie in between the two. Beyond the city, the interior stretches away, unbroken grasslands up to the horizon. It was from here that we first really appreciated the emptiness of the lands through which we would ride. Uruguay is about the same size as England and Wales combined, but has only three million people – and half of them live in Montevideo. All we could see was space. Take away the slums and the commercial glitz, and the view of the plains could scarcely have changed since Darwin's time.

As well as finding horses, we had to get some saddles made. Uriarte recommended us to the saddler, Pablo Maspoli. Maspoli's workshop was in a sleepy district near the centre, where rickety pick-ups and saloons rusted away on the roadside. There is no equivalent to the MOT in Uruguay, and geriatric lumps of metal shudder alarmingly along the country's roads. The most ancient ones, often more than forty years old, seemed to have congregated here. We went in and found a group of men working the leather, hammering, sewing stitches, casting their shadows over a floor covered in dust and old saddles.

Maspoli beckoned us through to his office, where there was a display saddle, an abandoned typewriter and a fax machine. He had bushy eyebrows and an even face, but there was something quirky about him.

We decided to buy Uruguayan saddles. They are very bulky and bear scant resemblance to their English counterparts, so Maspoli had to explain how they worked. As protection for the horse's back, there is a *yerga*, or woollen blanket, and a *carrona*, a thick leather cover for the *yerga*. The saddle is more rounded and much heavier than an English saddle, and goes on top of the *carrona*, and the brass stirrups are sewn over with leather and turned into boot-holes. The girth is fitted to an *encimera*, a strip of animal hide which is tied fast to the saddle to keep it in place. A sheepskin is placed on top of the *encimera* as protection from saddle-sores and the whole ensemble is strapped down by a second girth, known as a *sobrecincha*. So complicated are the shenanigans that a careful rider takes almost an hour to saddle a horse up.

Once he'd explained all of this, Maspoli asked us about packhorses.

'Are you taking much luggage?'

'About sixty kilos between us.'

'You must have a comfortable packsaddle,' he said. 'You need one with iron grips at each end, rather than one where you just sling the saddlebags over the horse's back.'

He fetched a packsaddle manual. It was German, filled with photographs of stout Teutonic men proudly displaying their packhorses. Maspoli launched into a comparison of the different styles, which sounded like Malay to me for all I knew of Spanish terms for saddlery.

'I've never made one before,' he admitted. 'But don't worry. I'll think about it this evening.'

'There is one other thing,' I said. 'Everyone tells us that we need four horses, but I thought we could use three. What do you think?'

'I think you need four,' he said.

II

The criterion of a good rider is, a man who can manage an untamed colt, or who, if his horse falls, alights on his own feet ... I recollect seeing a gaucho riding a very stubborn horse, which three times successively reared so high as to fall backwards with great violence. The man judged with uncommon coolness the proper moment for slipping off, not an instant before or after the right time; and as soon as the horse got up, the man jumped on his back, and ... they started at a gallop.

Charles Darwin

Through our contacts with Mac and the *Criollo* breeders, we met quite a few ranch-owners from around Montevideo. One of them was Jaime Solis. When I told Jaime about Maspoli's advice, he scoffed loudly at the idea.

'Pah! Maspoli – what does he know? He's never sat on a horse in his life.'

He was driving us out to his *estancia* (ranch) west of Montevideo. Jaime was a wonderful man, ebullient and opinionated, but immensely generous. He was tall and thin, and his angular face was defined by his dark beady eyes.

'Look,' he went on, 'I think it's a wonderful idea. But I'm a special case. I've always lived in the country. Most of the people you've talked to have never spent more than a week on their farms at once.'

'But Uriarte also said that we needed four.'

'Uriarte!' Jaime exclaimed, as if about to vomit with revulsion. Then he smiled conspiratorially, realizing for the first time how much there was to explain to us. 'Uriarte is a charlatan. He's barely ever sat on a horse in his life. Nor has Lockhart. Look at them! They all turn up to the Prado in suits and give prizes to each other's horses. The people with the best horses never win.'

'So you don't think the *Criollo* society will be much help?'

'The *Criollo* society? *Those* people? Listen, *amigo*, there have been *presidents* of the *Criollo* breeders who couldn't tell one end of the horse from another.'

'I'm sorry?'

'Listen. I'm going to give you one piece of advice. Those people only care about money. They're not real horsemen. The real test of a horse is what we call the *marchas*. That's when horses have to cover 750 kilometres in fifteen days, eating only grass from the same fields, without any days off. Sometimes the going is so tough that these horses die. Now I'm telling you that none of those people – Uriate, Lockhart, none of them – they've never had a horse come even in the top ten of the *marchas*. You go and ask them about their horses, and they'll say their horses are the best. Then ask them about the *marchas* and you'll see – they'll shut up soon enough.'

We reached his *estancia*, and Jaime asked us if we wanted to ride.

'We'll have to catch them first,' he warned us. We walked across a meadow to a small gallop, where four mares were grazing. One look at us saw them cantering quickly off as far away as possible.

'Spread out across the gallop,' Jaime told us. 'If they try to charge you, just stop them.'

He went up to one with a head-collar and began to whistle, clacking his tongue and trying to court her. His whistles and whispers sang with the puffing afternoon wind. Had there been a balcony this could have been a serenade, but the mare was in the empty space of the *campo*, unused to dancing to anything but the wind's tune. We stood a few metres away, on either side of the gallop, watching her balletic moves back and away from the entrapment of the lasso. We were petrified by the spectacle. As soon as Jaime tried to catch her, the mares careered wildly around in circles, veering away first from him and then from us. Occasionally they stopped to fix us with evil stares. Then Jaime would approach the mare surreptitiously, until she bolted and the whole terrifying business began again. There was no reason why they shouldn't just have battered us down and escaped. This went on for about five minutes, until the mare, flinching and backing away, but not bolting again, allowed herself to be caught, and the *gaucho* serenade ended with the reconciliation of song and dancer.

Jaime turned to us happily, as if nothing had happened.

Once we had caught the others, we saddled up and climbed on, our legs shaking. But the reins were separated into two nylon strands, and when I took one in each hand as is the English style, my mare moved around violently and nearly threw me.

'No, no,' Jaime laughed. 'Here we hold the reins together in one hand, and leave the strands to the left of the horse.'

Eventually we set off. As we went, Jaime continued with his advice.

'Look, you don't know anything. You're incredibly green. You'd be crazy to take four horses. You'll never manage them. At the moment, the only thing we all agree on is that you're crazy. *Loco, loco*. If you manage to go 300 kilometres, by that time at least you'll have certificates of craziness. If you still think you need a fourth horse, someone will give you one.'

Jaime had bought several kilos of steak on our way out from Montevideo. I had imagined that others were coming to lunch, but this was before I realized that Uruguayans usually buy one kilo of red meat per head for an *asado* ('or a little less if we have bread,' as someone told me). The *asado*, the national meal in Uruguay and Argentina, consists of every conceivable part of a cow, beginning with the guts and the heart and ending with the choice cuts, grilled over a fire. In the wealthier classes, the meat is served with salad. In the *estancias* it is served with bread, and oozes fat over the grate, spitting and crackling and leaving the lean hard life to the *gauchos* who chew at the carcasses.

Jaime prepared the meal, and we ate through what seemed like half a cow. Emily had not eaten meat for fifteen years, but as the guest of honour at a meal consisting of bread and meat, she could scarcely refuse.

'What's the food like in the country?' I asked, chewing on a particularly inconvenient piece of gristle.

'Terrible,' said Jaime. 'All they eat is fatty meat.'

Shortly after visiting Jaime's *estancia*, we travelled to two farms near Montevideo looking for horses. The first was owned by Willy Lockhart. Lockhart's driver, Roberto, took us to his *estancia*. As we drove out of Montevideo, we moved into what seemed like endless pastures and wheatfields. We turned off the main road after an hour and followed a long avenue of plane trees, past small farmsteads sheltered by windbreaks of eucalyptus, horses drinking rainwater at the roadside, sheep and cattle grazing in the yawning paddocks which stretched like an ocean to the horizon. The road cut down into a lush river valley, where copses of willows and *ombues** were in their spring renaissance, and the cleft was a flash of colours, reds and yellows and oranges, a break in the green that is universal in Uruguay.

'I love the emptiness,' Roberto said, ending a long silence. 'When I come here at night, I always stop at that ford. In all of this space, you can only ever see one light.'

We drove up to Lockhart's *estancia*. The peon was waiting, and led us through to the yard where we saw the horse: Ruso. Ruso was already saddled up, and the peon assured me that he was tame.

'I broke him in myself,' he said, to encourage me.

I grabbed the reins, put my foot in the stirrups and jumped on. Ruso didn't like this. He reared backwards and began to buck. Tiring of this, he decided that the best way of freeing himself from this ponderous encumbrance was to back towards a nearby fence and try to deposit me in the mire of dung that lay on the other side. Noticing the abject terror written across my face, the peon said something quickly to Roberto.

'Give him a longer rein,' Roberto said. 'He's not used to you, that's what it is.'

Ruso calmed down. The peon led me through a gate to a huge paddock, and looked at me curiously.

'If he tries to gallop,' he said helpfully, 'just let him go.'

Ruso definitely wanted to gallop. We rushed to the far end of the paddock, and then back. The only sounds were Ruso's hooves breaking the earth, his measured breathing and the wind.

I dismounted, and led him back to the yard. Two sheep were scratching away at the wiry grass, and beyond was the family's washing billowing in the ceaseless winds. Behind the yard was a circular corral bounded by a dry-stone wall. Here there were about twenty mares enclosed, some of them with their newly born foals. The peon unsaddled Ruso, and we discussed him.

'Did you like the horse?'

I pretended to sound as if I knew what I was talking about.

'He's got a nice pace but he's a little nervy.'

---

* The Uruguayan national tree, which is, botanically speaking, a bush.

As we spoke, Emily was trying to overcome her fears by stroking Ruso and talking to him. She was pleased when he stopped shaking, and her words continued to flow for some minutes.

The peon was clearly amused.

'He's a very tame horse,' the peon said. 'My six-year-old son rides to school on him every day.'

It was only once we had bought Ruso, and were riding across the country with him, that we discovered what a peculiar horse he was. A beautiful *gateado* beige colour, in many respects he was tame, and Emily got on especially well with him. Yet if you tried to catch him, he hid disgustedly behind the others, and was not averse to having a sly kick at you. The same was true if you tried to clean his rear hooves – he would even try to kick with his front legs as you tussled with the back ones. If he decided he did not like something, he was the epitome of stubbornness. Only once was his kicking useful, when he aimed deftly at an aggressive stallion. Ruso was clumsy and quirky. He tended to meander along slothfully at the back of our pack for some minutes, before suddenly bursting into a canter, ears pricked, overtaking the others and sending Emily careering past me in a flurry of hooves. He frequently tripped, once soaking our sleeping bags as he slurped from a puddle. When we stopped for a rest, he would graze contentedly awhile, and then, for no apparent reason, turn and begin to plod back the way we had come. He was not trying to escape, for he never bolted clear. He just walked on down the road, doleful and uncertain, until one of us caught up with him and led him back to the others. Then he would look at you out of the corner of a reddish eye, suspiciously, as if he wasn't sure he liked you, or even knew who you were.

It was only natural that we were still uneasy about Ruso when we went to the farm of Gonzalo Fulquét, another breeder, that same afternoon. Fulquét met us for lunch, and sat hiding his jowls beneath a checked trilby as we ate what seemed like another half-cow. He was a very proud man, and the soul of his Mediterranean ancestry washed through his jovial discourses on the state of Uruguay, his anecdotes from his travels in Europe and Africa, and the hyperbole which he span us about his farm.

'It's the most beautiful farm in Uruguay,' he told us. 'When my son came out here to check on the land, he rang me as soon as he had seen it. He told me that we must come here – there is nothing to match it in our country.'

Although Fulquét was not one to shy away from bragging – 'Both my ram and my ewe won the prizes for the best sheep in Uruguay at the Prado' – his land *was* beautiful. In a country where hills are almost as rare as trees in a desert, his farm lay in the lee of the highest uplands in Uruguay. Minerals flecked the hillsides with their iridescent shades, and in the blushing light of late afternoon colours spilled across the land, chasing each other as the sun chased the horizon. Beyond the house was a succession of eucalyptus copses, and the tips of the branches sent red flashes to tint the cold light towards evening. The kaleidoscope was completed by the garden around the *estancia* house, which was purpled by wisteria, purified by the white blossom reaching out with the spring and frazzled with the citric colours of oranges and lemons.

'My wife is a landscape gardener,' Fulquét explained, when he saw our admiration.

Fulquét's peon was waiting for us by the stables, as were the two horses which Fulquét was offering us: Chileno and Chimango. As soon as they saw us, they scampered into the far corner of the little paddock in which they were grazing, and sheltered beneath the boughs of a eucalyptus as they scorned our proffered hands. Chileno, who was by far the shorter of the two, hid behind Chimango, and they both succeeded in looking down their noses at us – even Chileno, who was almost smaller than we were. Beyond them was the corral where the *gauchos* broke in the horses.

'They really beat them up,' said Fulquét. 'They see it as a test of strength, as the best part of their job. It reasserts their identity.'

He shrugged, dismissing the horses and the land with his single expansive gesture, and then gestured to the peon, who helped us to saddle up. As soon as Emily was aboard Chimango, the regal chestnut – whom we would come to love – trotted beneath the eaves of the stable, and hoped that this would be enough to escape the inconvenience of having to go for a walk. Emily had to duck beneath the lowering roof, and she looked at me with an anxious smile.

At least he was a clever horse.

'It's just his way of saying hello,' said Fulquét.

Once I was aboard Chileno, we set off down the track away from the farm, Fulquét accompanying us on a proud gelding.

'Let's ride slowly to start with,' he said.

Barely a minute later, once we had passed the small copse by the house, Chileno and Chimango both broke into a rapid trot. When Emily and I tried to slow them up they cantered wildly down to the end of the drive, only stopped from gallivanting into the vast plains by the cattle grid over the track.

'Stop, stop!' cried Fulquét. 'You must sit back. If you sit forward, of course they'll go fast. They think that you want to canter.'

It was true, we were both hunched like Quasimodo over our reins, in the misguided belief that this would help. Of course, when we turned around to try to listen better to what Fulquét was saying, both our horses thought they were going home and broke into a very rapid trot.

'Stop!' cried Fulquét, watching us in utter bewilderment as we passed him. 'Let's try gently.'

But we couldn't. Both Chileno and Chimango wanted to canter when we wanted to walk, and walked when we wanted to go faster. After a few minutes, Emily turned to me, her face pale with terror:

'This is ridiculous,' she said shakily. 'I'm going to walk him back.'

She dismounted and led Chimango towards the stables, walking slowly and in loneliness through the plains, and I was left in the company of Fulquét. The horses were so much wilder here than in England that they had begun to scare Emily, who had not ridden for some years. Although I wanted to go after her, I had to sit with Fulquét as we rode around his *estancia*. He had taken us this far, and he had to show off his land to the visitor. We rode gently and the peace calmed me down somewhat, even though I wondered more than ever what on earth I was doing with this ridiculous project on my back.

'Once we've started,' I said to Fulquét, 'we'll get used to it very quickly.'

'You'll have to,' he said.

Incredibly, after this uncertain start, we ended by buying both Chileno and Chimango. I became happier with Chileno during my hour's ride with him, and despite spending another two weeks on the lookout, we never came across a horse as striking and noble as Chimango. We put our faith in the two horses who had been raised in this beautiful place, somehow believing against all contrary evidence that we would cope with them. We had to, and they did not let us down.

Chileno was a former polo horse. He was squat and tough, a *lobuno*, or greyish colour. He made tightening the girth nearly impossible by swelling his belly to a Dadaesque degree, grunting happily to himself as one of us wheezed with the buckle. He had a gallant, proud trot – the pace of a fast walk – and quickly turned himself into the lord of our herd. Neither Chimango nor Ruso ever dared pass him on the road. He was very short-sighted in his left eye, and terrified of wire. This was a fairly calamitous combination, since stray pieces of wire fencing abound in Uruguay, and he frequently trod on them. His response was straight from the polo-field. He would bolt off, startled out of his wits, and often turn viciously around in circles, tearing at his bit in rage. Yet he was also the tamest of horses. When we stopped for lunch, Chileno would stand where we left him, even if the grass was sparse. He would look at us expectantly, loyally, almost motionless. One of us would get up and lead him to better grass, where he would then munch happily.

Chimango was a lovely chestnut, very tall for a *Criollo*. He was an immensely powerful horse, who fought with every new rider, twisting and turning and wanting to break into an immediate gallop. Riding him was a challenge. When you dismounted to open a gate, he would always try to burst off again before you were properly on board. I once tried to hold him from this by tugging on his reins, and so he jolted his head back sharply and smacked me in the face. When he was carrying the pack, he would shove his ears back sullenly, and sometimes he tried to kick Ruso when he came past. But he was also the friendliest of them all. He always came up to us when we went to catch the horses in the paddock, ears pricked. Sometimes he came to the gate after we left them to graze, staring mournfully after us as we went away.

They were not the easiest horses, but after a few weeks in the Uruguayan countryside it became clear that horses here were not tame in the same way as they are in Europe. If we were going to follow Darwin, we would have to learn to do it in the *gaucho* style, on the same sort of horses that the *gauchos* themselves used. Evolution had not yet caught up with the taming of Uruguayan horses.

Evolutionary thought existed before Darwin embarked on the *Beagle*.

His grandfather, Erasmus Darwin, had been an influential proponent of evolution, and the ideas of Jean-Baptiste Lamarck were also hotly disputed. There was, however, no mechanism for explaining how evolution occurred – Lamarck's idea that external influences shaped evolution being open to too many criticisms – and most scientists were creationists, believing that God had created all species in their current state of perfection. Darwin's great contribution to science was not evolution, but his theory of natural selection. Although Alfred Russel Wallace nearly beat him to publication, Darwin's work and ideas had been evolving for twenty years. He was the first person to develop a theory explaining the process of evolution. Darwin's most famous book, *The Origin of Species*, prompted the great shift in thought – from creationism to evolution by natural selection.

Darwin's studies of the laissez-faire economics of Adam Smith – a very close cousin of natural selection – seem to have influenced him greatly. Darwin himself traced the catalyst for his ideas to 1838, when he read a paper by Malthus on human population growth. It struck him that because all species have a propensity for rampant breeding, and because there is a limit to the numbers of a particular species that the environment can support, there must be what he termed a 'struggle for existence' between the members of a species. Those individuals which inherit certain properties advantageous to their survival are more likely to win this struggle, and so pass these characteristics on to their descendants. So these individuals are selected by nature for survival, because of their properties. It is the variation between individuals of a population which allows one variant to be 'selected' ahead of another, and leads to species change. So variation is a key element of evolutionary biology.

Darwin's observations in South America were essential to his developing theory. This was especially true of the island groups which he visited – the Falkland (Malvinas)* Islands, Chiloé and the Galápagos – where he noticed that many of the species were unique, although related to counterparts on the South American mainland. This produced the idea that the species had simply evolved differently

* Because of the territorial dispute between the UK and Argentina, UN guidelines suggest this way of naming the islands. For simplicity's sake, I shall use 'Falklands' only from here on.

in response to the differing environmental conditions which they found. His geological discoveries, particularly in the Andes *cordillera*, were also crucial, as they suggested that there were important changes in the composition of the earth over extended periods of time which could explain the isolation of continents from one another, and therefore could explain how related species were found in discrete locations (following geographical changes), both being descended from the same ancestor prior to their geographical separation from one another.

Essential to Darwin's theory was that it was a theory of micromutation, or gradual change. Darwin insisted that evolution was not the result of sudden and large-scale changes in organisms – macromutations – but that the changes had developed slowly and over an unimaginably massive timescale. This distinction led to Darwin's theory of 'common descent', that all organisms on earth are descended from some one or few micro-organisms that developed in the primeval soup of the planet billions of years ago. Modern biologists have taken their cue from Darwin's micromutation theory, and evolutionary biologists are today almost exclusively micromutationists.

We should not naively believe that Darwin had no knowledge of evolutionary thought when he left Plymouth in 1831. Before studying theology at Cambridge, he had been a student of Robert Grant in Edinburgh. One day, as Darwin recalled in his *Autobiography*, Grant passionately expounded his admiration for Lamarck. This was a period of tremendous change, intellectually and socially, to which Darwin cannot have been blind. Darwin was certainly not an evolutionist in 1831, but he was aware of the idea, and five years of free time for study and thought converted him to believing in its truth.

Before we set off, Mac and Lucía invited us to their dairy farm. Mac was the manager, and they had a half-share in it. He had thrown himself into organizing things for us, arranging meetings, finding people with horses for sale, personally checking Maspoli's saddles, and so on. Mac was like an uncle to us while we were in Montevideo. He met us from the bus and drove us down the track to his farm. They had 700 cows, divided between two plots of land, overseen by a foreman and two peons. The cows were taken to the milking machine at six in the morning and six at night.

The farm was home to an aviary. There were partridges, rheas (South American ostriches), swallows, sparrows, doves and parrots. The parrots were bright green and cackled boisterously from the eucalyptus groves.

'They're a real pest,' Mac told us. 'They eat all the grass and the crops. They've been declared a national plague.'

There were also the tero-teros. These birds are quite pretty, a mixture of sharp black and white topped off by a tasteful crown. But when they open their mouths, the unfortunate result is an ear-threatening shriek of horrific discordance. Equally unfortunate is that tero-teros love singing. Whether it is because so many years of cacophony have deafened them or because they enjoy seeing people scampering over the plains holding their hands tight to their ears, I don't know; but they never stop. In their nesting season, which was imminent, they stand a little away from their nests, shrieking as a distraction, and dive for you if you come too close to the chicks. I often wished that I could shriek as they did, to communicate the fact that the last thing I wanted was a nestful of their wretched children.

We went to see the *estancia* of Mac's brother-in-law. Mac belonged to a co-operative of twelve farmers, who sent their calves here to be fattened up. The *estancia* dated from the 1870s, and behind the imposing iron gates its walls were beginning to peel and crumble. There were two *ombues* in the meadow beyond, tough and resistant against the winds. Beneath one of them was a dead terrier, its paws doubled up in an apparent plea for mercy. The terrier had been killed by the dogs on the farm because it was a stray. The murderers lay lazily in the long grass. Now they followed us, wagging their tails, as we walked down to the muddy corral where the calves were being weighed.

The animals were enclosed and then coerced a group at a time down a narrow chute which led to the scales. The chute had a succession of gates, opened and shut by levers, which allowed the calves onto the scales one at a time. Two *gauchos* stood on either side, prodding the calves viciously with sharp sticks to move them forward. Sometimes calves would whine and kick before reaching the scales, which caused them to be mercilessly flogged and berated until, terrified, they staggered onto the scales. Behind the terror was a green valley filled with poplars and parrots, and then the land swept up an undulation and disappeared into the endless field of the sky, soft clouds flecking the azure atmosphere so that the plains were chequered black and white.

A group of farmers was monitoring the weighing. Mac went over and introduced us, and then suggested we went for a ride. Two horses were tethered to the *ombues*. When we came back, the farmers were laughing.

'You still have time to hire a car,' one of them pointed out.

But they were worried about their livestock. The prolonged drought had left the pastures thin as cotton, and the animals were all underweight. Before the obligatory *asado* we went to see just how sparse the grass was.

'It's very serious,' Mac explained as we returned to his farm. 'Those animals are seriously underweight. What we've agreed is that the co-operative should buy some fertilizer, to make the grass grow properly again. This situation is no help to anyone.'

'Is the drought unusual?'

'Well, the weather is never predictable anywhere. But there's definitely been a change in the climate here. And in the species. That ought to interest you. When Darwin was here, he would have found pumas, but there aren't any left now. Only in the Andes and some parts of Patagonia. And then there are the wild pigs – they were introduced as a small experiment, and now they've gone out of control and are killing sheep.'

That weekend, with Mac and Lucía, we completed our rushed education in the proper *gaucho* style of riding. After trying out Ruso, Chileno and Chimango, we had been invited to stay at an *estancia* in the west of the country by another breeder, María Ieuwdiukov de Nín, and had galloped on two of the loveliest and tamest horses in Uruguay, up to thirty kilometres a day until even the prospect of saddle-sores became not too terrible. Now Mac and Lucía lent us two more good horses, Elefante and Zapicán, and we trotted gently through their paddocks. In the distance, we saw Mac and his foreman yelling as they chased after a herd of sheep. Elefante and Zapicán were so calm that even in spite of our lumbering weights they meandered contentedly through the fields. Whenever we turned back towards the farmhouse, of course, they pricked up their ears no end and trotted back twice as happily. Zapicán even broke into a spontaneous canter once, and I heard

Emily and him striking through the ground as they caught up with me. These horses were so calm that we relaxed into the riding, and became more confident about the journey.

It was at times like this that we convinced ourselves that we would succeed together. When, flushed after our day's riding on the Sunday, we watched the sunset over the plains, we knew that all the struggles were worthwhile. We sat silently on the porch, as the sun edged towards the horizon. As I rode across Uruguay and Argentina, this came to be my favourite part of the day: the wind hushing from extraneous noise to nothingness, with frogs garbling from the translucent puddles lying over the fields; owls hooting warnings to the imminent night; shadows tiptoeing from the eucalyptus plantations towards the slight valleys and rises in the plains – then running headlong towards the vanishing light beyond, before being swallowed by the bloodbath of the sun dying with the clouds.

Moments like this compensated for the drudgery of life in Montevideo. Whenever we returned to the city, away from our horse lessons in the camps, we found ourselves loathing the greyness and our dingy hotels. It was not really the city's fault, more a glimpse of the greyness and tension which we felt ourselves reflecting back to the world.

Finally, after almost a month of living in putrid hotels and learning the beginnings of this rural life, we left. Lockhart told us that we could set out from his *estancia*. We arranged for Chileno and Chimango to be freighted over, and at last we were ready to go. We said goodbye to the city with no regrets. We were through with the constrictions and depressions of places like the Torremolinos and the City, and we needed to stop the weeks of self-examination and find out if we could really do this. We collected the saddles from Maspoli's, and Roberto drove us out to the *estancia*.

Now the country looked greener than it had done before. The spring had been unusually damp, and the grass was lush. Brightly coloured *trébol* flowers spread out over the paddocks in a spray of purple, red and white. Although the task was immense, we were so relieved to be free of Montevideo at last that the atmosphere in the car was remarkably jolly. Emily practised Spanish with Roberto in the front seat, and the time passed quickly.

We reached a valley, and Roberto pulled into the roadside. He jumped down among the rocks. Beyond, the river was shallow and pure, scudding over a bed of minerals and flints. The sun beat down between the branches of the willows. Roberto picked up a stone, and held it to the light. It sparkled like a firefly flitting through the night.

'All over South America,' he said, 'in Uruguay and Paraguay, Argentina and Chile, we have these minerals.'

The stone was flecked with quartz deposits. He handed it to both of us.

'The mineral keeps the warmth of your force. It is always strong. On your journey, you will have many difficult moments. When you need extra strength, look for this stone, and hold it tight. Then, you will find that strength.'

His eyes shone with the spring-like optimism that comes with all beginnings.

PART TWO

Across Uruguay

The greater number of the inhabitants had an indistinct idea that England, London, and North America, were different names for the same place; but the better informed well knew that London and North America were separate countries close together, and that England was a large town in London! ... I am writing as if I had been among the inhabitants of Central Africa ... but such were my feelings at the time.

Charles Darwin on central Uruguay

Darwin made two separate horseback journeys in Uruguay. The first began from the 'quiet, forlorn, little town' of Maldonado, past the area of Las Minas, to the Río Polanco. The second was from Montevideo to Mercedes, running parallel to the coastline of the River Plate as far as Colonia, before following the Río Uruguay to Mercedes, and returning to Montevideo directly across country.

The empty land made a great impression on him. 'The whole country is so thinly inhabited,' he wrote during his first trip, 'that during the whole day we met scarcely a single person.' On this first excursion, he went with two armed *gauchos*, since the previous day a traveller had been found murdered by bandits. The security situation was precarious, and Darwin felt that 'the traveller has no protection besides his fire-arms'. They would ride all day over the plains, and then ask for lodging when night overtook them. Universally, they were well received. In some places, Darwin found that he could repay the hospitality through showing off his compass. This novelty caused widespread astonishment, since it was thought incredible that he could know the direction of places which he had never visited.

This first journey was made after the botched rebellion in Montevideo. The second came a year later, after Darwin's tremendous rides across the Argentine Pampas. Even the relatively level landscapes of Uruguay seemed hilly after the Province of Buenos Aires. He wrote that the undulations, although they were 'in themselves perhaps not absolutely great ... [were] as compared to the plains of St. Fé, real mountains'. Although he often pined for the tropical foliage around Rio, his experiences of living among the *gauchos* made up for the banal countryside.

We could not start riding from Maldonado, which has now been virtually swallowed by an exclusive resort, Punta del Este. All over the continent, I found that urban growth made following Darwin's precise routes dangerous and sometimes impossible, it being no joke to ride a fairly wild horse along main roads or through urban sprawls. Instead we left from Lockhart's farm since it was near the region of Las Minas, and as close as we could find to Maldonado. We would follow Darwin to Colonia, and then cut across the country to Mercedes.

Gustavo – Lockhart's peon – was waiting for us when Roberto dropped us off.

We spent five days at the *estancia*. Apart from us there was nobody there but Gustavo and his family. He lived in a small concrete building of three rooms, each with a distinct entrance, set a little apart from his *patrón's* farmhouse. Lockhart only visited once a month, and the rest of the time the expansive country house, full of equine memorabilia, lay empty. Yet there seemed no resentment from Gustavo or his wife, Rosana. They were self-sufficient. Whenever they wanted meat, they butchered a ram. Rosana milked the cows daily, and made butter and cheese. There was a small vegetable patch, protected by a spreading willow tree, where they grew lettuces and tomatoes. They had to buy *mate*, and flour for baking bread and making fritters, but nothing more. Rosana looked after their daughter, who was still a toddler, and did the cooking and washing, collected the eggs and milked the cows. Gustavo spent his time breaking in horses, rounding up sheep and patrolling the paddocks.

They seemed happy.

Gustavo spoke softly, with a sing-song voice. Sometimes his words vanished into a growling wind outside, or were swamped by the scratching of the white doves on the storehouse roof. His face was eager, his lip hidden by a black moustache which suited him. He always wore the same white cloth cap, which never got dirtied by its outdoor life; the same heavily patched *bombachas*; the same white checked shirt, creased and tainted by coarse earth; the same shy smile that accompanied everything he did or said, painting his face with the softness of sincerity. He shared this smile with Rosana. She would approach us cautiously, her smile preceding her wherever she went. She constantly kept an eye on her daughter, but this was unnecessary. Here there were no runaway cars to kill her, no labyrinthine shopping malls for her to get lost in, no malicious people to harm her; in fact, there were no other people at all.

Gustavo was a godsend. He shod the horses, refusing payment for this, and tested their tameness. He gave us countless tips and bits of advice, and he and Rosana were forever bringing us things. Mutton, milk, eggs, lettuce, even a special dish of country pancakes. At first, we didn't want to accept the constant offerings. But this was the sort of genuine generosity which could not be easily turned away. It was open-hearted, instinctive, a generosity offered so freely that it was simply rude to refuse.

When I did offer to pay Gustavo for shoeing the horses he said:

'What for? I had nothing better to do with the time.'

'But Gustavo – it was a hard job.'

'Nonsense. We all enjoyed it.'

He wouldn't hear of it, like the vast majority of people who helped out along the way. In the beginning, I would suggest payment for a service rendered, but the reaction was generally one of offence – had I really thought that money was necessary to induce a person to do a good turn to another in need? I quickly discarded all the rules of etiquette and commodities that I had ever learnt. The cobbler who mended the packsaddle wouldn't hear of payment; nor would the man who drove fifty kilometres out of his way to take Emily to the nurse when her TB jab became infected; nor would any of the people who allowed us to camp on their land and often offered us food.

Emily and I prepared ourselves for leaving. We worried about our safety, however much we reassured ourselves. But the whole journey was too imminent to do anything but concentrate, calm ourselves, and try – hard as it was – to believe in ourselves. This had been made even more difficult by an event on the day of our arrival. Gustavo had ridden with us over the plains, accompanying us as he showed us the further reaches of Lockhart's *estancia*. I rode Ruso, and Emily rode Chileno. To begin with, the ride was delightful and, interspersing our conversations with comments to our horses, we enjoyed the freedom of riding in the plains. But then, as we rode up a rise only distantly visible from the *estancia*, Chileno trod on a piece of wire and began to turn wildly in circles. Emily held on as her horse span, but eventually the real possibility of him bolting wildly like the good polo horse that he was forced her to slip her feet from the stirrups, deciding that it was better to cut her losses and fall off now rather than later on. I watched the accident from a short distance, and the incident unravelled itself in horrible slow motion.

There was a stricken silence, bellowing above the plains. Emily shook herself down, and then walked all the way back to the farm.

'It will be OK,' said Gustavo. 'It was just a little fall.'

But he dismounted from his gelding and rode Chileno awhile nonetheless, for a horse which has thrown its rider and got away with it can become very difficult.

In the evening we talked about the journey. Emily was bruised and had a crick in her neck, and was getting cold feet about the whole thing, especially since she didn't feel that she could back out:

'I wish we were doing something ordinary.'

'It'll be OK, Emily.'

'I just feel really nervous whenever I have to get on a horse. It's like I have had to learn three times: once at María's, once at Mac's and now here.'

'I know.'

'Why couldn't we have gone by bicycle?'

The accident was almost a disaster. We talked everything over, and Emily spent the next few days conquering her fears while I got used to riding with a lead rein. If it had not been for the space and time which we had to ourselves, the task might have been beyond us – but as it was we persevered, and almost managed to overcome our anxieties, for the umpteenth time, as the date of our departure approached.

The afternoon before we left, we sat with Gustavo in the storehouse. We were greasing our saddles with lard from a leg of lamb: taking a blob of the fat, bending it round either side of the leather straps, working the fat into the leather to protect it from the wearing weather. It was soothing work, feeling the fat ooze into the leather and leave its mark, before flaking like snow to the hard floor. None of us spoke at first.

Outside, the capricious spring was bringing more rain, lashing percussion against the roof. Wind blustered the storm clouds quickly overhead, but others replaced them. A ram bleated from the barn on the other side of the yard, lonely and worried like a lost child. Gustavo was about to butcher it, and the lamb was intuitively afraid even though it did not know why.

'Excuse me, *Señor*,' Gustavo said after a while. 'Could I discuss something?'

'Of course.'

'You know your spare set of stirrups,' he said. He was talking about a shiny brass pair which Maspoli had given us. 'I was wondering if you might sell them to me.'

Emily and I had already discussed this, and decided to give them to him. He and Rosana had done so much for us that we felt it was the least we could do.

'No, no. We'd like you to have them as a gift. To remember us by.'

'Thank you, *Señor*,' he said repeatedly, touching his cap deferentially. 'You see, I saw them. And I thought they were so beautiful. So much nicer than my own.'

He made his stirrup leathers from animal hides. I had watched him one evening, as he stripped the hair from the hide and cut the leather to size, his face furrowed in concentration. He made all of his own tack in this way.

'I only want them for special occasions. I wouldn't feel comfortable in them every day, but I want them for the Prado.'

Rosana came in and he turned to her, beaming.

'Look, look. They've given me the stirrups.'

Everyone was happy. Gustavo looked at us both.

'You know,' he said, 'I will remember this gift for my whole life.'

The *gaucho* has his origin in the battle for control of Uruguay. The *gauchos* – first known as *gauderíos* – became vagrants and Portuguese pawns in the fight against the Spanish. Uruguay was always in dispute between the two colonial powers – the city of Colonia changed hands several times – and the Portuguese tried to use the *gauchos* as spies and saboteurs.

By the time of Darwin's visit, the *gaucho* had adapted and was an established part of the region's folklore. Darwin himself loved them. Of the countrymen in Uruguay, he wrote: 'Their politeness is excessive; they never drink their spirits without expecting you to taste it; but whilst they make their exceedingly graceful bow, they seem quite as ready, if occasion offered, to cut your throat.' Then, as now, a *gaucho* never went anywhere without his knife. The knife belongs to a *gaucho* in the same way as his horse, or as laptops belong to businessmen. They don't carry them because of intrinsic violence, but for their work. They might need to cut a sheep free from fencing, or use it for butchering – some *gauchos* even use the knife's smooth back for grooming their horses. An old *gaucho* saying is that he who has no knife does not eat.

The problems arise when *gauchos* have had a few shots. Sober, the men would never be aggressive towards a stranger, but, when drunk, they are transformed. This life of loneliness consumes them and the alcohol spits out their rage. They become possessed by the drink. Every weekend, in every small town across Uruguay and Argentina, workers descend from the *estancias*, drink down their wages, reel drunkenly to a dance, and, as often as not, become embroiled with each other in a knife fight. The wildness of the plains emerges in collective, intoxicated catharsis.

Yet the *gaucho* is, still, a gentleman. There are many different types of *gaucho*, and neither the nomads nor the loyal peons are trouble-makers. It is the peon who flits from farm to farm that tends towards violence with drink. Darwin wrote that 'The *Gauchos*, or countrymen, are very superior to those who reside in the towns. The *Gaucho* is invariably most obliging, polite, and hospitable: I did not meet with even one instance of rudeness and inhospitability. He is modest, both respecting himself and country, but at the same time a spirited, bold, fellow.'

I found that every word of this eulogy still applies today, beginning with Gustavo. Of course, the *gauchos* today are different to those of Darwin's time. Their lifestyle is dying, as rural areas are progressively depopulated and, in some farms, the motorbike replaces the horse. *Gauchos* are now always old or in late middle age, and must watch the demise of their ways. More and more people disappear into the breadline

existence in the cities, leaving them to their plains. But their gentle-
manly character is still famous.

It is not for nothing that, in Uruguay and Argentina, the phrase *un
tipo gaucho* means 'a generous and trustworthy person'.

The time came for us to leave, and Gustavo helped us to saddle up. He
looked at our baggage in bafflement.

'Poor horse.'

We had far too many things. We had foolishly tried to bring enough
of everything for a year: books, razors, toothpaste, clothes, maps ...
However hard we squeezed and swore at the saddlebags, it couldn't all
fit in. So we tied the sleeping bags and a cavernous holdall on top. Now
we really were a travelling circus.

We hadn't gone fifty yards when I noticed that the sleeping bags and
holdall were slipping to one side. The bags looked about as stable as a
skiff in a hurricane. We stopped, and Emily tied Ruso to a hitching
post. Ruso recoiled, ripped the reins from the bit, and went for a stroll.
Chimango had a lopsided look as our saddlebags edged towards the
ground.

Gustavo ambled up slowly, bemused, and surveyed the chaos.

'It's no problem,' he said. 'There's a way out of everything.'

He cut a piece of wire from the fencing, and began to mend Ruso's
bridle. We readjusted the pack, tied the knots as tight as possible, and
started again. I tried to relax, and forget the impossible distances ahead.
This was just ridiculous. We still hadn't got a clue what we were doing.
I was riding a little ahead of Emily, when she called out:

'Watch out, Toby! The bags ...'

At this point the entire pack, including the saddle, slid right off
Chimango's back, falling to the left, until it was touching the ground
just next to his belly. Chimango startled, and leapt against the fence.
The wire jangled. Chileno pricked his ears up and jumped forward in
fright. I dropped the lead rein instead of being yanked backwards out
of the saddle by Chimango. Ruso stopped for a pee.

We had gone 200 metres.

Gustavo stopped the car, and walked up to us smiling evenly.

'The pack's slipped a little,' I said, trying to joke it off. We all began
to untie the straps, to free the stranded Chimango, who now showed

his tameness by staying still while we wrestled with the ridiculous
contraption.

'I've never seen anything quite like this,' Gustavo admitted. 'When
we travel by horse, we just take a hood to protect us from the rain.'

Gauchos sleep in their saddles. They don't have tents and sleeping
bags.

'We're just going to have to throw things out,' Emily said. Gustavo
said nothing. We squatted down on the track, then and there, and went
through everything. Naturally, the first bag I turned to was my wash
bag. Cleanliness would not be playing a major part in my journey. We
also dumped books, clothes, spare sets of shoes and rucksacks. In the
end, we still had to tie the sleeping bags on top, but at least we managed
to dispose of the holdall. We rode down to the end of the drive, followed
by Gustavo, Rosana and their children in the jeep. They followed us a
little of the way along the dirt road beyond. Then they turned back,
and we rode on alone into our journey.

These roads were dirt tracks which rarely saw more than ten cars in
a day. Fields flecked with farmsteads spread out in every direction, like
a giant quilted picnic cloth. Every so often, we passed a small copse of
eucalyptus, standing out above the plains as brilliantly as torches on
the night horizon. Everywhere was space, the unknown expanse of
Uruguay and limitless thoughts. The future now became an article of
faith. We had to believe that we would be fine, since if we had worried
about our safety we would probably never have gone anywhere. We
were heading for the town of Casupá, twenty-five kilometres from
Lockhart's. Yet we knew no one there, had no idea where we would be
able to stay with the horses, what we could eat or where we would
sleep. It became second nature to ask total strangers for permission to
camp, advice and directions. And sometimes, when I was alone, I asked
them questions just to speak to someone; to remember the sound of
my voice outside the vicious circle of my thoughts.

I will describe the first day in detail because it gives a good idea of
the sort of things that happened every day. As we went, we called out
to each other, asking how the horses were getting on, trotting over the
undulations that cut across Uruguay like a low-frequency wave. Every
twenty minutes or so, we passed a small house by the roadside, hidden
in shade. Dogs would emerge frenetically, barking crazily and yapping

away at the horses' heels; then plunging back into silence and padding back to their yards. After about an hour we were stopped by a police car, and three bemused patrolmen asked us what on earth we were doing. It seemed a reasonable question.

Before lunch, we stopped at least four times to readjust the saddle-bags, which had a life all their own. Chimango, whose load was much lighter than that of the others, kept trotting too fast on the lead rein, and Chileno wouldn't keep up. Chimango would get too far ahead, until we were forced to pirouette clumsily in the verge so that they were brought level again. Then he'd do it again a few minutes later, paying absolutely no attention to my pleas for him to go along at the same pace as us. Meanwhile, Ruso kept bounding away with Emily and then stopping next to a fence to stare wistfully at the fields. His intelligence was clear, for he knew that he was leaving on a journey and might never return – all he wanted was to bid his home farewell.

At lunch, we stopped to eat cold mutton next to a brook. As they grazed our triumvirate stared at us in utter bewilderment.

Near Casupá, the undulations became small hills, and plantations of pine trees cast shadows over the road. After a grey start, the sun was now burning gloriously across the rolling fields. We were stopped by everyone we met: a shepherd herding his ewes along the verge, children gawping at us as they walked home from school, farmhands emerging grimily from the fields.

They were all surprised when I told them we were heading for Tierra del Fuego.

Casupá was a sleepy place in which nothing much happened. A few streets fanned out from a surprisingly spruce plaza. The houses were all very neat, with the more well-to-do sporting manicured little gardens blooming with roses and blossom. It was a golden evening. The day had been so long, so filled with life, and this seemed the first chance to relax.

Unfortunately, as we arrived in the town it became clear that the horses had never seen anything like it before. Chileno became less and less responsive to the reins. All three pricked their ears, alert to dangers. They had never seen – or heard – mopeds, cars, houses, or so many people together. They started at the slightest sound. When we reached the main street, we dismounted to lead them through the plaza. Here, the school had just disgorged a rumbustious mass of junior pupils, all dressed in their uniforms of buttoned white tunics. They were busy fighting on the pavement, but as we passed they stopped at once. A small boy with a seamlessly round and cheery face asked us if he could lead one of the horses. Then we came to the railway track, and Chileno dug his feet in and refused to budge. Trucks were thundering past on the main road beyond. The boy gave up, and I coaxed Chileno gently over the thin strips of metal. Everything was unknown to them. All they had ever seen before were fields sprinkled with a few farms. They were intrigued by the hubbub, but it unnerved them. Like a rural migrant who first visits a city, the horses were suffering from culture shock.

Earlier, we had met a vet who recommended us to a friend's farm which lay just beyond this main road. When we arrived, though, the peon was reluctant to admit us, since the owner was absent. We waited near the farm, as the horses grazed and the sun curved towards the trees piercing the western horizon. We were nervous; still. Thankfully, the vet appeared shortly and persuaded the peon of our good intentions. We opened the gate of a large paddock, and freed our horses to graze for the night. There were unused rooms behind the *estancia* house, in which the farm manager allowed us to sleep. Behind our rooms was a muddy yard and several animal hides which had been strung between trees to dry, hanging like fleshy spider's webs from the branches. It was dusk. The sun was dropping behind a film of trees that rose from the bowels of a languorous evening mist. The mist met the steam rising from the grass already damp with dew, and embraced the night with its tangled layers of the imaginary.

The day had exhausted us. We crossed the road, barely able to talk or walk, our whole bodies aching, and ordered pasta and beer at a restaurant. With darkness, we slept.

Lockhart's *estancia* was near to Mac's. Since he had many friends in the area, Mac arranged us overnight stops for the next few days. We would arrive late in the afternoon, having tussled all day through our learning process. To begin with, it generally took at least two hours for us to catch the horses and then arrange all the saddles. The saddlebags were still a bloody nuisance, constantly falling to one side or the other, no matter how we arranged the sleeping bags and tied the knots. A succession of *gauchos* told us that they had finally provided the solution, only for the bags to list alarmingly twenty minutes down the road. I began to remember that Maspoli had never before made a packsaddle.

But, as before, small and unique moments made everything worthwhile. The day after leaving Casupá we rode into a farm with the sunset. The sky dissolved into a natural harmony of ethereal colours fusing with violent oranges and reds, the serene contrasts of the sky talking to our own doubts with love. Frogs croaked like a natural xylophone, as the plains dived into small brooks and copses before re-emerging unscathed. Eventually we followed a long and shadowy avenue towards the *estancia*, and rode in along with the shepherds. Hundreds of sheep were crossing the track, their shadows ebbing and flowing over the incipient night along with their bleats. The men cantered their horses up and down the flock, crying at the animals and pushing them into place. The yard was buzzing, men unsaddling their horses and hauling their tack into the stores. We dismounted, part of the thriving atmosphere for just one night.

Next morning we continued through wild country towards the town of Florida. It took us three days to pass the town and reach the last contact that Mac could give us. Although there had been precious moments, the stress had still been all but overwhelming. After an exhausting day's ride to Florida, we had to give a television interview. In the morning, we negotiated the town, which was several times the size of Casupá. But as soon as we had left it behind we were engulfed by the plains again, and the searing loneliness of these roads. Perhaps Florida hadn't been so bad.

Every day was so intense that it seemed to last for a week. There were times when we found ourselves riding through wild common land, bereft even of sheep and cattle, along old paths struck between fences. No one else rode this way, through the gates and past the stagnant ponds whose surfaces rippled in the morning wind. And then the next day the route would be different again: a metalled road being resurfaced, with banks of soft sand cast free by the bulldozers. Our horses floundered through the sand, and our progress slowed dramatically.

Even when the going was relatively straightforward, we were

constantly struggling with the blasted packsaddle, which was one of the most frustrating contraptions ever wrought. The frustrations were not just because it was complicated to use, nor because we had to whine and wheeze like bulldozers ourselves when it came to tightening the straps and girths, nor even because it was never straight and forever seemed on the verge of keeling over one way or another. The real cause of our infuriation with it was that it meant that we could never ride in peace, for we often had to be checking to make sure that it was not about to fall. If it had not been for the growing relationship of trust which we were developing with our horses, the trials of the packsaddle might have beaten us down completely. We had decided to talk to the horses as we travelled, so that they knew and understood us better, and this really seemed to work, calming them down whenever we had a problem.

In spite of the troubles we faced, we both felt that the journey made them a small price to pay. Some fascinating experience, or an unexpectedly beautiful spot, would revive our spirits as we rode, and we would fall into the tranquillity of the countryside again: the cloudscapes rising like mountains from the skyline, tremendous rainbows of light and dark, swirling with the birdsong that hummed incessantly from the fields and the copses, startled in its own tune by the rattled wings of a partridge escaping our tread, and flying like memories away from our eyes, out of reach.

Darwin's stay in Maldonado was relatively productive. Among other things, he collected eighty kinds of birds and nine species of snakes. Yet he found the scenery in Uruguay 'very uninteresting; there is scarcely a house, an enclosed piece of ground, or even a tree, to give it an air of cheerfulness'. There was nothing to engross him as there had been in the jungles in Brazil, or as he would find in places such as the Andes and the Galápagos. The lassitude of Uruguayans amazed him. He was sure that the perils of travel in Uruguay were due to laziness: 'Robberies are a natural consequence of universal gambling, much drinking, and extreme indolence. At Mercedes, I asked two men why they did not work. One gravely said the days were too long, the other that he was too poor.'[1]

Nothing could have been further from the situation in England. The country was reverberating with the industrial revolution, and Darwin had grown up in an atmosphere of industry and enterprise. The wealth of his father, Dr Robert Darwin, was founded on his being one of the first private money-brokers in England. He not only lent money to infant manufacturing businesses, but acted as a go-between for businesses looking for investors. Charles' cousins were the Wedgwood clan from the potteries. Economically, socially and intellectually, Britain was undergoing a revolution, and Darwin's life coincided with the birth of modern capitalism.

For many social historians, this is more than a coincidence. Darwin's was not the first theory of evolution; nor was it the first theory of natural selection. Darwin synthesized the two ideas, and produced a massive body of scientific observation to support his views. But for some, the key to the rise of Darwinism was the development of these ideas along with the world of nineteenth-century capitalism and industry. With the fierce competition between businesses, the misery, poverty, difficulties of survival in tenement blocks and so on, the potential battles in life were all too apparent. The phrase 'survival of the fittest', coined by Herbert Spencer, struck home. It tallied with life in the industrializing world. Social Darwinism, in fact, became – and still is – a justification for abominable practices. Capitalist entrepreneurs were not cruel exploiters, they were merely exemplifying the natural order; if they did not do so, then others would replace them in the rise to the top. As Rockefeller said in a speech at the turn of the century: 'The growth of a large business is merely a survival of the fittest ... This is not an evil tendency in business.'[2]

Can the rise of Darwinism really be dismissed as a social phenomenon? Many will reject this argument, pointing out that while the theory of evolution was accepted soon after Darwin published his main work, natural selection – the central plank of evolutionary thought today – was largely passed over; it was only through the fusion of Mendelian genetics and Darwinism that this idea gained credence early in this century. Natural selection was rejected by most of the scientists of Darwin's times, and it has only been through the rapid advances of scientific knowledge that we have come to embrace his original theory. Scientific discoveries since Darwin have shown us that his theory is more than a phenomenon of his times.

Certainly, science itself has replaced the sacred cow of religion which Darwinism helped to dismantle. The techniques of science's mass appeal are remarkably similar to those that religion used before the industrial revolution: science is claimed as being above human relations, as illustrating the universal truths behind the natural world, and it speaks esoterically. Scientific discoveries are our new pillars of faith in a quasi-religion. They are above the anthropomorphism of religious superstition. Many hail them as the paradigm of objectivity.

And yet when we look back over Darwin's thought, trying to understand how he reached what was an immensely controversial position, a paradox emerges. Despite the supposition that science should be above human relations, it appears that Darwin's anthropological discoveries played a substantial role in his development: the trigger for his theory of natural selection was reading Malthus' essay on human population growth; his vivid experiences among the Yámana tribe around Navarin Island were central to his developing beliefs surrounding the common descent of mankind from the apes; and, notwithstanding the importance of his investigations, the experience of a growing industrial society was a ready-made laboratory for the confirmation of his theory. Of course, the data which he collected in South America was also crucial. Darwin would later combine his geological findings with his natural history observations of the development of animals and plants in the isolated archipelagos which he visited to weld his theory together. Yet the significance of some of his observations, particularly in the Galápagos, did not strike him until he had had the specimens – most importantly the famous Darwin finches – analyzed back in London.

The fact that Darwin's cultural experience was incomparably wide surely aided his thought processes, enabling him to draw powerful analogies between men and other animals. In fact as many progressive thinkers are realizing, culture incontrovertibly influences our perception of facts. The more that Darwin experienced, the more cross-cultural his knowledge, the more creative his ideas could be. Stephen Jay Gould, one of the most famous evolutionists of today, writes that 'The most creative theories are often imaginative visions imposed upon facts; *the source of imagination is also strongly cultural.*'[3] If, as many philosophers and scientists are coming to see, theories are inalienably

cultural and cannot be 'objective', then the wider a theorist's experience
of cultures other than their own, the more generally applicable their
theory will be; and the clearest proof of this is Darwin's own theory,
which to this day unravels its implications in a bewildering spread of
fields.

From Florida, we went west across small tracks towards the village of
Cufre. The farms were small and mostly built of wood or adobe. Ancient
cars creaked past us once in a while, and everyone, including the driver,
would turn their heads 180 degrees to stare. We must have looked
incredibly strange. Hardly anyone in Uruguay journeys long distances
by horse any more; and even fewer wear riding hats.

As we travelled, we bought food in the *boliches*. A *boliche* is a
small store-cum-bar, descendants of the inns called *pulperías* in which
Darwin sometimes passed an evening as he went. They are never
signed; you have to know where they are in the maze of sandy tracks.
Invariably small, smelling musty and of age, inside we always found
the same select choice: bread, cheese, pasta, *dulce de leche* (caramelized
condensed milk) and, if we were lucky, some ancient oranges. The
bars next to the food were all old, sporting a row of cracked and
nearly empty whisky bottles and several pitchers of wine. Men came
at any time of day to down a litre of wine, escaping from the irrepressible
sun.

We lived mostly from what we could buy in these stores. This rarely
included vegetables, since any potato or onion lurking in the murky
light was invariably green with mould. Each night, we asked to camp
at a small farm. Camping wild was impossible, since the land was all
fenced off. People hardly ever turned us away, and nine times out of
ten they would invite us in to eat and drink *mate*. The farmers had
dairy herds, they were certainly not rich, but nor were they desperately
poor. They had plenty of food from their land, and most of them had
an old pick-up truck. We were often invited in to watch television –
The Simpsons – and tell stories about life in Europe. They all found
mad cow disease an impossible idea.

'So *why* do the cows go mad?'

'It's because they were given feed with diseased animal concentrate.'

'Why didn't they just let them out to eat the grass?'

It was funny, but also disturbing to them, since Uruguay will surely go bankrupt if it ever sees BSE. Then, as we sat and ate doughnuts or fried eggs, the perennial refrain was '*Sirvanse*' – help yourself.

'Behave as if you were at home.'

There was no running water in some of these farms. In the toilet would be a large jug floating in a pail, which was for washing and flushing. Children walked to school, or rode. Sometimes we passed them, galloping home, bobbing easily with the swaying rhythms of their horses. The farmhouses were set around sandy courtyards shaded by orange or lemon trees. When night fell, silence glittered with the shimmering stars. The men rose at three to milk the herds, while the women slaved away in the kitchen.

Sometimes we seemed to have fallen into the past. We'd sit and sip our *mate* in silence, our eyes peeled for the cockroaches on the floor. A peon or two, in-bred, faces hidden beneath flat caps, would stand in stricken silence against the wall, as we tried to talk with the family in this antiquated world which everyone was abandoning. We were fêted by some, offered home-made pumpkin jam and *dulce de leche*.

One man told me that the last foreigner to pass had been a *Norte-americano*, twenty years ago.

'But I don't really remember him,' his wife simpered. 'I was only a girl.'

Their daughter, blonde and blue-eyed – a genetic blip if ever there was one, judging by her dark parents – ran away from us when we came to the dining room in the morning, her eyes shining with shyness. Her father hustled into the living room with a camera:

'I insist on taking your photograph,' he said in a burst of optimism. 'You may die tomorrow, but the picture will still be here.'

Then they waved us off, and I thought I caught a glint of tears in the man's eyes.

'Yes,' he'd said, 'it would have been nice to talk for longer. But that's life! We each live the life which God allots to us.'

A week after leaving Florida, we reached Cufre, where Darwin stayed for a night. Here he met the postman, who had been delayed by floods. This was of small consequence, since he was only carrying two letters.

The day of our arrival was swelteringly hot. At lunch we rested at a small farm, where the couple insisted on our trying their wine and home-made pork sausage. The wine and the heat made us both flushed in late afternoon, and as we rode towards the village we passed a small dairy farm. Three dogs came tearing out, and leapt at Chimango, who started in fright, and jumped towards the side of the road. Emily fell from him and jolted hard into the earth.

I was riding a little way ahead when I heard the commotion. Emily was wearing a garish shirt of mine, which stood out against the green fields like a brilliant red admiral. She was sitting stunned on the road, unable to move, and for a desperate moment I thought that she was seriously hurt. As I went to help her we both began to cry, alone, with three horses in the middle of Uruguay.

For several minutes neither of us could speak.

'I think I'll just walk on my own for a bit,' Emily said, eventually.

Neither of us could believe that another accident had struck us, and for the first time we realized that we might not be able to complete the journey together. We could not think about anything except the awful pain we would feel if we had to part. When we reached Cufre, the local policeman, Waldo, took us under his wing and found us a place to camp with the horses. We were both exhausted, and emotionally shattered. Waldo's father, who had also been a policeman, took no notice of our bedraggled appearance. He drew us aside and gave us a strong warning.

'Listen, you have to be very careful here. There is a lot of drug trafficking! When people see you travelling like this, they'll all suspect you too. Always make sure that you report to the local police. That way, you'll be safe.'

Cufre, with its handful of cars, two shops, and a post office, did not seem a likely centre for narcotics operations.

Waldo disarmed his father's suspicions, and we finally had the space to cook dinner. Dusk hurried on as we sat by the fire, but five minutes after eating I threw the dinner up over the field – and that just about capped the day.

Hungry, ill and exhausted, we watched daylight relinquishing the sky. There was a sudden transformation as an aurora of fireflies descended, dancing madly every which way around us. Owls cried out over the night, and the stars began to shine from the blackness, fighting with the fireflies to sparkle brightest.

It was a very peaceful moment, which somehow managed to resuscitate our spirits.

'I'll be all right,' Emily said. 'But we've just got to take things slower.'

She climbed into the tent, and I watched the shadows of our three horses blend finally into the night, as they rustled around the copse at the bottom of the field, swishing their tails like scythes through the cooling night air.

II

I heard some men discussing the merits of those [representatives] for Colonia; and it was said that, 'although they were not men of business, they could all sign their names': with this they seemed to think that every reasonable man ought to be satisfied.

Charles Darwin

From the city of Colonia – a UNESCO site of world heritage for its well-preserved colonial layout – we rode north towards Mercedes. Here the small dairy farms vanished into the wild expanses of the large *estancias*. Many of the buildings were very old, with venerable tree gardens distinguishing the houses from the plains. There would often be towering firs, copper beeches, poplars, plane trees, silver birches and *ombues*, casting a wonderful umbrella of shade from the heat which became more oppressive by the day. The beginning of November heralded summer, and that seemed like an invitation to heatstroke. We couldn't ride all day any more; midday was torture. We always tried to find a shady spot where we could rest until the furnace cooled. We snacked on the bits and pieces that we'd found in the last *boliche*, and sometimes on what people had kindly given us for the day's journey. One day the gift took the form of a dozen eggs – not a recipe for happiness, since we later found that with the horses' motion they all smashed and leaked through everything.

Perhaps I had thought that this life would have no routine, that it really would be beyond boundaries. Now I realized my error. We always rose at half past five, when the tero-teros began to cry eerily over the plains as they glimpsed the first animals scurrying across the fields. The sky was still cast as a pale shadow of death, and lumbered uncertainly against the clusters of dark shadows which stood aloofly with the declining darkness. We would find our horses in the dark, dismantle the tent, cook breakfast, saddle up – and by the time we had finished the sun would be bright and searing already, high above the tips of the eucalyptus plantations. After riding all morning, we would stop for lunch, and then ride again in the afternoon, until we stopped for the night. Then we would have to unsaddle the horses, pick out their hooves, put up the tent, prepare dinner. By the time all the chores were done, the day was done with them and we were left to the night.

We mostly rode in silence. Sometimes we talked about some newly discovered trait of the horses, and then the outburst relapsed into the silence of our thoughts and the plains. Of course the plains weren't really silent – there was the wind in the grasses, the birds, the sounds of our horses, all stage-whispering like actors – yet still they seemed it; perhaps because of the immensity of the space, which swallowed up all your senses, and turned you so inward that you could no longer perceive anything external at all. You miniaturized the world in response to its vastness, so that you were only aware of yourself.

Four days from Colonia, we found ourselves on Uruguay's Route 2, the main road to Argentina. When I had asked a Montevideño which way we should travel he had said, 'Route 1, Route 2,' but he had no idea what it was like to ride horses along a main road. There were scores of articulated lorries flashing past with a fine disregard for the horses' sensibilities. It was scaldingly hot. The bitumen road was long, straight, and its mirages frolicked in the haze. The horses kept leaping and jumping with the constant stream of traffic. We were worried that they'd jump into the road and be killed.

It took an hour to reach the house of the Fuicas. Another man, Lito Cabrera, had recommended us to them, and I recognized the house from his directions. I walked up the grassy drive to ask Señora Fuica if we could camp. She had greying black curls and silver spectacles. She seemed to find life immensely funny; or perhaps it was just us. I showed her a letter explaining our journey.

'Ah,' she said. 'Darwin. The same name as my husband.'

'Dar-*win*,' she called, and Charles' namesake appeared. His face was all jowls, and his mouth was all gums; but Darwin had a heart of gold. He patted me companionably on the shoulder whenever he said something. His wife and he had the endearing habit of talking in tandem, as if one was an echo of the other, finishing the other's sentences as one mind and mouth.

'Why did your parents call you Darwin?'

'I really don't know. I've always asked myself the same question.'

'You know that Darwin was a scientist? He was here.'

But he'd never heard of Darwin. He and his wife had been neighbours of Lito Cabrera and his wife, all of them tenant farmers. But then the landowner had sold off the whole block of land to a rich Italian, and they had all had to move on.

'We were only able to move here because we'd been saving for years. The same with Lito. But everyone else had to go to Montevideo. That's why there's no one in the country any more. We weren't able to pay them enough money to keep them satisfied.'

When Darwin was growing up, there were ninety-eight pupils of his age at primary school.

'Last year there were two,' he said sadly, sipping *mate* beneath a shady orange tree. The oranges were ripe, and his wife gave us about fifteen.

'They're good for blood-pressure,' she said.

She had high blood-pressure, and ate fish all the time. She hated fish.

'I've always eaten meat,' she said. 'When I was a girl, we didn't know cholesterol. You ate what you wanted, then you died. Now they tell me to eat fish. Fish! Ha!'

Darwin looked at his wife pityingly. He would never eat fish, even if it killed him not to – which it probably would. In the morning, under an azure sky, he watched us saddle up.

'I should think there'll be a storm, today or tomorrow. It looks like it.'

Looks like it? I scoffed to myself, perceiving only the promise of another blistering day. And then, that afternoon, we rode into a mini-hurricane.

By now, we were only a few days from Mercedes. We headed for a small town called Risso. As we approached, a boisterous wind picked up, springing from thick calm. I looked southwards. Banks of ebony storm clouds glowered from across the wheatfields, spreading irrepressibly over the sky. And then the gales began, one hundred kilometres an hour and pummelling us like punchbags, gust after gust greeting us with fury. Dust was swept along the track and dashed into our eyes, rasping our faces like sandpaper. We couldn't hear each other, even when we shouted. I could barely hear the words of reassurance which I mouthed silently to myself; nature made language redundant. Clusters of vapour on the edge of the front whirled in chaos, confused as a breaking voice. We reached Risso, and the gales stilled, as if curtailed by magic. They seemed to have gone for good, but as we rode out of town we saw that the storm had turned in a semicircle and was coming straight at us. Thunder growled distantly, and the horses cocked their ears. When we saw the sheet lightening, we knew we had to find shelter. There are few things on the Uruguayan plains taller than a mounted horse.

We rode into the nearest *estancia*. An old *gaucho* had just finished rounding up sheep on an underfed white mare. He told us to tether our horses in the barn, and then he joined us. He was a slight man with a pallid face. Wind began to tear through the eucalyptus plantation beyond the corral, echoing and bellowing like an ocean spitting spume. Then came the rain, and then the hail. The horses started when they heard the hail assault the barn, twisting and turning, whinnying in fright. We were all frightened, but there was nothing to say. Rainwater seeped in and congregated in a depression in the earthen floor, so we all stood close together.

'You'll have to stay the night here,' the *gaucho* said, breaking the silence. He was pleased for the company. No other peon lived at the *estancia*, they all commuted from Risso.

'You'll probably have to stay tomorrow, too,' he said, with a trace of cheerfulness. He liked this idea, and toyed with it as the rain fell. The sound was almost soothing now. He had no concept of hurry. He did the same thing every day, and had done all his life. Like the old *gauchos*, he'd never seen anything but the farms.

In the corral was a group of sheep. The *gaucho* was going to butcher one for dinner.

'Then we can have *asado*,' he said.

The rain eased, and he ambled outside, squelching through the puddles and the softening sand. He chivvied the sheep into a pen behind the barn, and they scampered in eagerly. Then he shut the pen, and surveyed the wool and the quizzical faces. The sheep were uncomfortable with the wet and the cold. Dramatically, and without warning, he leapt in among them and seized a ram around the neck, one that was sleek and ripe for eating. He hobbled the ram and put him in a wheelbarrow. The rest of the flock began to bleat as he wheeled the ram to an enclosure a little way off; perhaps out of anxiety, or perhaps as a goodbye to their friend who was going, but not gone. The ram was remarkably passive, terrified into acquiescence: it was better to die quickly than to fear. The *gaucho* sharpened his knife on the whetstone and calmly stuck it into the jugular so that blood spurted in torrents. The ram shuddered and had convulsions, twitching for a while yet as the rain intensified and the man began to strip him from his fleece and cut the flesh free.

It was a few minutes before he stopped moving.

Then we went and ate in the peon's quarters. There were two dark rooms here, two rickety chairs and a fireplace spotted with ash. The man was sad and very lonely, and wanted us to stay. We could have another *asado* tomorrow.

'I butcher a sheep every day,' he said.

He had meat for breakfast, lunch and dinner; with a little bread.

'You don't want to go tomorrow,' he kept saying, sometimes with a mischievous grin.

But the storm abated with the dawn, and we went.

The *gaucho* is a symbol in Uruguay and Argentina, representing the nomad, noble human nature, wildness and animalism, bravery and kindness. The *gaucho* is a figure whose wisdom is not literate but transcends recognized learning, coming from the fields and their way of life.

Like many ideals, much of this is not based in reality. Until the turn of this century, *gauchos* were controlled through quasi-feudal laws and customs. Many had hoped that with the passing of Spanish colonialism, with the new republic, the servitude of the great estates would be a thing of the past. But nothing changed for a century. The Argentine *Código Rural* of 1865 enshrined the exact same tyrannical laws that had been introduced by the Spanish viceroys of the previous century. They had no bed but their saddles, and ate nothing but meat. If a *gaucho* was caught outside his *estancia* without the landowner's permission, he was returned and forced to pay a fine of fifty pesos – a considerable sum at the time, particularly since the *gaucho* was never paid.

Gauchos were in fact part and parcel of the extraordinary oligarchy which Argentina – in particular – became in the nineteenth century. In the 1850s a large *estancia* in the Province of Buenos Aires might have had 300,000 hectares. Towards the end of the century the price of meat rocketed with increased demand from Europe and the beginnings of refrigeration, and some people became obscenely rich in the space of a few years. So self-centred were the landowners that in 1854 an *estanciero* complained about the smaller landholders. He suggested to a government minister that their land should be appropriated, so that these nuisances could become peons or dependants, and thus be 'useful to society'.

The availability of unpaid but highly skilled *gauchos* was crucial in these developments. The average *estancia* had one peon per 2000 head of cattle, so there were rarely more than two peons in any farm. Those who did not work in the *estancias* – dismissed by the landowners as *vagos* – were wanderers who roamed the provinces around the River Plate, living from the livestock which they killed as they found it. But the *vagos* were targeted by particularly harsh laws, and often they felt it better to comply with a brutal *estanciero* than risk the wrath of the law. Perhaps the *gaucho* symbolizes feudal repression above all else.

Yet the wandering *gaucho* was the eulogized *gaucho*. Their nomadic lifestyle drew attention to itself. It was with these men that Darwin travelled when he rode across Uruguay and Argentina. Mostly, they specialized in taming wild horses. There were trackers, though (the *baqueanos*), thought by some to have mystical powers. A *baqueano* could tell the numbers of a mounted army, their speed, and which way they were travelling, from the cries of the tero-teros – even when the army was ten leagues distant. They could follow any track over any ground.

In the mid-nineteenth century a *baqueano* was away tracking for the police, when a thief came to his house and stole his saddle. His wife covered the thief's tracks, so that they should not be disturbed by the wind. On his return, the *baqueano* immediately set out to find the thief. He was gone for a year and a half, and returned with his saddle. He had tracked the thief across deserts, rivers, plateaux, and then through the mountains to the city of San Juan, 1900 kilometres away. Then he had walked grimly up a street on the periphery of the city, into one of the many nondescript houses, had walked into a back room, and found his saddle abandoned and unused amidst piles of fabric.

Sometimes you hear a peon being called a *tipo baqueano*. They're the proud old men who ride out bareback to round up the herds, and scarcely utter a word.

A day before reaching Mercedes, we camped at a police post. The policemen were bored speechless most of the day, since they worked in a tiny village where the only crime was very occasional minor cattle rustling. When I told one of them that we were following the trail of an English scientist, he said:

'It must be Darwin!'

There was a small town called Villa Darwin, fifty kilometres away up the Río Negro. He was the first person we had met since we had left Lockhart's who knew about Darwin.

'Aren't you going to go and see the monolith?'

We wanted to go, but Chileno's shoe had now worn out, and we urgently needed to get to Mercedes to change it.

'You should carry one of those small tape-recorders. Then you can ask people what it means to them that Darwin was here.'

'I've got one,' I said. So I got it out, and asked him what it meant.

'Well, I know that he was a scientist ... that he was in Mercedes ... but quite honestly I don't really care at all.'

He was a funny man. He used to smuggle goods over from Argentina to Uruguay.

'But then the exchange rate changed,' he said, recognizing the irony. 'So I trained to be a policeman instead.'

He treated us like royalty. He shared his dinner with us and insisted on giving us an old and intricately carved *gaucho*'s knife to remember him by. Then he found us a bed, and piled blankets on top. It was the first bed that we'd seen for a fortnight.

'With the weather like this, you'll need those blankets.'

He couldn't understand the weather. Usually mid-November was hot and dry, but now they had had this storm, whose tail-end was still sending cold winds and spots of rain across the plains. In Mercedes, the wind had resembled a cyclone, wrenching roofs from houses and flooring telephone wires. Everyone agreed that the climate was changing for the worse. We stayed at one farm where we did some washing, and hung it out to dry for the night.

'Will it rain?' I asked the farmer.

'Oh no – it never rains with this *pampero* wind from the south.'

So of course in the night there was a devastating thunderstorm, and our clothes were soaked through.

From the police post we moved on towards the Río Negro at Mercedes, heading for the Argentine frontier. Fray Bentos, the border town, was only a day's ride further on, and for the first time the prospect of leaving Uruguay seemed real. The journey was still a struggle, but we had become firm friends with our horses, and there was a bond of trust that we would always find them food, and they would always protect us while we were mounted. Even then, there were problems: once, Chileno got his foreleg caught in the lead rein tied around his breast, and bucked and heaved trying to free himself, so much so that he lacerated his mouth and cut himself so badly that we could not fit him with the bit until the wound had healed. And then, there were the dangers for which we could never legislate.

The bridge over the river at Mercedes was two kilometres long and extremely narrow. When we arrived the sun was at its peak, but there was nowhere to camp in the town, so we had little option but to cross it. We tethered Ruso and Chileno by the police post on the Mercedes side, and gingerly began to cross with Chimango. Even though this was a Sunday, the traffic was constant, and coaches and juggernauts kept passing us, the wind picking up and howling past, frightening Chimango with its presence. I kept him on as tight a rein as I could, but when we were about two thirds of the way across he whinnied at the sight of an articulated lorry and nearly leapt straight into it. He missed the side of the lorry by no more than twenty or thirty centimetres. The sun burnt down and frazzled us, and the stress of the crossing hurt us even more. We were so upset by this that we chose to lead Chileno and Ruso along the neighbouring railway track, stones and all. The policemen told us that there were never any trains, but in fact it turned out that freight wagons still plied along the line occasionally.

The whole nightmarish business took three hours, and when it was over Emily developed mild sunstroke. We rested the next day, which was as violently hot as the one before.

On the following day, three weeks after leaving Lockhart's *estancia*, we rode for five hours until we saw the bridge over to Argentina. We had saddled ourselves with Darwin, and followed him across Uruguay.

III

Nearly every public officer can be bribed. The head man in the post-office sold forged government franks. The governor and prime minister openly combined to plunder the state.

Darwin on Uruguayan government

Naively, I believed that arranging paperwork for crossing the horses into Argentina would be straightforward. After all, we had already had the horses' sanitary certificates produced before we set out, and Lockhart had promised to send them to Fray Bentos in time for our arrival. We camped at the nearest farm to the border, and then went to the Ministry of Agriculture the next day. Fray was a two-hour walk from the farm along a scalding bitumen road, and we arrived shattered from the walk, bathed in sweat. Nonetheless, I was feeling quite positive: we would only have to do this walk once or twice.

The Ministry was next to the famous but now abandoned meat-packing factory, overlooking the river.

'Hello, I think there are some sanitary certificates waiting for me here. I'm crossing into Argentina with three horses.'

They'd no idea what I was talking about. There were no certificates, which the attendant confirmed with the chief vet.

'Anyway, who's your customs agent?' he asked.

'Customs agent?'

'How are you going to get the horses over the bridge without a customs agent?'

'Can't I just arrange that now?' I asked, remembering that Lockhart had mentioned something about this, but had said that I could sort it out in Fray Bentos.

'No, no. You should have done all that when you cleared the horses for export at the Ministry of Agriculture in Montevideo.'

'Export?'

'You're exporting the horses, aren't you?'

'No, no. They're my horses. I just want to ride them across into Argentina.'

'So you're exporting them. Any horse going from Uruguay to Argentina is exported.'

'But that's ridiculous!' I fumed. 'You don't have to export your car when you drive across, do you?'

He shrugged, and then decided to give me a piece of advice.

'Listen, *compadre*, you'll waste time and money on this business. It'll be far cheaper to sell your horses and buy new ones in Argentina.'

'But I *like* my horses. I'm used to them.'

He gave up on me as a waste of effort and clearly mad. I ran off to telephone Lockhart, amazed at my misplaced optimism. I had had experience of South American bureaucracy before. When I taught English in Chile, I discovered that leaving the country required several weeks of meticulous preparation: several certificates from schools where I worked, from the place where I lived, as well as from the income tax office of my borough; and then I had to get a certificate for safe-passage from the National Centre for Detectives, in an office which was only open for two hours each morning – and I could only go on one of two days or all the other bits of paper were rendered invalid. I had even met one person who had been asked for her grandmother's birth certificate when she tried to open a bank account. And here was I, seriously believing that crossing horses from one country to another would be easy. I was obviously an idiot. I recalled, all too clearly, the reluctance with which Mac had endorsed the decision to keep the same horses. Mac *knew*, I realized. He lived here.

When I rang Lockhart, he promised to send me the papers the next day. But the real stumbling blocks weren't to be the sanitary certificates. Even though an Argentine government vet was going to have to make a special journey from Buenos Aires to the border to confirm the Uruguayan veterinary paper, everyone broadly agreed that the horses were clean, healthy and carrying no blemish of any kind – although you could have seen this just by looking at them. The real problem was that the customs' papers would cost about £1000, and still take another month to deliver.

It took a week of exhausting treks in and out of Fray Bentos for the fuse of this bombshell to sparkle down and produce the explosion, and when we became aware of the full extent of the problems it was all too much.

'But that's robbery!' I seethed to my contact at an export agency in Montevideo. 'That's as expensive as the horses themselves.'

'The problem is,' the man explained, 'that it costs the same whether you take one horse across or 300.'

'That's crazy! How can it be so expensive?'

'You're exporting the horses, right? You need an export agent in Montevideo and an import agent in Buenos Aires. You need a customs agent in Fray Bentos. Then you need to pay the Ministry of Agriculture in Uruguay and Argentina for processing the paperwork. And none of this is cheap. Listen, in my country's mitigation, all I can say is that this isn't the worst place for bureaucracy. Even if you could get the horses to Argentina, you'd never get them into Chile. The regulations are far worse over there.'

'But we went to the Chilean embassy in Montevideo. They said it was easy.'

'They are liars,' he said.

'I can't believe this,' I moaned pathetically. 'We're not really exporting the horses at all. It's not for profit.'

'I know that,' he sighed, 'and you know that. We both know it's absurd. But there's no way round it. I've tried to pull all the strings I know to get them to make an exception, but they won't. I'm afraid that all you can really do is sell your horses at Fray Bentos, and buy others in Argentina. All I ask is that when you get home, you tell people how impossible it is to work in this situation. There are so many regulations, and we have to pay so many absurd taxes. You know, you even have to pay a tax for every dog and cat that you own. All the money disappears into the government, and we never see it again. Please tell people.'

It was a disaster. Horses are prohibitively expensive in Argentina, and it was doubtful whether we could find any quickly that were good enough to do the journey. We had bought expensive horses in Uruguay, thinking that we would ride them for the whole journey, and now they were useless. No one would pay us the price that we'd paid for them, not when we needed to sell them quickly. If we had been able to smuggle them across, we might have tried that, but the Río Uruguay is four kilometres wide here, and the only crossing points are the international bridges. Someone recommended bribing the customs men at the border ('They all like that kind of business', he told us), but when we took into account the people in both countries *and* the veterinary people who also needed paying off, it would have cost even more than the legal papers.

There was no option but to sell the horses, which was a tremendous blow, for we had both come to love them. We talked with them every day, groomed them like prize pets, knew their quirks and recognized when they were in a bad mood, when they wanted to be affectionate, when they were hungry or thirsty or were ripe for a good day's ride. And now we had no chance of maintaining our friendship – we had to leave them, for good. The worst thing of all was that we had brought them away from their farms, which they had all loved, and now it turned out that the departure had been in vain. It made us feel both very irresponsible, and upset for the well-being of our horses.

The moment finally came when we could not escape the truth, and lay in our tent contemplating the horrid reality of what had happened. We would have to begin the whole acclimatization process again, with new horses, learning again to conquer our fears. We both cried. Then, Emily came to a decision:

'I don't think I'm going to be able to carry on,' she said.

We cried even more.

'If we could get the horses across, I would.'

'But...'

'I can't face going through the same learning process again. I trust these horses, but I'm not sure what it would be like with any others.'

There was nothing more we could say. We cried for much of the afternoon, but the matter was set. Emily waited with me in Fray Bentos until everything was arranged, but there was no longer any question of us completing the whole journey together. We both had to accustom ourselves to the prospect of more loneliness than we had ever known before, after having lived on top of each other for nearly three months. There was no intermediate point for our emotions, seesawing as they were.

After a few days at the farm by the International Bridge, where we had stayed in a disused water tower in which the water had dripped all night, we had gone to stay with an immensely cheerful woman called

Celia, and her children Román and Raquel. We had met Román in a bar in Fray Bentos, and he had invited us to stay along with our horses. So we sat with them, fuming to sympathetic ears about the mess, and trying not to let our own sadness filter through to our hosts. Celia, with her ample maternal girth and joyous bursts of laughter, was perfect company. Often we sat with her in her darkened bedroom, as she flicked through the armoury of the TV remote control, laughing at bad comedy, entranced by opera.

The horses were turned out into a six-hectare paddock, and they began hobnobbing with Raquel's gelding – Popeye – and a clutch of mares. We barely saw them for ten days, and by the time it came to leave for Buenos Aires they had all but forgotten what we were like. When we went up to say goodbye, we had to chase them over the huge paddock, littered with thorn trees, for half an hour. Their wildness had been returned to them, and it was quite painful: what right had we had to take them away from their fields? Only belatedly did they realize that this was something different, and stop. They allowed us to stroke them. We had come to love our horses, and perhaps they had come to like us just a little.

We still had to find good homes for them, and Mac's brother-in-law, Dr Chiarino, came to the rescue. He was a respected farmer from Mercedes, who had been a champion *Criollo* breeder. He thought the whole thing was laughable, but there was nothing to be done. We left our horses with him, and he sold them before sending me the money eight months later. He gave me a contact with breeders in Buenos Aires, who would help me find new horses, and spent ten days dashing between Mercedes and Fray Bentos, behaving as if it was his duty to resolve our problems.

The last thing we did before leaving Uruguay was to go to Villa Darwin. Laura, Chiarino's daughter, took us over from Fray Bentos. Darwin had ridden here from Mercedes, in the company of a local *estanciero*. At the time, there had been nobody living in this area at all, and Darwin wrote that 'the view of the Río Negro ... was more picturesque than any other which I saw in this province. The river, broad, deep and rapid, wound at the foot of the rocky precipitous cliff: a belt of wood followed its course, and the horizon terminated in the distant undulations of the turf-plain.' It had taken him a day from

Mercedes, but with all the palaver with the horses, Laura took us in her car.

Everyone who lives there today knows Villa Darwin as Sacachispas. The official name exists only in the welcome sign; but the school, police station, and bus office all affirm that this is Sacachispas. Nobody there knows or cares who Darwin was. We drove there on a day when the sun seemed almost too brilliant, making all colours shine with harsh violence. There was no monolith in sight, though; a man told us that it was at an *estancia* twelve kilometres away. Laura took us along a rutted, stony track, with the land fanning out in vast expanses on all sides. We passed two boys herding horses towards the town, but no one else.

When we reached the *estancia*, we were told that the only monument was to Artigas, Uruguay's independence hero. It didn't really seem plausible that the memorial could have been to both Artigas and Darwin, but we went to see anyway. We drove through a succession of fields, each larger and more desolate than the one before. There were obscure tracks over the grasslands which marked the way from one gate to the next. The sixth paddock was full of thorn trees, and there was a neglected corral near the entrance gate, overgrown with thistles and shrubbery like an abandoned garden. This was where we had been told to look.

'There it is!' cried Laura. She pointed at an old stone almost hidden by the undergrowth, on the rim of the river valley. The stone was dedicated to Artigas only; he had camped here in 1811 as he sallied over the country to begin the revolution. He'd chosen a stunningly beautiful place: the most beautiful that I saw in Uruguay. The Río Negro gurgled beyond a lush glade peppered with tall willows and hugging the banks for as far as we could see. As we watched, two flamingos soared away from us up the glade, pink petals in the green buds of the riverside. Over the river, the land stretched away unbroken and unpeopled to hills in the hazy distance, rising and falling in fat waves with the ponderousness which comes with immensity. The north of Uruguay is supposed to be far wilder and more uninhabited than the south, but I struggled to imagine such emptiness after that which I now knew. This emptiness inscribed itself indelibly on my mind, so that the emptier the land was the more content I felt.

Emptiness implied roaming, allowing the mind to roam with the land, rootless and wandering, the vagrant within.

But this glorious spot was irrelevant to Darwin. We had been sent on a wild goose chase from Sacachispas, which hadn't seemed the friendliest of places. When we went back, the same man that we'd met before came running down to us from his house.

'I'm so sorry,' he said. 'That stone isn't to Darwin, but Artigas. The Darwin stone is in the nearest *estancia* to the town. I remembered as soon as you'd gone.'

Laura drove us up to the *estancia*, where we were met by the peon's wife. She told us to pass an avenue of plane trees, and head for two hills, where we would see the monolith. But when we passed the avenue, there was a junction. Laura thought that we should take the right-hand fork, and I thought the woman had said left.

'There are more hills to the right,' she said. 'And anyway, women in the country don't know the land that well. Perhaps it's been a long time since she went there. Most country women barely ever leave the house.'

We followed the track over a ford beside a willow tree. Nearby was a watering hole coloured brown and white by Friesians, the water flashing in the sunlight. The cattle were slumbering in the midday sun.

'In England,' I said to Laura, 'we say that when cows lie down it's going to rain.'

'I don't think it's true,' she said.

There were no clouds, and the heat was yellow and constant. We followed a fence to a small congregation of thorn trees, and then, on a small rise above us, we saw the monolith. It tried to hide in the scrub, like the Artigas stone; but it was ten metres tall and it failed. We walked up to it through scrawny yellow grass, lizards and snakes escaping our path as we went. Their rustling was the only sound, the only movement in the heat apart from our own. There was no habitation within a radius of several kilometres. There was nothing to see but country and cattle.

And the stone. It was granite, and had hardly a blemish. It, too, was on the banks of the Río Negro. Here were the shady trees which Darwin described, here the tranquil river, here everything almost as it had been then.

Its legend was simple: '*Darwin – 1832–33*.'

PART THREE

Buenos Aires and the Pampas

I

It would do the whole tribe of you a great deal of good to come to Buenos Aires.

Charles Darwin, to his sisters

Darwin was in Buenos Aires three times. It was on his first visit that he appreciated the beauty of the ladies of the city, whom he saw as 'angels gliding down the streets'. That was in October 1832; but when he returned, twice, in the following year, the atmosphere had changed. He bemoaned the immanent muddiness of the city, and found himself caught up with internal Argentine problems. On his final visit, Darwin's arrival coincided with a blockade of the city. The *caudillo* Juan Manuel de Rosas was besieging the city in a bid to oust the Governor, and Darwin found the entrances barricaded. He had to find a way in to board the *Beagle*. He had caught a high fever on his journey down the Paraná River, and the last thing he needed was to negotiate his entrance to the city. Fortunately, in the south he had had an audience with General Rosas, and just the mention of this privilege was enough to spirit him past the guards.

Of all people in Argentina's history, Rosas is the most symbolic. He pioneered the expansion of *estancias* in the early nineteenth century. Having been bred and educated in the Pampas he was respected by the *gauchos*, primarily because of his horsemanship. Darwin himself noted this, in observing how the Argentines chose their leaders (including Rosas): 'A troop of unbroken horses being driven into a corral, were let out through a gateway, above which was a cross-bar: it was agreed whoever should drop from the bar on one of these wild animals, as it rushed out, and should be able, without saddle or bridle, not only to ride it, but also to bring it back to the door of the corral, should be their general.' Rosas used these amazing powers to become the most reviled tyrant in Argentina's history, eventually being overthrown in 1852 and exiled to England, where he lived in Southampton until his death in

1877. When he was prosecuted *in absentia* for treason, he was accused of murder, robbery, burning, destruction, sacrilege, perjury, forgery, imposture and hypocrisy.

Despite this he was widely popular, for he understood the *gauchos* and was almost one of them. A traveller through the Province of Buenos Aires in the 1870s, over twenty years after Rosas' dethronement, told of a drunk *gaucho* in a *pulpería* shouting 'Viva Rosas!' Argentina was a country of such shocking contrasts – effete sophistication in Buenos Aires, and the roughly hewn life of the provinces – that populism could always lead to a backlash from an opposing group. Rosas discovered this in 1852, as Perón would 103 years later.

In 1833, when Rosas' popularity was almost at its zenith, Darwin's earlier brief meeting with him was his passport to Buenos Aires. Ill and exhausted, he passed into the city. He was particularly worried about developments because his servant, Syms Covington, had stayed on at an *estancia* to complete the collection of specimens – now he would have to bribe the guards to find Covington a way in. So, with the city in turmoil and his body in fever, it is easy to imagine Darwin's despair when he discovered that the *Beagle* had left Buenos Aires before the blockade, and was across the River Plate in Montevideo. He had to spend several days holed up in Buenos Aires, a city which he had at first admired, and which now he could not wait to leave, before boarding a steamer to safety in Montevideo.

A pensioner ran the reception at our hotel in Buenos Aires. He was a diminutive man, with a slight hunchback and brilliant white hair flowing at the sides of his bald pate.

'Do you know what this country has always lacked?' he asked us, as we signed in. 'Good dictators, plenty of them!'

'Really?'

'Democracy's no good for us,' he said querulously. 'All the money disappears in thievery and corruption, and there's nothing left for the people. Heads need chopping off!'

'But you had a dictatorship here.'

'Yes, but they didn't do a good enough spring clean. We needed someone like Pinochet, in Chile. Pinochet did a good cleaning job, and kept the economy straight. The army worked for the people over there, they didn't steal. Over here, we're all a bunch of crooks.'

'The army killed people here, though.'

'Yes, but they stole everything as well. That's why this country is a disaster. *¡Es un desastre!'*

You could understand his bitterness. At the end of the Second World War Argentina was the sixth richest country in the world, but successive governments – beginning with Perón, through the military debacles of Videla, Viola and Galtieri, to the uncontrollable inflation under Alfonsín and the uncontrollable corruption under Menem – have brought Argentina to its knees, with high unemployment, hundreds of thousands of people living off rubbish tips across the country, and dark rumours about the drug Mafia's involvement in government. Barely a day seems to go past without a new scandal breaking: IBM bribing the Banco de la Nación to win contracts for government computers, journalists murdered or threatened, politicians constantly accused of embezzlement and fraud.

'There's always been corruption,' the old man said, 'but we've never had a bunch of thieves as shameless as this lot. There's just been a scandal about the customs agents. They've discovered that all the agents were bribed to waive import duties. Over one billion dollars of goods entered illegally.'

Everyone in Buenos Aires railed against the politicians. The taxi drivers gestured volubly towards the back of the cabs, their eyes flitting back to the road whenever we came across a near-death experience. The bakers would drip sweat over the bread with one hand and with the other give a passable impression of a drunken ballet as they expressed the failings of their politicians. In many South American countries it is customary to regale total strangers with your life story and philosophies, and I was confronted with one tale after another of political failure.

'*Che*, we should be one of the superpowers. And even with all their corruption, the politicians still can't destroy this country.'

'*Viste nene*. Until Perón came along and anarchized the workers, this was a great country.'

'The Peronistas are the only ones that protect this country. Look at Menem. How he's lifted up the country! Before, the streets were full of starving children, but now even the workers eat steak.'

'There's no work! Menem came along and privatized everything, sold it all off to the *gringos*, and now they've sacked everyone. We're all starving.'

They all disagreed with each other. The bars were full of men sipping coffee that was strong enough to make the beans jump out of the cup, expressing the caffeine with vibrant arguments and hand gestures that looked like punches. The disagreements were typical of a country torn between Europe and South America. Buenos Aires is called by some the 'Paris of South America'; the colourful Boca district, full of multi-coloured old houses, is more reminiscent of Naples; 40 per cent of Argentines are Italian in origin, 30 per cent are Spanish; and there are influential communities of Arabs, Jews, Russians, Poles, Germans and English, not to mention the famous Welsh community in Patagonia. This is a city of exile, of sadness and fond ideals about former homes, a city that straps down the spirit and tries to clothe it in urbane elegance, walking arm in arm with wistfulness. The tango, with its barely suppressed melancholy and existentialist longing, could only have come from Buenos Aires.

Elegance was everywhere, doubtless the corollary of Argentina's Italian heritage. Everyone was dressed perfectly. It seemed that none of them had sweat glands, for even though the climate was sticky and humid, and I had to change clothes twice a day, no one else seemed to sweat. My clothes were dirty, smelly and saturated with stale perspiration. I seemed to be by far the most inelegant person in Buenos Aires, judging by the glimpses I caught of a haggard and unshaven scruffian whenever I looked into a mirror.

Perhaps unwisely, Emily and I decided to go to the Colón Theatre the night before she left. This is one of the world's great opera houses, decorated with lavish extravagance: the gallery seems as high as a skyscraper and the ceiling (which we had a very good view of) is covered in frescoes. Everyone there looked immaculate. The women all had elaborate coiffures, apparently made especially for the occasion (perhaps, like Evita with her chignon, they believed that hair made a woman); they glittered like jewellery shops and wore silk dresses. It was a fair bet, I mused, that a reasonable slice of Argentine taxpayers' money was being exhibited here. We had both come dressed as smartly as we could, but our creased jeans and shirts did not quite hit the mark.

After the second interval, when I received evil stares from what seemed like half of Buenos Aires as I bought drinks at the bar, Emily and I decided that it was better to leave before the end.

This was where we had to say goodbye. Emily was leaving to stay with a friend of mine, Leslie, in Santiago de Chile, before travelling to visit cousins in Colombia and then returning home. We had supported each other through everything, and our love had grown across Uruguay. We had shared the tetchiness, the weaknesses, the joy and sadness of every moment, arguing and laughing, loving and sharing. It was horrible to part. It was impossible to imagine being alone after being with Emily for so long. Sometimes I cried when I thought about it. Now I would have to learn loneliness, learn how to live in my thoughts, confiding in myself only. She did not want to leave me either, but this was what we had decided was best. The opera was meant as a grand farewell, but its self-imposed exclusivity merely made us feel like shadows.

Confused, saddened, loving, upset: we parted the next day.

I would be alone for the rest of the journey.

To do everything exactly as Darwin did would probably cost several million pounds. Darwin generally travelled with guides and often with a team of, perhaps, six horses and several mules. The *Beagle*'s surveying duties meant that the ship constantly came and went. It first visited Tierra del Fuego at the end of 1832, but then returned north to the River Plate, and only finally emerged from the Magellan Straits into the Pacific in mid-1834, after its second voyage down the Atlantic coast. Before his second voyage to Tierra del Fuego, Darwin rode from Carmen de Patagones to Buenos Aires, continuing up the Paraná to Santa Fé. Then, when he returned to Buenos Aires and had to cross to Montevideo, he discovered that the ship still had a month's duties to complete in the area. It was then that Darwin decided to ride on to Mercedes.

Doing everything in the same order would have meant endless repetition and wasted time. And I had no *Beagle* to transport me backwards and forwards between Buenos Aires and Tierra del Fuego. I had chosen to follow Darwin in a geographical progression, first across Uruguay, and then inexorably southwards until I reached Patagonia. But I still needed horses.

No longer can you ride happily out of Buenos Aires along with the *gauchos*. Somehow, I had to find an appropriate and convenient place to begin from. I soon discovered that horses are five or six times as expensive in Argentina as they are in Uruguay, and that if I bought them here I would run out of money by the time I reached Chile. But Dr Chiarino had given me an introduction to a friend of his who was a *Criollo* breeder. A week after arriving in Buenos Aires, I was invited to the monthly meeting of the Breeders' Association.

The office was in an unprepossessing street of central Buenos Aires, on the third floor of a grey building. In the hall was a waiter in black tie dispensing whiskies to a pair of men with blotchy faces. I was invited to place my raincoat on the mahogany coat-stand, and then witnessed the end of the meeting. Unlike in Uruguay, where everyone had been trying to outdo the others with their cellular phones and new suits, here the breeders sat around in shirt sleeves. The room was masked by a thick cloud of cigarette smoke, and the discussions were continually interrupted by wisecracks. They were discussing the locations for various horse exhibitions across the province of Buenos Aires, and the meeting had gone on for three hours already.

'I've had enough of this nonsense,' a man said to me, soon after I'd sat down. 'Don't you want something to eat?'

He led me upstairs to the dining room, where we began to eat the *asado* while the business finished downstairs. Roberto offered me some wine and then asked what I was doing. I told him about the journey, and of the problems at the border.

'Ha!' he said. 'That means that the Uruguayans are almost as corrupt as we are!'

When the others came upstairs he told them all the joke.

'They skinned you, kid!'

It didn't matter, though, because I'd shared a bottle of wine with Roberto by now, and everything seemed rosy.

'What did you study at university, kid?' Roberto asked me, his voice already beginning to slur.

'Philosophy.'

'How many years?'

'Three.'

'Three!' he laughed. 'Three!'

He turned to Oneto, the secretary, who was sitting next to me.

'Three years. Oneto, isn't it right that a farrier studies for four years? And afterwards he has to do two years of practice!'

'Yes,' said Oneto. 'But they take one year over each leg.'

Roberto laughed and clicked his fingers clumsily at the waiter.

'More wine! So the kid wants to follow Darwin? What *is* Darwin's route, anyway?'

'No idea,' said Oneto. I explained that I had to follow the Atlantic coastline as far as the Río Santa Cruz, and then follow the river to the *cordillera*.

'You'd better not do that,' said Roberto. 'That's the ugliest route of all. There's nothing. *Nada, nada, nada.* Why don't you go somewhere nice and then just tell everyone you followed Darwin?'

'Because there's no point in that. I want to follow Darwin.'

'Well, where are your horses?'

'That's why he's here, *tonto*,' said Oneto. 'He wants someone to lend him some. Why don't you give him some of yours?'

'He could have a couple. But he'd have to give them enough fodder to feed an elephant at the end.'

'Hey, the kid's not stupid,' said Oneto, who was rapidly rising in my esteem. Some of the other breeders at the table had been listening, amid the decadent flow of wine and meat. Don Felipe-Juan Ballester began to take an interest.

'I might have a mare or two that you could have.'

Oneto leapt on him and began to turn the screw.

'Yes Felipe-Juan, he's even from Cambridge University. Look at the poor *nene*, he's upset because his girlfriend's going. He needs your help. You could give him a couple, and then he could leave them with a friend of yours in Patagonia.'

'How will he send the horses back?'

'It's easy! If he leaves them with the Hallidays at Río Gallegos, they can send them back with the horses they send to the annual exhibition in August.'

Felipe-Juan, who was a quiet man and a gentleman, didn't take much persuading. He would tell his foreman to arrange two horses for me, and I could begin riding from his *estancia* in a few days' time. The collected might of Argentine horse-breeding now began to relapse into sated inactivity, and we finished off what seemed like the tenth bottle of wine. We all fell into silence.

'*Che*, let's not talk about the war!' one of them said in the end.

'Oh, very diplomatic,' said Oneto.

'It's not the kid's fault, I know that. How old were you then, *nene*?'

'I was eight.'

'Eight! Just a little brat! Ah, well then, you probably wouldn't even remember it.'

'It was stupid,' said Oneto. 'We didn't think the English would care about those islands, thousands of kilometres away.'

'How were we going to fight the English? It was like fighting against a grandfather. The English built half of this country. And like a good grandfather, you beat us good and proper.'

They burst into spontaneous, self-pitying laughter.

I zigzagged home through deserted streets. I was accosted by one man, who I thought was about to mug me. But all he wanted was to entice me into a nearby strip club. The soft melodies of tango came into the street from somewhere, a tune suffused with hurt and self-loathing, with loneliness.

I spent another five days in Buenos Aires, trying to get used to my own company now that Emily had gone. Loneliness is most desperate in cities, where there are so many people and yet convention dictates that you speak to no one. I wandered from streets to plazas, staring at shop windows, drinking coffee or beer and laughing at my own thoughts, laughing about odds and ends, never knowing the rationale behind slivers of the past which I found flirting with my mind's eye. Sometimes all I felt was oppression. I would walk through the neon darkness after dusk, shut myself up in my bedroom, lie on my bed with neither books nor solace, and wonder why I was doing this.

I later found freedom in my solitude. In rural areas, where there were few people to judge me, I felt I could do as I pleased. I had no one else to consider, no one else to consult. I thought what I wanted, laughed at what I found amusing, laughed out loud, sang nonsenses to myself as I rode along. I invented myself anew, and then allowed my fictive ghost to die away with my journey.

But these days in Buenos Aires were the beginning of this phase of my life, and I was still learning about self-invention.

On one of my anonymous strolls through the city, I went to the Plaza de Mayo, the heart of old Buenos Aires. On one side is the presidential palace, the Casa Rosada – the 'pink house'; on the other the Cabildo, the historic town hall. In the middle were the mothers of the Plaza. These are the mothers of some of the thousands of *desaparecidos* who died during the military governments between 1976 and 1983. Every Thursday afternoon, these women walk anti-clockwise around the plaza with photos of their children pinned to their chests, demanding justice. The group has become an influential political force. They are mostly elderly, but march as the strength of Argentine society.

Many of the mothers clasped each other's hands as they walked slowly around the central fountain, in recognition of the lifelong friendships which their pain had brought them. Some of them wore white scarves of peace over their heads, the universal symbol of this protest group. They were impassive, and talked easily among themselves; impassive even in the face of the two TV crews that were filming them.

I wondered what they would have said to the hotel receptionist about the benefits of dictatorships.

II

One day, riding in the Pampas with a very respectable estanciero, *my horse, being tired, lagged behind. The man often shouted to me to spur him. When I remonstrated that it was a pity, for the horse was quite exhausted, he cried out, 'Why not! – never mind – spur him – it is my horse.' I had then some difficulty in making him comprehend that it was for the horse's sake, and not on his account, that I did not choose to use my spurs. He exclaimed, with a look of great surprise, 'Ah, Don Carlos, que cosa!' It was clear that such an idea had never before entered his head.*

Charles Darwin

Darwin frequently saw men flaunting their brutality towards animals. Although the *gauchos* learnt to ride before they could walk, they treated their animals cruelly. His opinion was that 'animals are so abundant in these countries that humanity and self-interest are not closely united; therefore I fear it is that the former is here scarcely known.' Most *estancias* had several thousand head of cattle, and horses flourished in the River Plate region. But in spite of their closeness to these animals, the *gauchos* never reached the Indians' own standard of horsemanship. The nineteenth-century naturalist W.H. Hudson spent the first part of his life in the Argentine provinces, living among the Indians and the *gauchos*: 'The Indian horse is more docile, he understands his master better; the slightest touch of the hand on his neck ... is sufficient to guide him ... The *gaucho* labours to give his horse "a silken mouth", as he aptly calls it; the Indian's horse has it from birth. Occasionally the *gaucho* sleeps in his saddle; the Indian can die on his horse.'[1] These differences intrigue me. Horses were brought to the area by Pedro de Mendoza in 1535, and by 1578, when Pedro Sarmiento de Gamboa passed through the Magellan Straits, they had been mastered by the Teheuelche Indians in Patagonia, over 2000 kilometres south of Buenos Aires. The durability of *Criollo* horses stems from the fact that they ran wild for centuries, and learnt to adapt to the very harsh climates of these regions. Yet why should the *gaucho*'s horse have been any different to the Indian's? No doubt it was due to the different attitudes and accumulated knowledge which each brought to their relationship with horses: an example of how culture can affect natural order.

The world of the *gaucho* wasn't one of logic. It was one of wildness and metaphor, senseless as their lives of wandering and bloodiness. The wildness of the plains – where you can see for many leagues with no houses or people, where the sweeping tablet of level land roars and whispers of the immensity of things – was expressed in the *gaucho*'s own wildness. With the plains and the threat of attacks from the Indians, they experienced everything as wild. Their knowledge, which was in no way rational, found its metaphorical expression in characteristics such as violence towards animals – for wildness was ubiquitous.

But the Indians had lived with this 'wild' environment for millennia. They didn't see it as wild, but as essentially theirs. Perhaps they were secretly aware of the metaphorical immensity of the plains, but they did not fear this. Their response was, inevitably, calmer than that of the *gauchos*, and this expressed itself in their attitudes towards their animals. Playing along with the endless stream of metaphors billowing in the plains presents the attitudes of the *gauchos* and Indians through a different eye-glass – curved like the earth, not straight.

I arrived at Ballester's farm on a clammy December morning, and Fernando – the foreman – met me. The Pampas were covered by a shield of cloud, which drifted close to the grass and disguised the land from itself. The mist made this place seem more mysterious and appealing than it really was, swallowing the grasslands and their uniformity, and returning your imagination to you intact.

I talked to Fernando about the plans, and he introduced me to Angel.

'Angel is our *domador*,' he said, 'the tamer of horses.'

Angel was a quiet young man from the northern province of Corrientes. His face was red with meat and wine, openness and hard work; dark with Indian blood. He hid his expressions beneath a wide-brimmed felt hat, which he rarely removed. The hat was tied to his stubble by a leather chinstrap. Now he and Fernando led me over to a muddy corral where a group of ten mares were kept.

'We have mares and geldings here,' Fernando explained. 'Angel breaks them all in, and then they go to the *patrón*'s other farm. He only keeps the mares, though. We sell all the geldings.'

Don Felipe-Juan owned 400 mares, and there were about seventy on this farm.

'I've picked two nice ones for you,' Angel told me. 'They're beauties.'

His brother went into the corral, and with a brief gesture of his hand isolated the two mares from the others. Intuitively, my mares knew that he wanted to catch only them. The others quickly galloped off to the far end of the corral, and the *Correntino* lassoed my pair one after the other. He communicated with them in a private language, which rose and fell with the clack of his tongue, shrill whistles, unseen gestures and unknown thoughts. Even though I saw their private world, it escaped me. I saw it but couldn't grasp it, like a person falling from a mountain and waving their arms at the fleeting cliff.

Horses have a special kinship with people in Argentina, a relationship which is not open to everyone. Hudson told the following story:

When Rosas, that man of 'blood and iron', was Dictator of the Argentine country ... deserters from the army were inexorably shot when caught, as they generally were. But where my boyhood was spent there was a deserter ... who for seven years, without ever leaving the neighbourhood of his home, succeeded in eluding his pursuers by means of the marvellous sagacity and watchful care exercised by his horse. When taking his rest on the plain ... his faithful horse kept guard. At the first sight of mounted men on the horizon he would fly to his master, and, seizing his cloak between his teeth, rouse him with a vigorous shake ... man and horse would vanish into one of the dense reed-beds.[2]

My mares were tethered near the chicken coops, and I now spent half an hour getting to know them. They were unsure of me, quaking when I stroked their manes. That afternoon, the farrier was coming to shoe them, and I wanted to leave the next day. I couldn't quite understand why the horses seemed so afraid, until I watched them being shod.

In most parts of the Argentine plains and Uruguay, horses never have shoes. The earth is soft and free of rocks, so there is no need for them. Invariably, teaching a horse to put up with the farrier banging away with a hammer on their feet is not easy. But in Uruguay, where our horses had trusted and liked us, it had taken the farrier one and a half hours to shoe the three horses in Mercedes. Now I watched the Argentine farrier take four hours to shoe two horses.

He was an overweight man in his fifties, who wheezed and sweated, mopped his brow with exaggerated sweeps of his hand, and panted slightly as he set about his business. A cotton waistcoat hung airily over his belly, as if puffed out by the wind, disguising his paunch. His *bombachas* were heavily embroidered, and tucked into pristine leather boots. My two horses – Cartera and Carta Brava – took it in turns to receive his attentions. They both looked unhappy and worried as the man prepared.

Cartera went first. She was a *lobuno*, like Chileno, and had a long fringe that hung over her eyes like a bridal veil. As soon as the farrier bent down to pick up her front leg, she tried to edge away. One of the *Correntinos* held Cartera by a short lead rein; Angel had picked up her leg, and the farrier was filing and cutting the nail before matching the shoe to the hoof. But Cartera was mistrustful, and she backed away and began to kick out with her hind legs.

'*Hija de puta!*', swore the farrier. He picked up the broad wooden handle of a riding whip, which was as hard and wide as a rolling pin, and beat her over the back with it.

'Behave yourself, or you'll be sorry.'

Cartera jumped back, her eyes crying with fright. I was standing near to her head, and tried to whisper to her and reassure her, but she struggled with these hands on her legs like a petulant child. She kicked and neighed loudly. Carta Brava neighed back in fright and support, only too aware that her turn was to come. The men swore and worked for a while more, until Cartera tried to kick and stamp with her front legs as well.

'*Vamos, puta, vamos.* Come on, we'll sort you out,' yelled Angel. The farrier picked up the whip and laid into Cartera again, as the other *Correntino* held onto her firmly and smiled at me. Then Angel stood back, only to run up and kick her in the belly as hard as he could. The farrier copied him. They were both yelling and swearing, but neither Fernando nor Angel's brother said a word.

'It's too hot,' the farrier complained. But the day was as cool as it had been earlier. The crown of his bald head shone with sweat, and he glowered and moaned at the intransigence of the horses. The only heat was in his mind.

'I used to work with polo horses,' he said as he got back to work. 'I was in one of the best polo stables. I used to ride bareback, galloping, with six or seven of them on lead reins.'

He spoke as if trying to convince himself as much as us of his talent. He had no time for this work any more. He cared not for the horses but for his belly. He discussed a recent night when he'd met Angel at the local *boliche*.

'It's the first time I've ever seen you drink beer,' Angel told him.

'Yes, I don't usually have beer. I'm a real whisky man. Put me in front of a bottle of whisky and there's no stopping me.'

Looking at this performance I could believe him, but I wasn't sure how much this was helping the horses. I felt terrible, because it was my fault that they were being put through this. But I could not intercede, because the mares weren't mine, and this was the Argentine way. If Cartera had been difficult over her front hooves, when it came to the hind legs she was impossible. She kicked and bucked and shook from one side to another. Not ten seconds went by before she had another attempt at kicking herself clear. The man kicked her again, smacked her again with the whip. At one point he looked so livid that I honestly believed that he was going to knife her in the ribs. Then they devised a new torture, wrapping the thong of the whip around her nostrils and twisting it as tight as possible. Cartera seemed near to fainting from pain, and she slowed her complaints. Eventually they finished the agony, and rested. We sat and sipped *mate*.

'You see,' said Angel, half-apologetically, 'it's the only way to teach them. The more pain they're in, the less they'll worry about what we're doing to their feet.'

The violence, steeped in bloody tradition, continued as Carta Brava was shod. The farrier's sweat stung our bloodstains, mingling with ghosts of a wildness that was over, but which lived stubbornly on. We could not wring the wildness from history, nor wipe the sheets clean and recall ourselves to forgotten calm.

Fernando led me away and introduced me to the tractor driver, Rodriguez.

'You can eat with them this evening,' Fernando said. Several of Rodriguez's eight daughters played around in the garage as we discussed the journey. Later his wife confided in me.

'All we wanted was a son,' she said. 'But we just had daughters. Then we had twins, but they were both girls.'

Their ninth child, a son, had been born two weeks before, and so the couple were radiantly happy. Dinner was a chaotic affair. Eleven pairs of hands dived into the towering pile of meat in the middle of the table. The baby boy started to cry, desperate at this sudden diversion of attention away from his cot. Some of the girls rose and fussed over him, while others ate. The eldest girl, a teenager basking in puppy fat, finished her meal and stared at the rest of us triumphantly almost before we had started. The radio droned out more scandals from Buenos Aires – Maradona's agent had been cleared of drug trafficking, despite having been caught with cocaine hidden in a vase in his room; he was known to have friends in the government.

'Thieves,' said Rodriguez. 'Thieves. We work and the people from Buenos Aires steal it.'

The radio signal began to crackle and buzz with electricity, heralding a tremendous storm. Sheet lightning lit up the skies like flares at a battlefield. The rain hammered at the roof without ceasing, and deafened us all into silence. Then the house shook in shock after a bolt tripped down the lightning conductor. We were thrown into darkness and fear.

'We never used to get storms like this,' Señora Rodriguez said. 'Not at any time of the year.'

'It's crazy,' her husband said. 'We've had a drought all winter, and now when we're about to start the harvest we get the rain we've been praying for.'

There were nearly 200 millimetres of rain that night. It rained so much that Fernando had to park his car in the neighbouring *estancia* and walk to work over the fields. In other parts of Buenos Aires Province there were 400 millimetres of rain. The harvests were ruined. The fields were flooded and there was no grass to be seen. It rained for much of the next day as well, and we sat sipping *mate* and grumbling about the weather. Only the frogs were happy, and they croaked joyfully all day since their Christmas had come early.

'You see, that's what happens with agriculture,' said Rodriguez. 'I only became a tractor driver because it pays better, but I've got no time for these crops. You get a year's bad weather and it's all lost. You didn't get that when we concentrated on livestock.'

The rain delayed my departure by a day. When the storm finally cleared, I rode out at dawn along the track away from the farm. Although the skies were opening, there was still a chill wind, which gusted sporadically over the plains and reddened my complexion, chasing wispy clouds overhead. Angel rode with me for a league or so. He seemed to feel more at ease on a horse than anywhere else. He knew that no one was more capable on horseback than he. It was his Indian blood, Fernando had told me. Angel excelled. He was Ballester's champion rider, who was taken to Brazil and Chile for the international *marchas*. His deferential calm was now expressed in complete control over his situation. Whereas I was always keeping an eye on my horses, to make sure they did not get caught up with each other and that they kept at the pace I wanted them to, he rode effortlessly.

We rode in silence for a while. The floodwater had evaporated, and the fields were boggy and chequered with puddles. The tero-teros picked their way through the mud, squeaking uncertainly – now their cries were only occasional, punctuation marks against the garrulous breeze. The space was immense. In the very far distance, dark specks across the plains marked the herds of cattle from the pastures. Telegraph poles marched in regimental order up to the horizon. Once Angel had gone, there would be nothing to keep me company but the silence.

'At this speed, how far do you think I'll go each day?' I asked him.

'Oh, you should go forty or fifty kilometres. Perhaps a little less with rest.'

'It's difficult to judge distances here, it's so flat.'

'Yes. The best way to tell is by how many hours you ride for. Never go more than three, three and a half hours at a time without giving your horse a break.'

'Right. I'll always judge things by the time.'

'You don't have a watch, though,' Angel noticed, looking at my wrist. 'How will you tell the time?'

'I suppose I'll look at the sun.'

We rode on silently for a few minutes, and then Angel began to fiddle with his own watchstrap. We had reached a minor junction in the tracks across the country.

'Here. Have it,' he said, handing his watch to me. 'You're going to need it more than me.'

Fernando was waiting for us at the junction, and filmed me for posterity's sake. Then Angel shook my hand with sincere strength, refusing to let go of it for some seconds. He would not meet my gaze. His eyes blinked with a lost emotion, and I realized that Angel was worried for me.

'*Dios te va a acompañar*,' he said softly, as I left him to his horse in the Pampas, and he and Fernando waved me on my way.

The track away from Ballester's farm was as solitary as life can be. For the first three hours I saw only one house, a deserted rural school skulking in the lee of a windbreak. The rest was grass. Windmills whined like sirens, cavorting with the gales, metallic sounds spitting jarring music at my ears. Faraway, at the embrace of the horizon and the plains, banks of black clouds loomed at the periphery of my thoughts. The darkness was real, as real in the sky as in my mind. There was going to be another storm. I was so exposed here. There was no one even to ask the time of, to converse with desultorily, out of duty, passing a few minutes of our journeys in an exchange of drifting loneliness. I had imagined myself pondering – a mounted wonderer. But I did not articulate my thoughts to myself. I contemplated. I stared at the grasses, the wind toying with the ears of wheat, twisting them into graceful bursts of ephemeral beauty before the game died into stillness, absence. Memories sometimes played with me before lapsing into the forgotten. My identity came in bursts and then danced away over the fields into the arms of the storm.

Perhaps the storm had nothing to do with my mood. But after four hours of suppression, the clouds hurtled towards the lonely road. I saw several forks of lightning away across the plains. Now I came to a *puesto* – one of many shepherd's houses scattered across an *estancia* – and rode up the drive to find shelter. The *puesto* was hidden in a copse of eucalyptus, but the windows were cracked, and the house's roof had fallen in. No one lived here. The windmill, more rust than steel, lay defunct in the thistles and weeds. There was a semi-stable barn, where I thought of sheltering. But I had no food, and it was better to reach the nearest village than to wait for the storm to assault me. I rode an hour across the plains to the mask of buildings that winked at me mischievously all the while, wagering that I would not reach their sanctuary in time.

In the thick stillness before the thunder broke, I reached Juan E. Barra, a one-street village built to service the railway line. But the trains ran no more, and the town was dying. The station was overgrown and abandoned. I left the horses loose, as we had done with the triumvirate in Uruguay. But Cartera and Carta Brava were still only two hours' gallop from the *estancia*, and once I had left them they instantly began to run around, highly excited at the prospect of returning home before dark. As I came back from the shop, I saw them gambolling along the platform (my saddlebags shaking with Carta Brava's over-excitement), trying to work out how to cross the tracks and head home. I grabbed them just in time, and walked in embarrassment through the village. Everyone stared at me.

Then the rain fell, fat drops dripping deliberately onto my cheeks at the onset, followed by a downpour of water that infiltrated everything. This was real misery. The thunder roared all around the skies, and everyone but me had disappeared indoors. I was stranded with my two horses and nowhere to camp. Desperate, I rode out into the torrents towards the nearest farm, a kilometre beyond the town. The rain streamed down my neck and turned my back into a bed of goosepimples. I felt awful. I bellowed at the thunder, in a futile desire to answer fury with fury. Having said hardly anything all day, I wanted to scream now that the thunder swallowed my words with its own wishes. I spurred the horses on, terrified that we would be struck by lightning. Then I couldn't see how to open the gate into the farm. The storm closed in. I was half-sure that the lightning would kill me, half-despairing at the thought of all my belongings made sodden by the rain. I didn't know if I could cope with this, so suddenly alone as I was.

Darwin rode across the plains in the midst of Rosas' campaigns against the Indians. In 1830 only a third of the Province of Buenos Aires was occupied by landowners – the rest was held by the Indians, who roamed from place to place and periodically attacked the settlers. Rosas had made it his aim to occupy the whole region. Only recently he had ridden with his militia from Buenos Aires to Bahía Blanca, setting up military camps – *postas* – at regular intervals along the route. Teams of thoroughbreds were kept at each *posta*, so that the soldiers could gallop from one to another, changing horses as they went. It was often wandering *gauchos* who were conscripted to guard the *postas* in these dangerous areas. So Darwin did not keep the same horses as he rode across the plains, but changed them at each military camp.

Ballester's farm was in the middle of the Province of Buenos Aires, roughly level with the old road from Bahía Blanca to the capital. I started from here, and rode north as far as I could until I had reached the Darwin route, near the Pampas crossroads of Olavarría. The border regulations had put paid to my chances of following Darwin up the Paraná River to Santa Fé, but these new difficulties were instructive in their own way. Although Darwin's route is now, in many ways, tamer and easier than it was in the 1830s, difficulties have not been removed – they have only been altered. Instead of bellicose Indians there are bureaucratic regulations which make those in *The Trial* seem reasonable; I had no cholera epidemics, but I had to cope with the nervousness of my horses when faced with busy roads, for journeys in the 1830s were designed for horses and not motors – the roads had then had watering and feeding stations at regular intervals, not petrol stations.

Reading through Darwin's journals, I realize that the Pampas changed him. There is a thrill here which can be dissipated in the rest of his writings: 'There is high enjoyment in the independence of the *gaucho* life – to be able at any moment to pull up your horse, and say, "Here we will pass the night." The death-like stillness of the plain, the dogs keeping watch, the Gypsy group of *gauchos* making their beds round the fire, have left in my mind a strongly-marked picture of this first night, which will never be forgotten.' The freedom of nomadic *gauchos* always fascinated outsiders. To travel with these men was to see a world without boundaries. You could point your horse in any direction and gallop, killing whatever cattle crossed your path. The agile shadows of the flames dancing against the charcoal night, glaring at the brilliance of silver sparks in the sky; the immediacy of life; the experience of riding with the day, eating what was hunted and caught, sharing and joking through this rough life of ages: these moments left a profound impression on Darwin.

As in Uruguay, the land in the Province of Buenos Aires is all fenced today. You cannot camp in the plains, killing cattle and not caring whose it might be. Instead of camping alone in the fields, I was obliged to enter *estancias* and ask for permission to pass the night. This is an old custom in Argentina, which began as a way of protecting livestock from wandering thieves. I was always welcomed, for the conversation of a stranger is always a diversion in these lonely farms.

But the romantic in me still wished for the *gaucho* freedom of the past: for the freedom from fences.

In Juan E. Barra, the farmer put me up in his storehouse, divested me of my wet clothes and hung them, steaming like kettles, over the fire in his home. My state of mind was salvaged by the humanity of this man and his family. They invited me in to eat dinner and watch videos of the national *jineteadas* (rodeos) where *gauchos* cling to stallions that are deliberately trained to be as wild as possible, a demonstration that the horsemanship skills of the era of Rosas still live on. Deaths are not unknown in these rodeos. The horses are tethered to stakes, and the men mount them bareback, to stay on for as long as sanity or bravura dictate. In Patagonia I saw a *jineteada* – one of the horses was so wild that when it was freed from the stake, it reared so far backwards in fury that it lost its balance, toppled over, and fell directly onto the jockey. I happened to know this boy, who was no older than sixteen, and he had to be carried away from the arena. Having been nearly crippled, though, he was quite happy to get on again for the second round.

I quickly found my rhythm riding through the plains. In much of Uruguay, there had been farmsteads every couple of kilometres, but here I had to ride two hours between houses. The fields were full of thistles and the prickly Pampas grass. Sometimes a flock of wild ducks or geese flew overhead. Bird life is rich, as in Uruguay. But even though I was used by now to the startled whirring of a partridge's wings, humming like propellers as they sprang away from me, and to the tero-teros' siren calls, the suddenness of organic cries wrestling with silence startled me. I was happier with the silence, when there were no details to notice. One day I rode forty kilometres, and the sole break to the plains were three dead armadillos, lying upended on their backs with their legs towards the sky, drunk with their death, surrounded by swarms of flies.

The tracks were unerringly straight. For a while I followed the old railway line, punctuated with abandoned stations every fifteen kilometres or so. Shortly after leaving one station behind I would spy a blur of shadow on the horizon, a small pinhole of darkness in the plains' plate of light, and realize that these were the eucalyptus surrounding the next station along the line. Distance seemed to disappear into a concept for maps only: you could always see your target, even if it took three or four hours at a good pace to reach it. Time, which always makes itself known through the passing of changes, vanished into the constancy of the spaces and the grasslands.

With few specific details in the land, I concentrated on my mares. In Argentina, horses are not broken in until the age of four or five, which means that they never lose the uncontrolled freedom of their youth. Neither Cartera nor Carta Brava had ever been a packhorse before, and after the initial thrill of novelty they both decided that this inferior role was not for them. They both took to trying to kick me with their hind legs when they discovered that it was their turn for the packsaddle. Then, when I had finally managed to cajole one of them into being saddled up, whichever one was packhorse thought it great fun to suddenly stop dead in her tracks as we were riding along. There is not much that you can do when half a ton of horse refuses to move, and the first time this happened, with Cartera still trotting forwards happily, I tried to drag Carta Brava along anyway – she ended by pulling me backwards out of the saddle and dumping me humiliatingly onto the verge. Then I tried the traditional technique of tying the lead rein through a ring on my saddle's girth, so that the horses did the work. But then, even though I had tightened the girth as much as was sensible, Carta Brava was so stubborn that she pulled it right to the back of Cartera's chest, and my saddle began to slip.

However, in spite of our minor disagreements about these matters, we shared moments of happiness together. One time, a group of ten horses came thundering towards us from the other side of a vast paddock, whinnying and throwing up spray from the grass as they came to greet us. We all loved the peace of the grasses, mottled dark and white by the cattle, where little moved except us and the whispering winds, and the grass ebbed and hummed like a score at the wind's command. Even our occasional accidents had to be taken with a pinch of salt in the face of the onslaught of this calmness. Once, Carta Brava got caught in her own lead rein (which was tied around her neck), and she suddenly reared up to almost ninety degrees and deposited me effortlessly in a puddle. Even my ritualized soaking, and the loneliness and fatigue, were worth it for this journey.

I met new people every day, which offset my solitude. I stayed with *puesteros, domadores, alambradores* (makers of fences); in the yard of a tractor mechanic; with caretakers of the abandoned stations. When I was in the virile presence of the *gauchos*, we ate meat in silence – morning, noon, night. Sometimes my gut would try to rebel, and I protested that I couldn't cope with the meat.

'We don't eat this much meat in England,' I'd say. The men would say nothing, but they mocked me silently as they wiped the grease from their lips with old newspaper. I would throw the excess fat to scavenging dogs, whose diet of scraps of blubber was even more unhealthy than my own.

Most people revelled in finding humour in their own sadness. A *puestero* of Italian descent cackled when he thought of my journey. He had been born and brought up in Coronel Pringles, the local town.

'I've only ever been to Pringles,' he said, bursting into a sharp spree of laughter as his son assaulted him repeatedly with the blue beret that the man wore habitually.

This was typical of the children. They ran freely about, and did pretty much as they wished. Their mothers were mostly young – one woman still had so much puppy fat that I actually mistook her for the older sister of her two young sons – and did not want to be too harsh. Life in the Argentine country is so hard that parents do not want to deprive their children of what little freedom they will ever see. The kids were kings and queens. They played with the horses, brawled enthusiastically with one another in the meadows, and ran off when their parents told them to calm down. I often fascinated them.

Luciano was an example. In Coronel Pringles, he followed me everywhere. He was an eleven-year-old, blond and a tearaway.

'No one can control me at school,' he told me. 'My mother doesn't know what to do.'

He hung over me like a sycophantic servant, begging to put things away, release my horses into the paddock, filling jugs of water unasked. He stayed near to question me as much as he could. Did we have Coca-Cola and 7-Up in England? How big were the drinking troughs for the cattle in my country? Did I really miss my family and friends? And wouldn't I like to visit his aunt's *estancia*?

'*Che*, if you can ride horses, she can give you a job as a shepherd. Then you could stay here. Don't you want to stay? I want you to stay.'

Then two cousins appeared, and he told them that I was from England.

'Where's that?' asked one.

'North America,' said the other.

'*Boludos*,' yelled Luciano; and they ran off to fight.

Hospitality was everywhere. If I asked for permission to cook, I was invited to eat. One *alambrador* was genuinely upset because there was nothing he could give me to remember him by. Another man gave me a special bit to carry as a spare. People divided into two camps when I told them of my journey: half were certain of my lunacy, and the other half expressed a desire to join me.

Darwin was also struck by the warmth of the men on the pampas. Of one man he wrote: 'My host, the lieutenant, pressed me much to stop. As he had been very obliging – not only providing me with food, but lending me his private horses – I wanted to make him some remuneration. I asked my guide whether I might do so, but he told me certainly not; that the only answer I should receive, probably would be, "We have meat for the dogs in our country, and therefore do not grudge it to a Christian."'

The kindly lieutenant was in charge of the *posta* nearest to Bahía Blanca, in what is now the small town of Saldungaray. From here, Darwin climbed one of the few highlands in Buenos Aires Province, the Sierra de la Ventana. He had few good words to say for the hill, which was so barren that they could not make a skewer with which to grill their meat over the fire. Darwin climbed the hill during a delay, owing to renewed attacks by the Indians. The peak of the Sierra is divided into three summits, and Darwin was so dispirited by the bleakness of the climb that he could not be bothered to reach the highest of them, even though he believed himself the first foreigner to make the ascent. It was on this ride that Darwin developed the apparently universal loathing for tero-teros, and noticed quantities of swans and plovers; but in general, he wrote, the country 'is inhabited by few birds or animals of any kind'.

Darwin may have been unimpressed by the Sierra de la Ventana, but he would be rendered speechless if he saw it now. In place of the desolate and blasted scree slopes, the area has been developed for local tourism. There is a small town, La Arcadia, which is overrun by expensive houses owned by businessmen from Bahía Blanca. As I rode into the town, a man stopped his car and asked me if I was hiring out my horses. I smiled at the thought of the mayhem which might have broken loose if I had taken him up on his offer – for my horses were still far from tame, and stubbornly refused to warm to the packsaddle. Now, as I led them gently through this town of tour buses and ice cream stalls, the mares were very nervous. As I crossed over a bridge, a local bus came rushing at us from the other direction, and Cartera nearly jumped sideways into it. I found a farm to stop, where I met a cattle trader whose father had been Scottish.

'If you're heading for Bahía Blanca,' he said, 'you should go and visit this family that I know. They're both English. He used to live in Patagonia, like his father and grandfather before him.'

I had time to spare, so I rode around the edge of the Sierra, and headed for this farm. The Scot had told me that I couldn't miss it, it was the only farm in the area which was on a hill (it was probably the only farm for several hundred kilometres which was on a hill). I could see it from a distance of several leagues, a pretty chalet surrounded by acacias in blossom. When I reached the gate, I looked down over the valley. The farm must be one of the most beautiful in the Province of Buenos Aires, with clear views of the Sierra de la Ventana behind it, a billowing golden pond of wheat filling the valley below, clusters of livestock grazing in the haze towards Bahía Blanca, and the only Jersey cows in Argentina in the field below the farm.

I tethered my horses, and went to introduce myself. Susan answered the door.

'Goodness,' she said. 'The last person who just turned up like you was Bruce Chatwin.'

Chatwin had come to stay with them on the journey that produced *In Patagonia*.

'He just appeared, like you. He wanted to talk to James, you see, my husband. He was brought up on one of the great sheep stations in Patagonia.'

They had lived here for thirty years, and 'Bruce' had arrived just as they were putting the finishing touches to the chalet.

'Bruce was the first person to sleep in it,' said James. 'We were still living in the prefab. And when he wrote about us, he only talked about the prefab.'

'He *wanted* us in the prefab, you see,' said Susan. 'He had this idea for a story, and fitted us all around it.'

They invited me to stay in their guest house, which was weighed down with old copies of the *Daily Telegraph*. They both had strong English identities. They drank tea, and ate mutton with English mint sauce. They did not have *asados* over fires of thistle stalks. They hadn't been to England for nearly twenty years, but they read English books and English newspapers. They were both charming reminders of my faraway home, and I stayed for two days, talking of Darwin, England, Patagonia and Chatwin. They constantly remembered little details.

'So fastidious about his food,' she said. 'He barely ate a thing.'

'He didn't speak much Spanish either,' he said. 'He spent his whole time hunched over his dictionary and making notes.'

'But then he stayed again on his way back from Patagonia. He was much more fun then.'

'He was a great walker.'

'I don't think people realize how much he walked. He hitched with truck drivers too, but he did so much walking. One day he walked right over to those hills in the distance. And I said, "But Bruce, *why*?" "Just to see what's beyond," he said.'

On my second day, I followed Darwin – and Chatwin – up to the Sierra de la Ventana. James had warned me against pit vipers, but the only animals I saw all day were two hares and a few hawks and finches. In the whole ascent, up a steep canyon littered with boulders and thistles, and then up a saddle to the peaks, I passed only one tree, a conifer. The barren slopes were just as Darwin had said. The plains were the same, empty of most wild animals, endless and eerie.

But something was missing.

Rosas' *Campaña del Desierto* won the Pampas for Argentina. In a
relatively short timescale, he subdued the Indians and paved the way
for Roca's wars of extermination against the Patagonians in the 1870s.
Darwin's visit coincided with the height of the campaign. At Bahía
Blanca he wrote about the Indians he met there: 'Indians (*mansos*, or
tame) ... passed the night here; and it was impossible to conceive any
thing more wild and savage than the scene of their bivouac. Some drank
till they were intoxicated; others swallowed the steaming blood of
the cattle slaughtered for their suppers, and then, being sick from
drunkenness, they cast it up again and were besmirched with filth and
gore.' Darwin predicted that there would be no more wild Indians north
of the Río Negro in another half-century: 'It is melancholy to trace how
the Indians have given way before the Spanish invaders ... Not only
have whole tribes been exterminated, but the remaining Indians have
become more barbarous: instead of living in large villages, and being
employed in the arts of fishing, as well as of the chase, they now
wander about the open plains, without home or fixed occupation.' The
foundation of Bahía Blanca was instrumental in Rosas' campaign. With
a supply line now running from the port to Buenos Aires, and militia
press-gangs rounding up the *gauchos* for armed service, the Indians
were cornered. They were either forced into assimilation with the
Europeans or murdered. Darwin's prediction was accurate, which is
why Argentina is the most European country in Latin America. He
found the business appalling. He discovered that all Indian women aged
over twenty were murdered in cold blood: 'When I exclaimed that this
appeared rather inhuman, he answered, "Why, what can be done? they
breed so!".'

Thirty kilometres from Bahía Blanca is the bay at Punta Alta. It was
on the beach here, just below the headland, that Darwin made one of
the most important discoveries of his whole journey. Within the space
of less than 200 square metres, he found an incredible variety of fossil
bones: the giant Megatherium (an extinct quadruped as big as an
elephant), giant sloths, an extinct variety of horse and much more. He
spent several days painstakingly collecting the bones, and packing

them up carefully into crates. As he later wrote, this showed 'how numerous in kind the ancient inhabitants of this country must have been'.

Darwin's careful collection of fossils on his journeys were critical to his developing thought, and the discoveries at Punta Alta occurred at a crucial juncture. During his five years away from Britain, Darwin made sure to obtain the three volumes of Charles Lyell's *Principles of Geology*, a ground-breaking book which seriously challenged the biblical version of creation and the accepted age of the world. The existence of fossils which were clearly much older than the date of the beginning of the world as accepted by the Church – which had been calculated by Archbishop Ussher to 4004 BC – was hard to contradict. Darwin's extraordinary catalogue of discoveries on the beach added fuel to the theory's growing popularity.

This realization of the earth's antiquity was essential to Darwin. The idea of variations evolving across billions of years was impossible when the world's beginning was seen as 4004 BC. But when Darwin's own discoveries taught him that the earth had to be infinitely older than the dogma maintained, he saw that there was no reason to stop at any particular magnitude. If the world was not merely 6000 years old, and the biblical picture was simply wrong, the earth could well be unimaginably ancient. This shift in his thought, and the immediacy of having ideas confirmed by what he had seen, created a fever in Darwin's mind. Perhaps if he had simply read Lyell's book and been convinced of the theory's rationality, he would have taken his own thoughts no further. Seeing the theory's reality spelt out before his eyes galvanized him into thought.

And yet the fossil record was something which later bothered Darwin as he put the final touches to his theory, not because of any doubts over the earth's antiquity, but because the palaeontological record is incomplete, and it is therefore impossible to prove conclusively that changes in organisms occur through micromutations bridging species groups with their predecessors. In fact the fossil record shows, as modern palaeontologists admit, that many species simply appear suddenly, without any indication of a gradual evolution from an earlier and related species. Stephen Jay Gould circumvents this problem with a theory of 'punctuated equilibrium': the idea is that organisms could have changed suddenly because of rapid bursts of genetic activity, which led to very quick organic developments within species. He uses this theory to explain what palaeontologists call the 'Cambrian Whoosh', one of the great leaps forward in the anatomical design of organisms, about 600 million years ago. There are bound to be gaps in something as hit-and-miss as the fossil record, but the fact remains that the evidence for the particular mechanism favoured by Darwin – gradual natural selection – is murky in the fossil record, and it is dangerous to give any more than a cautious reading of the fossil data. Otherwise, the theories may slide dangerously down the avenue of fitting the facts to the theory, and not the theory to the facts – as is so often the case in all spheres of theory.

Bahía Blanca and Punta Alta made a profound impression on Darwin. His experience of the Argentines' cruelty towards the Indians and the finds at Punta Alta shaped his thought in different ways. He consolidated his belief in the earth's age, and saw how one race of men could be eradicated by another in what seemed to be essentially the competition for the same resource.

Before I rode into the modern city of Bahía Blanca, I had heard it called many things: ugly, dirty and full of thieves. The thieves were probably too drunk to bother me (it was between Christmas and New Year). But the petrochemical plant on the beach belched pungent smoke across the city, whose only agreeable quality was a plethora of shops selling fantastic ice creams. Bahía Blanca was grey and boring. Nothing happened here. There were no bathing beaches for seventy kilometres because of all the industrial waste.

So I went to Punta Alta, hoping that things might be better. Here, the beach was lined by forlorn and windswept rows of thorn trees, sheltering peeling attempts at picnic tables. The beach was littered with broken glass and half-buried bottles, and was absolutely revolting. At one end was Argentina's main naval base at Puerto Belgrano (the bay in which the *Beagle* docked the first time it reached this part of the coastline), and at the other end was an oil refinery.

Today Darwin would find the Indians gone for ever and his fossils buried in the polluted mess. Some of the more fertile seeds of his theory have been thrown irretrievably into the wind, and now lie scattered in the lost lanes of the Pampas.

III

From Bahía Blanca, I rode south towards Carmen de Patagones. The near-300 kilometres between the two cities is just a short hop in Patagonian terms. This is the beginning of the desert. A desert of bushes and emptiness; deserted but for sandspace.

Now in midsummer, the days glowed like embers. By eight in the morning I had to smother my face with sun cream to avoid the blush of sunburn. I would rise with the first dash of light against the rim of night, knowing from the fading starlight that dawn was near. But even getting up before five in the morning, I found it difficult to get away before half past six, and by then the sun was already high and harsh. The road was even emptier than it had been north of Bahía Blanca. It drifted past lagoons filled with mosquitoes which seemed to have no notion of survival. They swarmed onto me and the horses carefree, blackening us like slapdash artists, oblivious to the fact that I generally ended by killing them all. They were so numerous that in the early mornings I regularly killed several every ten or fifteen seconds, for one or two hours, perhaps two thousand daily, brushing the death from my body stoically, automatically.

Many of the labourers in this area were migrants from Bolivia and northern Argentina. They had mostly come on foot, taking several months to cover the imponderable distances. They worked slavishly, and were then swindled by their bosses. I met one Bolivian who claimed that his *patrón* owed him $16,000; but this man did not have the money to take him to court, and he had no other work.

'I have to stay,' he said. 'I came here to earn money. I can't return without it.'

The workers were mostly alcoholics. A succession of small and unpleasant towns followed the road south, where the men congregated to drink. Some of them came to work and ended up living in railway sidings. They asked the council for corrugated iron to build a shelter, then they sold the metal and bought wine with it. In Villalonga, a town of four or five thousand people, there had been three murders in the space of six months.

It wasn't easy to camp here, because landholdings were smaller and the owners were suspicious. Many times I found a farm waterless, abandoned to parch and wither in uselessness, or the owner would tell me that he was going to lock up and I could not stay. Sometimes they would recommend me to a *tipo gaucho* who would surely allow me to camp, but they might live several leagues down the road. I would struggle on through the unbearable heat, as the grass gradually thinned and was eclipsed by haze, dried-out earth and stunted sterility.

It was always the old men who helped me out. One was Martín Laprada. He lived in a shabby mud house next to a diaphanous canal, one hundred kilometres from Bahía Blanca, cultivating a vegetable patch which he irrigated from the canal. Near his left temple was an open mole, an ugly excrescence across his face. He was eighty-three, and lived with a lunatic who helped him about the house.

'Yes, I'm not surprised that you couldn't find a place to stop,' Martín said. 'People around here used to be good, but now...'

He shrugged. It was realism, not desire, that had resigned him to his old age. His shrill voice rang incongruously with his hardiness and the perversity of his continued existence, when all those near him were dead.

'My wife died thirty years ago. My daughter died recently. I've got six grandchildren in Bahía, but they don't often come here.'

He laughed, as if to say 'who can blame them?' We sat and talked in the shade cast by old willow trees, and Martín's helper hovered nervously around us. The man left and bicycled unsteadily along the road, before returning with two enormous sheets of cardboard.

'Here,' he said. 'I found these in the ditch. I thought they might make your bed more comfortable.'

He was from Bahía Blanca. He had black eyes which never stilled for more than a few seconds, speaking uneasily for his spirit. All his actions were troubled. He experienced the world as impossible, illogical and disconnected, as if it was a babbling torrent which vaporized into slowly vanishing steam whenever a person tried to decipher it, hanging weightless, like an incipient thought, over their comprehension.

'He's mad,' Martín whispered to me when the man was chopping wood at the far end of the copse. 'If he touches a drop of alcohol, he goes crazy. If I didn't look after him, he'd be killing people.'

The helper bicycled to Martín's in two days from Bahía, sleeping out in a field on his way. In the night, as I tried to sleep, he fidgeted and fretted beneath the hurricane lamp. He flitted from his bed on a decomposing mattress to the door of Martín's room, where the old man was slumbering to the soft growl of tango music.

'Martín! Martín!'

The man whispered urgently, speaking to silence.

'Martín! Martín!'

He brushed his knuckles against the door in a parody of a knock, standing awkwardly, as if he had forgotten why he was there, whispering insistently. After sixteen or seventeen goes, Martín replied.

'*Qué!*'

'I can't sleep.'

'Just try,' Martín told him, knowing that it was the indiscriminate madness in the man's mind that never allowed him rest.

Before the morning *mate* the man fell asleep. Martín and I sat on the porch, eating cold stew and watching the prospect of another blistering day. Martín's cap was already low over his eyes.

'I have to be careful with the sun. I've already had skin cancer,' he said, gesturing at the open mole and laughing bitterly again. 'This is all going to end badly. The weather heats up every year as if God has forgotten to turn the oven down. Before, it was an exceptional day in summer if you had thirty degrees centigrade. Now it's thirty-two, thirty-four, thirty-six ...' he laughed. 'Thirty-eight! We're going to fry like steaks. The sun just carries on burning us up. I don't care though, I'll be dead before it happens.'

I asked him what the area had been like before.

'Green! Fertile! All the fields were planted with alfalfa. Now, everything's arid. Even when it rains, nothing grows. In fact, the grass looks as though it's been burnt after the rain. All that industry at Bahía makes it acid. This will end badly, I've seen enough in my life to know that. There are some Christians who say that the world will end in the year 2000. Perhaps it'll be earlier!'

Darwin wrote that from Carmen de Patagones to the Río Colorado, 'the whole line of country deserves scarcely a better name than that of a desert'. But I was still a day's ride north of the Colorado here, and the soil ached with the daily onslaught from the sun. The earth was flimsy, crumbling pathetically as the horses passed. It was difficult to see how it could support any agriculture at all, far less livestock. But somehow, the farmers soldiered on, loving their earth as it cracked like dry lips.

The Pampas Indians used to sight the Sierra de la Ventana from the Río Colorado, 200 kilometres distant, and Darwin tells that the hill is 'visible at an immense distance'. He also noted that his guide saw it long before he did. I had noticed a similar trait in the region. When I had been well to its north people had pointed out the Sierra to me, saying that they saw it easily, even though all I saw was the sky. Now I looked back from the bridge over the river, but saw nothing once again. With the Indians gone, no one could see the Sierra from here.

It was at his camp on the Río Colorado that Darwin met Rosas. Following his meeting, he described Rosas as 'enthusiastic, sensible, and very grave'. He later retracted these favourable views in a footnote to the 1845 edition of *The Voyage of the Beagle*, where he admitted that his prediction of prosperous rule for Argentina under Rosas had been 'entirely and miserably wrong'. Yet Darwin did recognize the seeds of Rosas' terror, writing that his unbounded popularity made him 'in consequence a despotic power'. An English merchant had even told Darwin that 'a man who had murdered another, when arrested and questioned concerning his motive, answered, "He spoke disrespectfully of General Rosas, so I killed him." '

I found it difficult to picture the mayhem of Rosas' camp at the Río Colorado, which was peopled by some of the most bloodthirsty and cruel men that Darwin met in South America. The river cut a tranquil ribbon through a band of willows and eucalyptus, catching and eddying around banks of rock and moss and flushing itself sluggishly out to sea. It was a tranquil place, attracting visitors to splash and lie on the narrow sandy beaches, in the shadow of a monastery dedicated to a local saint.

I spent New Year's Eve sleeping in a tiny abandoned shower cubicle belonging to the monastery. Then I crossed the river, and entered Patagonia. Before me, the small plots of land around the river gave way to emptiness. As it was New Year's Day, the only cars which passed came wobbling alarmingly across the road. As I neared Carmen de Patagones the greens elided into browns and yellows, dreary beginnings of the Patagonian desert. The verges on the roadside were no longer billowing sails of grass; they were beds of sand, strewn with stunted bushes. My emotions felt throttled with excitement: 'At last, Patagonia! How often had I pictured in imagination, wishing with an intense longing to visit this solitary wilderness, resting far off in its primitive and desolate peace.'³

Patagonia greeted me with troubles, as it has so many. When I reached Villalonga, I camped in what must have been the greatest wood for hundreds of kilometres: several acres of lush grasses for the horses, resting in the shade of healthy poplars, willows and eucalyptus. The small farm was bisected by a canal. But in the morning, as I prepared to saddle Cartera and Carta Brava, I noticed that Cartera had a small cut from the packsaddle on her back. She was delicate, and travelling on with her was unwise.

'Stay for the day,' said Don Guzmán, the Chilean peon. 'You don't want to make that any worse, not with such a long journey before you.'

Guzmán was in his seventies, a grandfatherly figure with a spreading paunch. He was deaf as a post, and would cock his good (or better) ear towards you when you spoke, squinting with the effort and misfortune of having to listen to the nonsense of others. He worked alongside Alejandro, a Bolivian in his late fifties. They did very little: pottering about the yard; hurling abuse at the owner's wolfhound that stole their food; cutting weeds with a machete for feeding the pigs; preparing dinner; strangling the day's silence with the raucous stutter of the radio.

Having applied antiseptic to Cartera's wound, I sat with them all day, and their lives unfolded.

'I came to Argentina eighteen years ago,' said Alejandro. 'I hitchhiked 4000 kilometres to Puerto Deseado. My *patrón* in Bolivia treated me

like a dog, so I came here. Here we're more equal. The *patrón* eats
asados with us here, they muck in. He's a good man here.'

'He wouldn't mind you being here,' said Guzmán to me. 'That's why
we let you in. In some farms, the peon would be sacked for less.'

'But sometimes they don't pay us.'

'Some of them are *porquerías*, worthless scum.'

'They tell you they haven't got any money,' Alejandro chuckled. 'Or
their wife stands at the door and tells you he's gone away. Still, we get
our food.'

'We don't starve, no we don't. No man should want more than work,
food and a family. I'm lucky, I've had all three.'

'Why did you leave Chile?'

'There was no work! The Communists infiltrated the unions, and
threw out everyone who didn't agree with them. So I decided to come
to Argentina. I spent three days in third class on the train to Bahía
Blanca, and then we arrived, three of us. There was work there,
but nowhere to live. Then someone told us to come down here, to
Villalonga, Stroeder.'

He'd found work, and been here for forty years. He'd never gone back
to Chile ('what for, when I was working here?'). He trusted his God,
who had brought him everything he had wanted from life.

'As a worker, I was always going to be poor. God chose this life for
me, and I'm happy with that. It was the godless, the Communists, who
tried to destroy the workers. They raised our hopes, but then couldn't
deliver. They were worse than the *patrones*. In Perón's time they burnt
a farmer to death just near here. Because the poor man couldn't afford
to build clean houses for the peons!'

Guzmán looked disgusted by the whole affair. All he wanted was to
be left to work in peace until his death. Alejandro was busy smoking
and spluttering like a bronchial chimney. Whenever he laughed,
he burst into a hacking cough. He liked laughing, his face reddened
frequently from a secret stash of wine, and our even conversation
was often interrupted by his throat's staccato lament.

'It'll kill you,' Guzmán said quietly, but Alejandro said nothing.
'You'll have a heart attack.'

His wife had died of the same.

'She was with one of my grandsons. He was only four. They'd gone out to throw corn to the chickens. I was out in the fields, mending a gate, and I saw my grandson crying and shouting. I ran over, and saw that she'd collapsed. She was still clutching the little bowl of grain ... the bowl she used to feed the chickens with ... the handle had caught in her hand. I went to get the doctor, but it took an hour, and she was long dead when he arrived.'

His voice never wavered as he told me. It was a part of life, which he had learnt from the country.

I ended by spending three days with the old men. Cartera's sore improved slowly. I helped with odd jobs, collecting the weeds for the pigs, and helping the men chop down an old acacia tree. There was little else to do but swat flies, a task at which Guzmán was supremely skilled. As we talked, his eye jumped to dark specks in the air, which quickly decorated the red plastic of the swatter. Unruffled, Guzmán would turn his good ear towards us again, and wait for the next victim.

I left, wanting to impose no more. Cartera was still delicate, but the sore had improved a little. I risked it. That day – a Sunday – I rode until I found a farm where I could camp, thirty-five kilometres north of the Río Negro at Patagones. All day, vicious gusts of wind vied with each other across the plains, enervating the sand so that it eddied and swirled about me, dashing itself into my face, dallying timelessly against my lips before falling to the ground. My hair gelled with the grit, and the plains were transformed into a yellow haze, opaque and unforgiving. The wind was warm and wrapped my body in surrogate comfort. I could see that there were no real clouds, beyond the Hollywood fog that lay over the beginnings of Patagonia. With the land vanishing beneath the dust storm and the sky invisible, there was nothing of the world left to notice, no details at all.

The family were having lunch when I stopped. The *estanciero* brought me a plate of cold beef, and watched me unsaddle. His son-in-law, Señor King, followed him, and gave me his advice.

'Darwin – mad. You – madder. Why are you going by horse? Horses belong to the past. Why not take a motorbike?'

He flexed his wrists and mimed revving up the motor.

'Have you been to Patagonia?' he asked. 'It's ugly. Uglier than the ugliest thing you've ever seen. Flat,' – he made a sweeping arc with his flat hand – 'empty. No women. Just desert.'

'Where would you go?'

'The USA! Vegas, Miami. Or Mexico. Cancún, Acapulco. You can have a good time there.'

I took Cartera's saddle off, and saw to my horror that her sore was much worse.

'The sore!' I said, cursing my stupidity. '*Ay, ay!*'

'That's not good,' the *estanciero* said, shaking his head. 'How did that happen?'

He started to look at the packsaddle.

The wind picked up again, hurling sand by the truckload over the corral. King gritted his teeth and looked evilly at the horizon.

'*¡Es un desastre!* No rain, no wheat, no Toyota. Just the old Ford. It's like a museum in there.'

He gestured towards a huge old barn, where the abandoned shells of old Fords and Chevrolets were hanging from the walls. I looked out at the wheatfields, which were desert-fields, sprayed with stunted wisps of wheat deemed too stringy to have been harvested.

'It's the fourth year in succession that the harvest has failed,' King said. 'Drought, drought, drought.'

'There's no money,' his father-in-law joined in, lifting his head from the packsaddle. 'We pray for rain, and we just get wind. Wind and dust.'

The winds scattered the topsoil and turned the lands to desert. They did the same every year. It was a geographical case-study of desertification, before my eyes.

'I'll tell you why that horse has injured herself,' the man went on. 'Who made this packsaddle?'

'A saddler in Uruguay.'

'Well, look at it! The wooden cross at the front is cut far too low to the horse's neck. With so much travelling, it's rubbed and rubbed and rubbed, and this is the end result.'

Cartera had fistulous withers, an inflammation which would take at least two months to heal properly. At first, I hoped and prayed that the injury would miraculously cure itself, but the pus continued to flow out. I swore at myself. I swore at Maspoli for pretending he knew how to make a packsaddle, which had turned out to be nothing but trouble. I felt desperately guilty for the injury to Cartera, which was entirely the fault of my journey.

I shared my troubles with Patagonia's laughing, mocking winds.

I was allowed to sleep in the barn. The wind was my only companion; Patagonia was greeting me. Left alone, with no one to speak to, I personalized the wind and made it speak even more volubly than in Uruguay and the Pampas. If I went outside in the day, it laughed at me with dust. If I stayed inside, it chattered from all sides of the barn, laughing and acting the buffoon, running away and playing with the windmills, whining and rattling like a baby, roaring like an old man in fury. Sometimes it even slept, at night, knowing that I was too tired to answer its impersonations. Then it dropped from its breathless monologue into the stillness of poetry, the hush of night when its spirit fell away and allowed me to dream. By day it tore through my mind and stripped me of thought. I thought of nothing. I had nothing to read, nothing to do. I fed the horses three times a day, and tried to make them believe that this misguided adventure would turn out for the best. I fed myself three times a day also, even though I was doing nothing that warranted feeding. I diminished into a shrivelled kernel of myself, listening to the wind and my self-pity.

I could not continue with these horses. If I waited for the sore to heal, I would arrive in Patagonia with the winter, which was suicide. But I could not afford any other horses, not in Argentina.

Never in my life have I felt as desperate as I did then. The loneliness, the days without talking to anyone but the wind; they were close to making me mad. I walked through the deserted fields, staring morosely at the emptiness. One day I nearly trod on a black widow spider in my bare feet, and the start of fear revitalized me.

This was absurd, I told myself. I had all but reached the southernmost point of Darwin's rides in Argentina. I shouldn't jeopardize the whole journey because of this setback. I decided to send the horses back to Ballester, and continue into Patagonia under my own steam. I would aim to walk as much of the distance as I could (I ended by walking nearly 1000 kilometres in Patagonia and Tierra del Fuego), and do the rest with my thumb. I arranged it all in two days, and thoughts flooded back with the decision. I still sat in the barn for most of the day, but I no longer felt alone.

I thought of Darwin. I had seen so much of his horseback journey in Uruguay and Argentina. Scientifically, his most important discoveries had been at Punta Alta. It was not just that the fossils and bones showed the age of the earth to be far greater than was imagined by Christianity. Many of the species that he discovered were related to modern species: there had been bones of a prehistoric guanaco and a prehistoric horse – what did these suggest about the existence, development and extinction of species? And the fact that so many of the animals unearthed no longer existed? Darwin's mind raced down one track after another. But the experience of riding in these places was as memorable for him in its own way, certainly at the time. We should not discount the import- ance to Darwin's thought of seeing Rosas' wars against the Indians, and of experiencing such a wild way of life. It was everything that he felt and saw which contributed to Darwin's growth on the journey.

I had had a similar experience in some ways. The wildness was more 'civilized' than it had been 165 years before, but it was still there. Many of the customs and traits were clear descendants of those which Darwin witnessed. The *gauchos* still ate little but meat, were still expert horsemen, and could be extremely cruel to their animals; autocratic governments and populism had plagued Argentina until only recently; tero-teros still dominated the plains. But the plains themselves were changing.

Everyone in Uruguay and Argentina told of the changes to the environment. This was to become the constant factor of my journey. The world was hotter, and indigenous animals were dying out. All over Uruguay, we were told that the sun had become 'bad' – and then we had run into the vicious storm near Mercedes. Furthermore, it wasn't just the climate that was different. In Uruguay I saw not a single deer, nor a capybara, both of which Darwin noted as abundant; the caymans had all but been hunted to extinction; and, as Mac had told us, there were no pumas left. Now in these parts of Argentina described in such detail by Darwin, there were no longer any guanacos or hares between Patagones and the Río Colorado; and, as in Uruguay, there were neither pumas nor deer. Sometimes you smelt the skunks, but they were rare.

Now that the droughts had come, perhaps even the cattle would eventually die out in some parts. Near Bahía Blanca I had been told that the droughts had killed thousands of cows. Of course, there have been droughts before. Darwin himself tells of a great drought in the Argentine Pampas, where no rain fell between December 1828 and

April 1832. The British Consul-General, Woodbine Parish, told him that so much dust had been blown about that landmarks were obliterated between estates. But there are differences between those droughts and the modern ones: droughts then were never as widespread as they have been in the past decade or so. Every region that I visited in the course of my journey complained of drought, and this is visible in the area north of the Río Colorado, which is becoming almost as dry as the land to the south. Darwin tells us that the river used to mark a boundary, but as the crisis sweeps the wheat-growing region, the towns are abandoned. Within a hundred years, the desert may well have reached Bahía Blanca. Climate change closes in, and the wildlife which Darwin observed is dwindling into the growing heat.

Some people couldn't explain it. Others had heard of global warming and the hole in the ozone layer, and cursed industrialization from their farmsteads in the burning haze. Just reading through some of Darwin's notes, you discern a difference between then and now. Darwin used to gallop his horses for most of the day, sometimes covering a hundred kilometres, day after day. Although most of his rides were in spring and autumn, he rode from Mercedes to Montevideo – about 280 kilometres as the crow flies – in three days at the beginning of summer. But you couldn't even think of doing this any more, because the horse would die from heat exhaustion. The middle of the day is, generally, a sultry oven, when nothing and nobody moves. Before the workers realized the gravity of the changes in the climate, they carried on working through the heat of the day. I was told that dozens died of heart failure.

'It's a disaster,' people would say, sipping their *mate*, with melancholy brooding on the fringes of resigned smiles.

'God created harmony,' said one woman, 'and the scientists have messed it up.'

The bitter irony is that Darwin's theory, as an integral part of the industrial and scientific enlightenment of the nineteenth century, is one of the intellectual ancestors of the economic revolution whose disdain for ecology is now – beyond reasonable doubt – causing untold damage to our planet. Many of the features which he observed and annotated so fastidiously, and which were so critical in the development of his thought, are gone – or are going – and a creeping aridity clutches the earth and the hearts of those who live there and know it, seeing it crumble and flake and vanish like time, into unremarkable specks of sand.

PART FOUR

Hotfoot in Patagonia

In calling up images of the past, I find the plains of Patagonia frequently cross before my eyes; yet these plains are pronounced by all to be most wretched and useless. They are characterised only by negative possessions: without habitations, without water, without trees, without mountains, they support only a few dwarf plants.

Charles Darwin

After leaving the horses I walked to the Río Negro at Patagones, before hitchhiking west to San Antonio Oeste. I was determined to walk between here and the Peninsula Valdés. This is the next port on the Atlantic coast which Darwin mentions after Patagones, writing that here he observed guanacos swimming from island to island. I wanted to follow the *Beagle* along the coast. I had no boat, and now I had no horses, but I still had my feet.

San Antonio was a smudge of drab concrete hanging forlornly on the rim of the desert. I asked the police about the route south.

'Oh yes,' they said. 'You've got no problem. Lots of people live down that way.'

I was up at five thirty the next morning, and by seven I was heading south.

I walked out of the small holiday resort of Las Grutas, next to San Antonio. The track hugged the shore. I crested a slight rise, away from the town and the mangy flea-dogs that yelped after me; then I was gone into the desert. I walked fast. I was carrying six litres of water, which had to last the three days which I would take to reach the next village. My pack was leaden, and dragged my feet back as I tried to march through the ridges of soft sand. After an hour and a half the track heaved itself up a low cliff, and vanished into the plateau. The sun was high and burning by now. I could see for thirty kilometres or so straight ahead, into a blur of dreary colours that merged with colourlessness, an amorphous mass with no defining features at all, featureless as the gulping haze. The only sign of people was the track, parallel lines disappearing long before they hit the horizons of nothingness.

I walked for two hours more until the sun stung the sweat that clung to my body. There was no wind. Patagonia, so resonant of tempests and savage cold, was sweltering. By now the track had become bogged down in the tall dunes next to the beach, and every pace was twice the torture of before. My throat was even drier than the desert. All morning I had seen just two signs of life, a grey tortoise and the sinuous treads left behind by snakes aching along the track. But now I saw the remains of an abandoned windmill, sheltered by a cluster of stunted trees that managed to cast a sliver of shade over the land. An old watering hole for the sheep, this, a few metres from the tumbling ruins of an abandoned *puesto*. I rested, and pondered the sanity of continuing. My water carrier had leaked and my supplies were down to three litres. I had kept on because of the tyre marks in the track, which had made me think that *someone* must live here. But now these were faint as a moon's halo concealed by a turbulent night. I could carry on, run out of water, and not know where I was. I felt like turning back.

I stopped for an hour.

Then I heard an engine, groaning with the fatigue of its journey. A geriatric pick-up truck was plunging towards me through the sands, heading back towards Las Grutas. I ran out, and got the driver to stop.

'What are *you* doing here?' he asked me, incredulous.

'I'm walking to Puerto Madryn.'

'*This* way? You're mad.'

I asked him if there were any *estancias*, and to my astonishment discovered that there were at least three between here and the next village.

'What about traffic?' I asked.

'No one. No one but us, looking for squid.'

He told me that there was an *estancia* twelve kilometres away. I set off again, and my mind emptied itself. I could have thought of anything – if I had been able to think – but I met emptiness with emptiness. I saw only my feet, regular as little robots, moving disembodied down the track. I saw the space with my eyes but not with my thoughts. My identity was immersed in that desolate, world-weary place. Time disappeared, and I don't know how long passed before another engine groaned.

This was another pick-up, laden down with Mapuche Indians. I mistrusted the driver on sight, a squat man whose eyes hung close together and flitted away from my gaze like a lost fly when he spoke to me. He offered me a lift, though, and I was not fool enough to spurn this in the baking midday sun.

This man lived from the Mapuches. There were scores of these families, spread out along the coast at intervals of a few kilometres, living in shanties built of driftwood and covered with plastic tarpaulins. The families owned virtually nothing. They lived scouring the rock pools for squid when the tide was out. Zorro – as he was known – bought the squid from them for a pittance, and sold it in Las Grutas. In practice the Indians never saw a peso, since whatever they earnt they'd use to repay him for the goods they ordered whenever he went to town. The squidcatchers lived without water, and washed in the sea. They were among the poorest people I met on my journey, lost and forgotten, absent from every public record of poverty or literacy, all but slaves, living and burning themselves to death in their shanties by the sea.

Zorro took me to the *estancia*, where he introduced me to Aníbal: the foreman. He worked with one other peon to cover the farm of 15,000 hectares. They still worked the land with horses, even though the grazing was sparse, verging towards non-existent, and the animals nearly died of hunger every winter. Aníbal greeted us bleary-eyed, scratching his hair and fond memories of a siesta with his right hand. He invited us in reluctantly. I could tell he didn't trust Zorro either. But Zorro made himself comfortable in the kitchen.

'Isn't there any *asado*?' he asked.

'No,' said Aníbal sullenly. 'I haven't butchered any sheep for a while.'

'*Che*,' growled Zorro, disappointedly. 'I'm owed some meat. I lent you that petrol last week.'

Aníbal's car had run out of petrol on the track to Las Grutas, and Zorro had lent him some to rescue the situation.

'*Si, si*,' Aníbal muttered stroppily. 'But if you want sheep, I'll have to go and catch them from the plateau.'

'I know,' Zorro trilled happily. 'But I need that meat today. By this evening, *viejo*. I need to give it to the squidcatchers. They've ordered it, and I don't want them to go short. Perhaps I'll come by at seven.'

'That means we'll have to go straightaway to get them.'

'You know how it is,' said Zorro, feigning guilt. 'Those thieves in Las Grutas. They pay me hardly a peso for the squid, and then you should see the prices they sell it for themselves. They rob me. I have to keep this old pick-up going, I have to help the squidcatchers survive...'

'*Si, si,*' said Aníbal.

Zorro talked desultorily about this and that. The desert hummed its unique song through the cracks in the wooden door, wistful as a harmonica. Aníbal didn't offer Zorro any *mate*; he wished that the wily old thief would leave him alone. Eventually, he offered us some squid in jelly, and I chewed it ravenously, sitting silently with my heat and hurt. When Zorro left, he turned to me.

'I'm going a little further up the road this evening. I'll take you if you want.'

Once he'd gone, Aníbal relaxed visibly. Now we did drink *mate*, and the bitterness revived me. He was an intelligent man with a coarse, mole-ridden face. He was only in early middle age, but the rough life of Patagonia was ringing him with age. He told me that it was the sun, the ozone (or lack of it): the drought. His work was a swollen vein bursting with faint tragedy. The grass had gone; the sheep were vanishing along with it. The ewes were too thin to suckle their lambs, and the *estancia* had only produced 400 this year – the year before there had been 1300.

'If it goes on like this, sheep farming will die in Patagonia. Ten, twenty years, that's all that's left. It gets hotter and hotter.'

I asked him about dangerous animals, just to reassure myself. Patagonia had the image of ice and snow for me, not venomous snakes.

'Well,' he said, 'it never used to be bad. But with the heat, we've now got everything. Coral snakes, rattlesnakes, pit-vipers. There are also tarantulas and black widows. There are more snakes than sheep nowadays.'

Later, we drove towards the plateau with the other peon, to catch the sheep. This was a place of dry river canyons, an almost uninterrupted thicket of wiry shrubs, grey-green. All was boundless: the skies and the land, the knots of mountains rising up away from the sea like towering waves in a storm. The *estancia* was so big that we drove for half an hour and did not reach anywhere near its limits. As we neared the enclosure where the sheep were kept, we came across a guanaco, alert and fleeing the car straight down the track. Aníbal opened the glove compartment, pulled out a revolver, and aimed steadily with his left hand as he sped up. He pulled the trigger twice, missing each time. Then the guanaco had the sense to dive off into the thicket.

'¡Mierda!'

The sheep lived in a desertified enclosure that had become all sand. I wondered how they lived. They cantered chaotically away from us, but Aníbal and the peon herded them into the smallest pen, and began to select the ones which they would butcher.

'They're all too thin,' Aníbal exclaimed, disgusted. He picked one up, eyeing it distastefully, and then letting it drop. 'No,' he said, with a trace of humour, 'I'm not inviting *you* to the banquet.'

They took twenty minutes to throw eight sheep into the back of the pick-up. A few spots of rain had begun to fall, but the main body of the shower could be seen looming over the plains, perhaps twenty kilometres distant. The moisture merely softened the sand and darkened the sky, and the sun quickly won the battle, tinting the desert golden once more. Beyond the edge of the plateau we saw a rainbow curving in a complete arc from north to south, falling to its pot of gold in the ocean.

'¡Mierda! Those fucking rainbows always stop it from raining.'

At the *estancia* house, the sheep were kept in a pen, hobbled, loaded one by one onto a wheelbarrow, and then wheeled to a stone slab in front of a barn where the peon slit their throats. Aníbal concentrated on decapitating the twitching bodies and preparing the carcasses for Zorro. They worked fast in the fading light, since Zorro was due soon. These sheep, like the one in Uruguay, were immensely passive in the face of death. They could not see the murders from the pen, but when they were wheeled out to the killing stone they must have seen and smelt the blood, seen the fleeces of their erstwhile friends, must have sensed the sordid need for blood whetting the edge of the peon's knife, its greed, must have guessed what was to happen, and yet still did not flinch, nor kick out, nor writhe in prescient anguish at the thought of death, not like the rainbow trout flipping madly on its killing stone by the riverside, nor the cows lurching in horror onto the scales in Uruguay. They did not feign death, unlike the Patagonian foxes and skunks. They were still before it, respectful but resigned, perhaps because they believed that you cannot love life if you fear death.

When Zorro arrived, the men had finished their fourth sheep. He was in a hurry this time, and did not stop for conversation. He loaded the carcasses on top of floursacks, and put the sheep heads into a navy blue bucket. We left in a matter of minutes, for a tour of the squidcatcher settlements. At each one he weighed the squid on a rusty (and probably loaded) set of scales, and then handed out bread and meat in return. The children in the shanties were malnourished and dressed in rags. The teenagers were also dressed haphazardly, but they'd filled out and could collect fifteen kilos of squid in a day. The adults had aged before their time; their eyes were clouded with fatigue, their hair whitening with every year in spite of their dark faces.

We stopped at one settlement, and ten children and adolescents leapt into the back of the truck, for the thrill of the ride. The pick-up was a messy mass of limbs and sacks and barrels, stilled by the petrified gaze of the sheep heads. The wind hurtled against our faces, and smacked us with exhilaration.

I felt so free.

The sun was creeping towards the horizon now, casting shadows over the plains even though nothing seemed tall enough to cause them. Some flamingos coloured the sea iridescent pink as we drove past them, and the day died a violent death. When Zorro dropped me off, it was nearly nine o'clock, and there was a maximum of forty minutes' daylight left.

'Just follow the track,' he told me. 'The *estancia* is six kilometres down the road.'

I walked fast. The desert was no place to be at night. This was not just because of the frequent forks in the track where it was easy to take a wrong turn and get hopelessly lost in the plateau, nor for the chances of coming across wandering serpents. The night would bring me fear. Being alone in the daytime, when your sight protects you and reassures you that the desert will end in some goal, is possible; but at night, with the fears of ages and spirits coursing through me, and neither sound nor sight to stall them, the desert would wound me. The sun was gone, and the light was fading into the afterglow of day. I had no water left. I had not expected Zorro's shopping expedition to take so long.

But as I went, willing myself not to worry, the road petered out and disappeared into a pebble beach. I had gone wrong. I double-backed over thickets and sand, worried, convinced that the track must be somewhere inland, and stumbled over it after five minutes. I squinted ahead hopefully towards the farm, but saw nothing but scrub.

I walked on and on until I was almost running.

Then I came to a fork in the track, blank, without signs. Each sandy strip was punctured by treadmarks, like a field etched with faint paths. I turned right, but after ten minutes the track became progressively narrower and the treadmarks dwindled away and vanished.

I was overcome by a fever of fear. I could hear the fear, I embodied that fear – everything about me defined fear. My burden was fear, so I no longer even noticed the weight of my pack. My panic, my thoughts running with my feet, only heading backwards and forwards, decisions contradicting each other within a few seconds. I would turn back and take the other track. No, I would go on. Or turn back. Or pray. Perhaps there were no demons with me, but I almost began to believe in them.

I kept going.

The two tracks merged. I calmed myself again. This had to be the way. Now that I believed this, I would find the farm and the water. Just as my shadow began to be cast by the brilliant full moon, and not by the dregs of the sun, I caught sight of a windmill's silhouette. Beyond the windmill was a light, and the strain of a dog barking its wistfulness into the embers of the day.

During the five years of the *Beagle*'s voyage, Darwin was only actually at sea for eighteen months. He loathed the ocean. In a letter to his friend Fox, he wrote: 'I hate every wave of the ocean with a fervour, which you who have only seen the green waters of the shore can never understand.' He was often seasick, even after he had been travelling for some years. As soon as the ship made landfall, Darwin would busy himself finding suitable lodgings and arranging collecting expeditions. When he was on the ship he annotated and analysed his collections, but it was the time that he spent on the continent which educated him best. Almost all of his shore visits were for lengthy periods, sometimes as prolonged as four months.

The *Beagle* made two journeys down the Patagonian coast. Both in 1832 and 1833 the ship set sail from Montevideo. The second time FitzRoy made several landfalls, both before and after reaching Tierra del Fuego: at Port Desire (Puerto Deseado), Port St Julian (Puerto San Julián), the Falkland Islands and the Río Santa Cruz.

By the time of his second visit to Patagonia, Darwin had ridden across the plains of Argentina and Uruguay, and had cheered himself up immensely. Now he was able to explore the vast unknown of Patagonia also, and make important discoveries. At Christmas time in 1833, at Puerto Deseado, Conrad Martens – the new ship's artist – shot a rhea, and the crew happily tucked into an impromptu *asado*. At the time, Darwin thought this bird to be merely a part-grown example of the ostriches found further north. It was only a few days later that he recalled having been told of a different type of rhea here in Patagonia, a smaller relative of the northern ostrich, and he realized that this was what they had eaten. Fortunately the feathers, wings and some of the skin had been preserved. Darwin was able to salvage the bird and send it to London – it was named *Rhea Darwinii* in his honour. The excitement of this, and of the first European journey up the Río Santa Cruz (which was made by the *Beagle* crew), made Patagonia an important part of the journey.

Comparing the second journey to Patagonia with the first, we can sense a shift in Darwin's state of mind. FitzRoy made no breaks in the first journey to Tierra del Fuego, sailing constantly from Montevideo to Cape Horn in under a month. The return involved a visit to Berkeley Sound on East Falkland, only two months after the English seized the islands from Buenos Aires, before the *Beagle* returned north to Uruguay. No wonder Darwin chafed at the routine in some of his letters home. In May 1833 he wrote to his sister Caroline that 'I most devoutly trust that next summer ... will be the last on this side of the Horn: for I am become thoroughly tired of these countries ... I have lost all interest in this part of America, and I feel more inclined to growl than write civilly to any-body.' The inability to make investigations ashore frustrated Darwin terribly. He must have stared at the desolate coast of Patagonia wistfully, wishing that he could break the monotony of the sea voyage. We can imagine his relief on returning to the River Plate, when he was able to spend several months ashore embarking on more-or-less continuous excursions. Having developed his physical strength on the rides across the Pampas, Darwin was determined to explore the Patagonian shores on the *Beagle's* second voyage.

Yet apart from the journey up the Santa Cruz, Patagonia's interior went unexplored. FitzRoy's brief was to chart the coastline, and the area was so vast that there was little time for other exploration. Even at the time of the great rush of Patagonian colonization, in the first decade of the twentieth century, vast tracts of land remained which had been largely unexplored. Although Antonio de Viedma had nearly reached the Andes in 1783, the first expedition from the Atlantic to reach the *cordillera* was not until the 1870s. The expedition up the Santa Cruz was brief, and did not reach the river's source, but it put the *Beagle* crew in the ranks of Patagonian explorers.

These expeditions infused Darwin's memory with images of Patagonia which never left him. He did make important scientific discoveries – such as the rhea, and the skeleton of an extinct quadruped (the Machrauchenia Patachonica) which was related to the guanaco – but it was seeing the vastness of lands without limit which affected him most.

'¡Hola! ¡Buenas noches!'

I called out into the night. The peon, a quiet man whose shadow only just broke the darkness of the barn, growled at his dog and stepped out into the moonlight. I could not see his face as I spoke to him.

'I'm walking to Madryn,' I said. 'Aníbal at the last *estancia* said you might give me some water and let me camp here.'

Aníbal had told me to say this. The peon was a good man here, he'd said, but he would be wary of me.

'Aníbal?' he said. 'Well, you'll have to ask my *patrón*.'

The owner was from the city of Trelew, and he came to greet the visitor with his wife.

'Walking this way?' he asked. 'Well, come in and warm up.'

I went inside and sat with them at the dining table. Covering the table was a garish and florid tablecloth, but the colours were aged and weakened by the sickly light from the hurricane lamp. The room was cramped, and decorated with memorabilia of Patagonia: old stirrups, photos of *jineteadas*, famous books on the region. The man had lived in Patagonia all his life. He was getting old now, and his face was red with the sun, crinkled around his lips and his cheeks. His wife was a solid woman with golden hair and a happy demeanour, indomitably talkative in spite of the thickness of the night and the loneliness of the farm.

'Give the lad something to eat,' he told her. 'Where have you come from?'

'Las Grutas.'

'By foot?'

'Half walking, half in pick-ups.'

'With the squidcatchers,' he said knowingly.

'That's terrible,' his wife said softly, bringing me a plate of stew. 'Terrible, the lives of those people. We didn't know anything about them until we moved here.'

'They're thieves,' he said. 'They kill our sheep.'

'It's a disgrace to Argentina that people live like that. The government should look after them,' she said.

The night was still, after so much motion. As in the Pampas, the wind dropped with the sun like a raucous voice ebbing into the soft heat of song. When we paused in our chat, and slurped the stew, the only noise was the suppressed roar of the hurricane lamp.

'Which of their bosses took you along?' the man asked.

'Zorro.'

'That scoundrel! There are several of them that live from those Mapuches. They rob them blind.'

'He was bringing them their food. That's why I arrived so late.'

'What does he get them?'

'Lamb, bread, *mate*. He got the lamb from the other *estancia*.'

'Ah yes. But he'll charge them the supermarket price. Or else sometimes, I'm sure that he comes here and steals my sheep at night. With the way things are, that's all we need.'

'Things are bad?'

'Terrible. I've lived in Patagonia all my life, and I've never seen it like this. We've had a drought for ten years.'

'No rain at all?'

'Well, of course it rains,' she said. 'But not properly. Not enough to get the grass to grow again.'

'This farm,' he said. 'It's going to go under. We only had one lamb this year. One! All our sheep are dying. Or dead.'

'Dead?'

I was exhausted, and could barely bring myself to understand what he was saying. This day had transformed itself into a lifetime.

'Yes! They used to die before, of course they did. When there was a bad winter, snowdrifts. But now they just starve to death. It's awful.'

'Terrible,' she said. 'They just get weaker every day. They fall over. Then they can't get to the watering holes and they die.'

'Everywhere it's the same,' he said. 'All over the world. But the politicians pay no attention.'

'They talk of this that and the other,' she said. 'This problem, that problem.'

'But they don't realize that the way things are going, there won't be much left for them soon.'

'The world's in a bad way,' I agreed.

They nodded.

'And why?' he asked. 'Why?'

'It's because of money,' she said. '*El dinero es una porquería.*'

'Men are so foolish,' he said. 'Look at this technology. We tell ourselves that we are advancing and unlocking truths, but what are we *doing*? We've forgotten what we're doing to the world.'

'We've forgotten the world,' I said.

'Yes! People think that with the new way of thinking they unlock truth. But all they use is logic, and logic is useful in offices and libraries – not in the world.'

'When everyone lived in rural places,' she said, 'they thought differently. They understood things differently.'

'And now we say that that was wrong, that we're right. But look at what we're doing and what they did, and then ask who is right.'

'Who's to say,' she said, 'that one way of thinking is better than another? It all comes from up here.'

She tapped her head.

'But how do you know that scientific technology has got anything to do with the drought?' I asked.

'Of course it has! Anyone who says it hasn't is blinded by money,' he said. 'They want to think that they can carry on, greedily, richly, just the same as ever, living from the workers. Some scientists say it is caused by industry, others that it isn't. They don't know, and yet still they tell us that they're always right.'

'The difference is,' she said, 'that science controls everything now.'

'It's eating everything else up.'

'We're losing everything,' she said.

'Listen,' he said. 'We used to have a farm in Gastre, in Chubút Province. We had it for twenty years. Every summer, in December and January, the sun always used to rise over the same point of a hill that was across from our house, above a pointed rock. I went there five years ago, and that had changed. The sun now rises above a point that is half a kilometre from that rock.'

'Are you sure?'

'Of course! I may be old, but I remember it well. It's all changing.'

'All changing,' she sighed.

We were silent again. I could not bring myself to go to sleep in the barn. I wanted to talk on and on, but my exhausted mind prodded my voice with nothing that it could say.

'What *are* you doing here?' she asked. 'Nobody comes this way without a reason.'

'I'm following Darwin's route,' I said. 'The *Beagle* along the coast.'

'Darwin!' he exclaimed, scornful.

'How long will that take?'

'A year.'

'That's wonderful,' she said. 'You must meet so many people. So many that you could write a book.'

He laughed.

'That's what he's doing,' he said. 'Hadn't you guessed?'

He laughed again, and I went to sleep soon afterwards, on a pile of sheepskins mounted up like bales of hay in the inertia that enveloped the dusty barn.

I walked all the next day; and the next; and the next. There were generally five or six hours between *puestos*. I would arrive, ask for water, rest; and then leave. The track curved without apparent rhyme

or reason over the desert, always towards the next hill southwards –
the hills straggled dustily down to the sea. The view was always the
same, always would be the same in Patagonia: sand, scrub, space-spree
of freedom, singing with the cry of guanacos in the wander of their
loneliness. And sometimes, there were animals. They punctuated my
contemplation with thoughts of their own, dragging me away from the
emptiness which my head became as I walked.

I came across these same guanacos, startled, terrified of this person,
bounding away from me; or I was jolted by the unexpected cackle of a
gaggle of parrots flying overhead. Sometimes I'd look up and eye warily
the drifting circles of carrion hawks piercing the plains with their laser-
vision, waiting to pounce on whatever death was left to them.

And then, one morning, I stared into the translucent eyes of a pit-
viper, still as death, acting death, as I nearly trod on it.

This last was a shock. It was long and brown, featureless: 'I do not
think I ever saw any thing more ugly,' Darwin wrote of it. It had been
sunning itself on the track, and stilled in terror, as did I. I retraced my
steps slowly, and drew a wide circle around it. With no one ever passing,
I would have been a vulture's meal had it struck at me.

In the farms, I drank water by the gallon. Families watched me, in
the stillness, listening to the flies. They told of the drought, always the
drought. When I told one group that I'd nearly trodden on the pit-viper,
they told me these snakes had been unknown before Patagonia began
to heat up. Then I'd move on to the next *puesto*, and be met by furious
dogs, snapping at my heels and desperate to take a nip; or by uncanny
silence, drowned by the invective of the suddenly howling wind, when
the buildings were abandoned. One old *puestero* lived alone, with no
teeth, and a vest full of holes. His yard was a cemetery for cars. No one
ever came to visit him, and I thought of how long his corpse might
wait to be discovered after he had died.

I rarely came across more than two *puestos* in a day. Sometimes I'd
see the track rising up through the plateau; then, for example, it would
swoop down to the remains of an abandoned village by the sea, Puerto
Lobos. This was the old road south, but no one ever came past and the
settlement was gone. Many of the settlements marked on my map did
not exist; nor did the roads, which had been chained off by the *estancieros* because they were unused.

If I stopped to rest, I heard nothing. I was the only source of sound. When I moved, I could hear and feel my labours – when I stopped, the world stopped working with me. Once I saw a vulture quite clearly, motionless on one of the bushes. Nothing moved but me. I felt as if I was breaking a law of the desert, by moving and being alive.

I loved this place, but it scared me. My pack weighed thirty-five kilos, with all the weight of food and water which I carried. There would be no one to see me collapse with exhaustion, writhe, and retreat into my skeleton. There were many skeletons along the way, their bones picked clean by scavengers, like the earth itself. Sometimes I felt that the vultures were circling over me deliberately, waiting for their meal to begin.

I walked on and on until I reached the main road near Puerto Madryn. It took another five days from the first *estancia*. When I reached the town, having hitched a lift the last kilometres with a local *estanciero*, I was shocked by the growl of the city. Madryn was a modern, booming tourist town. People came to see the sea lions, right whales, penguins and elephant seals.

I looked over the bay, knowing there would not be any guanacos swimming from island to island any more. You never find guanacos near a town in Patagonia, since they know that they will all be shot.

I tried to make sense of all that silence and solitude.

Then I met a German, the first European tourist I had met since leaving Montevideo three months earlier. I asked him if he liked Argentina.

'No,' he said. 'There are too many cities.'

II

All was stillness and desolation. Yet in passing over these scenes without one bright object near, an ill-defined but strong sense of pleasure is vividly excited.

Charles Darwin on the plains near Puerto Deseado

Puerto Deseado was always one of the main harbours on the Patagonian coast. Together with Puerto San Julián, it was an obligatory stopping point for early mariners heading for the coasts of Chile and Peru. While San Julián was the site of the execution of traitors by both Magellan and Drake, Deseado has seen ships burnt and penguins and sea lions culled almost beyond recall. Its name – Port Desire, as it was called by John Davis – rings hollowly against bloody Patagonian history.

One of the earlier European expeditions was made by the Spanish brothers, Bartolomé and Gonzalo García de Nodal, who visited the harbour in 1619. On one island of the harbour, there were so many sea lions that the brothers dared not land. There were so many gulls, cormorants and penguins that they covered the island completely. Exactly 150 years later an English frigate, the *Wager*, docked at Puerto Deseado on its way to a messy shipwreck in the South Seas. One of its crew was John Byron, grandfather of the poet, who later wrote how very profitable the seals could become if they were hunted for their skins. Not long after Byron's visit, the first hunters arrived, particularly interested in the worth of the skins of the fur seals.

The marine life at Puerto Deseado had already suffered a pounding at the hands of its baptist, John Davis. Davis and his men had culled 10,000 penguins from the island at the entrance to the harbour – now called Penguin Island – on their way back to Britain from their abortive mission to Tierra del Fuego. But the penguins developed worms which devoured everything in the ship, and Davis limped back to Britain with virtually the whole crew dying of scurvy.

The history of Europeans in Patagonia is a destructive one. It is not just that the Tehuelche, Ona, Yámana and Alacalufe Indians have been virtually wiped out (in the Ona's case, completely so). The wildlife has been devastated. Guanacos, rheas, sea lion, penguins, *huemules* (indigenous deer): the list of casualties is interminable. All of these species still exist, but their numbers have been devastated. H.C. Gardiner, the first European to reach the source of the Río Santa Cruz at Lago Argentino, in 1867, estimated that he saw 10,000 guanacos and rheas on his journey. Doing the same journey today, I cannot have seen more than two hundred guanacos. I did not see a single rhea. In fact I did not see one *Rhea Darwinii* in all the time I was in Patagonia.

This is not entirely due to overhunting, since both guanacos and rheas are known sufferers of the drought (particularly the rheas). But the decimation in their numbers is everywhere apparent. Along the Patagonian shoreline, there are now only two colonies of fur seals. There are still sea lions at Deseado, but their numbers are restricted to a few small colonies. Together with the culling of the animals has come soil erosion from intensive sheep farming – desertification is so extreme that in many parts of Patagonia an *estancia* can only cope with one sheep per three hectares of land.

Obviously, humans have always been hunters. Together with artificial selection, hunting forms part of the armoury with which people affect the world. In *The Origin of Species*, Darwin distinguished between artificial and natural selection: 'Selection by man, whether intentional or unintentional, combined with the strong principle of inheritance, played a most important part in adding up very slight variations in a given direction.' Darwin was thinking here of animal breeders, who breed specimens that possess a particular feature which the breeders want to maintain. In this way, men control the development of animals in particular ways. This selection is artificial because it is chosen by men, and not left exclusively to the whim of genetic mutation. In fact, Darwin repeatedly suggested that men possess characteristics which make them 'artificial' in some way: 'Unlike men,' he wrote, 'other organisms cannot artificially increase their means of support.'

Darwin later touched on the capacity of men to destroy products of natural selection. Men are capricious, he says, and kill off beings for no reason other than their arbitrary quirks, so that each being is not allowed to live and procreate according to its kind: 'He selects any peculiarity or quality which pleases or is useful to him, regardless whether it profits the being & whether it is the best possible adaptation to the conditions ... See how differently Nature acts! By Nature, I mean the laws ordained by God to govern the Universe ... Nature's productions bear the stamp of a far higher perfection than man's product by artificial selection.'

Famously, Darwin felt bound by both the devout faith of his wife, Emma, and by the cultural climate of his times. These qualifications were designed to allay his religious critics. His lead has been followed by modern evolutionists such as Ernst Mayr, who skates over the distinction in two pages and says that Darwin saw artificial selection as an accelerated analogue of natural selection.[1] Another modern evolutionist, Richard Dawkins, has followed Darwin by using artificial selection as a model for natural selection.

However, the distinction between artificial selection and natural selection remains a clear one – Darwin depends on artificial selection in his argument for natural selection – and the short shrift which is given to it by some evolutionists smacks of dogmatism. Having written that every evolutionary biologist understands this process to work through natural selection (thus bypassing artificial selection), Dawkins claims that all evolution is to be understood in terms of the 'selfish' desire of DNA combinations to propagate themselves from generation to generation.[2] Seeking to explain how there can be nothing but genetic material behind the development of all organic matter, he gives what he admits to be a 'speculative account' of the formation of life, claiming that the few raw materials on earth before life 'at some point' formed a molecule with the extraordinary capacity of creating copies of itself. These 'replicators', says Dawkins, became our genes.

What was initially presented as a 'speculative account' is now, a little bewilderingly, presented as unalloyed truth. The agenda is to show how we humans really do have common descent from the same molecular beginnings as all creatures, that our impulses are at heart born of the selfish genetic thrust which characterises all life-forms. The main evidence for this theory is that genetic material is transferred from parents to offspring, and that there is a natural urge to procreate and reproduce that genetic material.

At some points in this account it is difficult not to wonder how often facts are structured around the theory, and how often the theory is actually beholden to the facts. In *The Doctrine of DNA: Biology as Ideology*, a highly respected scientist, R.C. Lewontin, casts a cauldron of hot water onto some of the more popular assertions made by genticists.[3] Lewontin claims that sociobiology – the attempt to explain human behaviour in terms of natural selection and inbred genetic selfishness – is in fact simply an attempt to enshrine conservatism and convince people of the necessity of the status quo. He argues that biological theories often have a deeper agenda, which is to convince us of the justification and inevitability of the inequalities in modern society:

> The claim that all of human existence is controlled by our DNA is a popular one. It has the effect of legitimising the structures of society in which we live, because it does not stop with the assertion that differences in temperament, ability, and physical and mental health between us are coded in the genes. It also claims that the political structures of society – the competitive, entrepreneurial, hierarchical society in which we live – is also determined by our DNA, and that it is, therefore, unchangeable.[4]

Lewontin then proceeds to provide alternative interpretations, and in some cases rebuttals, of accepted genetic arguments. The key step of sociobiologists is to identify universal human characteristics – but, says Lewontin, there is no evidence that human universals are in the genes, and in fact it is often simply asserted that because they are universal, they must be genetic. This argument also debunks the subsequent claim, that these features, as coded in our DNA, are unchangeable. The analogies drawn between human and animal traits which supposedly support genetic continuity as the crux depend entirely on how the analogies are read. Often, an analogy is alleged between humans and animals which in fact depends entirely on language and interpretation. A word – 'aggression', for instance – is applied to the behaviour of rats, and then by analogy is used to 'discover' the same trait in humans; as the same word is used the same feature is supposedly described, although whether what humans and rats are doing is really the same is in fact highly debatable.

In fact, as Lewontin's ideas suggest, genetic *theory*, and its role in natural selection theory, is based mainly on complete assumptions of the theory's validity. One of Dawkins' central ideas is 'kin selection', the theory that our altruistic acts are based on the desire to propagate our own DNA, and consequently that acts of apparent selflessness towards family members are actually driven by this urge, which he characterizes as 'selfish'. Not only does this approach fall prey to the dangers of linguistic confusion, but this interpretation of behaviour also depends on a prior belief that selfishness underlies the behaviour – otherwise, Dawkins would simply see altruism as altruism. Assuming that there can be nothing more to explaining our behaviour than genetic constitutions, Dawkins assumes that this characteristic of DNA is enough to explain everything human as selfish. However, what he uses as evidence for this behaviour (the explanations of altruism through the selfish gene) actually depends on a prior belief in his theory. Lewontin concludes: 'Science consists not simply of a collection of true facts about the world, but is the body of assertions and theories about the world made by people who are called scientists. It consists, in large part, of what scientists say about the world whatever the true state of the world might be.'[5]

With much of sociobiology, this statement rings very true. As I saw the destruction that people had wrought on the fauna of Puerto Deseado and on the indigenous peoples in all of this region, the fact that it is people that have a great power to select was reinforced, and the dangers of a dogmatic rejection of artificial selection as a mere analogue of natural selection seemed to be highlighted. Patagonian history appears to contravene the idea of a uniform evolution of ecosystems with only one element – the intrinsic selfishness of DNA – determining development. For the history of Europeans in Patagonia is one of people whose genetic development has not adapted them to these climates and conditions, systematically destroying races of people and animals which – according to our understanding – should be better adapted in consequence of their long interaction with these surroundings, and the genetic mutations which have long been favoured by this environment. People seem to have transcended the power of natural selection in this case – in so many cases – and subordinated it to their own power to wreak change. Humankind, as Darwin said and as is so often said, is the only race to exert control over its environment.

This is the influence of culture. Stephen Jay Gould – to name only one modern evolutionist – consistently plays up the distinctions between cultural and evolutionary change throughout his work. Although natural selection may have been behind the development of culture, culture unquestionably now affects natural selection. This is obviously the case with the slaughters in Patagonia, and is a paradigm for the human capriciousness so scorned by Darwin. The effects of culture on nature are everywhere apparent: in industrialization, pollution and the demise of many species which otherwise would be flourishing. These species have not been replaced by species better naturally equipped to cope with the conditions in a particular place, but by a species that is better culturally adapted – in that it has a culture at all.

It has become a dogma of recent times that only something that is scientifically proven or verifiable is justifiable as a channel of enquiry. But this, like most dogmas, is a cultural fact and not an actual fact. Scientific observation tells us what is happening to the tattered fabric of the world's environment, but not why it is happening. In order to understand this, we must return to a study of culture, since culture has replaced natural selection as the defining force of evolution.

I hitchhiked from Madryn to Deseado, and was there in a day.

Everyone knew everyone here. I wanted to follow the *Beagle* along some of this coastline. I decided to go south, towards San Julián. Roberto Cis owned some land this way, and I found him at his hardware store. As we were discussing the route, a man in drainpipe cords appeared who ran the farm next to Cis. Then they thought of someone who might be able to give me a lift part of the way, and I roamed through the town's back streets, knocking on the doors of total strangers as I looked for José-Ricardo Juanola, the foreman of a big *estancia* who was rumoured to be in town. People were baffled by my appearance: a strange and shabbily bearded man with an appalling body odour problem, knocking on their doors and asking for the address of a man he'd never met.

When I found his house, Juanola helped me to draw a map of the *estancias* between Deseado and San Julián.

We talked for several hours over lunch, and then José-Ricardo's son said:

'Well, if you're interested in local history, you should meet my grandfather. He knows more than anyone in Puerto Deseado.'

'He doesn't want to do that,' his mother said. 'The old man may be rude. He often doesn't like to talk to strangers.'

'Let's take him along,' her son insisted. 'Grandfather will enjoy it. He likes talking.'

So I went to see him.

José-Ricardo's father was ninety-one. He was a Galician, but had moved to Patagonia when aged four. Despite a measure of decrepitude, he lived alone, walking steadily and looking fifteen years younger than he was. He wheezed constantly with bronchitis, but braved the hardships of his age as well as he could, and until a few years before he had regularly ridden horses around his farm. His face was red with knots of veins that had the effect of making him look innately cheery.

This was unfortunate, for the old man's hard life had made him a cynic. He bridled with rigid opinions, most of them self-taught. He was a polymath of sorts, who selected what he learnt and enjoyed his prejudices. His laughter came from the soul of a man who does not see humour in the world, but blackness and the absurd. Yet you had to forgive him all this, for he was clearly a good man.

He loved to throw rhetorical questions at me, wait for a hesitant answer, and then beat me to it. He often talked without a break for minutes at a time, and then reluctantly recognized my existence.

'Where were the first aborigines from?'

'Well ... there are lots of different theories...'

'What do you think?'

'I know that most scientists think man originated in Africa...'

'No! Patagonia. Do you understand? Patagonia. The home of man, his oldest roots. *No se si me explico.* Do I make myself clear?'

'*Si, se explica.*'

'What about the petrified forests? Do you know how old they are? ... Two hundred and fifty million years old! Two hundred and fifty million years! And still scientists think they can come and unlock her secrets! Her wisdom! They're all fools. Rich fools, but fools. *No se si me explico.*'

'*Si, si. Se explica.*'

He laughed.

'Ha, ha! And why do they bother? Why? Why do you think? ... To distract us ... To distract us from the world. The more that industry distances men from their roots, the more they have to be distracted that they may forget themselves ... Look at those cities. Bigger and greyer. More and more artificial entertainment. Entertainment! Ha! Why do people need entertaining anyway? So that they aren't bored. The greater the tragedy that's in store, the more we're hidden from it. Well, all they need to do is come here, and then they'd see! Ha, Ha ...'

He burst into a violent cough, and I looked at his convulsions nervously for half a minute. I did not want him to excite himself to death before me.

'Oh yes,' he resumed, 'we're only just beginning to realize that, but it's true. We're heading for the apocalypse ... Patagonia! I never thought I'd see it reduced to this ... Never thought I would see this desert. It stopped raining. Do you know when it stopped raining?'

'No.'

'In 1925. It used to rain every summer until 1925. Since then, just disaster, disaster. Oh it's the apocalypse, that's for certain. God has lost patience with us. *No se si me explico.*'

'*Si, se explica.*'

'Before, you left a horse to graze for an hour in the plains, and it was full. Now you leave it out for a month, and it's dying of hunger. There's nothing, nothing. No grass. No animals. When I was a boy, we'd hear the whales calling to each other in the creek. But they're all dead now ... History repeats itself you see, young man. Everything goes in circles. What do you think? ... There was poverty and hunger, and then there was wealth. Now, within two generations, we'll have mass anarchy again. More poverty, more hunger, overcrowding. Too many people. You know the only way out?'

'No.'

'We need a ruthless dictator, a tyrant. Someone like Pinochet in Chile. They must come along and kill 90, 95 per cent of people, and then we can start properly again. But before that happens, the sun will burn us all to death. Natural law or human law, one way or another there won't be much left soon enough.'

He laughed at the folly of it all.

'And anyway, if they don't kill us, then the UFOs will do instead. All the powers pretend that there's no truth in UFOs. Ha! Do you know why we see so many here in Patagonia? Do you know what? They've got their bases in Antarctica, under the ice. A man left Madryn in his car about five years ago – twenty minutes later they found him in Salta [3000 kilometres away], covered in slime, with no idea how he'd got there. How do they explain it? How do they explain that?'

He laughed, scornfully, at 'them'.

'The thing is, young man,' he dropped his voice from the didactic rant which was his favourite, 'the thing is that what they don't want to tell anyone ... what they don't want us to know ... is that they don't know the answers. We don't know the answers. No one knows. We're all alone here ... The world is so much more complicated than we can ever see ... And yet they pretend they've discovered everything.'

'Have you ever written any of this?'

'Oh yes! I've written. But never published. You should never publish anything either, not if you've got any sense. It's best not to go against money and power, people always end up paying for it. Look what's happened to Cuba! ... There's a Communist country that works. People have work, they study, they're healthy. But the politicians can't accept this, because the Cubans are the only ones that don't scrounge off the people ... So they try to shut them up ... Oh, I've written things, yes. I've written a book. I wanted to publish it, I did. But then, I thought there's been so much evil here in Patagonia. So many terrible things. Is it a man's fault if his grandfather was a poisoner, or lied in court to steal another man's land? It's not, is it, young man? But no, tell me: what do you think?'

I did not know; my thoughts unravelled like a spool of thread, labyrinthine and unforgiving as a spider's web as I left the old man, and looked for someone who could take me up Deseado's inland creek, which stretches fifty kilometres away from here into the Patagonian wastes.

When the *Beagle* stopped for Christmas here in 1833, Darwin accompanied the ship's bowman – Mr Chaffers – in a yawl to explore the inland estuary. On a walk up to the plateau, Darwin wrote that 'There was not a tree, and, excepting the guanaco, which stood on the hilltop a watchful sentinel over its herd, scarcely an animal or a bird.' They continued up the creek, until the yawl ran aground in the narrowing muddy stream and they transferred to a dinghy before camping by some cliffs – this campsite was drawn for posterity by Martens. I wanted to find it.

By a stroke of massive good fortune, I met Marcos Oliva Day. Marcos was Deseado's public prosecutor, an environmentalist and a Patagonian explorer. He runs a unique voluntary project in the town, giving free kayak lessons to the children in the summer holidays – the school has produced two Argentine national champions. For ecological ends, he and members of the kayak club have kayaked to Cape Horn, along the whole length of the coastline of Santa Cruz Province, and across several remote lakes in the Andes. Marcos is also a local historian, and only two years earlier he and a group of divers had discovered the remains of the *Swift*, an English sloop of war which sank in Deseado in 1770.

Marcos took me up the creek in his motor boat.

'Look at it,' he said, as we bounced over the waves. 'You can see them all. Magellan, Schouten, Darwin. Close your eyes and they are sailing past us.'

We stopped in Bahía Uruguay, and climbed a small promontory. From here, we could look down at the island where Schouten and Lemaire, the Dutch navigators, burnt one of their two ships – the *Hoorn* – when they landed here in 1615. They had planned to burn off the growths of barnacles and weeds on the ship's hull with a fire built of brushwood. But the wood had burnt too fiercely, and the fire had blazed out of control, reducing the *Hoorn* to ashes. They sailed on down the Patagonian coast, and on 29 January 1616 they rounded an extremity of land with nothing beyond it but the ocean. Realizing that this must be the southernmost tip of America, Schouten named it Cape Hoorn, after the unfortunate ship and the city where they were born.*

The island was a slab of land much like the rest of Patagonia: sandy and scrubby. It did not look like an important site for global maritime history. From the promontory, we could see the unending plains that I would see everywhere in Patagonia, in Madryn and Cabo Blanco, San Julián and the Río Santa Cruz, the same sense of sterility and lifelessness clutching the mind through the immutable views that extended on all sides.

We carried on up the creek, in the golden evening light. A school of

---

* Whether it was Schouten or Drake (in 1578) who first discovered Cape Horn is still disputed.

Commerson's Dolphins followed the boat, breaking through the waves and casting their spray over us like the bows of a boat breaking the water. There were thousands of South American terns screeching overhead, the sound of a devil's orchestra, twirling around and around and then hovering so close to the boat that you thought you could touch them. In the cliffs were several species of cormorant – the imperial, rock and grey cormorants – aloof and disdainful of the terns' cacophony.

'This must be one of the richest places in Patagonia for wildlife,' I said.

'Yes,' Marcos replied. 'But think what it would have been like when the first explorers were here.'

The roar of the engine drowned most of our conversation, and we stopped trying to bellow into the breeze. The further inland we went, the closer the cliffs converged around us. They shone brilliantly, their glare burning like lightning as the creek crept towards them. Many of the cliffs looked as though they might have been the ones in Martens' drawing, and we kept thinking that we had spotted the campsite.

'That's the one,' we'd say, pointing a kilometre or so up the valley; then, seeing further and further: 'No, *that's* the one, I'm sure.'

We went on, squinting into the haze between us and the sunset, now sailing deep into the reaches of Bahía Concordia. The creek narrowed, cutting between banks of glutinous sinking mud that broke off with the surf and coloured the creek chocolate. And then we saw a prominent, almost phallic rock, and beyond it, around the sweep of a meander in the creek, a vertical cliff falling to the mud below. A flock of ducks garbled their way over the water, shaking the air like the shudder of crumbling earth. Marcos cut the engine, and we were welcomed back into the fold of Patagonian silence.

He was right. Close your eyes, and your ears, and you could see Darwin and the others, chatting laconically, in dribs and drabs, keeping their spirits up by the evening fire, warding off the stillness and wisdom of the plains beneath the stars.

As I reread Darwin's notes, I realized that although no landfall was made between Deseado and San Julián, some *Beagle* officers had seen a herd of guanacos drinking briny water from a salt-pan near Cabo Blanco. Cabo Blanco was eighty kilometres north of Deseado, and I decided to walk there instead of south to San Julián.

It took me two days. On the first day I got lost. Someone had told me that I would cut distance by following the beach, and then heading inland to an *estancia* that was clearly visible from the shore. I walked for four hours out of Deseado, returning to wilderness. A track followed the beach, layered with stones which cut into my feet and blistered them. I saw one sheep and a clutch of horses grazing faraway in the flats, distant as the shore glimpsed from the sea. The ocean's scraping rattle against the pebble beach kept me going. I dreamt of the *Beagle* keeping me company, a phantom pouring realism over my journey. After a while I passed a couple of rotting chairs and a cardboard crate full of smashed wine bottles, sitting in derelict loneliness in their private auditorium at the edge of the ocean. Then the track split in two, and the beachside fork disappeared into a sandy hollow bereft even of animal tracks. I stared myopically at the scrub – I had lost my glasses, and only had a new pair made up a week later – screwing my eyes together, trying to pick out a gleaming white *estancia* on the hillside (even if it was a mirage); but my squints spotted only stillness.

I retraced my steps to the fork, and tried the other branch.

This track headed directly inland, away from the beach. I knew that there was an *estancia* a little way inland so I decided to make for it. But then this track also disappeared, and I was left to follow the line of the fence. After twenty minutes, the fence turned a right angle, and I tried to find my way on through the featureless blur of Patagonia for the short-sighted. There were a few hillocks standing out from the scrub, but even they all looked alike to me.

I had no compass.

I took my bearings from what hills I could, and carried on. A cold sheet of rain began to shiver down. Every time I reached a hillock, I climbed it, and looked into another mass of featureless land tangling with the greyness of the sky, mingling with the clouds until each disappeared into the other's gargantuan entrails. I repeatedly dreamt that I saw the *estancia*; but repeatedly I did not. The rain pressed against me, unwelcome as night on the road, and my mind cooled and slowed and tried to talk my feet out of walking on. But I had to continue, and after an hour marching through the desperate absence of signs, I stumbled by chance onto the road to the *estancia*.

I arrived there after ten hours' walk, and spent the rest of the day talking with the *gaucho*. Miraculously for Patagonia, and because it was sited above a subterranean spring, the house had one of the richest orchards I had ever seen, with hundreds of trees stuffed full of plums, pears, apples, cherries, apricots and peaches. We scoffed the fruit until dusk, and then in the morning the man filled my rucksack with about ten kilos of apricots, since he had three crates of them to eat before they all went off.

'No, no,' I tried to protest.

But he insisted, however much I complained that the weight would kill me before I reached Cabo Blanco. As it was, it took me another ten hours to reach the Cape, aching every step with the fruit but loath to throw away any of the *gaucho*'s gift. After five hours I saw the light-house which marks the cliff perched high up and shimmering in the haze. Although I knew how deceptive distances were in Patagonia, I somehow thought that I would arrive within two hours. I walked and walked, and the lighthouse never seemed to get any nearer. It glim-mered in the desert, always seeming just too far away to be near. I crossed the dry plateau, then fell into salt-pans crusted white, like spring earth sprayed with frost – the only thing that I could see or hear or smell. I walked for another five hours before I climbed up the steps and knocked on the lighthouse door. It was a terrific place: a black outcrop of rocks, crashing and twisting down to the seas, raised tortuously above the waters that fought and assaulted it. Below the rocks, I heard the howls of the fur seals, Cabo Blanco being one of the Patagonian coast's two colonies. I could see them sitting indefatigably on their rocks, showered by wave after wave of the growing storm, immobile as the cliff before the advancing roar of watery fury.

The marines who manned the lighthouse let me stay. There were plenty of spare rooms in the rattling old shell where in the old days ten men had been stationed at once. No one lived within thirty kilometres of Cabo Blanco, and hardly anyone ever visited, so they were delighted to have company. One of them, a morose man with thick lips from Tucumán in the north, decided to cheer me up by speaking irrepressibly about his health problems.

'I have terrible cholesterol,' he said. 'The doctor says that I shouldn't eat any meat at all.'

'No,' I said, leadenly, longing for sleep and thinking of the last five months of *asado*.

'Dairy products. They're terrible as well. Milk, cheese.'

'Yes,' I said, thinking of the creamy cheese and *dulce de leche* that I took with me on my walks.

'But the worst, they say, the worst is to eat eggs.'

'Yes.'

I often took several hard-boiled eggs with me as well. Perhaps it was then, as the gathering wind howled through that lonely lighthouse at the end of the earth, that I decided to become a vegetarian when I returned to Britain.

III

Why, then – and the case is not peculiar to myself – have these arid
wastes taken so firm possession of my mind? ... I can scarcely analyse
these feelings, but it must be partly owing to the free scope given to
the imagination.

Charles Darwin on Patagonia

In early 1834, the *Beagle* continued down the Patagonian coast from
Puerto Deseado. They spent ten days at San Julián in January, and
returned to the Río Santa Cruz in mid-April from the Falkland Islands.
Here, while the *Beagle* was undergoing repair work to her false keel,
FitzRoy mounted the expedition up the valley.

At San Julián Darwin demonstrated his strength. A party of men,
including FitzRoy and Darwin, set out from the ship to search for a
water source marked on an old Spanish map. The weight of the guns
and measuring instruments that they were carrying, combined with
the heat of the middle of the day, meant that the men were quickly
exhausted. From a hilltop they caught sight of what seemed to be lakes
a little further inland. Darwin was the only one with the strength to
continue, and they watched in alarm as he stooped down at each lake
and then returned with the news that the water was brine. FitzRoy was
still in a very bad way, and he stayed behind with one of the sailors
while Darwin and the others returned to the *Beagle* to raise a rescue
party. By the time he reached the ship, Darwin had been walking
continuously for eleven hours without a drop of fresh water. He was
the fittest man on ship.

When I reached San Julián, after hitching there from Deseado, I
followed him over the plains towards the lakes which are now known as
the Salitrales de Cabo Curioso. Everything was as always in Patagonia.
I walked what I estimated to be forty kilometres in the day, and then
made for the Santa Cruz.

Since leaving Buenos Aires the Santa Cruz had loomed over me. I knew that the river would be more lonely than anything before. Although the walks to Cabo Blanco and Madryn had been solitary, I had always camped at a farm for the night. But I was told that there was only one *estancia* near the river in the 300 kilometres that I had before me.

It was tempting to think that nothing might have changed since Darwin's journey. They set off up the river on 18 April 1833 with three weeks of provisions and twenty-five people. Straightaway they saw that the river current was rapid. They had three whale-boats with them, and hoped to sail upstream. But the current required them to fasten the boats head to stern, taking it in turns to haul the boats upriver from the banks. It was slow work, and Darwin estimated that they covered fifteen to twenty miles a day [twenty-four to thirty-two kilometres], but only ten in a straight line. The expedition had to turn back on 4 May within sight of the mountains, since their provisions were low – it only took three days to return with the current, as opposed to seventeen days against it.

Darwin estimated that when they turned around they were 140 miles [220 kilometres] from the Atlantic, and only twenty miles [thirty-two kilometres] from the *cordillera*. The exact point which they reached is not known, although they cannot have been as near to the mountains as they thought, since even Lago Argentino is still about forty kilometres from the first peaks of the *cordillera*. They certainly did not reach Lago Argentino, and it is unlikely that they reached the Río Bote, since Darwin would almost certainly have mentioned this (it is the only tributary on the south side of the Santa Cruz between the Atlantic and Lago Argentino). I decided to walk on until I reached the Bote, within clear view of the Andes, and then hitch the rest of the way into the town of Calafate.

I set out from the small town of Comandante Luis Piedra Buena. I bought four kilos of bread, three sticks of salami, six packets of biscuits, and two kilos of *dulce de leche*. That would have to do me for ten days.

'Aren't you afraid of the bandits?' the baker asked, as I ordered the bread.

'Bandits?'

'The men who come over from Chile and rob the *estancias*.'

I asked Tino Peralta, a friend of Marcos Oliva Day, about this.

'Oh no! Don't worry. The only people who'll kill you there are the Indians,' he joked.

Then I suggested ringing him from Calafate when I had finished walking.

'If I don't ring you within two weeks, perhaps you could tell the police?'

'Don't worry, amigo. If anything happens to you, the hawks and condors will find you first.'

Tino was a funny man. He cooked me an enormous quantity of steak one night, and then when I declined a second peach on the grounds that my intestines would burst he complained that I hadn't eaten anything.

I left early the next morning. I crossed the road bridge to the south side of the river, then cut under a barbed wire fence, down a steep bank, and onto the only grass which I saw on the whole journey. I had not walked a quarter of an hour when I slipped, and the buckle on the shoulder strap of my rucksack snapped. The strap dangled loosely, unattached. Although I could have interpreted it as a bad omen, I did my best not to.

I sat on a hillock, already breathing heavily from the weight, and tied the strap to the broken buckle with some twine before continuing.

The valley is its own world – independent country. On each side are cliffs reaching 300 metres up to the plateau, soaring disdainfully away from the width of the snaking eel below. The river meanders its ribbon through the plain, sweeping sinuously from side to side as it retreats to the Andes, winding extravagantly, like a languorous drunk, and cutting a valley between fifteen and thirty kilometres wide out of the Patagonian plateau. Continuously following the meanders would have killed me, so I tried to spot the river's curls further up the valley, and cut across towards them.

The days blended naturally into one another. They were all alike. I got up, banished the lethargy of exhaustion, and walked. I followed the river, cutting over the blank plains where I could, until I could walk no more. Then I rested, closing my eyes to my tiredness and the emptiness. Walked on. Rested. Perhaps I ate something now, because I had no energy left. And eventually I camped when I could face it no more. The more I eat, I told myself, the lighter my pack will become, and the easier the journey will appear. It weighed far too much, as usual, when I set out. It was killing me. As soon as night came, I crawled into my tent and slept, too profoundly to remember my dreams, until the guilt-trigger of my alarm recalled me to the emptiness of each day.

The scale was immense, much worse than at Cabo Blanco. I would turn a curve in the valley walls, and spot a cliff in the distance. I would know that it was far; but never know how far. I would walk all day and still not reach it. Then the river would cut right under the banks of the cliff, and in the morning I would have to climb up onto the plateau, avoiding the ravines, and the crumpled knots in the valleys and mountains, skirt the cliff, and find my way down the far side. On average, I had to climb onto the plateau once a day. High up, when I had left the river below, the drabness of Patagonia greeted me with even more force; the spirit of a beloved old friend, grasping my hand with unashamed warmth and refusing to relinquish it. The greys and whites were greyer and whiter. The plains were vaster than before, vaster than my mind could grasp.

Sometimes the days were still. If I stopped to rest, the despairing entropy of the world suddenly died along with its moving dance.

On other days I walked headlong into terrible winds. These were the worst of all. The winds whistled down from the Andes, threatening a storm, buffeting me unceasingly from the moment I set out. If I opened my lips to speak to myself, my voice cut into the air and died, drooping pathetically to the ground, lost before anyone could hear it.

There was never anything novel in the scene. There had been one *estancia* on this side of the river, at Los Guindos, but this was now abandoned. I arrived, and saw some pear trees. But the pears were hard and unripe, so I left them. The fence was up, and broken glass lay hollowly around, ringing like bells in the wind. Other than these pear trees, there were only two trees on the south side of the river in the 300 kilometres between Piedra Buena and the Río Bote.

Darwin was similarly impressed after his journey up the river valley: 'The complete similarity of the productions throughout Patagonia is one of its most striking characters. The level plains of arid shingle support the same stunted and dwarf plants; and in the valleys the same thorn-bearing bushes grow. Everywhere we see the same birds and

insects ... The curse of sterility is on the land.' This last sentence
has been popularized in Spanish as 'Patagonia, la tierra maldita' –
'Patagonia, the cursed land' – implying that Darwin loathed Patagonia.
He is famous for this in Argentina and Chile. In fact, as I have said,
Darwin found that it was the memories of Patagonia which stayed with
him most insistently. He was never able to forget this limitless place,
and put this down to the freedom of the imagination which comes with
such space.

This sort of space changes you irrevocably. Alone in the plains, I had
looked forward to being able to think over anything I wanted to in a
logical way. But when it came to it, I just contemplated. Days passed,
and I did not really think about anything. My diary entries were curt.
What could I say? I walked on, silenced by the silence, a mirror to the
nothingness around me. There were no new features in the landscape,
no new people, no animals, just these 'plains of arid shingle', my
companions day after day. The only break to the plains was the river
itself, as welcome a change as an oasis dancing in the desert. If I stopped,
I secreted my tiredness into the ground. I did everything without
thinking, or at least without articulating my thoughts to myself. I had
no need of articulating them. I knew my thoughts, and there was no
one else to bother telling. This was a similar experience to that of
Hudson: 'During those solitary days it was a rare thing for any thought
to cross my mind ... in that state of mind I was in, thought had become
impossible ... At the time, I was powerless to wonder at it or speculate
about it; the state seemed familiar rather than strange, and although
accompanied by a strong feeling of elation, I did not know it ... until I
lost it and returned to my former self – to thinking, and the old insipid
existence.'[6] However, thought does not become impossible. It is only
the old analytical thought which drifts away. You still think. You just
have no need for language any more. Swallowed up by the plains,
everything seems transparent, like a mountain stream sparkling in
clear sunlight. Hudson went on: 'That instinctive state of the human
mind, when the higher faculties appear to be non-existent ... is then
like a highly polished mirror, in which all visible nature – every hill,
tree, leaf – is reflected with miraculous clearness; and we can imagine
that if the animal could think and reason, thought would be superfluous
and a hindrance.'[7] I wrote nothing in my journal, because words could

not express my experience. Even now, I struggle with the vastness and peace which comes with the Patagonian solitude. There were no novelties to articulate, and so language gradually became redundant. My mind was no longer cluttered. Arguments and thoughts no longer revolved around the definition of words, thoughts no longer became embattled in webs of logic and assumptions; they became themselves – vanished into the valley.

In cities, there are so many things that the world becomes a confused jumble of signs which seem impossible to disentangle from each other. Everything is a distraction, because you are forced to notice things: the flashing lights, the raucous orchestra of dissonance, the myriad anonymous faces which fleetfoot their way into consciousness.

The hubbub invades our consciousness. So many images are thrown at us that we forget our own identities. In the desert, where there are no new images at all, nothing to distract us, we are forced to return to ourselves, speechless, wondering, calm. We need say nothing at all, we need only watch.

Because in watching the desert, we return, and watch ourselves.

On the third day from Piedra Buena, I came across a new *puesto* by the river. Leandro and Cristián, the *puesteros*, were flabbergasted to see me.

They'd never seen anyone walking up here.

'Come in,' was the first thing Leandro said. 'Have you eaten?'

I hadn't. I was ravenous. I spent most of the afternoon eating the remains of their *asado* and remembering what my voice sounded like.

'Darwin,' Leandro said. 'The name sounds familiar.'

'He discovered evolution,' I said, in an approximation of the truth. Leandro burst into a guffaw of laughter.

'That nutter! Crazy man! The bloke who said we all came from monkeys. *He* came past here?'

It had to be impossible. How could such a man, such a thinker, have come past here?

Leandro told me that there was another *estancia* forty kilometres down the river. I walked all the next day until I came across two poplars standing incongruously by the riverside, breaching the solitude of the desert with their own loneliness. This had to mean that the *estancia* was near; a track clambered up to the plateau, and in the morning I followed it.

The hill was steep. By this time, my legs were biting me with acid pain. I longed to rest. When I set out, I climbed up the track because I had to reach the plateau and skirt some more cliffs. But when the poplars of the *estancia* came into view, clustered together in a low hollow, they were too tempting to scorn. I kept to the track, and now caught sight of long barns beyond a network of dusty enclosures, collapsed at either end, all their windows cracked and the masonry crumbled as if Patagonia was at war.

An elderly peon was working in one of the corrals. When he saw me shuffling up the litter-strewn path past the corral, he simply stared.

'Go on into the kitchen,' was all he said.

I passed the back of the barn, where the yard was full of debris. There were sheets of iron rusting in the wind. Guanaco legs lay next to a small stream, scraps of fur matted with congealed blood clinging gorily onto them. Sheep skulls lay everywhere, discarded like bleached ashes from a fireplace.

I climbed a few steps into the kitchen. Dust and darkness poked through the windows at lunch time (I had risen late). There was an Aga in the corner, with a voluminous kettle whistling on top and a pile of moist and louse-ridden wood at the side. An old wooden cabinet stood next to the door, where the man kept sugar and salt and tea.

I sat in the dark room for some time.

Then the old peon appeared.

'You can stay in the room at the back,' he said. He hadn't even heard me speak. He showed me an old bed with a disintegrating foam mattress bolstered by several filthy sheepskins. Then he left me for a few minutes, and I sat silently once more. He was getting dressed for lunch with his *patrón*, who had come for a few days from Piedra Buena. He put on an immaculate checked shirt, grey cloth trousers and pointed black shoes that were shinier than desert flints in the sunlight.

'Excuse me,' he said. 'I have to go and eat with the *patrón*, but I'll come back later. Feel free.'

He shuffled down the hill to the main house:

A short while later he came back.

'They've invited you to eat,' he said.

I finished my tea, and walked with him to the orchard below the house. Matías – the *patrón* – was eighty-one, a slight man with forests of lines on his forehead and piercing green eyes. He had come to the *estancia* with his nephew, Coco, and Coco's two daughters. They all looked after lunch, while old Matías held forth.

Matías had been born at the *estancia*. They'd once had eight peons, but now there was just the one man. The peon was sitting silently on a tree stump, slightly away from the others, by far the smartest dressed person there.

I offered him my position at the table, but he would have none of it.

Matías talked about the hole in the ozone layer and the collapse of sheep farming.

'There's nothing left,' he said. 'There's an oil company prospecting further up the valley. They're prospecting on my land as well. I hope they find oil, don't I?'

He laughed evilly.

'Isn't that right, Coco? If they find oil, they'll *have* to pay me, won't they? Ha ha! Those are the rules now. Aren't they? Aren't they?'

He was bleating like the sheep he lived off and ate. His nephew ignored him and let the old man go on. Sometimes Matías fell into silence, and Coco would talk about the desperate state of Argentina, as Argentines love doing. But mostly, we all let the old man rant. When we finished eating, Matías told a joke.

'There was a group of monks in a monastery, eating a meal,' he said. 'When they finished, the Abbot said: "Well, we have eaten, we have drunk, so now let us give thanks to God." But the cook is listening, and he said: "Well, I haven't eaten, and I haven't drunk anything. So to the devil with all this shit!" Ha! *A la mierda, y a la puta que lo parió!* Ha, ha! Do you get it, Coco? Ha! *He* hasn't eaten, *he* hasn't drunk anything. So, *a la mierda, y a la puta que lo parió!*'

He went on and on. He laughed so much that his eyes really began to water, like cataracts.

'What's this sauce which you put on the lamb?' I asked after a pause, pointing to the relish of chillies, oil and oregano.

'It's *salmuera*. Ask the old man,' said Coco derisively. '*El viejo sabe todo*. The old man knows everything.'

'Ah yes!' said Matías, cheering up at once. 'Do you know how many types of *salmuera* there are? Eighteen...'

The peon excused himself after lunch, and left me to pass the afternoon with them. In the evening I returned to spend the night on the sheepskins. When I went into the kitchen, the room was empty. The peon appeared shortly afterwards. He had been chopping wood with a heavy axe, and he mopped his brow with a colourful handkerchief as he entered. The room had given up the battle with daylight now, and was illuminated by the half-light of a hurricane lamp. At least the darkness hid the dust and the poverty, the absence of possessions, hiding us away in our cave, where others could not see or judge us.

He stooped over the Aga and slid the logs into the fire, to heat up the leftovers from lunch – more steak.

'The *patrón*,' he said quietly. 'Did you like him?'

I didn't know what to say, so I was silent.

' "There are eighteen different types of *salmuera*," ' he mimicked. '*El viejo de mierda. Salmuera* is *salmuera*, and that's it.'

So he doesn't like him.

'Have you worked here long?'

'Too long! That old fool, he's never done a day's work in his life. He's just lived off his *estancia*. He's inherited everything. No wonder he's so old,' he laughed softly to himself.

The exaggerated shadows from the hissing hurricane lamp heightened his rubbery face, his piercing black eyes, the air of heaviness. Everything about him was heavy: his face, his speech, his life.

'But he's paying for his laziness now,' he went on. 'He's so old that his life hurts him. You see it in his eyes. Everything about it's been easy, so now it's harder than ever.'

He spoke easily, slowly, with the uncertainty of a man who does not often speak to others.

'What about you, *paisano*? How old are you?'

'It's my birthday tomorrow, actually.'

'How old will you be?'

'Twenty-three.'

'Twenty-three,' he said in soft surprise. 'I thought you were nearer thirty.'

My beard had grown, and Patagonia was ageing me.

I stayed the next day, trying to recuperate. There was never any pressure on me to go. I helped the old man with some odd jobs around the house: chopping wood for the fire, moving a table from his kitchen down to where the shearers had stayed when they had come to work the week before. Shearers were the worst form of life according to the *gaucho*.

'Terrible,' he said. 'Pigs. Thieves. Look at these beds,' he said, gesturing at a flea-infested pile of skins, 'they're too good for shearers.'

He had never been educated, but he possessed a wisdom of sorts. He told me his life story on the second night, perhaps because he never met anyone else who would listen. He had begun work when he was twelve, on an *estancia* in Chubút. There had been 400 workers. There were six men solely responsible for butchering enough meat for the workers. Thirty sheep a day were killed for their meat. There had been 300,000 sheep and 6000 cattle. Each section of a hundred men slept together in the same barn, huddling together in winter because of the cold. They had always eaten outside, on long wooden tables beneath some poplars, whatever the weather.

'All the farm managers were English,' he said. 'They treated us like animals. They didn't care if a man died. If one died, another would replace him. They beat you if you didn't do what they wanted. The last thing they wanted was for us to be educated. We weren't allowed to have radios. If they found a man with a radio, they beat him, sacked him, and destroyed his radio. What do you think of that, *paisano*?'

I had said that I was Canadian. I often did, to avoid unpleasantness over the Falklands War.

'*Qué hijos de putas,*' I said.

He laughed bitterly.

'*Si, qué hijos de putas.*'

'Before,' I said, 'there were more peons in the *estancias*.'

'That's because we were treated like dogs.'

I left with regrets the next morning, and carried on walking. It was another four days to the Río Bote. I met nobody here. I tried to imagine all that the old man must have seen and learnt, because I was sad to leave. Once I reached Calafate I would go to Chile, and I knew that things would be different there. I walked on in the same space as further down the valley, the winds still assaulting me as if I was a criminal.

The mountains drew nearer, pushing the *gaucho* out of my mind with the arrogance of vain beauty. The splendour of the *cordillera* was an incredible sight after over five months' travelling through wild plains. My legs were aching even after the rest, and it was only through willpower that I made the end of the journey. When I reached the Bote, I followed it south to the main road, and hitched into Calafate.

I still think of the *gaucho*. He was the last of his kind that I met. Wildness had followed me from the Pampas to here, expressed enduringly in all the people I met and everything I thought.

I want to describe him in detail, because his goodness and knowledge was only defined by everything about him, sleeping in all the twisted branches of his stories and habits.

His life was terribly hard, and he was exploited. But he was incomparably human. When I lost my jumper he insisted on giving me one of his own. When I left, he told me that it was no problem for me to stay as long as I wanted to.

Sometimes, when we talked, our differences caressed us. He was old, I was not. I was educated, he was not. I had many of the things that are valued by society, and he had none of them. And yet I still felt bottomless, inferior, whenever I listened to the flow of his self-awareness and passivity, his acceptance of the indiscernible forces that, in their ravishing power, hold no regard for our arrogance or theoretical transcendence, and indeed pause only to offer the briefest respect to the humility of the leap of faith.

At one point I had told him that Canada was the second biggest country in the world.

'No,' he said. 'I don't believe you, *paisano*.'

'It is.'

'Well, that's what happens when you talk to an educated person. You learn things.'

He'd hardly been to school at all. The teacher had travelled by horse, from village to village, staying for three months and then returning the next year.

'Then, when I was older, I learnt to read and write,' he said. 'Maybe I should go and learn something again.'

Then he laughed again, a laugh of dry irony.

'Ha! Go back to school! Now that is funny. *Estoy para la muerte no más.* Death is all that's left to me.

He was gouging the brain out from a sheep's head that had been sitting in the oven for hours. I had wondered at the profusion of sheep's heads, but he was convinced that they constituted the greatest of culinary delicacies, and, as I watched with no little incomprehension and disgust, he ate the brains as if they were sweetbreads.

PART FIVE

In the Bowels of the Earth

I

It was most ludicrous to watch through a glass the Indians, as often as the shot struck the water, take up stones, and as a bold defiance, throw them towards the ship, though about a mile and a half distant!

Charles Darwin, near Port Famine

When the news of Francis Drake's presence in South American waters reached Lima, Pedro Sarmiento de Gamboa was ordered to chase him by the Viceroy of Peru. Sarmiento chased Drake's shadow down the Chilean coast but the Englishman had already set off across the Pacific, in an attempt to repeat Magellan's circumnavigation. So Sarmiento passed through the Straits of Magellan and returned to Spain across the Atlantic. Possibly to distract from his failure to capture Drake, on his return to Spain Sarmiento began to persuade King Philip that a colony should be mounted on the Magellan Straits. This would take Christianity to the furthest confines of the known world.

Sarmiento's imagination played tricks with everyone. He claimed that he knew for certain that cotton and cinnamon grew in the interior of these regions. This proved, he said, that the climate was temperate. The colonists would be able to live on the indigenous fruits and roots that were abundant. With the quantities of wild berries and fish to be had, it was inconceivable that the colonists could go hungry; inconceivable.

He persuaded King Philip to colonize the Straits. Twenty-three ships were assembled, carrying 3000 people. They set sail on 27 September 1581.

It is impossible to imagine a more disastrous expedition. Before even leaving the Bay of Biscay, a storm arose and scattered the fleet, sinking seven ships and killing 800 people. They reached Rio de Janeiro in March 1582, by which time 150 people had died of plague at sea – a further 200 unfortunate souls were to perish of the same in port. By the time they reached the Straits, the expedition's size had contracted to two galleons and three frigates. The headwinds were so furious that they could not enter the calmer waters. Florés de Valdés, the captain-general of the expedition, ordered its return to Rio, whereupon he wrote to Philip that the enterprise was hopeless.

Sarmiento was not discouraged. He set out again in December 1583 with three galleons, two frigates and 500 colonists, and reached the Straits in two months. They were beset by gales, and as Sarmiento was unloading supplies the winds pounded one of the ships to pieces and left the others far out to sea. Diego de Ribera, Sarmiento's second-in-command, tried for several weeks to re-enter the Straits, but eventually he was forced to return to Spain. The colonists were left to their own resources, with one ship.

Sarmiento founded two cities, Nombre de Jesús, at Cape Virgins, and Ciudad Rey Don Felipe two weeks' march down the coast. The men were already suffering from hunger and poor hygiene, and a plot was mounted against Sarmiento. He discovered the plot and executed the ringleaders in the Plaza of Ciudad Rey Don Felipe.

Sarmiento was unperturbed, even by the polar winter which had by now begun, and he sailed with thirty men to visit Nombre de Jesús. Unfortunately – and this seems a common adverb where Sarmiento is concerned – as he prepared to disembark the most violent gale which they had yet encountered arose, breaking the ship's moorings and carrying her out into the Atlantic. Try as they might, there was no way back into the Straits. Sarmiento arrived in Rio with his crew half-dead from starvation. When he despatched a ship with provisions for the colonists, the ship sank. So he set off for Pernambuco for more supplies, and his ship unfortunately also sank – he only escaped by clinging to a raft. Sarmiento chartered ships twice more for the South Seas, but was defeated first by the weather and then by a mutiny. Despairing, he decided to return to Spain to make a plea on the colonists' behalf. When he finally reached the court, eight years after leaving for the Straits, no one cared about the colonists any more.

By this time, the Spaniards were all dead bar two. After their Governor's departure the men at Ciudad Rey Don Felipe waited for two months in the perishing sub-Antarctic winter with no news of him. Their food supplies evaporated, and they lived off shellfish. The men at Nombre de Jesús had to walk down the Straits to the other settlement, since most of the provisions were kept here. They waited all winter, and then all of the following summer. At the end of the first winter – 1585 – only eighty were left alive. A year later, the number was down to eighteen. At this point, a sail was sighted as the party were halfway between the two settlements.

The ship belonged to the English corsair Thomas Cavendish. A rowboat was sent to talk with three of the colonists. One man – Tomé Hernández – took up the offer of rescue, but the others were too suspicious of the British. Cavendish tells that the men planned to travel overland towards the River Plate.

But this is not the full story. After many further trials Hernández reached the Viceroy's Court at Lima, where he claimed that once he had boarded the ship the weather had improved dramatically, and Cavendish had determined to set sail for the Pacific, leaving the others to die. Only one of the remaining colonists survived, who was picked up by another British ship under Andrew Merrick. But this man perished along with most of the crew before they returned to Europe.

Cavendish wrote of the colonists that 'they died like dogs in their houses, and in their clothes wherein we found them at our coming'. He named the place Port Famine.

From Calafate, I crossed the Chilean border and caught a bus to Punta Arenas, on the Magellan Straits. My plan was now to walk to the *Beagle's* anchorage at Port Famine, and then cover Darwin's land routes on the Falkland Islands and Tierra del Fuego, as well as his maritime routes south to Cape Horn and north to the island of Chiloé through the Chonos archipelago.

I rested up for three days in Punta Arenas, trying to recover from Patagonia. As I left on the road to Port Famine (or Puerto Hambre, to give it its Chilean name), I passed a succession of disused ships, salvaged shipwrecks left to rust with the gulls on the shoreline. The rocks by the beach were green with algae. There was very little traffic along this road, only a few tour vans carrying tourists to the extremity of America. They were taken to Fuerte Bulnes (the first Chilean settlement on the Magellan Straits, founded in 1843), then for a brief cameo visit to Puerto Hambre, before returning to the city in time for lunch.

It was only fifty kilometres to the ruins of the Sarmiento colony, and

I enjoyed stretching my legs after the rest in Punta Arenas. Grey clouds hung low over the Straits like risen banks of fog, masking the cormorants as they skated over the sea. A few fishermen's shanties were built on the shore, lapped by layers of seaweed and the freezing waters where a person can only live for ten minutes before icing in their own grave. The road cut through forests of Magellanic beeches. Sometimes the clouds showed inclinations for parting, and I glimpsed the higher snows encircling the sea, above the thick whorls of forest which rose like opaque breath from the earth.

The journey seemed short, even though I walked all day through the sullen clouds. When I reached the junction for Puerto Hambre, I walked through an aisle between the forests. In this cathedral for the south they spread chlorophyll over the track even though the sky tried to shade the trees with darkness. I walked on until the track gave out into a grassy hollow decorated with two football goals and a semicircle of wooden chalets: Puerto Hambre is now a collection of holiday homes for the top brass from Punta Arenas.

As I walked on to the ruined fortifications of the chapel, to see the saddened lumps of rubble lying uselessly on a grassy headland set out to sea, the shouts and screams of the children playing football filled the cold air of the settlement. No one lived here permanently any more. The military sent a sergeant and a few cadets to keep the chalets in order, but they came and went every week. Now, you could hear the thump of the football, the shouts, the whirr of the generator from the military post. You could listen awkwardly as the caterwauling echoes of the present swallowed the famine and death of the past, swallowed the misery, and replaced it with the blank sheets of an endless football match.

I spent three days at Puerto Hambre. On the first day after arriving I climbed the hill behind the settlement, Mount Tarn, which Darwin struggled his way up through the forests. It is a great deal easier now, since logging companies have moved in and much of the hillside is scarred with emptiness. Then, in the afternoon, I walked to the graveyard of Captain Pringle Stokes, the man whose suicide preceded FitzRoy's appointment as captain of the *Beagle*. The grave was set on a rise fifty metres from the straits, cleared of the native forest and blinking its white cross against the bleakness of the day.

I looked down the channel. The straits opened out from here, and mist rose ponderously up to the sky. I could see for fifty kilometres further down the channel, almost to Cape Froward itself, the southernmost point of the American continent. The mountains were covered in dark welts of forest which dispersed into summits of snow. They fell in successive chains, and you could imagine them continuing on, and on, until they teetered over into the chasm that bridges present and future ends.

I walked on until the track gave way into the forest that stretched unbroken to Cape Froward. Later I heard of a German who had tried to go on through the forest. He had fallen and broken his leg, and his corpse had only been found three months later.

Back at Puerto Hambre I made friends with the sergeant and the cadets, and we chatted in the evening about Chile and England. They told me dirty jokes and Chilean swear-words. Chileans love to compare their swear-words with those from other languages, and it is quite possible to have conversations of an hour and more which sound like an inter-linguistic congress of obscenities.

'What's the strongest, strongest thing that you can say in English?' the sergeant asked me.

'C—t,' I said.

'Yes, but what's that in Chile?'

'*Chucha.*'

'*¡Chucha!*' he said in disappointment. 'Is that all? That's really soft here. The strongest thing you can say in Chile is *hijo de puta*. If someone insults my mother, I hit them.'

This man, who was lewd and unpleasant, made me go through long lists of our swear words, and their translations into Chilean slang. He couldn't believe what he was hearing.

'But it's incredible,' he said. 'How do you say *culiado*?'

'Fucker,' I said.

'So it's the same! That's unbelievable. Swear words are the same everywhere.'

The sergeant loved to dominate the conversation. He was round, and had evil little eyes. He talked about his wife, his affairs with prostitutes in Punta Arenas, and moaned sporadically about having spent fifteen years of his life on the Magellan Straits.

'It's all the fault of the bloody Argentines,' he said. 'When they invaded the Malvinas, we all got sent down here.'

'Why?'

'Because after they invaded there, they were going to move on Chile. Didn't you know? At all the borders down here, they put up a sign saying "First the English, then the Chileans". So Pinochet sent thousands of us down here, and we've been here ever since.'

He grinned at me.

'That's why I like you,' he said. 'You're English, and you English taught the Argentines a good lesson. Now they know they're not king of the roost any more.'

He offered me raw sea urchins for dinner, and made a tasteless joke about seafood and virility. Afterwards, I walked back to my tent. The clouds had been chased away, but now the waters in the Straits were perfectly calm. A waxing moon had risen; it drew from a quiver of golden arrows, and shot its lyrics over the darkness.

The *Beagle* passed through the Magellan Straits in June 1834. By now all were desperate to reach the clear skies of central Chile. They had already visited the Yámana tribe in southern Tierra del Fuego, and there was nothing to be gained by remaining much longer in the area. Much of the survey had been completed, and they had already been at sea for two and a half years.

They had paused briefly in the straits in February, before heading for the Falklands. Darwin recounted to his sister Catherine that 'we had a very interesting interview with the Patagonians, the giants of the older navigators ... They have so much intercourse with Sealers & Whalers, that they are semi-civilized. One of them who dined with us ate with his knife & fork as well as any gentleman.' Now, on this second visit, they witnessed the antithesis of the civilized Tehuelches, as they were greeted by Indians hurling stones at them (these were probably Alacalufe Indians). They did not stay long, and by July they were in Valparaíso and among the delights of Chile. They were all glad to be gone from this part of the world, of which Darwin wrote: 'In the Strait of Magellan, looking due southward from Port Famine, the distant channels between the mountains appeared from their gloominess to lead beyond the confines of this world.' It is difficult to think of any

European explorer who had anything even slightly complimentary to say about Puerto Hambre. All was hunger and hardship. Winter started at the end of February and wasn't over until the end of October. Winds of up to a hundred and fifty kilometres an hour were commonplace, and piled the snow into unshakeable drifts. It could snow in midsummer. The misery of the desperately short winter days in this outpost of the world, a month's journey or more from the nearest city, was despair enough for many. Men deserted their ships, plotted to kill their commanders, died of pestilence or pain. This was no place for them.

On 1 June 1834, as the *Beagle* made its way through the straits, they picked up two sailors who had deserted ship and had ended up living for months with the Patagonians. 'I dare say they were worthless vagabonds,' said Darwin, 'but I never saw more miserable looking ones.' Every European who by some misfortune ended up here deserved sympathy.

I left the scene of the unilateral massacres to walk back to Punta Arenas.

I walked for several hours, and was then hailed by a woman from a house above the road. She owned a small plot of land, and had come from Punta Arenas to plant rhubarb. She was intrigued by this stranger walking along the track, and invited me in for a coffee. She talked all afternoon, about her life and her country. She was an extraordinary woman, brushing aside Chilean mores with disdain, saying what she wanted to say and not caring what others thought of her. This was why she had achieved a great deal in life. She knew much Chilean history, and recounted it impartially, amusingly, because it was no good getting distraught over people's inevitable mistakes.

She had been brought up by her grandfather, a few kilometres from Fuerte Bulnes, growing up with the last of the Indians.

'There was one girl, she was my age. We used to play together. They still lived in their animal skins, and the women still went diving for oysters. In the same way as ever. This is forty years ago, I'm telling you. *Claro*, they all died soon after I was a girl. They all died of TB ... and everyone says what a disgrace, they killed the Indians. But think about it. What would the Indian be if she was alive today? A thief and a drunkard! Indians and alcohol are a disastrous mix. They were terrifying whenever they saw some alcohol. They killed each other, really killed each other...'

Her grandfather had been a fisherman. They'd never gone hungry, for there were always shellfish for them on the beach.

'Chileans are lazy,' she said. 'There's no need for us to work. It's only the women that keep this country going. We'd spend days doing nothing really, and whenever I told my grandfather that I was hungry, he'd just go and pick some mussels or sea urchins off the beach. We've got every climate in Chile. Here, if we're hungry we find seafood. In Santiago, they'll look for fruit. That's the mentality of Chileans. *Claro*. If someone sees my husband building a house for my children next to this one, they'll say: "*Puta huevón*, why are you building a house when you've already got one?" Or if we build a well because the source runs dry in December, they'll ask why we're building a well for one month of the year. This is why the Communists did so well here. When Allende* came in and said that everything belonged to the workers, the workers all rubbed their hands together in glee. They could eat the meat they've always wanted to, take the *patrón's* antique clock, and so on. But then one day, one of them gets up late for work, and everyone says: "*Puta*, if that man didn't get up, neither will I." They're all *patrones* now, you see. So they all stay in bed and the farm collapses. Then one day, they realize that there are no vegetables left, but "*Puta*, the *patrón* never said anything about planting vegetables", and so on; and so the whole thing collapses.'

She had held a position of importance in the Pinochet government.

'Of course,' she said, 'it was all the rich landowners who stirred up the trouble. And the CIA. They bribed the union leaders of the truckers to foment a strike, so the union leaders were fine but the poor truckers were starving. Everything stopped. You couldn't even buy bread. It was all fixed, of course, we weren't stupid. Until the coup you couldn't find anything to eat, and then within a few days the shops were all full – that was no accident. But still, we couldn't govern ourselves so someone had to do something. That's why the military intervened.'

---

* Salvador Allende, the Marxist president of Chile elected in 1970, who was overthrown by Pinochet's coup in 1973.

'What about all the people who died? All the *desaparecidos*?'

'No one cared about them. They still don't. What people care about is that the country was pulled away from disaster.'

'Were people killed?'

'Of course they were. But listen. If you went up to a soldier and said: "Listen, you *hijo de puta*, you fucking soldier, you're full of shit," – well, of course you got in trouble! The thing is, at least they weren't corrupt. They didn't steal from the people, and the people knew that. That's why Pinochet was always popular.'

Under the military government, she'd worked all over the country.

'Anyway,' she said, 'you English aren't innocent of a few killings when it suits you. You gave the Argentines a good beating in the Malvinas War!'

Most Chileans feel a virulent antipathy towards their Trans-Andean neighbours, and the Falklands War guaranteed me a friendly reception everywhere.

'I know,' I said. 'But I was only eight then.'

'Ha!' she laughed. 'Well, I can tell you that you certainly weren't innocent little babies in any of that.'

And then this is what she told me.

In 1982, she had been working very near the Argentine border with Chile. One day, about five weeks before the Argentine invasion, the place where she worked had been radioed from Punta Arenas and told that two men were coming to do some tests. This woman, among the hierarchy at her workplace, was in the welcoming party. They were all immediately suspicious, since the men were clearly *gringos* – 'American, British, I don't know' – and very much on edge. A Chilean commando had come too, and he told the officials that the men were going to do a little 'birdwatching'.

Then the officers saw that there was an extensive array of electronic equipment, including radio antennae and satellite dishes under a tarpaulin in the back of the truck.

They demanded to know what was going on, and the commando told them.

'He told us that he didn't know exactly what was going on, but that he'd heard that the Argentines were going to invade the Malvinas.'

'What did you say?'

'I told him: "They're idiots." How did they think that they were going to beat a country like England?'

The commando told her that the men had come to spy on the Argentine movements, hence the electronic equipment. Five weeks later the Argentines invaded, to widespread international disapprobation. To listen to the emergency parliamentary debate in London the next day, you would have thought that the possibility of an invasion had only really surfaced since the incident on South Georgia on 18 March 1982, two weeks before. But, as Defence Secretary John Nott protested: 'No other country in the world could react so fast, and the preparations have been in progress for several weeks.'¹ In fact, by tremendous good fortune for the war effort, two British warships, the *Invincible* and the *Hermes*, happened to be in Portsmouth undergoing maintenance tests, so they were able to sail for the South Atlantic at three days' notice, much more quickly than might normally have been expected.

The woman gave me a lift back to Punta Arenas, and I left for the Falkland Islands the next day.

We arrived here in the Falkland Islands in the beginning of this month.
We found to our great surprise the English flag hoisted. – I suppose the
occupation of this place, has only just been noticed in the English
papers; but we hear all the southern part of America is in ferment
about it. By the awful language of Buenos Aires one would suppose
this great republic meant to declare war against England.

Charles Darwin in a letter to his sister Caroline, 30 March 1833

The *Beagle* made two visits to the Falkland Islands, each time harbour-
ing in Berkeley Sound off East Falkland, near Port Louis. On their
arrival in March 1833, they came as representatives of British authority
in the islands. The British ship HMS *Clio* had arrived on 3 January,
finding fifty Argentines there, most of them mutinous convicts. Captain
Onslow raised the British flag on the shore, delivered the Argentine
flag wrapped in a bundle to Captain Pinedo, and told him to leave.

There was no constituted authority as such on the island, but a
British flag had been left in the charge of Dickson, an Irishman, who
presided over a motley crew of settlers and *gauchos*. All aboard the
Beagle felt that the situation was highly unsatisfactory. On their return
a year later, they discovered that a group of *gauchos* and Indians had
rebelled and murdered Dickson and three others. A Lieutenant Smith
was now acting as Governor, trying to protect the thirteen settlers –
who had meantime escaped to Hog Island on Berkeley Sound – from
the eight men accused of the mutiny. 'When we arrived,' Darwin wrote,
'we found him in charge of a population, of which rather more than
half were runaway rebels and murderers.'

Darwin was disgusted at the gory struggle for this 'undulating land,
with a desolate and wretched aspect ... every where covered by a peaty
soil and wiry grass, of one monotonous brown colour'. He wrote to his
sister Caroline: 'All the economy at home makes the foreign movements of England most contemptible. How different from old Spain.

Here we, dog-in-the-manger fashion, seize an island and leave to protect
it a Union Jack; the possessor has been of course murdered ... we shall
leave this scene of iniquity in two or three days.'

Nothing but misery greeted their time in the islands. Preceding the
bloodiness which coincided with their second visit, during their first
stay the ship's clerk Mr Hellyer drowned amid the thick kelp in the
Sound, whilst trying to salvage a duck which he had shot. 'Mr. Hellyer
was buried on a lonely & dreary headland,' Darwin noted. During this
stay he spent some time on the beach at Port Louis looking for shells,
and wandering around the shores of the inlet on both sides. The
desolation was unbroken, and the whole crew was relieved to leave
on 6 April.

'This is one of the quietest places we have ever been to,' Darwin
noted on 17 March. 'Nearly all the ships are gone: & no one event has
happened in the whole week.'

I flew to the islands in a daze since with me on the plane were fifty or
more crew members of a seismic survey ship, all of whom were British.
I had only met three other British people – or even native English
speakers – in the past five and a half months (other than Emily). My
fellow passengers were all talking in *English*, and as the plane cut
through the scarlet clouds of sunset above East Falkland, and the light
poured like claret over the chequered lakes and fjords of the islands, I
realized that I was about to go into reverse culture shock. I had almost
forgotten what it was like to be British. I listened to them gossiping
away about football and the forthcoming general elections, and found
that my English mouth had frozen. When I reached Port Stanley and
found that I had to speak in English, my sentences kept developing
Spanish quirks. I finished every phrase with a quizzical and very Spanish
'*no?*', and then resolved to keep myself quietly to myself if I could.

I walked around the place, incredulous. There were real pubs, serving
bitter and stout, and one of the first things I insisted on doing was to
have my one and only Guinness of the year. There was fish 'n' chips, and
the tell-tale smells of fry-ups lurking everywhere. There was everything
that a British person longs for when they are far away from home,
dangling tantalizingly before me like forgotten desires. Stanley was
characterized by vegetable patches kept tidily and unobtrusively behind

neat little fences, sheep grazing on the golf course, petrels wafting away from the line of shipwrecks in the harbour, people rushing hurriedly along the drab pavements, heads bent and sheltering faces blankly from the winds, and the Co-op, selling Chilean *dulce de leche*, the prices marked in Falkland Islands pounds and pence.

My landlady was Kay, a jocular grandmother and chain-smoker. She had been born on West Falkland, and had lived in the archipelago all her life. She spoke quietly, and then would rattle off into a spurt of laughter when she told a joke. Another of her guests was Søren, a German backpacker who had arrived on the same flight as me. The next day we were to go to Port Louis. I wanted to walk across the isthmus to Darwin, named after the point which he reached on his journey across the island, while Søren wanted to visit one of the only king penguin colonies outside Antarctica, at Volunteer Point, two days' walk beyond Port Louis.

In the evening, Kay spoke of the war.

'It must have been terrible,' said an English doctor who was also staying, 'when they just moved in.'

'You had to feel sorry for them,' Kay mused. 'Most of them were kids really, they didn't know anything about it. They were starving. My father used to work at the Municipal Rubbish Tip, but he had to stop because of the numbers of conscripts that came hunting for food there. We used to see the officers eating meat and chocolates while the poor lads starved.'

She had spent most of the war at the ranch of a friend of hers, to the west of Stanley.

'Twice, conscripts fled to the farm. First time, we came back to the house to find this big Indian fella, just sitting behind the house. We were petrified, but then we saw that he was too downtrodden to do anything. Poor guy,' she said. 'He was from the tropics. He'd just been walking along a road one day when a truck came along, picked him up, and threw him in the back. He didn't even know where he was. He'd seen our house and fled from their positions because he'd had enough. We told him that he'd better return or he'd probably be shot as a deserter. So he went back.'

Her face was drawn as she spoke.

'I mean,' she said. 'You'd have thought that if they really wanted the islands they'd have told the soldiers where they were going. And you wouldn't have sent them in our winter, not when they were from the tropics.'

I only spent one full day in Stanley, because I had to walk across the island in a week. It was a quiet, somnolent sort of place, where you could not imagine much happening, ever – not invasions by Argentina, and certainly not battles in the street. The atmosphere was full of a sense of Britishness which I found extraordinary considering that Britain was not far short of 15,000 kilometres away. I had been so long in South America that the hush and reserve was only comprehensible to me when I heard a murmured comment in one of Stanley's pubs:

'Of course,' said a middle-aged woman. 'We're all on pills after the war. All our nerves were shot to pieces.'

Darwin's mood was similarly bleak during his stay on East Falkland. Following the nondescript stay at Berkeley Sound and Mr Hellyer's death, things did not improve when Darwin rode across the island. He set off on 16 March 1834 with two *gauchos*, the only two Spaniards who were not directly concerned with the murders. After passing the tremendous stone run just south of Port Louis (which today is called Prince's Street), he breached the range of hills which runs across the island – at either Smoko Rocks or the Cliffs – before camping near Mount Pleasant, and arriving the next day at the narrow isthmus which is now the site of Goose Green sheep station.

The weather was appalling. On the night of the 16th a barrage of snow and hail assailed them. On the 18th 'it rained nearly the whole day, so that at night it began to be very miserable work'. The *gauchos* made fires from the bones of a bullock if they found them, or with bushes if they didn't. They kept as warm as they could with their saddles, but, wrote Darwin, 'the ground on which we slept every night [was] more or less a bog'. On the 19th, unspeakably miserable because of the weather, Darwin and the men were desperate to reach Port Louis: 'I was determined to make a push & try to reach the ship before dark, which I succeeded in doing. From the very great quantity of rain this boggy country was in a very bad state. I suppose my horse fell at least a dozen times & sometimes the whole six were floundering in the mud together ... Even the *gauchos* were not sorry to reach the houses.' What was more, to add to the misery of the conditions, it was not as if the journey was fruitful for his collections. Other than horses and rabbits, the only quadruped was a large wolf-like fox, which was commonplace. However, Darwin intuited with now characteristic misery: 'Their numbers have decreased rapidly ... Within a few years after these islands shall have become regularly settled, in all probability this fox will be classed with the dodo, as an animal that has perished from the face of the earth.'

The last Falklands Fox was killed in 1876.

I made my way to Port Louis with Søren, and we introduced ourselves to the farm manager. Søren told him that he was planning to continue on to Volunteer Point:

'Oh, you can't do that. The land's closed.'

'Closed?'

'Yep. George [the farmer] has stopped everyone going there until the government builds him a road.'

'How can he do that?'

'Oh, it's his land all right.'

Søren looked evilly at him. There was another wildlife sanctuary at Seal Bay, eight hours' walk north.

'What about Seal Bay?'

'Oh no,' said the man. 'We don't allow anybody to go there any more. You can only go with one travel agency in Stanley.'

He got on with his work.

'*Unbelievable,*' fumed Søren. 'I *can't* believe it. What kind of place shuts its two major tourist attractions and doesn't tell you until you get there?'

It was, I had to agree, a long way to come in order to make this discovery. If I hadn't been there I worry to think what Søren might have done, but as it was he fell in with my ridiculous journey after Darwin and accompanied me across the island.

We followed Darwin round towards Johnson's Harbour for an hour and a half. We didn't go any further, since this was George's territory. Berkeley Sound was incredibly calm. Low clouds beat against banks of grass and heather, above a rocky beach which was black with mussels and strewn with green tangles of kelp, the only forest on the islands. There were some small oystercatchers picking daintily over the shore-

line like fastidious Victorians still stuck in the 1830s. A few bald sheep
ran wildly away from us, bashful in their nakedness, but their bleats
struggled hopelessly to quell the peace. It was so quiet that even the
disturbance of a flurry of upland and russet geese hovering over the far
side of the Sound carried clearly across to us, echoing with startled
discordance.

When we returned to the farm it was evening, and bitterly cold. This
was the very end of summer, and the breeze was icy, while the daylight
faded like stars into dawn. We shivered our way up to the house to ask
the manager a little about Port Louis. The settlement had been the first
capital of the islands, and their house had been the government house.
One of the walls was clad in a great frontage of ivy, patrolled by a
massive ginger cat. The man pointed out the lines of the fortifications
made by the French and Spanish, now just mounds of earth peering
from the hillside like an overgrown grave. We were frozen, and inside
I could see people drinking and eating. This man had a knife tucked
into his belt like a *gaucho* – but he was not a *gaucho*, and he did not
want to do much talking.

'*Unbelievable*,' said Søren, as we walked away. 'I mean it's pretty
strange already that he didn't ask us in. It's not as if he can ever do
much talking most of the time.'

He went to shiver in his tent, and I walked around the bay, below
the former battlements. A farmhand came out of a barn, and I said
hello. We talked quietly about farm work for some time, and he hid his
sawdust-coloured face from my gaze.

'Going for a wander are you?' he asked.

'Yes.'

'You'll find it plenty boggy that way, towards Goose Green,' he said.
'Mind you, they do say as they've built some roads recently.'

The roads had been there for ten years and more, but I wondered if
he had seen them.

Søren and I took three days to walk to Darwin. We were an incon-
gruous pair. I walked faster than he did, and became annoyed at his
constant need for breaks. He loathed the flatness and uniformity and
found walking here incredibly boring, but after Patagonia I was used to
it and quite liked it. Or at least I might have quite liked it if it hadn't
been for Søren.

'This is no fun,' he'd moan, as we squelched our way though a bog. When we came to a brook he took twenty minutes looking for a place where he could bridge it without doing what I had done; taking off his shoes and wading through.

'This is no fun,' he complained, when he reached the other side and his feet almost began to shiver.

It *was* pretty miserable going. There were no trees, no breaks to the grasslands except rocks and heather. There were wild red berries – diddly-dee berries – but they were unpalatably bitter; there was also a sweeter sort of berry – the teaberry – which hid in banks of moss and tasted a little like blueberries. Whenever we came across the teaberries, we feasted on them and wished that they were as common as the ubiquitous diddly-dees. The land was divided into three types: tussocks, which grew unevenly so that your feet constantly slid up and down and banged into them, shredding your boots and feet as if they were bare rocks; bogs, disguised cunningly as beautiful beds of red and purple moss – so much so that the first time I marched happily onto the 'moss' I found myself with freezing water up to my chest; and stone runs such as Prince's Street, chutes of erosion-fed boulders often over a kilometre wide, littered with holes and crevasses where you could easily fall and break a leg. After we had crossed over the most precarious of these we passed down to Colorado Lake, above Mount Pleasant, and saw that a storm was brewing over the Wickham Heights. Winds blew black banks of cloud in our direction, and they looked certain to engulf us in a Darwinian downpour.

'This is no fun at all,' Søren decided. He flung his rucksack next to a brook, and so we camped there.

The next day was eased by meeting Mel, a warm and loquacious farmer who invited us in for a cup of tea as we walked towards Darwin. He showed me all his saddle equipment, and I saw that he used the same type of saddle as the Argentines.

'Oh yes,' he said. 'We even use the same terms for the saddlery.'

In fact, as I walked on, I realized that there was really very little to differentiate the lifestyles of the Falklands from those of Patagonia. The farmers still use horses to round up the flocks, although the wealthier landowners use motorbikes; the land is almost exclusively used for sheep farming; and the towns (or town, in the case of the

Falklands) are essentially administrative. Buenos Aires might have very little in common with the Falklands, but the islands are like a cousin to southern Argentina.

As we walked down the new road between Mount Pleasant and Darwin, I left Søren some way behind me. I looked over my shoulder to see if there was any point in waiting, but he looked so thoroughly miserable about the whole thing (we were heading straight into a gale at the time) that I left him to it. The next thing I knew, he was waving and grinning cheerfully from a jeep which had picked him up. I had meant to walk all the way there, but now here was my smiling friend waiting for me and the sure accusation of insanity if I walked on. So I cheated the last fifteen kilometres.

When we reached Darwin we went and introduced ourselves to the farm manager.

'Hello,' I said. 'I think Kay rang from Stanley about me. I'm doing Darwin's route.'

'Ha!' he said. 'You weren't doing much walking last time I saw you.'

'No, I cheated the last bit.'

This mollified him a little (at least I wasn't a *lying* vagabond), so he said we could camp in a neighbouring valley.

'Where Darwin was,' he said. 'You can take the water from the wells. Or if they're no good, there's plenty of water by this windmill.'

So we pitched our tents in the valley, and had a look at the wells. The first was dry, and the second was covered in a green film of algae that looked several centimetres thick. Then I went and looked around the windmill, but all I could find was a concrete tank covered by a rusting piece of corrugated iron, beneath which was another green layer of vibrant organic life.

Thinking that there must have been some switch for a water supply, I went over and disturbed the man from watering his garden.

'Excuse me,' I said. 'Where did you want me to get the water from?'

'The windmill!' he said, as if talking to a child. 'If you go in there, and look in the concrete tank, ye'll find enough water to drown in.'

Later, I watched him driving away from his farm. When he saw a line of upland geese on a hillside near the road, he stopped the car, pulled out his rifle, and shot them one by one with amazing calmness. The geese just sat there and waited to die. Not one of them flew away.

Either they were terrified or just ignorant of their danger. It was a sickening sight to see them perish in a swirling flutter of feathers.

'I can't believe all those people died so that that man could kill geese,' I said to Søren.

'And deny us water,' said Søren.

Søren went to walk towards Goose Green on his own, while I decided to cut over the moors towards the site of the Goose Green battlefield. It was only a short distance from our campsite. The field was empty, bounded by gorse, rustled by the wind like autumn leaves. On each side of the isthmus pearly sea water shone in the late afternoon, polishing the dreary scene. As I walked, I remembered that this was an area of minefields. Although these are all fenced off on the Falklands, there are some stray mines which are periodically discovered. Just as this thought was leaving me, I came across a rusting coil adjacent to a piece of sinister-looking plastic. 'I'd better be careful there aren't any mines,' I thought to myself. And the next thing I knew I came across a small black square of plastic protruding cautiously above the grass, in the middle of which was what looked like a button.

My feet possessed their own survival instincts, and carried me swiftly backwards away from the battlefield. I had been to the army's display of mines in Stanley, and this piece of battle residue was similar enough to terrify me.

I went down to the farm manager, since I thought he might like to know that there was an unmarked mine on his land.

'I've just come across a mine,' I told him.

'Never!'

I described what I'd seen.

'Let's go and have a look,' he said.

We drove off up to the field in his jeep, and when he discovered that I hadn't marked the spot he grumbled.

'Bloody stupid,' he said – which was true, but then I wasn't used to stumbling across landmines on an afternoon walk.

We drove around the field for five minutes, and he became thoroughly impatient. I looked desperately on all sides, but all I saw was grass. Everything looked the same. He was clearly seething at the idiocy of this bloody visitor, and I was soon more worried by him than by the mine. Eventually, I came upon a twisted piece of metal, which looked vaguely as though it might once have been in a battle.

'Oh,' he said. 'Is that it?'

'Yes,' I lied.

'That's just a bloody cluster bomb,' he scorned, and we drove back to the farm.

I should have carried on the search, but the evening was hurrying on, and his irascible impatience was getting to me. And anyway, the Battle for Goose Green was not worth continuing.

It is probable that Darwin rode from here towards Bodie Creek, five kilometres south of Goose Green, before turning back. Søren decided to visit a colony of Gentoo penguins the next day, while I followed Darwin to Goose Green and beyond.

Goose Green was a tidy settlement, still shaded by lingering memories of war. There was a minefield next to the golf course, and a long shed with 'POW' marked in straggling white paint, now fading like memories in the sunlight. But the village green was neatly mown, and several whitewashed houses were congregated around the jetty. I wanted to buy some food, but all I found was a shuttered-up kiosk with a No Smoking sign.

I knocked on doors around the settlement in an attempt to discover when the shop would open.

'Come in,' said the first person I found. 'Have a tomato sandwich.'

The tomatoes had been picked that morning from the greenhouse. I had breakfast with John and Lizzie, who had both lived all their lives in the Falkland camps.

'It's falling to pieces,' Lizzie said. 'The farm I was brought up on, there used to be about thirty people there. Now there are seven.'

'The whole of Lafonia,' said John, 'there's only that Walker Creek farm, and North Arm. Twenty-seven people.'

'Used to be lots of houses in the camp,' she said, 'but now they're ruined.'

'Have another tomato sandwich.'

I walked on to Bodie Creek, and crossed the bridge. This is the most southerly suspension bridge in the world, but it had rusted beyond repair and John was going to close it for good that afternoon, welding iron bars across each end of this era. I crossed over the bridge, onto the immense peninsula of Lafonia, the southern tip of East Falkland: a hundred kilometres long and forty wide, inhabited by twenty-seven people. I walked on for two hours, and saw only sheep and geese. I passed two ponds, a beer bottle tossed into the grass, and the skeleton of a horse bleaching like the grass in the wind and sun. The horse's innards had dried into a thin hide over the ribs. A diddly-dee bush was growing on the hide, life's laugh at death lost in the absent vastness – lost almost as I might have been. From the skeleton, I could see no house, no track and no animals at all. Beyond the rising ground on the horizon, where the grass kissed the sky, the mountains of West Falkland rose remote and half-concealed by the turbulent clouds eddying in between. Beyond the mountains, magnificent and foreboding, the sky curved and fell into the unknown.

Back at the bridge I met John. He was going back for lunch, and gave me a lift to Goose Green.

'The sun's strong today,' I remarked, since most people in the south had interesting views on the weather.

'Always is these days.'

'Do you get burnt?'

'Do I get burnt? 'Course I bloody do. Terrible with this damn ozone hole.'

'You notice that?'

'Oh yes! Haven't got a bloody clue what the weather's going to do. It'll be terrible hot one month, and you burn like a bleeding tomato, and then it'll rain for a month and ruin the vegetable garden. The grass is like kindling now.'

'It's drier now?'

'Oh yes. It ain't wet here, the earth, not like what it used to be. That place which you walked over, on the way from Port Louis – time was when you'd have had a job getting over here at all, that was how boggy it was. Terrible! Now it's hard as a road.'

We drove on. Everywhere was grassland and sheep. It was just as I imagined the Orkneys or Shetlands, except that it was faraway from home.

'See that,' he said, as we drove over a scrap of cloth buried in the dust. 'Argentine sleeping bag, that is. Poor buggers.'

'Were you in Goose Green in the war?'

'We were in the bloody village hall, with the rest of them. But they were good lads. No one got raped, no one got hit. The number of men there were, we could have watched our wives being raped sixty or seventy times a day. A hundred and nine people in the village hall there were, and nothing happened to them. The only civilians that got killed were killed by the British.'

He was silent for a while.

'After the British won the battle, there were some that wanted to kill the poor lads. But I said, "Listen, they treated us well, so now you've got to treat them well." Poor lads, they were only seventeen or eighteen. They didn't know what they were doing.'

We drove up to Goose Green, and John went inside. I chatted for a while with Lizzie, over the fence. She was watering the flowers.

'You been to Argentina?' she asked.

'Yes.'

'Did you like it?'

'Yes.'

'So did we,' she said. 'We went there in '78, before all this nonsense. Good people.'

'So generous,' I said.

'Yes. It's ridiculous, isn't it? I mean they're 300 miles away, and we're not talking to them. After the Berlin Wall came down, we both said, "Right, that's it, everyone's got to be friends with everyone else." How long do people think it's going to go on for? It's so needless.'

She was vehement about it.

'The island council just say "No" to everything. They *assume* that we don't want anything to do with them. And those relatives, they just want to come to see the graves of their children. Who can blame them? There should never have been a war in the first place. It was our government's fault for not paying enough attention, really.'

I thought of the woman I had met near Punta Arenas.

'Sometimes I take my granddaughter to the Argentine cemetery. It's so beautiful in the evening there, with the sunset. So peaceful. Once, she looked up at the graves and said "Granny, why do people have to do such terrible things to each other?" '

When I read some of the accounts from the Argentine conscripts, I could not help but be angry at the history of blood which came back to

Walking
towards
Puerto Madryn,
Patagonia

A windswept
Navarin Island

The *gaucho* prepares
dinner during the
storm, near Risso,
Uruguay

The last *gaucho*,
Río Santa Cruz

Children, near
Cañete, Chile

Mapuche family,
near Hueñelihuén,
Chile

Guests of the Carabineros (author with Martillo)

Apple

Above left
Chimango,
near Mercedes,
Uruguay

Centre left
Carta Brava,
Cartera and the
Pampas

Below left
Chileno and Ruso,
near Cardona,
Uruguay

The coast near
Curanipe, Chile

Looking north
– near Puerto
Saavedra, Chile

Giant tortoise at the Darwin Research Station, Isla Santa Cruz

Galápagos sea lions, Isla Santa Fé

Blue-footed boobies, Isla
Española, Galápagos

Top Portrait of Charles Darwin, 1849
Above The author near Wollaston Island
Right Darwin plinth, Villa Darwin, Uruguay
Below HMS *Beagle* in the Straits of Magellan

drip over the fields 150 years after Darwin visited the islands in the aftermath of the British takeover. The conscripts starved while their officers ate *asados* and drank wine. There are many stories of officers stealing their conscripts' rations, of conscripts having nothing to eat or drink but *mate* which had been reused for three days, being equipped with useless waterproofs, having to sleep in puddles during the icy Falklands winter. Then, after their capitulation and surrender to the English, the soldiers discovered about forty barns stuffed full of all the food and equipment which they had needed so desperately during the preceding three months. Some of the barns were so full of food that the conscripts could not even get inside. The brutal futility of the whole gruesomely stage-managed episode is difficult to comprehend.

From Darwin, Søren and I made our way back to Mount Pleasant. Our flight back to Punta Arenas was leaving the next day, and we had been given permission to stay at the military base next to the airfield. The 2300-odd inhabitants of the islands are now protected by rather more than 3000 members of the armed forces, in one of the last strongholds of the British empire. Since much of Britain's wealth was founded on its colonies, it seemed sweetly ironic that one of the few overseas dependencies the country has left now costs a fortune to keep hold of. When we got to the base, it was almost more of a shock than Stanley had been. I had never been to the NAAFI, or drunk with the Gurkhas at the services' bar, or read warnings about trying to pass off as Falkland Islands currency coins minted for Ascension Island, St Helena and Tristan da Cunha. I had never even imagined that the mint might make currency specifically for use only on three of the most isolated and thinly inhabited places on earth.

None of these things could have existed apart from my home country, but they were some of the oddest and most alien aspects of Britain that I could have come across anywhere in the world. I might have expected to feel homesick while on these islands, homesick as I had been on the only other occasion during which I had been away from Britain for such an extended period of time. But those few reminders of Britain which I came across on the Falklands were so unusual that they barely reminded me of home at all. I was so far from Britain that leaving the Falklands, and returning to South America, seemed far more natural to me than the obliquely British life on these distant islands.

III

I shall never forget how savage & wild one group was. – Four or five men suddenly appeared on a cliff next to us, – they were absolutely naked & with long streaming hair; springing from the ground & waving their arms around their heads, they sent forth the most hideous yells. Their appearance was so strange, that it was scarcely like that of earthly inhabitants.

Charles Darwin on the Yámana Indians

The *Beagle* visited Tierra del Fuego in 1832 with the purpose of founding an evangelical mission among the wild Yámana tribe of Tierra del Fuego. Ever since leaving Plymouth, the crew had been accompanied by three Yámana who had been captured during the *Beagle*'s previous visit to Tierra del Fuego, and had been living in London learning the rudiments of English, Victorian manners and Christianity. They had even been introduced to King William and Queen Adelaide. Now they were returning home with Richard Matthews, an eager young missionary. Their names were Yokcushlu, Orundellico and El 'Leparu; but the English knew them as York Minster, Jemmy Button and Fuegia Basket.

In 1829, soon after assuming the *Beagle*'s captaincy, FitzRoy lost a whale-boat, stolen by the Yámana. In revenge, he kept four Indians captive, hoping that the boat would be returned to him. But when nothing happened, he determined to take them to England so that Christianity could percolate even to this extremity of the earth. The sojourn of the Yámana was extraordinary for everyone. They were first taken to lodgings in Plymouth, but one of them – 'Boat Memory', so called because he was the most intelligent of the four – contracted smallpox and died. The others went to London, where they moved to Walthamstow and began their education. FitzRoy met them off their coach at London, and wrote in his journal of the voyage that 'They were glad to see me, but seemed bewildered by the multitude of objects. Passing Charing Cross, there was a start and exclamation of astonishment from York. "Look!" he said, fixing his eyes on the lion upon Northumberland House which he certainly thought was alive, and walking there.'

Darwin described the three in detail.

York: 'a full-grown, short, thick, powerful man: his disposition was reserved, taciturn, morose, and when excited violently passionate; his affections were very strong towards a few friends on board; his intellect good.'

Jemmy: '[was] merry and often laughed, and ... remarkably sympathetic to any one in pain ... He was of a patriotic disposition ... short, thick, and fat, but vain of his personal appearance; he always used to wear gloves, his hair was neatly cut, and he was distressed if his well-polished shoes were dirtied.'

Fuegia: 'a nice, modest, reserved young girl ... very quick in learning anything, especially languages ... York Minster was very jealous of any attention paid to her; for it was clear he determined to marry her as soon as they were settled on shore.'

The *Beagle* returned with them to Tierra del Fuego on 17 December 1832. On 21 December, they rounded Cape Horn, and anchored for Christmas off Hermit Island, not far from the Cape. FitzRoy's plan was to sail up the south side of Hoste Island and leave York Minster at his home on Christmas Island. However, the weather proved so appalling that they spent twenty-four days advancing just twenty miles [thirty-two kilometres] in this direction, and Darwin recounts seeing spray from the sea clearing the top of a cliff that was 200 feet [sixty metres] high. York then announced that he and Fuegia were prepared to be landed at Jemmy's home in Woollya, and so the *Beagle* changed tack and made for the south-western coast of Navarin Island.

They harboured at Goree Roads on Lennox Island, and approached Woollya in three whale-boats along the eastern arm of the Beagle Channel, sleeping in a succession of inlets on the northern side of Navarin Island before turning into the Murray Narrows and reuniting Jemmy with his family. Darwin was underwhelmed by the spectacle of Jemmy's greeting with his brother: 'The meeting was less interesting than that between a horse, turned out into a field, when he joins an old companion. There was no demonstration of affection; they simply stared for a short time at each other; and the mother immediately went to look after her canoe.'

The *Beagle* crew estimated that there were about 120 people living at Woollya. While Matthews worked at establishing a hut for the mission, Darwin observed the Yámana. 'The women worked hard,' he wrote, 'while the men lounged about all day long, watching us. They asked for everything they saw, and stole what they could.'

For three days, as Matthews' camp was established, relations with the Yámana seemed amicable. But then, following a dispute with an elderly man which culminated in his miming the cutting up and skinning of a human body, the tribe vanished from Woollya. Nevertheless, the *Beagle* crew decided to leave Matthews to set himself up. A party left to reconnoitre the western arm of the Beagle Channel, which they covered for over 200 kilometres to Stewart Island. On returning to Woollya, they found chaos. Having left Matthews with a zealot's enthusiasm for his evangelical mission, they returned to a cowering wreck. The Yámana had consistently stolen from his hut, flooding in as soon as the *Beagle* had left and threatening his life. At the very moment that the ship had returned they had been yanking out the hairs of his beard using mussel shells as tweezers. Matthews fled on board and refused to return ashore.

Jemmy was disparaging and apologetic about his compatriots. Darwin recounts that Jemmy's own brother 'had stolen many things from him, and as he remarked, "what fashion call that": he abused his countrymen, "all bad men, no sabe [know] nothing" '. Jemmy was far and away the most popular of the Yámana among the *Beagle* crew, and they appear to have been genuinely sorry to have had to leave him. But leave him they did, returning to the River Plate to complete the survey of the Atlantic coast.

Returning in February 1834, they met Jemmy again in the area around Woollya. He canoed over to the ship from Button Island, but initially he was so far changed that no one recognized him. Darwin wrote: 'It was quite painful to behold him. Thin, pale, & without a remnant of clothes, excepting a bit of blanket around his waist: his hair, hanging over his shoulders; & so ashamed of himself, he turned his back to the ship as the canoe approached.' Jemmy dined aboard ship, but he had no

wish to return to England, partly since he had recently settled down
with a wife. Jemmy had taught the woman some English, and seemed
quite happy to remain in his land at the uttermost part of the earth.
When the *Beagle* left in the morning, they saw a huge spiral of smoke
on the beach where Jemmy had landed after taking his leave: they took
it as a sign of farewell. Although all his possessions had been stolen by
York in what Darwin described as an 'act of consummate villainy',
Jemmy seemed content.

Jemmy had fallen into an adventure as tumultuous as any. Now he
had chosen wildness, as opposed to the constrictions of civilization.
Perhaps he agreed with Hudson that the latter was '[a life] of continual
repression, although it may not seem so until a glimpse of nature's
wildness, a taste of adventure, an accident suddenly makes it seem
unspeakably irksome; and in that state we feel our loss in departing
from nature exceeds our gain'.[2]

After travelling for six months, I had become putrid and insect-ridden.
I had lost all interest in my personal appearance, and sleeping regularly
in barns and on sheepskins did not help matters. I had stopped shaving
months before, and my face was covered in sticky hair which grew
unevenly and looked like patchy and badly tended clumps of straggly
moss. My clothes smelt as if I had accidentally thrown them into a
skip, and had only just salvaged them by rooting through stacks of
rotting vegetables. I smelt as if I did this sort of thing every day. Even
my shoes were falling apart, try as I did to stick them together with
superglue.

Increasingly, people asked me why I was doing this. They pitied me.
Not infrequently, they took one look at my revolting appearance and
proffered me a shirt or some trousers.

'It fits you perfectly,' they'd insist – 'You really need it,' agreed their
noses. *Why*, they said, *why* are you doing this?

I needed distance. Often it is only when you step outside something
that you see it most clearly. Bound up in the machine of my life, in its
inalienable expressions and ways of seeing things, I couldn't look at it
impartially; couldn't see the wood for the trees, nor even see how few
trees were left. It was the same with travelling. By the time I finished
my journey, it had become second nature to undergo fear and trauma

and loneliness and love and happiness and joy at the ineffable beauty of the world, day after day. I needed distance and the perspective of the old routine to understand anything of what I had seen. But while I was travelling, the old language of logic and analysis vanished into the endless vistas of the Pampas and Patagonia, buried beneath the multi-coloured ocean dissolving into sunsets.

The journey had a rationale and internal propulsion all its own. When I returned from the Falklands to Punta Arenas, I went and called on the Chilean navy, and managed to get a passage on the only naval ship visiting Cape Horn for the next three months – the ship happened to be leaving the next day. I would be taken through both arms of the Beagle Channel, to Cape Horn, as well as to many of the islands in the archipelago: Navarin, Wollaston, Picton, Lennox and Nueva. I was going to follow the *Beagle* through the channels. The small supply ship left Punta Arenas late at night, sailing south towards the Pacific Ocean, crowded with marines and their families. Although it was bitterly cold outside, I stood and listened to the spray frothing like a geyser as the ship's prow sent it cascading into the clear cloth of the water. Above the sea, the mountains rose into the unwavering whiteness of permanent snow, and the summits blinked bleakly in their purity, like distant lighthouses, as the land was enveloped by the night.

After four hours' sailing we stopped at Puerto Harris on Dawson Island, and unloaded many of our passengers into the drizzle tumbling through the illumination of the settlement's dim streetlights. After sailing through the rest of the night, in the morning we headed out into the Cockburn Channel. This was the open sea, with the Pacific yawning out in self-controlled turbulence towards the west. I ate a roll, drank a cup of milky coffee and went out on deck.

The seas were rough. The waves were three or four metres high, and regularly sloshed over the sides of the deck. The ship shuddered through the waves, breaking blankets of spray over the containers and the few fools out on deck. We lurched from side to side like a drunk toying with the imprudent dream of falling over and leaving himself in the arms of God. Out on deck before the ocean, I awoke from the sleep of calmness, and tossed along with the fulminating waves. Thoughts emerged tumultuously along with this experience, in which the tearful world could pour out its anxieties and emerge becalmed in the divisive channels of thoughtlessness and cosseted security beyond the storm.

With the mood as it was I could not stay long on deck, and swayed inside through the door which slammed open and shut with each motion of the sea. I found that most of the passengers were being violently sick, and when I reached the kitchen I began talking with an old sailor who was chuckling at them all.

'I've been a landlubber for six years,' he said. 'I'm getting used to the sea again.'

He looked scornfully at the regular procession of people running to the toilets.

'These seas aren't rough. You should see what it's like down around Cape Horn.'

'I'm going there soon,' I said.

'It's twice as bad! I once saw a swell twenty metres high. You'll struggle like these people when you go there.'

'They're not enjoying it, are they?'

We were having to grip hard onto the units in the kitchen to avoid running up and down with the swaying ship. We spoke some more about the seasickness.

'It's at times like this,' he said, 'that we realize how small man is.'

'Mm,' I said, slowly noticing a growing heaving motion in my gut.

'What can man do against the power of God?' the man asked rhetorically, emotion ringing through his voice.

'Mm,' I said, attempting to shrug my shoulders and constrict my chest simultaneously.

'We are nothing,' he mused.

'Mm,' I said, and went to retch with the rest of the ship.

As soon as we passed beyond the ocean into the Beagle Channel, the seas calmed. Mountains soared up on all sides, twisting into bunches of ice and rock. Where the slopes lessened some Magellanic beeches huddled together, their branches beaten low by the wind. The channel seemed to head permanently towards the walls of the mountains, but the walls bent and curved and extended like a stretched spring, and the mountains ahead parted and allowed us into further reaches of water. Where the cliffs of the channel finally levelled above, ice-sheets covered the Darwin *cordillera*. Some of the glaciers descended almost to the water, culminating in a battle of icy pinnacles and moraine on the cliff top. One of them spilt into a waterfall that plunged like torrential rain from the vertical cliffs straight into the sea, disturbing the channel with a splutter of ripples that cascaded into the surreal stillness. A few albatrosses swept past us like giant straws fluttering with the will of the wind, zigzagging effortlessly above the water. It was hauntingly, unimaginably beautiful, a place swaddled in blankets of peace and silence.

Late at night the ship docked at Puerto Williams on Navarin Island. We collected a statue of the Virgin Mary, and after restocking we set out for the isolated islands south to Cape Horn. Now the winds were stronger and funnelled harshly through the channel, whistling stoutly and frothing up the water into white horses. We harboured at Puerto Toro, the southernmost permanently inhabited settlement on earth, and the crew prepared an *asado* to prepare for the morrow's strike at Cape Horn. The commander spoke to the men.

'It's a tremendous honour,' he said resonantly, 'for us to carry the Virgin's statue to Cape Horn.'

Everyone looked suitably respectful.

'Unfortunately,' he went on, bowing to the irrepressible humour of Chileans, 'we'll probably be throwing all this food up as a present to the fish tomorrow.'

As the *asado* was being prepared, I explored the settlement of thirty-five people (including the five policemen and their families). A muddy track climbed from the jetty piled high with crab-catching nets, past the wet and chipped wooden boards around the houses, and quickly disappeared into the wilderness of Navarin Island. The track ended when it came to the cemetery, marked by a bare cross hewn from two branches, guarding four unmarked graves from the oncoming southern winter. When I asked later in Puerto Toro, no one knew who was buried here. I walked on into beds of springy moss, red and purple and yellow and orange, collapsing like rotten wood when I stepped on them so that the water beneath bubbled up around my feet and chilled me through to my socks. The moss tumbled and sprang through the concealed bogs, glaring through its colours, until it vanished into the endless forests enveloping the rest of the island. I reached a bare tussock, and sat just above the moss bed. Nearby the moss was sprinkled with the white and mauve spots of the teaberries that I had already come across on the

Falklands. I stuffed myself with them absent-mindedly, waiting and watching the utter stillness and silence for quite some time, amid the gathering chill folds of the night. It was not for nothing that Darwin wrote to his wife Emma, just before his marriage, that 'during the five years of my voyage ... which from the active manner in which they have been passed may be said to be the commencement of my real life, the whole of my pleasure was derived from what passed in my mind whilst admiring views by myself.'

There was a crescendo in the wind overnight, until at daybreak the water was more white than blue, and the gales whipped the furious waves into a kaleidoscopic sheet of spray above the ocean. Apparently, at the Horn, the winds were sixty knots strong. Towards the sun the water glowed so golden that it burnt my eyes. In the morning, I sheltered in the kitchen, watching the clouds tilt from side to side through the porthole as we struggled through the seas. Whenever anyone burst inside from the deck, the wind blustered so eloquently that you felt it was visible – you could hear the gales beyond the thick glass. Once I went outside, but it was no place for a person and I staggered backwards and forwards with the will of the wind. The only animals that I could see were a pair of giant petrels, circling and occasionally alighting on the waves. It was too dangerous to cross Nassau Bay, so we sheltered and waited for the storm to abate.

Next day, we pushed for the Horn. Conditions were good at the Cape itself, but poor in Nassau Bay. On beginning, the ship straightaway began to roll from side to side, like a marble in a saucer. Water continually crashed over the sides of the boat, and we desisted. Even this modern naval supply ship felt unstable, so what must the *Beagle* have been like? We harboured in Banner Bay, on the eastern shore of Picton Island. The marine infantry had to retrieve an old fuel drum here, so I went ashore with them in a motorized dinghy. Amid the Magellanic beeches and the teaberries and the moss, almost hidden by the enveloping tentacles of Picton, there was a small shrine. It stood next to the old fuel drum, and the marines unloaded the Virgin so that she could survey the scene of worship – not that anyone is left to worship her here.

This was another site of human misery at the bottom of the world. The publication of the diaries of FitzRoy and Darwin precipitated a wave of public interest in Tierra del Fuego, and missionaries resolved to continue the evangelical work among the Yámana. In 1850, Reverend Allen Gardiner and a group of fellow missionaries landed at Banner Bay with this in mind. They sailed over from the Falkland Islands, having chartered a ship to bring them supplies the following October. This was Gardiner's second attempt to found a mission among the Yámana.

When the supply vessel arrived as agreed, all it found was a wooden board with the message: 'Dig Below – Go to Spaniard Harbour – March 1851'. Underneath the board was a bottle with a message telling of hunger and illness. The ship sailed to Spaniard Harbour, and discovered the bodies of the missionaries, scattered there among driftwood, empty medicine bottles and various bits and pieces of the now obsolete equipment. The disaster had been precipitated by an unbelievable error: the ship which had dropped them off in Banner Bay had managed to overlook unpacking the ammunition for the men's firearms, which meant that they had had no means of self-defence, and no way of hunting. The Yámana were so hostile that the missionaries had had to move to somewhere more protected. The Antarctic winter descended with characteristic force, their rations dwindled beyond repair, and the men died before the supply ship's arrival.

Darwin had been cautiously optimistic about FitzRoy's mission to 'civilize' the Yámana. Although he feared that 'it is more than doubtful, whether their visit will have been of any use to them', he went on to say that 'Every one must sincerely hope that Captain FitzRoy's noble hope may be fulfilled, of being rewarded by the many generous sacrifices which he made for these Fuegians, by some shipwrecked sailor being protected by the descendants of Jemmy Button and his tribe!' Yet even the tone of this suggests that Darwin had his doubts. With the disaster at Banner Bay, they seemed to be confirmed. And then, in October 1859, a subsequent missionary party was butchered at Woollya in a massacre probably instigated by Jemmy himself. It was only when Reverend Thomas Bridges became proficient in the Yámana tongue and was able to communicate with the people in a language and expressive field which they understood that the evangelical project had any success. The shock of seeing a European speaking to them in their own tongue ultimately converted them into being his allies during the early years which he spent with them in the 1870s. Bridges became the figurehead of the Yámana, having, in the words of his son Lucas, 'in twenty years ... transformed these irresponsible savages into a law-abiding community ... Murder was now almost unheard of and, owing to the strength of public opinion and increased civic consciousness, lesser crimes had greatly diminished.'[3]

Tragically, despite Bridges' efforts, civilization killed the Yámana. Almost as soon as the Argentines arrived to found a sub-prefecture at Ushuaia, in 1884, a measles epidemic broke out, killing three-quarters of the population within two years. The Ona people of northern Tierra del Fuego were completely eradicated, although, in contrast to the Yámana, they were largely killed by the European *estancieros*, who did not like them hunting their sheep. There is only one pure-blooded Yámana now, a seventy-year-old in Puerto Williams. Ursula Calderón's photograph featured in the 1997 Patagonian exhibition in London's Museum of Mankind, perhaps uniquely – a living person acting as an exhibit in an ethnographic exposition of a dead culture.

In Puerto Williams, there is a moving collection of photographs of these peoples that are now no more. You can trace their descent to a lukewarm interest in life, which exactly mirrors their own journey to pseudo-civilization. One family picture, taken on Hoste Island in 1883, shows them all half-naked, with the father bearing a broad and open smile. But then there is a later picture of a girl self-consciously covering her private parts. The most telling photo of all was taken in the 1920s, of the Yámana grouped with a missionary, all dressed in smart clothes. The men are wearing flat caps and jackets, the women dresses. Their bodies are slumped, their faces sullen and melancholy. A glance is enough to demonstrate the depression and death that came with civilization.

I was sharing my quarters with a group of young Chileans doing their military service, all bitterly complaining about having been posted to this ultimate extremity of their country.

'I wanted to go to Valparaíso,' one wag told me. 'The sergeant told me that that was where I was going, but the bastard commander didn't like me – "You're going to Punta Arenas," he said.'

He was homesick and longed to be back puffing dope and ripping through the city streets in loud cars with his friends in Chile.

'I want to go back to Chile,' he said. 'We're a long way from Chile here.'

When we returned to Williams, waiting for the storm to soften, I found myself talking more and more with them. We kept ourselves company in the howling loneliness and alien air all around us. Two days later, when the conditions had calmed and the commander announced another foray towards the Cape, I stood on deck with one of the conscripts as we set out. The night before we had all watched the most sublime sunset, as the Beagle Channel had dissolved into scarlet, running blood red as if the Yámana had only just been killed. Now the channel was skulking in a surreal yellowish light, the sun hidden by the banks of scaly clouds above the mountains, the water pasty and overcast by the looming shadows of the mountains all about, the darkness heightened by the inextricable shadows beneath the beech forests that covered the islands as readily as earth. We watched the beautiful scene in silent awe for some minutes, and then my new friend turned to me:

'You see, *Señor*,' he said. 'I may be a long way from Santiago and my family, but sometimes I think that the beauty here makes up for it. Not many Chileans can ever say that they have had the chance of going to Cape Horn.'

The journey took eight hours. I spent the last hour of it on the bridge, talking with the officers, watching the prow ride the waves and spray the ship with water. Mist hung low over the nearby islands, and drizzle spat against the windows. Eventually a hulking shape appeared before us.

'Cape Horn,' said the commander.

The dinghy was winched over the side of the ship, and the marines climbed down with supplies. Here we were to leave three lifeguards for a three-month stint guarding this last outpost of land. We bounced over the waves, towards a steep rocky beach and the three men that we were taking off the island. They waited for us with broad, almost ecstatic grins – they had had enough of watching the same videos over and over again, and drinking and washing in rainwater. Next to them was the lighthouse dog, the only permanent inhabitant of Horn Island.

The mongrel scampered up to me as I disembarked, whimpering and dashing away, begging me to play with it. Its eyes were round and human, and seemed to speak. I ignored it and climbed the battered wooden steps hammered into the cliff, past bearded moss dangling from the rocks like broken spiders' webs. The officers were toiling up behind me with the statue of the Virgin, and it seemed certain that they must overbalance, with the weight and the wind – and yet they did not. Perched on the cliff was the lighthouse, a chapel and a monument to the Albatross. Here the land was unprotected, and the grass was being shorn by a squall and fifty-knot winds. The rain assaulted me horizontally, and I could see nothing through my glasses.

It was a thoroughly miserable last outpost of land, yet its wildness and freshness were invigorating. I thought of the *Beagle* limping into similar winds as it struggled in vain towards Christmas Island, and my admiration for Darwin, and the past, leapt with my imagination. Darwin was a thinker and a gentleman, who after returning from the *Beagle*'s voyage put his adventures behind him and never again showed any inclination for travelling. The contrast between the adventurer in South America and the sedentary thinker is one of the most intriguing things about him. Few people are able to travel so far and experience so much of the wildness of life, then to leave it behind them so finally as he did.

I did not stay long above on the cliff. I signed my name in the Visitors Book, and then hurried down to the shelter of the cove. Back on the beach, the mongrel jumped towards me as soon as I returned. I went and sat on the slippery rocks, waiting for the dinghy to return to the ship, and it sat with me. I could not be rid of it, this black sign of humanity, pleading and playing with me in the shelter of its home.

IV

While going one day on shore near Wollaston Island, we pulled along-
side a canoe with six Fuegians [Yámana]. These were the most abject
and miserable creatures I anywhere beheld ... these Fuegians in the
canoe were quite naked, and even one full-grown woman was absol-
utely so. It was raining heavily, and the fresh water, together with the
spray, trickled down her body. In another harbour not far distant, a
woman, who was suckling a recently-born child, came one day along-
side the vessel, and remained there out of mere curiosity, whilst the
sleet fell and thawed on her naked bosom, and on the skin of her
naked body! ... Viewing such men, one can hardly make oneself
believe that they are fellow-creatures, and inhabitants of the same
world.

Charles Darwin

We sailed back to Puerto Williams, via Wollaston and Lennox Islands. It was darkening as we docked, and I told one of the officers that I was going to walk to Woollya. The marines knew it well, for they often patrolled through that part of the channels, and they knew how desolate the place was.

'Walk to Woollya,' he said. 'Phew! What does a man think about, walking for a week on his own?'

With the return to Williams was the return to my own company. Before I disembarked a wave of sadness clung to me. I had been aboard the ship for a week, and for the first time in months I felt that I belonged somewhere. I had made friends and shared the voyage with the marines. On reaching a base, I helped with the loading and unloading of supplies, and we went to fetch each other's food from the kitchen, squeezing up to allow more people onto the bench in the mess, nattering in the darkness of the ship pitching through the waves, pensive and prostrate on the bunks. I had been accepted, and returned instinctively to the inalienable human reality that an experience is more endurable for being shared.

The only way to reach Woollya these days is along an imaginary horse trail through the jungles of Navarin Island. To give an idea of how difficult it is to follow this track, when I met the farmer of Woollya he told me that he himself regularly got lost cutting across the island. I had to keep to the rough road which heads west from Williams towards the tip of Navarin Island at Puerto Navarino, and then find my way.

I set out along the track on the afternoon after returning from Cape Horn. It took only ten minutes for Williams to disappear into the rises and depressions that humpbacked along the shore of the channel. The clouds hovered above the world, but in the distance a fan of rays from the sun struck the sea with silver, a diaphanous light stilling in the timelessness of perfection; there, far away from the field of contact, the water bounced with colourful reflections. The hills of Navarin Island were almost saturated with unending and apparently impenetrable jungles. The forests were so dense on some of these islands that from afar the tangled treetops could look like a full covering of grass. Away from the whine of the ship's engine, silence reclaimed the land. The only sound was the grating crunch of my feet floating over the sandy road. Sometimes I stopped – and could imagine the Yámana following me in the silence, immutability, sameness of this slippery vision of light still as death in the calm of late summer; their paddles clutching eddies in the lilac waters as they came.

I walked for twenty kilometres, and then passed a woodcutters' shanty set aside from the track. The sun was falling behind the mountains of Tierra del Fuego, and it was time to rest. The shanty was encircled by logs, like a miniature fortress, and the lumberjacks invited me to sit with them for their dinner, sharing with me their *sopaipillas* (fried bread) and fresh sea urchins. Two men worked here all week, cutting down the beginnings of Navarin's forest and selling the wood for fuel in Puerto Williams. Then they drank their earnings away in the town's one and only wine bar.

'It's good money,' the older man said, 'when they pay you.'

'*When* they pay you,' his friend agreed. 'I've been on bloody Navarin for fifteen months, and I still can't save the money to leave.'

He'd met a North American tourist in Williams a few months earlier, and she'd given him her address in the States.

' "If you ever get the chance to visit the States, come and visit me," she said. Ha!' he scorned, 'I can't even leave bloody Puerto Williams, so how the hell am I going to get to the United States?'

The older man was silent, his winebibbing face glinting in the flames. He was from the island of Chiloé, and had lived on Navarin for thirty years. When he had come, there had been less than a hundred people on the island, and now there were still only two thousand.

'You get used to it,' he said.

I slept in the same room as them. The shanty had a porous roof made of damp beech trunks, patched up with an orange plastic tarpaulin. Dust layered the floor in thick carpets, and smothered the twilight with darkness even before night fell. We listened to Argentine football on the radio, crackling and spluttering across the channel from Tierra del Fuego. Occasionally we spoke to one another in the flickering candlelight. Then they fell asleep, and proceeded to snore and fart harmoniously all night.

Although Chile has long claimed the land south of Tierra del Fuego, and once nearly fought a war with the Argentines over it, the land has only ever really been home to the Yámana; and now they are all but dead. Those who live here have either been sent by the Chilean navy, and live out their postings in grumbling acquiescence, or have come because they can find no work elsewhere. These last hack down the forests, or trawl the channels for fish. But there are few enough people needing fuel and seafood that the population of these islands remains minuscule. On Hoste Island, which is over 160 kilometres long in both directions, there are four people. The terrain does not permit civilized society. Were it not for the territorial dispute between Chile and Argentina, the land would be virtually uninhabited.

Who else can belong here but the Yámana, ghosting their own canoes in our stumbling wake?

In the morning, I walked on from the shanty towards Puerto Navarino, another thirty-five kilometres westwards. It was a staggering day, without a cloud to hinder the view. The snows of the Darwin *cordillera* glinted almost purple in the effervescent light. Everything shone in meta-force. The forests were mists, hanging loosely against the hills, bouncing back through themselves to the sea, reflecting into the eaves of the atmospheric light. And, as I walked on with my solitude, the serenity made my heart ache with the world's beauty.

I passed the Yámana cemetery at Mejillones, the graveyard of this race, tidily and tastefully done up. Mejillones was a bay set back from the channel, perhaps one of the campsites made by the *Beagle* as they sailed towards Woollya with Jemmy in January 1833. As I walked towards the cemetery, I noticed an incredible profusion of turkey vultures flying over my head and perching in the trees. The white flashes of their wings were everywhere. The pointed heads of these birds seemed to stare at me suspiciously, as soles swept the journey from beneath my feet. Nowhere else on this road did I see more than one or two of them.

It was as if they were the reincarnated spirits of the Yámana, who had finally found their resting place.

It was near Puerto Navarino that Darwin had one of a series of encounters with the Yámana: 'A small family of Fuegians, who were living in the cove, were very quiet and inoffensive, and soon joined our party round the blazing fire. We were well clothed, and though sitting close to the fire, were far from too warm; yet these naked savages, though further off, were observed to our great surprise, to be steaming with perspiration at undergoing such a roasting.' The highly distinctive sense perception of the Yámana intrigued Darwin throughout the time he spent with them. This experience on the Beagle Channel showed him clearly that they had developed different capacities in accordance with the harsh environment in which they lived. The woman who stood naked and unconcerned in the sleet on Wollaston Island betrayed the same feature. It was also apparent that the three Yámana on board the *Beagle* had infinitely more perceptive senses than the English. They could spot sails long before anyone else, and, when they reached Woollya, Darwin noted the 'astonishing distance at which Jemmy recognised his brother's voice'. Later, in *The Descent of Man*, Darwin argued that these acutely developed senses were essential for preserving life under harsh conditions.

The extraordinary differences between himself and the Yámana exercised Darwin's mind more than any other experience of humanity on his journey. How was it possible to explain the vast gulf in intellect and capacities between members of the same race? The idea that these discrepancies resulted from successful development according to the relevant conditions which races came across made immediate sense of what Darwin had seen. Even when I went on deck one evening off Wollaston Island, wrapped up in all my thermals, I was frozen to my bones. A European would easily perish in the sleet and cold of these channels, as Sarmiento and Gardiner – to name but two – discovered. But the Yámana thrived in these conditions. Darwin wrote that 'Nature by making habit omnipotent, and its effects hereditary, has fitted the Fuegian to the climate and the productions of his miserable country.'

But what the Yámana were not adapted to were the external diseases and customs brought by the Europeans; it was these introductions which killed them off. Yet – and this seems paradoxical – as history shows, the Europeans themselves had been more likely than not to perish in this part of the world. The fact seems to be that the Yámana have been killed off, not to be replaced by a competitor for survival from their natural resources, but by a race that is not adapted to compete for those resources.

In other cases of introduced species affecting an ecosystem – as with the feral dogs and goats in the Galápagos Islands – the species instantly adapt to their new habitats, and their existing features give them a large share of success. But with the case of the eradication of the Yámana (and with the Tehuelche in Patagonia, and the Alacalufe in the Chonos Archipelago), the successful competitors replace them in spite of their existing features. The few people who live in these islands do not adapt to them; rather, they bring what they are used to, and live in the freezing cold notwithstanding, wishing that they could go home, since Navarin is home to no one now.

The eradication of the Yámana has been followed by the installation of people who will never allow themselves to reach their level of wildness, since human civilization does not now allow itself to be overturned. To be properly adapted to these climates, people would have to return to wildness. But nowadays it seems as though people do not have to follow the 'natural rules' of corporeal adaptation, since the culture of technology allows them to behave differently.

When I reached Puerto Navarino, I discovered that I had come too far. Once, there had been a police post here, but now it was abandoned. The population consisted of three marines and their families, who told me that there was no trail from here to Woollya – that the path only continued for a couple of hours along the shoreline. Nevertheless I set out through the forests, but the wood was denser than lead, so progress was impossible. When the forest gave out into a cliff which plunged vertically into the Murray Narrows, where two petrels played like ghosts in the chill bay below, I realized that I would never reach Woollya this way.

The marines advised me to return twenty kilometres back towards Williams, and then cut along the 'trail'. The day after failing at the Murray Narrows, I returned that way. They told me that where I came to a stream with a shanty on the hill above the bay, I should ask the peon how to reach Woollya.

I reached the stream at midday, and walked up the slope to the corrugated iron shack. There was a path marked faintly in the grassy slope, which fell down on one side to a bright glade shielding the stream. Beyond the shanty, the island dissolved into forests, and a man was chopping wood next to the building. Outside there was a pile of logs, a small bucket for washing in, and a gas canister. As I walked up to him, his back was turned to me, unaware of my presence, but perhaps instinctively shy of his drudgery.

Ramón was overjoyed to see me. He was a powerful man with a tragic face, his jowls hanging ponderously on each side. He lived alone with a tiny ginger terrier, his only companion. He spent his day chopping wood, mending fences and making *sopaipillas*.

'You're looking for the path to Woollya?' he asked. 'That's bad luck! I've only been here for two weeks and I've not been over there yet.'

He invited me into his hut, to eat some *sopaipillas* and drink sickly sweet tea, and we discussed the journey. He decided to go with me, some of the way, and see if he could help me. We set out through the forests, forded a river, and then crossed through thickets of *calafate* thorns which tore my clothes to shreds. The terrier scrambled along beside us, squeezing with difficulty through the bushes, yelping and whimpering whenever we went too far ahead.

'Now which way do you think we should go?' he kept asking me. All we could see was a low range of hills, covered in forest. Neither of us had a compass. He looked for animal droppings, and we would follow them when we found horse trails, until they were engulfed by the forest. Sometimes we found beaver trails leading away from lakes, wide paths that seemed sure to continue; until they too embraced the jungle. After an hour and a half of companionable wheezing, we breached the hills, and they folded down into a bog of purple moss. We descended, and our feet squelched through the colours. The island stretched away in unbroken forest beyond the bog.

Ramón climbed a steep hill, and we watched the trees together for a minute. We could see no sign of a harbour at the far side of the island.

'Now,' he said, 'I'm just looking for a landmark. We seem to have come quite high.'

We looked down to a lower valley in the east.

'I wonder if that wouldn't be the way over to Woollya?'

The journey was incredibly slow through the forests, and I couldn't face hacking my way triangularly back to the valley.

'What about continuing on up to the higher ground?'

I pointed to the highest forest that we could see, and Ramón shrugged.

'It could be,' he said. 'From there, you'll get a view of the island. At the very least, you should be able to see Woollya.'

He couldn't continue any more, since there was work to do at the *puesto*.

'If you get in trouble,' he said, 'make a fire. If you get lost, follow a stream, and you will reach the shore. Don't forget that God is with you. I will wait for you. We will meet again.'

I continued. The forest was so dense that I rarely saw anything but trees. The only guides to direction were my instincts. There was no trail. Occasionally the trees dispersed and were replaced by streams and their beaver dams where the water had spread out over the mosses, producing marshes and mud. The deciduous leaves were turning orange and red, and with the purple moss the forest looked gorgeous.

But all I could think about was going on; not losing myself; not twisting my ankle, as a prelude to a vulture's feast.

After three hours I reached a pass, and the hills fell away to the channel on the far side of Navarin Island. I could see Button Island, whence Jemmy had paddled over to the *Beagle* in 1834. As I climbed down, I realized that the coast was nearer than I had thought. I scrambled down a gully, and came to another chain of beaver dams. I trod carefully through the moss, wary of a sudden pool like those I had found in the Falkland Islands, until I came to what looked like a narrow strip of mud, three metres wide.

I tested its surface gingerly, with one foot, careful to keep enough weight on my other leg in case this was sinking mud.

It was exactly that; my leg fell straight down through the mud; I could feel no bottom to it at all. Despite the care I had taken, I felt my whole body begin to fall. Desperately, I flung myself backwards, and clawed at a tree stump on the bank behind.

I hauled myself back to life.

A slight breeze brushed the dampness of the mud against my skin, and I shivered. It was getting late. I walked on again, praying to find a way down to the channels. I tried to go down a steep ravine, but its angle became sharper with every few metres, until I had to turn back. Then I found an extremely narrow river canyon, the only way down. The canyon was littered with fallen trees, so I had to squeeze beneath them or clamber over them to go on. Then it narrowed into a chute, which I had to climb down along with the water.

My legs were exhausted. I had been fighting the forest for nine hours by the time I limped onto a stony beach, littered with mussel shells, frozen by the half-light of dusk. All around me mountains disappeared into the sky. There was no sound; even the breeze had blown itself out.

I camped on Useless Bay, and the next day continued for two hours along the shoreline. But I had no idea which way I was going. I didn't know if I had struck the shore above or below Woollya. Any of these bays could be Woollya, I thought, launching through the *calafate* bushes and covering myself in scratches and thorns. There was no path, no people, nothing but the mountains and the calm waters. So still was it that the passing of time had no relevance. With nothing happening, nothing changing, I imagined myself in a world apart.

I could see no sign of a settlement and I had to turn back, or I would have run out of provisions. There was no one to guide me, since the last spirits have left to scavenge what light is left, chuckling away with the turkey vultures deep in the forests.

Of one of his first meetings with the Yámana, Darwin wrote:

[Friendship] was shown by the old man patting our breasts, and making a chuckling kind of noise, as people do when feeding chickens. I walked with the old man, and this demonstration of friendship was repeated several times; it was concluded by three hard slaps, which were given me on the breast and back at the same time. He then bared his bosom for me to return the compliment, which being done, he seemed highly pleased. *The language of these people, according to our notions, scarcely deserves to be called articulate* [my italics].

Forty years after Darwin's visit, in order to further the mission's aims, Thomas Bridges began to compile a dictionary of the Yámana language. The completed work had 32,000 words and inflections, the number of which could have been greatly increased according to Lucas Bridges. Listening to a constant flow of incomprehensible sounds, Darwin thought that he was hearing the same words and phrases over and over again, and estimated that about one hundred words covered the whole language. Lucas Bridges wrote: 'We who learned as children to speak Yahgan know that, within its own limitations, it is infinitely richer and more expressive than English or Spanish.'⁴ Bridges' book is a wonderful illustration of why travellers rarely give more than a superficial representation of the places which they visit. He was born in Ushuaia, and lived much of his adult life among the Yámana as they died away, speaking their language from an early age. He dismisses many of Darwin's observations of the Yámana. Far from being unused to fires, as the instance near Puerto Navarino implies, the Yámana loved fires and spent the whole day huddling around the flames when not otherwise occupied. Also, it was untrue that the men did nothing but lounge about, as Darwin implied from what he saw at Woollya: 'There was a fair division of labour,' Bridges wrote. 'The men gathered the fuel and fungus for food, whilst the women cooked, fetched water, paddled the canoes and fished. The men tended the fires, made and mended canoes and prepared material for them. They also attended to the hunting ... The women were by no means slaves, for what they caught was their own. The husband used only what his wife gave him, and she did not ask his permission before making gifts to her friends.'⁵

The most shocking misunderstanding of all, though, concerns the Yámana practice of cannibalism. The whole crew of the *Beagle* knew for a fact that the Yámana were cannibals: a boy had explained to them that they ate old women instead of dogs in times of famine, because 'Doggies catch otters, old women no'. Yet Bridges says that cannibalism was unheard of among the Yámana. Thomas Bridges tells in his journal of eating thongs or hide moccasins in times of hunger, but they never proposed eating a person: 'They would sternly rebuke anyone who, when pressed by hunger, ate a vulture, however fat and nicely roasted, on the score that it might, at some time, have fed on a corpse.'[6]

How can it be, then, that Darwin – whose powers of detailed observation were extremely strong – returned from Tierra del Fuego with such misplaced perceptions of these people? Bridges suggests that the idea of cannibalism must have been placed in the heads of the Yámana by the Englishmen during the voyage. He paints the following scene: the English, convinced that these barbarians must be cannibals, prod the Yámana with questions about this until the three Yámana decide to create wild stories about their dastardly practices as a game, and tell increasingly extravagant versions as their responses are enthusiastically received, since this was what the English wanted to hear. In other words, Bridges puts the 'shocking mistake' down to cultural prejudice.

The case of their language is probably the same. Yámana was a language that did not work like English, atomizing objects into one logical symbol. Instead it was a perspectival language, recognizing that what we see depends on our position. Lucas Bridges says that there were at least five words for 'snow', and an even greater variety for 'beach'. These words depended on the object's relation to the speaker: 'A word used in a canoe might differ from that used to describe the same thing when the speaker was on dry land. Further variations were brought in by the compass direction of the hearer and whether he, too, was ashore or afloat.'[7] They had a wealth of words for related actions which English defines with phrases: *Iúa* meant to bite; *Iúashéata*, to bite off or bite in two; *Iúagámata*, to bite in passing, bite instead of, or bite slightly; *Iúawiela*, to leave something instead of biting it. There were also some wonderful words which English could do with inventing: my favourite is *Mamihlapinatapai*, which meant to look at each other, hoping that either will offer to do something, which both parties much desire done but are unwilling to do; *Tutukuralagöna* meant 'to abstain from giving when using food in the presence of those who would like a share of it'; *Tutuwöraxgamata* meant 'to land a person at any place when on one's way to a place beyond'. These are only a few examples. A reading of the dictionary of Thomas Bridges gives a clear view of how perspectives are transformed by language.[8]

Perhaps, then, we should not be surprised that Jemmy Button all but forgot his language when he returned to England with the *Beagle*. Darwin wrote: 'We had already perceived that Jemmy had almost forgotten his own language. I should think there was scarcely another human being with so small a stock of language, for his English was very imperfect. It was laughable, but almost pitiable to hear him speak to his wild brother in English, and then ask him in Spanish ("no sabe?") whether he did not understand him.' As the ship's favourite, Jemmy had more exchanges with the Englishmen than York or Fuegia, and consequently his attitudes were most affected by the cultural abyss between the English and the Yámana. The two languages and conceptual frameworks were so distinct that Jemmy naturally forgot much of his own language. There was very little common ground which English and Yámana could share.

The Yámana were the nearest thing to man's apish beginnings that Darwin ever saw, showing him, as he thought, our origins. Yet these people were neither savages nor barbarians. They had a rich language, many social customs and an oral historical tradition which Lucas Bridges also documented. They were different to Darwin, and Darwin's cultural prejudices more than tinted the way that his eyes viewed these people – his prejudices *were* his eyes. This is a paradigmatic case of why no study can claim objectivity. Darwin was far more liberal and fair-minded than many of his contemporaries, and no doubt saw himself as a dispassionate observer. Yet his culture got the better of him, and his 'scientific observations' were on this occasion prejudices.

The Yámana language is an instance of a language close to earth. Many languages have evolved to a stage where the speaker's perspective is irrelevant: a tree is a tree, and that is all there is to it. But it is this atomic generality which encourages the wide and sweeping generalities – theories – to which contemporary culture is so prone. How much easier it is to invent theories about selfishness and genetics when these things are categorized as wholes in our language. But sociobiological and genetic theories could never have arisen among the

Yámana, for they would have scorned generalizations about objects that we *see* as manifold, however much we try to unify them in a single word. Language deludes us into believing that our theories are general, when in fact it is our language which is general. As we try to generalize and impose order on the world, our language generalizes. But in so doing, the words become further and further separated from their particular beginnings, whereas a perspectival language, which is closest to the first ostension of a word, is closest to the beginnings of the word.

With the development of culture and artificial selection people have started to affect the process of natural development, wiping out species adapted naturally but not culturally to a location. As language has evolved and generalized, culture has done likewise, until it is now cultural evolution which changes the world more than anything else. The beginnings of culture, ensconced in the beginnings of perspectival language, were thus closest to the time when we lived – like all other species – by the rules of natural selection.

No wonder that poor Jemmy forgot his own language so rapidly. He was being asked to assimilate into a totally different mindset, where the language he learnt was that of forgetfulness before nature, not the acceptance of the natural order. Language, in transmitting culture more than anything else – this culture which was rapidly evolving beyond itself – swamped him with this forgetfulness. In his oblivion, at least, he assimilated with the Europeans.

I made my way back to Ramón's, losing my bearings in the forest again, and finding myself turning blindly through tunnels in the trees. Eventually, I found a stream hurling itself down towards the Beagle Channel, and I followed it until I hit the track to Puerto Navarino. But I had strayed off line, and I only arrived, exhausted, with nightfall.

I spent two days with him.

He had been many things in his life: an alcoholic, a fugitive from the Chilean coup in 1973, a wanderer, from Panamá to Scotland, a fisherman, a cowhand, a wild man and then a repentant Mormon missionary.

'I'm still young,' he told me. 'I'm forty-eight. I can find a wife.'

He was in love with his *patrón*'s daughter, and thought she loved him too.

'She's twenty-one,' he said dreamily, 'and so beautiful. Ximena. What do you think, Tobías? I can't think of any reason why God has destined me to stay on this island other than that I must marry her.'

Ramón had been converted to Mormonism in Punta Arenas, when he had fallen in love with a North American missionary.

'It was on 31 May 1986,' he told me. 'We were walking along towards each other, along the street in my *barrio*. We looked at each other, and it was love at first sight, Tobías. She taught me everything about myself, showed me the damage that I was doing to myself by drinking. She taught me about God, Tobías. Before I met her, I never believed in the Lord.'

He talked incessantly about this, the most beautiful and the most tragic episode in his life, which coursed through his thoughts and his soul interminably, unendingly – impossible that he should ever be converted to any other passion. He thought of her as he read his Bible, as we talked in the profound darkness of the night, as he fried *sopaipillas*.

'She went back to the States, and never wrote to me,' he said. 'Why not? Why would she do something like that? We were in love, and she forgot me completely. Why didn't she write when she went back to Kansas?'

The pain was struck out by his writings. Chileans have a saying that in their country there is a poet hidden beneath every stone, and Ramón was one of them. In the morning, as we sat clutching our blankets in the clammy cold of autumn on Navarin Island, he showed me his poetry, scrawled passionately, painstakingly, lovingly, in one of his exercise books. I lived his life with him, through his poetry. He discovered himself in his writing, in expressing himself to the paper. His poems were full of the love of God, of his love and anguish: a man's attempt to set life in perspective.

'Love,' he said, 'is like a child. Children can't help crying, and neither can lovers.'

Love flooded his face, passion and pain puckering his lips and cheeks and exorcising itself through tears. Ramón cried like a child, and then wiped the tears clean from his face with a hand thick as a door and strong as a hammer. In strength, was his human – all too human – weakness.

As he read his poems, his life, he shook with the pain and the eternal recurrence of pain, pain that burst through every action and thought and desire that he had ever had, burst irreparably into life, to be released only with breathlessness. In every sentence that he spoke was pain, desire and contradiction.

He was a good Mormon, yet he was irreducibly lewd and possessive: 'When I see a woman that I want to sleep with,' he said, 'I don't stop until she's mine.'

He told me that he had trained as a chef; then that it had been as a painter/decorator.

He told me that under Pinochet he had lived for fourteen years outside Chile; then that he had met the North American in 1986, in Chile.

He said that his passion for the North American could not be quelled; then that he was in love with the *patrón*'s daughter.

He embodied unsystematic, irrational humanity.

Ramón encapsulated something human, *because* he was irrational, kind, humanist, empathetic and suffered incessantly. He didn't care that something should be coherent. He talked sporadically about his life, without reason, trying to grasp its beauty and rhythm with the imperfect pincers of language. Often he talked for ten minutes or more at a time, and his words smouldered slowly in the shanty, with the fire in the rusting Aga, stopping and starting with his shaky movements which betrayed an alcoholic's stagger, as he spoke and rose to toss more wood into the grate, spoke whilst wiping the tears from his face as the smoke billowed into the room and made our eyes smart, spoke while listening to the deep, somnolent crackle of the fat frying our bread until it was the colour of dark tea, or of the bark of the woods beyond the shanty. Then, just as the wave of words touching us from his past was vanishing ephemerally, beautifully, like an idea into the thickening arteries of history, the flow stopped, and Ramón would turn his glistening face to meet my gaze. The words no longer came, but his eyes spoke even more eloquently in the vanishing power of their expressions: 'Why should I be judged against coherency,' he seemed to say, 'when we are all inconsistent in our actions and beliefs? When no rational system could ever be coherent?'

Just as precious to me as his garrulousness were the moments of silence which we shared, expanding to fill the holes in the day which yawned and stretched out into the invisible arms where night should have been. We talked and sat and stilled so much that the colour of the light beyond the windows vanished, with time, into the subconscious picture of memory. With every passing moment, the goodwill which he felt towards me, as a representative of the human race come to this most far-flung extremity of its consciousness, swelled, like a tree burgeoning in springtime.

Darwin wrote in the last paragraph of *The Voyage of the Beagle* that the traveller 'will discover, how many truly kind-hearted people there are, with whom he never before had, or ever again will have any further communication, who yet are ready to offer him the most disinterested assistance'. No one who saw the way in which I was treated by people like Ramón could have accused them of being xenophobes, not when they said that they would rather trust a foreigner than a local, since a foreigner was less likely to steal. They were not selfish in offering food and hospitality to someone they knew that they would never see again. They would have laughed had I told them dogmatically that human characteristics are irrevocably selfish, and that self-interest governs all morality.

This idea is plausible only because our contemporary society thrives on self-interest. But where beliefs and language and customs are profoundly different, and the consumptive ethic is absent, experience is profoundly different. Many times self-interest does not underscore experiences of life. The theory of the selfish gene is only so plausible to us, as Lewontin implies, because of the characteristics of our entrepreneurial and hierarchical society. For the purposes of coherency, sociobiology claims that all human actions are intrinsically self-centred, and of course the importance of the self ensures that many of them are. But it is an unjustified generalization to say that they all are. Theories are alarmingly general, despite the inconsistency and incomprehensibility of our experiences. It is not that everyone is good, but that 'good' is not an empty term; good people do exist. No dogma or coherent theory can gainsay the experiences of goodness, whilst trying to generalize about a world which has no generality open to theory.

The history of the uttermost part of the earth is essentially one of ceaseless human tragedy, from the Sarmiento colony, through the history of the Yámana, to the Falklands War. All those who live there today have not evolved to the harsh conditions, nor are they suited to them. Yet still, even in this desolate extremity of civilization, I was generally received with the same warmth and generosity as everywhere else on my journey. Possibly it is true that the isolation of these places makes people keener to talk to strangers; but equally possible is that this desire follows from the experience that people are, often, good.

PART SIX

Chiloé and the Chonos Archipelago

I

We obtained from the brow of a steep hill an extensive view ... of the great forest. Over the horizon of the trees, the volcano of Corcovado, and the great flat-topped one to the north, stood out in proud pre-eminence ... I hope it will be long before I forget this farewell view of the magnificent cordillera fronting Chiloé.

Charles Darwin

After turning its back on the Magellan Straits in June 1834, the *Beagle* passed the Chonos Archipelago and Chiloé Island, before heading for Valparaíso. After an eventful period, when FitzRoy nearly abandoned the captaincy,* the brig returned southwards down the Pacific coast to Chiloé at the beginning of November. The expedition spent much of the summer in the archipelago, returning northwards in February 1835. Darwin visited the main island of Chiloé, as well as the smaller islets of Caylen, Lemuy, Quinchao and Tanqui. This was the southernmost point on the Pacific coast where he rode across country again, travelling from San Carlos (now called Ancud) to Chacao, and then to Castro; from Castro, he rode across the island to the chapel of Cucao on the Pacific coast.

One of the things which most struck Darwin about the island was its immense poverty. Of Castro (which has today replaced Ancud as the island's capital) he wrote: 'The poverty of the place can be conceived from the fact, that although containing some hundreds of inhabitants, one of our party was unable anywhere to purchase either a pound of sugar or an ordinary knife. No individual possessed either a watch or a clock; and an old man, who was supposed to have a good idea of time, was employed to strike the church bell by guess.' The poverty struck Darwin everywhere, as did the noble humility of the Chilotes. And yet,

---

* This was caused by the Admiralty's refusal to pay for the *Adventure*, an American sealing vessel which FitzRoy had bought for £1300.

despite – or possibly because of – the poverty, Darwin found the Chilotes polite, respectful and immensely generous people: 'I never saw anything more obliging and humble than the manners of these people.'

Interestingly, he clearly distinguished Chiloé from the rest of Chile, saying that here the Andes are not nearly 'so elevated as in Chile'. In the 1830s, Chile was still fighting the Mapuche Indians, the fiercest tribe in the Americas. Chilean control only reached south to Concepción, since other than the small fort at Valdivia the land beyond the Bío-Bío River belonged to the Mapuches – and Chiloé, with its distinctive folklore and history, was yet further south.

But today Chiloé belongs to Chile. Now that Chile has extended itself more than 2000 kilometres beyond the Bío-Bío to Cape Horn, the whole of my journey along the Pacific coast would be Chilean. I returned from Navarin Island to Punta Arenas, and then caught a boat that followed the *Beagle* through the Chonos Archipelago towards Chiloé. Once I was through the tortuous Fjords I would be able to buy a horse again and renew my horseback journey, as Darwin had done, beyond the southern tip of mainland Chile. The thought was difficult for me to come to terms with, since I was now so accustomed to walking and living without even the company of horses; but the journey required horses, and I knew that I would get used to them quickly.

The voyage through the channels took three days, silenced by the walls of the mountains rising in foreboding magnificence on either side, draped in thick forest. The density of the trees etched the mountains with a blackness which strangled colours with almost a musical melancholy, and the melancholy seeped through to me, for even though I made friends on the voyage and chatted and laughed and drank, I knew that I would soon be alone again, and blankly reclaim the loneliness of contemplation. However, I was not alone just yet, since the period of the boat journey north was my longest stay on the mainstream tourist trail during the whole year. There were many more foreigners than Chileans on the boat, and I enjoyed speaking English on a daily basis, partly because I knew that shortly I would be in the Chilean heartland, and would not speak my own tongue regularly again for many months. I made good friends with three of the travellers – Amanda, Dave and Serena – and they came to watch me buy a horse.

They thought it might be funny.

We went to the small village of Queilen, opposite Tanqui Island and near the southern extremity of the archipelago. This was a good place from which to begin, since it was opposite one of the southernmost islands which Darwin had passed. I could ride past Lemuy, and then travel across to Cucao.

We arrived in darkness, the rain lashing against the wooden houses in the main street. A light, lonely and pale as a shroud, filtered its dullness through thin strings of rain. Sporadic gusts of wind chuckled down the street, rippling the puddles with a lithe, foot-free dance; steps of ghoulishness that hurried us into the first lodgings we found – a large house next to the pier, shapeless and soundless as we knocked on the door along with the rain.

The owner had a flabby face, and he led us up a rickety narrow staircase and threw open a pair of doors. We settled our things, and then looked at the house. It was full of paintings bent sinister by ugly images of malice: a jetty in the moonlight, sheltering the oscillating shadow of a blood-red body floating in the sea; an image of religious terror: a beaming priest adjacent to a quiet and surly fisherman, holding a girl (the fisherman's daughter?) dressed in virginal white, whose frizzy hair and face start in terror; an idyllic country scene, which is too perfect but to be evil, with the fisherman helping his sons unload the nets, and dark thoughts lurking in the recesses of our suspicious minds, knowing that, so it is said, there are still witches on Chiloé.

Whether or not their charms work, people still practise witchcraft on Chiloé. Chilotes believe that witches can fly, transform themselves into any animal, put others to sleep, make rivers wax and wane, and kill. They are said to plunder the cemeteries at night, stripping skins from the recently interred, dressing themselves in them, and then flying between the islands. It is said that you can see a witch in the dark because of the shining lights whirring through the air.

Typical of the techniques used to unmask a witch is the custom in the area of Chullec. Here, when a Chilote travels at night, they carry a knife, and if the flashing lights appear they make the sign of the cross next to the light, and another on the earth before striking the knife at the heart of the cross. At this point, the witches transform themselves back into their human person.

There are so many stories of the supernatural that empiricism is as alien to a Chilote as mysticism is to an Anglo-Saxon.

> Many years ago ... when I was very young, I went fishing with my father
> and an uncle ... we passed near some cliffs, when my father suddenly
> diverted the boat so that we were hidden behind the nearest rocks. He took
> me by the hand, and told me softly: 'Hold on, don't move and don't speak!'
> Then he added: 'Wait, and you'll hear the wonderful music of the mermaid.'
> I withheld my breaths. Hidden, almost invisible, we saw a woman of
> great beauty, with long blonde hair which almost seemed golden in the
> moonlight; she was playing a beautiful instrument which gave out gold
> and silver melodies, her hands were lovely; then I realised that she had no
> legs ... her body had the shape of a fish, and ended in a fin.[1]

Chilote faith in witchcraft is unquestioning. Witches belong to their
lives like the rain which sprays their fields, real or imaginary. They do
not tell even their closest family members that they have joined the
coven – and the secrecy can occasionally bring even themselves into
danger:

One afternoon two brothers drove to the hamlet of Pid-Pid. They
told their mother that they were just going for a drive, but really they
wanted to drink some *chicha* (apple cider). As they drove off, they
discovered a goat in the back of the truck, which cheered them
immensely since now they would be able to pay for their cider with an
asado. They tied up the goat, but when they reached Pid-Pid it had
transformed itself into a vicious dog. They beat and kicked it, fearful
of witches, and then cut out its vagina and left the dog by the roadside.
They returned home in the evening. In the morning their mother did
not emerge from her room. They entered her bedroom and found her
dead, with her vagina horribly mutilated. From her bedroom a trail of
blood led to the verge where they had left the dog the day before. Their
mother had never told them that she was a witch.[2]

In one of the homes where I stayed, a little girl gave me a pitying
stare when I spoke cautiously about witches:

'Don't you believe in witches?' she asked incredulously, as if talking
to a fool.

People who had seemed perfectly sane would tell me incredible
stories: a waitress told of her grandfather coming across a coven of
witches eating a baby's body; a fisherman mentioned an old lady in the

village who had been killed by witches; a teacher told me that her father had only been saved from a supernatural death by an extra-ordinary meeting of the Witches' Council.

Where were they, these witches, if not walking through the invisible walls of these paintings?

After some minutes the owner of the guest house appeared, and we stopped admiring the artworks. We all felt awkward, uneasy, as we pondered the reputation of Chiloé for black magic.

I tried to enliven things.

'I've come here to buy a horse,' I told him. 'Do you know anyone who has one?'

'Oh yes,' he said. 'I've got just the man for you.'

And in the morning, he introduced us to Don Segunda Segovia – horse salesman extraordinaire.

The morning was sunny, and with the improvement in the weather our moods lightened. Don Segunda rode up to the guest house on a pregnant mare, dressed in a silk waistcoat and immaculate felt hat, and asking a high price.

'Too high,' I said.

'She's very good with traffic,' he replied. Just then a large truck trundled past, and his mare turned wildly around in circles, whinnying in fright.

Don Segunda looked annoyed. When he looked annoyed his gaze heated up, his whitening stubble shone, and he looked vacantly at your eyes as if he didn't see you.

'I've got another horse in the countryside,' he said. 'Let's go and see it.'

So we hired a truck, and drove for half an hour outside Queilen. Amanda and Serena came with me, and we were soon walking through the lush fields of Don Segunda's land.

'There she is,' he gestured, pointing at a chestnut mare. 'I'll go and wait down by the river. You just herd her down here.'

The mare was the only tame horse in a herd of twelve. He walked off. As soon as he next opened his mouth, I knew there would be trouble.

'Herd 'em all down here,' he shrieked, waving his arms like a wind-mill and looking every bit the impatient and irascible little man which he was. I tried to concentrate on the mare, thinking that we would probably be better off without the wilder ones, when he yelled at me again:

'All of them! All of them! Come on,' he cried.

The horses were circling wildly, but I managed to channel five of them down a muddy chute towards the river. Mud flew everywhere, since the land was saturated from the night's soaking. I slid my way down the chute, and found that the horses were trapped in a ribbon of river that was fifty metres long, sandwiched between bushes at one end and a tangle of driftwood at the other. Don Segunda was standing with a lasso on the opposite bank, making ineffectual sallies at catching the mare. The rope glanced against her leg, and virtually every other part of her body except her head. The horses ran away from him down the river.

'*Puta*,' he swore. I hadn't heard him swear before, since until now he had maintained the appearance of a gentleman. He had told me how he had worked thirty years in Patagonia, and that he had worked with animals all his life. He always addressed me with consummate politeness.

'Stop them escaping,' he yelled at me.

I was standing at the mouth of the chute, and it was my job to wave my arms and stop them from running too far. But I was up to my knees in mud. I didn't want to move too much, since every time I did there was a sporting chance of my foot and shoe bringing their intimate and smelly partnership to an end. Nevertheless, I heaved myself around, and tried to get them to return to him.

Then he'd miss again with the lasso. Once he was a metre away, and managed to hit the wrong horse.

'Fucking horse,' he said. Then he threw the lasso over to me, but lacking his thirty years of experience I didn't do too well either.

'Fucking horse,' I agreed.

'Can't you get any closer?' he asked. If I had moved, this time I really would have drowned in mud.

'Why don't you throw some mud at them?' he suggested. Suddenly enlightened by this stroke of genius, the animal expert began to hurl great clods of grime at the poor horses, who blinked and splashed around, but did not return to their master.

'Tell the girls to throw mud too.'

'This is stupid,' Serena muttered.

Amanda found a tree that had fallen across the river, and she stood on it and shooed the horses back towards Don Segunda. Finally, after an hour or so, we caught the mare. I tried her out along the road, and then we drove back to Queilen.

This was not the only time that I witnessed Don Segunda's great skills with the lasso. One day I happened to see him trying to catch a pig. This pig was big and slovenly, and waddled slothfully around a field, yet still managing to escape Don Segunda's rope. Then, when he was caught with his snout in a trough of rotten potatoes that Don Segunda had cunningly planted to entice him near, the pig ran into a screaming fury, careering around the field and dragging his captor up and down the hill like a yo-yo, before the man tripped and was hauled along the ground for twenty metres. His helper, an enormous woman who looked likely to give birth to quads at any moment, punished the pig by hitting him over the head with a bucket. Then, when Don Segunda tried to tie the pig to a tree, he was pulled off his feet and dragged merrily along the ground again.

It must have been great fun for the pig. I enjoyed it also, chortling away from a safe distance. Perhaps it should have crossed my mind that buying a horse from such a man might be an error.

I had to return to Argentina for my saddle. This was a nuisance and involved me sitting for days on buses, but there was no way that I could have walked around Patagonia with an additional twenty kilograms on my back. Ten days later, I was back in Queilen, preparing to leave.

I arrived with autumn – and in Chiloé this means rain. 'In winter the climate is detestable, and in summer it is only a little better,' wrote Darwin. 'I should think there are few parts of the world, within the temperate regions, where so much rain falls.' The morning after I returned, the rain began, continuing torrentially for thirty-six hours. It chattered constantly, a replacement for Argentine wind, dripping from the eaves of the houses, bursting invigorated against the windows with new gusts of wind. It spat, and spattered the village grey in its inestimable melancholy. Yet, looking out of the window, it was sometimes possible to imagine that the rain was negligible, even that it had ended, as if rain was so integral to the essence of Chiloé that the downpour could neither be seen nor heard. The clouds hung deceptively high above the bay, so that you could see the lush slopes of Tanqui Island, the fields falling to sea, interspersed with dark copses. You could even see the houses across the bay quite clearly, and the yellow spire of the church fighting upwards against the rain like the rising steam from the chimneys. Sometimes the drips and leaks hushed for a few minutes – before beginning again in their repetitive strain.

Occasionally I watched people hurrying along the street, their faces grimacing against the weather, yet not appearing to be incommoded by the deluge. This made me think of a family which Darwin came across in Castro: 'They had no shelter during the rain. In the morning I asked a young Indian, who was wet to the skin, how he had passed the night. He seemed perfectly content, and answered, "Muy bien, Señor." '

Sometimes at times like this, with the same weather touching the timeless beat of a place which seemed frozen in history, it seemed that things could scarcely have altered in the intervening years. This delight was always most true in these places far from urbanity, where the chords of nature's crumpling accordion still ground through the gathering gloom.

Don Segunda had left my mare at the farm of his neighbour, Angelino, and I went one afternoon, carrying my saddle in the hold of the local bus. When I reached the stop, I had to haul it 500 metres up the steep hill to the house. A Chilote woman helped me with my own bags, while I heaved the saddle on my head. She was very cheery.

'We Chilotes are always good to strangers,' she said. 'When I was a girl, my parents told me never to deny anything to anyone. God created us all. We're all of the same blood. We have to share.'

We climbed through countless layers of thick greenery, ferns and brambles and trees and the grass shading each other, as if there was no colour in the world but green, and no need to look beyond verdant variety. Angelino was her godfather, and she took me to him. His house was built of dovetailed planks, and in the boggy yard were several huge sacks of apples for making *chicha*. I wanted to sleep in the barn, which lay between the house and the sodden branches of the orchard, but Angelino told me that it was infested with rats.

'Come inside,' he said. 'Have some *chicha*. Stay with us.'

The *chicha* went straight to my head, which was just as well because it looked and tasted like urine. After a few glasses, though, this did not matter. All over Chile, alcoholism is a serious problem. More than once I was told (not without a tinge of pride) that Chile was second only to France in the global alcoholism stakes – though quite who would take the trouble to investigate such a thing, and be sober enough to make a report afterwards, went unexplained. In Chiloé, the ratio of grown men to alcoholics often seemed to be one to one. In every bar, at any time of day, groups of men could be found getting blotto, telling each other increasingly improbable tales as they did so, along the lines of 'close escapes I have (not) had with killer whales'.

At Angelino's, things were little different. A group of workers appeared for dinner, and ate greedily, drinking *chicha*, and arguing loudly about football. They mostly had more than a shadow of Indian blood. The light was cast by a roaring hurricane lamp, which glared in the reflection of the clear soup which we were served. Then came the meat and potatoes, and the silence which often falls with food. There was a studied intensity amid the clatter of knife and fork, and the hollow stares of the huge white cat. The cat was shaggy and clearly adored by everyone there, and to break my unease I asked Angelino's niece what she was called:

'*Blanco*,' she said. 'White.'

They played cards after dinner, and I sat in silence. Sometimes I overheard one of the men whispering to a newcomer:

'See that gentleman over there? He's bought a horse from Don Segunda, and he's going to try to ride to Copiapó.'

Then the recipient of the news would crane his head round and stare at me.

As in Uruguay and Argentina, people still thought me mad, or at least extremely peculiar, wherever I went.

It poured all night. With the grey film of daybreak came a finer drizzle, and then a pause in the rattle of the rain pounding against the roof like nails. From my room, I looked hopefully out into the backyard, at the steaming hills streaming back towards a break in the forests. Surely the weather would improve. I left to ride again.

Amazingly, I did not find it difficult to get used to the renewal of my horseback journey. My mare, who was a lovely chestnut colour, was very tame, and began with real purpose. Although my legs ached at first, the softness of travelling along the dampened tracks through the island made up for any pain. There was nothing quite like riding for discovering the countryside all around, for without the physical demands of walking, the eyes could really wander where they wished.

To begin with, though, they could not wander very far. Within twenty minutes the rain was reinvigorated. The clouds clung together, and shielded each other in mist. The permanency of the island beneath the rain gave it an image of peacefulness. Yet the land still told me that a different strain of wildness was, will o' the wisp, hiding from me as it followed me through the hills; it lay in the dense and dark forest clambering up on all sides, the steep folds of the island, the solitary gravel road winding through the hamlets like a dream.

This place could not have been more different to Uruguay and Argentina. Here, I regularly passed through small hamlets of lean-tos with gleaming aluminium roofs, where matronly women stared incorrigibly at me as I went. Divorced from the generality of the plains, in Chiloé there were a thousand and one details to entertain me: people, hamlets, horses chewing furiously in the rain, small and precarious churches on the roadside. In a way I felt less solitary, for I could always see a plume of smoke betraying a chimney in the distance – but the fact that there were more people also reinforced my loneliness.

That morning I came to Lemuy Island, across a small channel from me, rolling down to the sea. When Darwin arrived at Lemuy, he found the inhabitants desperately bartering for tobacco and gunpowder. The latter was 'for a very innocent purpose: each parish has a public musket, and the gunpowder was wanted for making a noise on their saint or feast days'. The rain was still teeming down, and I was soaked. Across the channel, Lemuy displayed the same green attractiveness as the main island. The road still rose and fell with the hills, and its principal village, Puqueldón, was built on an immensely sharp slope down to a bay. As in all towns in rural Chile, it was a place where you could imagine nothing dramatic occurring, a place where people would probably drink the same spirits in the same bars in twenty or fifty years' time. Skiffs were piled up in the little port, lethargic, waiting for something to happen; there were some men unloading king crabs; a few old Chilotes sat covered in blankets and ponchos waiting for a bus; schoolchildren chased each other up and down the streets.

I moved on from Lemuy to Chonchi, where Darwin broke his ride from Castro to Cucao. Chonchi fell from the forests to the sea, mirroring Lemuy across the water. I found some oats for my mare, and wandered into the telephone office to ask where I could camp. Just as the woman was giving me advice, a girl came rushing in:

'Look, look,' she said, pointing at my mare, 'some silly old *campensino* [country person] has tethered his horse in the main square.'

I rushed out in embarrassment, and camped not far from the town. The mare – who was nameless – was tired by the journey. Don Arturo, the landowner, cackled when I told him my destination.

'Copiapó! You're going to have to change your horse.'

The mare, who was extremely likeable, neighed appreciatively as I brought her oats.

'Why? She looks fine to me.'

'Too thin,' he said, even though she was quite sleek.

He invited me over to watch them putting a nose-ring through the pig's snout.

'He's too greedy,' Leonel – Arturo's son-in-law – told me. 'Once he's finished eating the straw, he starts on the mud. The ring will stop him.'

The pig was a tame brute and a handsome soul, mottled white and black, who grunted happily as Leonel approached and bustled him under the shelter of his corrugated iron pen. Then, Leonel straddled the pig and pulled his lasso taut around the snout. The pig shrieked. Leonel sat on his head now, his boots laced with mud, his face sweating since the pig was strong. Leonel's wife passed him a piece of wire, and then turned her face away from the gruesome scene. Leonel used his brute strength to force the wire through the rubbery flesh of the snout. The pig was in agony, and I winced with its shrieks. It screamed eerily, with its lips pulled as far back as they could go, baring the impotent agony of its taming. Leonel pushed the wire through a second time so that he could make the ring, and then twisted the two strands together so that they could not be undone.

In the morning, I rode to Cucao. Darwin had followed a very poor trail to Huillinco, and then transferred to a canoe which took him along the tremendous arm of Lake Cucao to Cucao itself: 'The periagua is a strange rough boat, but the crew were still stranger: I doubt if six uglier men ever got in a boat together.' At Cucao, he found thirty or forty pure Indian families living at Chiloé's only settlement on the Pacific coast. His companions, the governor and Commandant of the island, treated the Indians like dogs, and they responded with extreme humility. In the morning, Darwin rode north along the beach to Huantamó Point, before returning to Castro.

The road from Chonchi to Cucao breaches the rolling hills of the Chilote interior. Thick forests are everywhere. Darwin found that, after more than three years' voyaging, 'this undulating woody country, partially cultivated, reminded me of the wilder parts of England, and therefore to my eye had a most fascinating aspect'. The road today continues on from Huillinco to Cucao, and I followed it as it stuck to the south side of the great lake, which winked at me through intermittent drizzle. Beyond Huillinco I found fewer hamlets, until the gravel gave out into a few score houses deafened by the ceaseless drumming thunder of the surf beyond the dunes. It had taken a whole day to cross the island, and it was almost dark. The main square was really just a glorified field. I left my mare to graze, and found a campsite for myself.

In the morning, I crossed the huge suspension bridge over the Río Cucao with care, and rode along the beach towards Huantamó. This is a vast expanse of sand, perhaps thirty kilometres north to south and unbroken. Once I came across an Indian woman riding towards the village from one of the desperately poor farmsteads strung out north along the beach. The point at the end of the bay loomed through the haze of spray, remote and tremendous like an island's shores seen from afar on the ocean. Absorbed into the wild space and terrific sounds of fury bursting from the seas, I began to see how you could view the ocean as legend.

Chilotes do not only believe in mermaids and witches. They also believe in a ghost ship called the *Caleuche*, the witches' ship. The *Caleuche* patrols the islands, whisking shipwrecked sailors into its bowels. It is not only Chilotes who believe in it, since there have been reported sightings by the Chilean navy and the merchant navy. I met a man in Queilen who claimed that he had once been fishing at night on the beach, and the witches' ship had come within metres of the shore.

Together with his friends he had frozen all night, and watched the spectacle of the dancing mulattos, the bright lights and strange sounds, wafting through a thick mist towards them.

'There must have been something there,' he told me. 'In the morning, our nets were filled with the biggest fish I've ever seen.'

At times, the *Caleuche* is supposed to come ashore for repairs. Then it is transformed into a log of wood, its crew into a flock of birds. As I rode along the beach at Cucao, beset by the shrill cries of tero-teros, this did not seem such an improbable idea.

In *Patagonia Revisited* Bruce Chatwin tells a story from Cucao. He talks of the legend of the boatman, a mystical figure that is said to pole the dead spirits of Chilotes across Lake Cucao and out into the Pacific. The man who tells him the story mentions that he had known one cynic, who had – in defiance of the legend – gone to stand on the shores of the lake and called out for the boatman. The boatman came.

When I returned to the village, I found a house selling bread and *empanadas* (mince turnovers). The owner was a silent man, who threw wood into the Aga and waited for the huge brass kettle to boil.

I asked him about the boatman.

'Oh yes,' he said. 'That's an old story.'

We were silent once more.

'I saw the boats myself, once,' he went on. 'Six or seven years ago, poling along the far side of the lake. I called out in surprise, and they vanished.'

II

In a short time we were surrounded by a large group of the nearly pure Indian inhabitants. They were much surprised at our arrival, and said one to the other, 'This is the reason we have seen so many parrots lately; the cheveau (an odd red-breasted little bird ...) has not cried "beware" for nothing.'

Charles Darwin, on arriving near Lemuy Island

On San Pedro, one of the islets near Chiloé, Darwin captured a fox which was apparently endemic. As an undescribed species, this was an important discovery. Put together with the discovery of the fox endemic to the Falklands, Darwin glimpsed the first indications of an important strand to his ideas: that, if separated by a geographical boundary, members of the same species evolve differently as they adapt to their new habitats. The perfect example of this would come on the Galápagos, where Darwin found that the giant tortoises had branched into fourteen species on islands that were almost all visible one from another.

By this stage of the journey Darwin was leaning ever further towards evolutionism. His many discoveries all pushed him in the same direction: the extensive fossil finds at Punta Alta and in Patagonia which supported Lyell's geological theses, and showed that the earth must be far older than religion supposed; the human experience with the Yámana and the Pampas Indians which pointed towards the discrepancies in capacities within a race, and set him thinking about how these changes came about; and now, the observation of how species on islands differed from – and were yet related to – their continental neighbours, which implied some process of change after their separation.

The long periods spent in Patagonia and Tierra del Fuego were the wildest and most lonely. Now, as he headed north into Chile and came across frequent pockets of civilization, the character of his journey changed. Chile was the site of many crucial experiences for Darwin, such as the earthquake at Valdivia, the tidal wave at Concepción, the discovery of a petrified forest during his passage through the *cordillera* to Mendoza – which Darwin was sure had once been on the Atlantic coast – and the discovery of this fox on Chiloé. Away from the wildness of the south, Darwin intensified his reflections. The combination of the tidal wave – when Darwin measured that the land had risen by eight feet [two and a half metres] at Talcahuano – and the discovery of the petrified forest showed him that the earth was immeasurably ancient and that geological transformations could account for its upheavals. This explained the separation of islands from a continent, and so showed how island species were able to evolve differently with time.

So Darwin, never one for superstition, paid scant attention to Chilote beliefs. Here, at Lemuy, he learnt that this bird had the mystical powers to inform people of the arrival of visitors. But he saw the poverty, indigenous traditions and superstitions as part of the same phenomenon. The long winters, when the days were short and it could rain for a month on end, gave people the opportunity to invent fables. I came across Chilotes who believed the same.

'It's all rubbish,' some would say. 'Long winters, nothing to do, so people come up with nonsense.'

I rode along, trying to put black thoughts out of my mind. It was not pleasant to imagine that any of these animals could be a witch come to do the dirty on me, or that the next person who allowed me to camp in the glade beyond their house might put a wicked spell on me. But then, just as my thoughts were returning to normality, the casualness of chance would throw oddities into my path.

I returned from Cucao to the east coast of Chiloé, and made for Castro, which was nearby. When I reached the town, I noticed that my mare was limping slightly. I was cold and fairly miserable, since my clothes and all my provisions were soaked through with the rain, and now I was worried by her injury. I asked the police where I could camp, and they directed me to their own stables. I hired a truck to transport my mare. It had been raining all day, and I was soaked through again, spoiling for a cold. The stables were run by a delightful couple, Ramón and Teresa. I couldn't afford a hotel, so I asked them if I could camp.

'OK,' said Ramón. 'But come in and have a cup of tea first.'

Then they invited me to stay. They gave me their children's room, and bustled the boys to sleep with them in their own room. I was bewildered, but grateful for the kindness. As I sat in the kitchen, warming myself by the Aga, Ramón said:

'Of course, we knew you were coming today.'

'How?'

'The bird told us,' said Teresa. 'The little red bird came and pecked on the window. It always tells us when strangers are coming. I thought: "Who on earth is going to come today? There are no visitors any more. It's cold and raining, all the tourists have gone now." And then you came.'

In the morning, the mare's injury improved. Some *guasos* [the Chilean equivalent of the *gaucho*] examined her near the stables.

'She's fat, the mare,' one man said. 'But she's OK. She's just had a bang on the heel, look.'

I had been worried by a slight crack in one of her hooves. But now he parted the skin and showed that the crack was just a continuation of a slight cut in her leg.

'It's already healing,' he said. 'It was just the hard road which made her feel the cut.'

The day before I had been forced to ride along the main tarmac road to Castro.

'Give her a day's rest, and she'll be fine.'

Ramón had no objection to my staying.

'Come back to the house,' he said. 'Have some *mate*.'

Unusually for Chileans, he drank *mate*. In the heyday of the Patagonian *estancias* many Chilotes left to work as shepherds in Argentina. Castro was full of old men tipsy on *pisco* (Chilean firewater) or *chicha*, reminiscing about the old life in Patagonia as they cackled in the dim bars on a misty afternoon, talking about God and the sorry state of humankind, reddening their faces every minute with another slug of spirits. They had returned from Patagonia with the habit of the bitter drink, and passed it on to their children.

'We all went over there,' Ramón told me. 'There was no work here, but plenty in Argentina. Especially under Perón.'

He had left home when he was fourteen, in the hold of a cargo ship bound for Punta Arenas.

'My father had died, and my mother told me that if I wanted shoes, I had to get them with my own sweat,' he told me.

We spent most of the day in the kitchen. He was a chatterbox, rambling from one topic to another without a pause in the steamy warmth around the Aga while Teresa busied herself with the household tasks. She spent all day cooking, collecting firewood, making cups of coffee, sweeping the endless spread of dust that seemed magnetized to the furniture like flies to sweat, her face radiating with shy smiles as she bustled past – she was a cheerful woman, initially shy of me but then confiding more as time passed. They fed me constantly, refusing absolutely any payment. The radio was on all day, crackling an eclectic mixture of tango, samba, Mexican and Chilean folk music through the house. The whole family seemed to live in the kitchen: Ramón with his twitching face of tension and endless *mate*, Teresa coming in and out, the children fighting and screaming, squirming and crying and belatedly listening to the admonishments of their parents after they had hurt themselves. The ginger cat slept all day, and then indulged in a vicious fight in the night, the scratches and hisses knifing through the house's paper-thin walls; in the morning, it limped bloodily into the kitchen, and cowered behind the Aga.

My cold worsened overnight, until it was serious and I had a hacking cough. Ramón and Teresa refused to let me go anywhere.

'You're crazy,' they said. 'You'll catch pneumonia in this rain.'

It was still raining, always raining in Chiloé. And yet, they said, this was nothing to what it had been like before.

'It's only been raining for a week,' said Ramón. 'Before it rained for a month at a time. We even had to ration the water this summer, something we never did before. The Lord won't visit the earth any more, he won't return. Don't you think? Not now that we're destroying creation. We will have to wait until the apocalypse.'

In the afternoon, a neighbour came to drink *mate*. Her face was thick with Indian blood, and her black curls flopped over her face like a veil. They were soon discussing traditional Chilote topics for a rainy winter's day: life, death, witchcraft and food.

'You have to capitalize on life,' the neighbour said. 'You never know

when you're going to die. That's why in winter you've got to concentrate
on eating and keeping the fire going. Then at least you won't die yet.'

She cackled.

'Unless a witch puts a spell on you, of course.'

Ramón scowled.

'That's all rubbish,' he said. 'Or eighty per cent of it is. My cousin
once told fishermen that he'd seen the mermaid. He shouted "I've seen
the mermaid!" to them all, and they fled, leaving their nets on the
beach. Then he just stole all their fish and went home.'

The woman wasn't so sure.

'I've seen some pretty strange things myself,' she said. 'And you
should know,' she said turning to me. 'Everyone knows that horses can
see spirits.'

'Oh well, horses!' Ramón said. 'They're completely different. We all
know about that! I knew a man in my village who was riding one night,
when he passed the cross which marked where an old enemy of his
had died. The horse stopped and refused to go any further. The man
dismounted and tried to lead it past, but he couldn't. The horse had
seen the dead man's spirit, and knew that the spirit had an evil plot
against his rider. He could have tried to kill the horse, and still it
wouldn't have moved.'

Darwin rode straight from Castro to San Carlos, but I decided to make
a detour via Dalcahue to visit Quinchao Island, which he reached from
the *Beagle*, before heading along the coast towards Chacao.

As I rode, Chiloé's mystique came and went with the rain. I was still
soaking myself daily, but I had overcome my cold. The island flickered
before me through the drizzle and cloud. The rain was finally a comfort,
since it was always with me. Sometimes I met a father and son herding
ewes along a track, or I was assailed by madly barking dogs when I
passed a farmstead, but mostly the only noise was the rain's patter
dampening down the grass. Only rarely did a bus or pick-up pass me.
There was something soothing about the rolling hills, forests, fields
and hamlets; even about the greyness. Perhaps, like Darwin, I was
reminded of home.

On the first day I reached the village of Achao, on Quinchao Island,
by nightfall, and treated myself to a bed in the guest house. I looked

for someone to share a few words with through the night. The barman seemed a likely candidate, since he was a gabbler and an incurable alcoholic. He served me beer without telling me that he had poured half a tumbler of *pisco* in it as a special surprise to burn my mouth off.

His grandparents had been Scottish.

'Thompson!' he said. 'You must have heard of them.'

'Don't be silly,' said an old man with a Brillo Pad beard, the only other customer in the bar. 'There must be hundreds of them in his country.'

'So what's England like?' the barman said, pouring himself a shot from the secret stash of liquor he stole from the bar owner. 'What do you think of Chile over there? You think we're all Indians, don't you?'

He roared with laughter, and the old man was silent.

'Isn't that right, Don Bernardo?'

'So what if it is?' he snapped. The barman, whom everyone called 'Inglés', mocked him.

'What's the matter, Don Bernardo? Don't you like being called an Indian?'

'Inglés,' he said softly. 'You know nothing about it. Forgive me, *caballero*,' he turned to me, 'but you English joke about the savage Indians and piratical Spanish, but who was the worst pirate of all? Wasn't it Drake himself? He came here and helped himself to what he chose.'

The barman laughed openly at Don Bernardo, and served two fishermen who had come in for wine.

'Hey, Inglés,' he called over to me. 'Come and meet my friends.'

They were from a remote island, three hours by launch from Achao, and they invited me to return with them. I could stay for four days in their island free from foppishness. I shook hands with them and planned to go the next day. I would leave my mare with Don Bernardo. When they had gone, I called over to the barman and told him my plans.

'No, no,' he said. 'You must be crazy!'

'What?'

'You mustn't go with them!'

'Why not?'

'Haven't you heard of the witches? These islands are full of them!'

'What's that got to do with me?'

'They particularly prize white skins. You didn't think that he was inviting you over just as a favour, did you? They want to use you in some ritual.'

I laughed. He had to be joking. I couldn't take him seriously, not with his tales of death in the arms of a carousing clan of witches.

'I'm not joking, Inglés,' he said, looking at me earnestly. 'I wouldn't joke about this. Don't go with them.'

I looked anxiously from him to Don Bernardo, and the old man rose and began to walk slowly down the stairs that led out of the bar. As he left, he called out:

'Take care of the lad,' he said.

So I did not go. The next day I retraced my steps to Dalcahue, and continued north towards Chacao. The day after leaving Achao I passed by Quicavi, supposed to be the site of the Witches' Cave; here the witches congregate for their Council. There are some eyewitness accounts of proceedings at the Council:

'I am sixty-nine years old,' says Don Chato, 'and I was born in Chaulinec, one of the islands of the Chiloé Archipelago. When I was a young man, my parents moved to Chuit Island. I remember that some neighbours on Chuit had a daughter who was very ill, and the parents suspected a witches' spell. They asked me to accompany them to Achao, and then to Tenaún, in a rowing boat, since I was a very good oarsman. There were four of us...

'When we arrived at the cave it was lit, and we introduced ourselves; there was a doorman who charged us to go in ... inside was the Judge and a secretary around a table.

'Doña Isidora Leviñanco presented the case and the other three of us were witnesses, we had to give our names, surnames and addresses. They charged Doña Isidora 200 pesos to cure her ill daughter ... [the Secretary] opened a window, and a dove appeared, receiving the Secretary's message ... and then flying away quickly. We waited an hour, and when this was done, the Judge and Secretary fetched a basin filled with water, five glass balls and a mirror, and there in the mirror we saw the face of the witch ... she died a year later, and Doña Isidora's daughter got better.'[3]

These legends flash through the islands, furrowed deep into the muddy stew of earth, there to be unearthed if only the digging is done. At times

I agreed with a Spaniard I met, who said that people invented the stories to make the island more interesting. Or I thought that the dreams depended on the drunken sprees that leave the islands stumbling at every step, as uncertain and insane as the mirth of a megalomaniac. But I was playing along then with the rationality which toys with the shards of these stories, and consents to their rubbishing, claiming that myths are irrational, superstitious, groundless; and analysable as such, as mere cultural frippery, only meaningful in anthropological theories of exchange and coherence, inherent meaning and belief; with nothing core and existential to be left dangling beyond.

Yet these people were thoroughly sincere. If I made a friend in a village, sharing a drink or three in a bar and chattering late into the russet glow of wine, I would leave with my hand aching from the iron grip of goodbyes, as if these people knew that it is always the untrustworthy and the devious who leave their mark with limp hands. Would they invent these stories? I didn't and don't believe it. Would any amount of *chicha* or firewater lead to someone imagining a witches' council?

But there couldn't be anything to their tales. Witchcraft is the preserve of peoples fastened to tradition, only tardily touching the reality of material and technological advances. If brought to the irreducibly material world, they would remove the senseless rags of their superstition, wouldn't they?

Ah, says the African witch doctor: but the reason that there are no witches and devils in the industrial West is that they don't like electric lights.

Or, they might say: when a space rocket crashes to earth, like Challenger or Ariane, we don't say that technology based on scientific research was wrong – we say that we can explain what went wrong. Yet when a spell fails to work, witches too have their explanations. In Chiloé they say that those with 'thick' blood cannot be touched by black magic.

If, as Lewontin says, science to a large degree consists of what people called scientists assert, aren't they then the surrogate witches and shamans of our own world? Witchcraft works along the same lines after all. The spells are those which the witches – who supposedly know about these things, because they are in contact with the spirit world –

say will work. If a scientific prediction is wrong, the scientist explains it, whilst if a spell fails, the witch explains it: each according to the assumptions and beliefs implicit in their mindset. The logical structures of the two sets of beliefs are exactly the same.

Of course, empirical observations are a crucial way of forming beliefs about the world, and have led to immeasurable technological advances. But there is a growing trend to dismiss any other way of looking at the world as unfounded *because* it is not scientific. This surfaces most self-evidently in the mass globalization of Western political and economic systems, which are founded on empirical scientific rationality. Although culture begins in localized, specific situations, and survives through oral transmission, there is now an unconscious project to universalize its tenets. As culture generalizes and words generalize along with it, both try to spread their influence: we see this clearly in globalization. And yet, in generalizing and removing us from our perspective, we yawn further and further from the natural evolution which made us.

We constantly see objects looked at differently all around us. No two people see the same thing in a picture or hear the same movement in music. Our experience shows that there is generally more than one way of viewing something, and that the same thing can often have infinite layers of meaning and interpretation. In mainstream Western culture, we largely engage scientifically and technologically; in Chiloé, they largely engage mystically and supernaturally. And, with its strong cultural traditions, there is nothing to suggest that Chiloé is any the worse for it.

In Castro, I had removed several months' supply of hair – but I was still a mess. Perversely, though, I enjoyed the scumminess: it wouldn't be with me for ever, and it somehow went with what I was doing. Of course it was easy for me to idealize this tremendously harsh physical life, which I was only living for a year – how easy it was for me to do that. I was tremendously lucky, free, able to wander and then return to my comfortable little existence. How pathetic I felt, sometimes; how lucky, at others; how desperately lonely; or proud and defiant in my loneliness. These people, humble and meek, good in the extreme, seeing me in the comparative hardship which I had chosen, helped me out because they knew what it was to struggle, to be cold and wet and to go hungry. I always carried food, because I never wanted to impose, and yet with a horse I had to ask people for permission to camp in their fields, and with the permission came the bubbling generosity.

My mare began to limp again, more pronouncedly than before, as I neared Chacao. Doubtless, the witches were having their way with me. I noticed this as I climbed a steep hill past the hamlet of Linao. I had been riding in the archipelago for nearly two weeks, and was now used to its ways. I was used to the clouds which smelt of rain even when they withheld it, the endless rolls of hills dissolving into each other's murky shoulders, and the forest flecked with fields. Today, miraculously, the clouds were clearing, and I could see across the Gulf of Corcovado to the *cordillera* on the mainland. It was a wonderful sight, this unbroken chain of green mountains, occasionally throwing their power into the whitened cap of a volcano as sailors soar to a mast-head enveloped with frost. The sky was as calm and blue as a river stilling for dusk. The beauty eased my despair at my mare's injury. She was limping more and more pronouncedly, and I had to stop.

When the *guasos* had told me that she was fine, I had trusted them. But Don Segunda had sold me a lame horse, and I in my foolishness and carefree idiocy had bought it. Now when I asked the first *campesino* I came across to look at her, he shook his head sadly:

'You've been had, I'm afraid. When did this horse start to limp?'

'Well, she first began about a week ago, but it got better so I continued.'

'Yes,' he said. 'I'll tell you what's wrong with this horse. She's got a fungal condition in her hooves. I've had horses with it before.'

'What does it mean?'

'It means that if you cure the limp in one leg, it transfers to the other. Look, she's limping in her left leg.'

'But before, the limp was in her right one.'

'That's what happens with this infection. But whoever sold her to you must have known. It's only something that you notice after a few days.'

We led the mare gently to his farm, and I unsaddled.

'You can leave her here if you want,' he said, 'but you can't carry on with her.'

I had taken easily to riding again after the time in Patagonia and Tierra del Fuego. I loved my chestnut mare, and always tried to find her the lushest meadows, always bought her oats to keep her strength up. She was fatter than she had been when we had set out, especially after our rest at Castro, and I was devastated to discover that I had been conned by Don Segunda. The *campesino* took pity on me and invited me to stay with him, feeding me pork chops ribbed with strips of popping fat and a huge mound of potatoes, and throwing open a spare room along the low hallway. The room was designed for dwarves, and I had to stoop as I peeled off my filthy clothes and my socks washed through with rainwater. My body smelt of horses, dirt and fatigue. Outside the rain was lashing down interminably, hounding me with its power. I lay prostrate on the sagging mattress, sobbing helplessly into the pillow.

PART SEVEN

The Southern Chilean Coast

I

*We had an opportunity of seeing many of the famous tribe of Arau-
canian* [the European name for the Mapuches] *Indians; the only men
in the Americas who have successfully withstood for centuries the
conquering arms of the Europeans.*

Charles Darwin in a letter to his sister Caroline

Darwin's next call on the Chilean coast was at the town of Valdivia,
about 220 kilometres north of Chacao. He visited the forts at Niebla
and Corral, experiencing the great Chilean earthquake on 20 February
1835. Darwin had been passing his time very pleasantly in the small
town, where the ship's crew were entertained by Valdivia's *intendente*
(Commandant). He went shopping, was invited to balls and embarked
on excursions. On one of these journeys, Darwin was astounded at the
density of the native forest around Valdivia: 'I wanted to go to a house
about a mile and a half distant, but my guide said it was quite impossible
to penetrate the wood in a straight line. He offered, however, to lead
me, by following obscure cattle tracks, the shortest way: the walk,
nevertheless, took no less than three hours!' It was on one of these
walks that he felt the earthquake: 'I was on shore & lying down in the
wood to rest myself. It came on suddenly & lasted two minutes ... The
rocking was most sensible ... There was no difficulty in standing
upright; but the motion made me giddy.' This experience, as we shall
see in Talcahuano, gave Darwin definite evidence that the physical
world could be changed by natural occurrences. Of further importance
was that for some while there had been intense volcanic activity in the
area. From Chiloé, Darwin had witnessed the Osorno Volcano and
others emitting great jets of steam in November, whilst the Antuco
Volcano (between Valdivia and Concepción) was extremely active con-
currently with the earthquake and tidal wave. These impressions began
to show Darwin how geological activity might be inter-related. Two
days after the earthquake, the *Beagle* was in Concepción, 350 kilo-

metres north of Valdivia, where they witnessed the aftermath of the great tidal wave. 'In my opinion,' Darwin wrote, 'we have scarcely beheld since leaving England, any other sight so deeply interesting.'

Darwin was, in a macabre sort of a way, extremely fortunate to witness this sequence of events. Tidal waves – *maremotos** as they are known locally – only occur in Chile once every hundred years or so, the most recent striking in 1960. Witnessing the concatenation of these terrific geological forces irrevocably changed the way that Darwin thought about the world. It was impossible to see it in such a benevolent light with these tragedies occurring around him, and his measurement of the changes in the earth's formation pushed him irretrievably towards a Lyellian view. 'An earthquake like this,' he said, 'at once destroys the oldest associations; the world, the very emblem of all that is solid, moves beneath our feet like a crust over a fluid; one second of time conveys to the mind a strange idea of insecurity, which hours of reflection would never create.'

Since Darwin did not touch the coast between Chacao and Valdivia, I travelled to within two days' ride of the town before looking for a horse. It was already the end of April, and my time and money were running out. Horses, saddles, expensive flights to the Falklands: none of these came cheap. I had had to leave my mare with the *campesino* on Chiloé, and cross the canal at Chacao. Now I travelled to the region around Osorno, which is known as the best in Chile for tough resistant horses: the type I needed. I contacted a vet and he suggested a local breeder to me. I went to the man's *fundo* (a Chilean *estancia*), and there fell in love with a grey gelding, tough as old boots, faithful, strong and obedient, yet characterful also; with eyes that spoke like beacons and had their own ineffable dictionary. He was called Martillo – meaning 'hammer' in Spanish. I thought this a good name for my horse.

I was with Martillo for two months. I talked with him as I went, interspersing our conversations with songs for the winding road. He had a tremendous weakness for apples, and whenever I reached a town I bought several kilos in a market. He would devour them all at once, puckering his lips up and leaving them quivering in my hand when I had no more to feed him. He was the tamest animal imaginable. Once

* Literally, 'seaquakes'.

we stayed in a place where there was a young puppy, only two months old, who began to tease Martillo's hind legs, tussling with them and trying to take a quick nip at his ankles. As Martillo walked, he lifted his legs as exaggeratedly as a royal guardsman, making sure not to tread on the puppy – rather than kicking him, which is what many horses would have done. On setting out, Martillo had never even seen a bridge before, as I discovered when on coming to the first one he shied violently away, so that I had to dismount and lead him across. Yet he became incredibly calm with traffic, and only a few weeks later we were travelling on flyovers and dual carriageways as we rode into Concepción.

I loved Martillo. I loved his immense size, his habit of breaking free from enclosures and going for a wander, his intelligence, stoicism and nobility. He had not decided to explore, yet he took to our challenge zestfully, and, I could see, revelled in the beauty that he saw, pricking his ears up whenever we came to a new site of interest. I loved him because he was both gentle and strong. He was a tremendous brute and yet he was completely without malice. When we set out, he was so fat that he could barely crest a rise of a hundred metres without wheezing at the effort of it all; but by the end of our time together, he bounded up the steepest of hills with nothing I could do to stop him, as we learnt the mountains and forests of Chile together.

I spent only two days in Valdivia, since the winter was hurrying on and I was keen to head north, away from the rain. I found a *fundo* where I could camp outside the town, and then visited Corral and Niebla. It was near Niebla that Darwin found the impassable tract of virgin forest, whilst across the estuary, at Corral, he discovered a unique species of frog. The two forts are today Valdivia's principal tourist draws, and I shared them with day trippers from nearby towns in southern Chile. The forts are well preserved, and their cannons still point threateningly out to sea. Yet now they have no function but to be stared at, and the tragic tranquillity of uselessness has settled over them, a peaceable bit of calm which fits only too well with their new role as a tourist attraction. Their real purpose vanished along with the subjugation of the Mapuche tribes in the area; with the coming of civilization to this distant pocket of America.

Although the Spanish quickly conquered most of the peoples in their path, the Mapuches in Chile proved to be a different proposition entirely. The *caciques* (chiefs) only finally ceded to their conquerors in a treaty of 1881, 340 years after Pedro de Valdivia's founding of Santiago provided Spain with its first colonial base in what is now Chile. The treaty of Quilín, in 1641, had recognized Mapuche autonomy south of the Bío-Bío river, and the Spanish were only allowed a right of passage along the coast between their forts at Concepción and Valdivia. These forts near Valdivia had been the only Spanish strongholds that withstood Mapuche defiance, and it was near here that Darwin had his brief opportunity of seeing them.

Now I was going to follow the *Beagle*, and the old Spanish right of passage, along the southern Chilean coast. I set off north from Valdivia, and within two days I was into Mapuche territory.

Chile has two mountain ranges: the Andes, and a coastal range which rises in places to 3000 metres. Riding north from Valdivia, I was almost instantly amid the beauty of the coastal *cordillera*.

Rarely have I felt so calm and contented as in these parts – with the ubiquitous forest cleaving the clouds with its greenbacks; the glimmer of puddles bouncing in the sunlight sweeping up a shower; the clefts and clearings in this crumpled carpet of land that never straightens; the golden light painting brilliance and clarity, to compensate for the frequent squalls unleashing themselves over the defenceless country. The coast pitched all along its line, thrown down from cliff to shore and then climbing anew, unable to determine its character, whether high or low, even or uneven, rough or smooth; the waves rushing in and receding in their conversational dialectic; conflicts bursting at the seams of the natural panoply; drizzle dampening my face and mistifying my glasses, as if shielding reality from discovery. In the constant dichotomies lay the Chilean national character: the land rising into the furthest celestial reaches, yet unaccountably drooping helplessly from frigidity to fertility in the Central Valley, splattering itself in lakes and forests and then losing these in the peaks again protruding at all edges of its vision; mountains that toss the volcanic spume of ire aside with disdain – let it fall, frenzied, on the lives below.

Within an hour of crossing into the land of the Mapuches, I noticed differences. The Mapuches drove their oxen along the dirt tracks, the lumbering tread of the animals spitting up dust to cloud the sunlight.

The oxen were yoked together with saplings, and driven forward by their owners with sharp sticks. There were small farmsteads sprinkled regularly alongside the road, outside which might be a few pigs and the obligatory yapping mongrels. It was a glorious day, and I was following the coastal track which hugged the Río Queule, a beautiful waterway that runs parallel to the sea, a short distance from the surf, for fully thirty kilometres, before reaching its frothing death in the estuary. At regular intervals, rickety wooden ferries crossed over the river to reach the Mapuche communities strung out along the shoreline.

It didn't seem like an area in which I had to be mistrustful. As with everywhere I went, people often called out, sometimes stopping me for a conversation by the roadside to hear the stranger's story, once or twice offering me some fresh *chicha* to ease the journey. After five hours' ride, I began to look for some oats for Martillo. I asked the first men I came across where I could buy fodder in the area; they asked me my purpose, and I explained; and then one of them, Armando, a Mapuche, said:

'Yes, there is a man near here who sells oats – but why don't you come to lunch?'

He lived in a comparatively wealthy house. Between the house and the track was an apple orchard, with a carpet of lush grass where Martillo could graze awhile. Carlitos, the local teacher and a friend of Armando's, showed me where I could buy oats (although the farmer refused to charge me for them), and then we sat down to eat.

Armando's wife and daughter served lunch. They had been preparing the meal all morning in their kitchen painted red with strings of chillies, and ornamented by clumps of heavy pots hanging like fat sausages from hooks in the ceiling. As well as Armando, Carlitos and myself, there was another guest, Don Chilo. Don Chilo was ninety-four years old, and an experienced old fisherman whose lips were splayed and cracked, the rubber stamps of his life's wisdom.

As we ate, he told a story about Mocha Island, a small spread of land lying about fifty kilometres offshore:

'We made a journey to Mocha, once. In those days we just had wooden fishing boats, they were hopeless in a storm. We were very lucky, for as soon as we arrived a huge storm blew up, torrential rain, gales and thunder. If it had blown up whilst we had been at sea we would have sunk. The storm lasted two weeks and we were stranded. We had no food, but the people were kind, they fed us and gave us shelter, so we didn't go hungry. I rode with them around the island, and they showed me many beautiful places. I'm sure it must have changed after the *maremoto*, though. People don't believe me when I tell them how much the *maremoto* changed everything. When I tell them that you used to be able to walk across the estuary at Mehuín, they laugh at me. You'd sink if you tried it now. But it's true.'

'I was here when we had the *maremoto*,' Armando said. 'We saw this almighty wave crashing over the dunes and coming straight for us. Only, thanks to God, it was in the daytime, for if it had been at night many more people would have died. We ran up the hills, and sat there for days until the water subsided.'

'You must have been terrified,' I said.

'Well, not really,' said Armando. 'You see, we thought it was the end of the world, so all we did was drink wine and *chicha*.'

They hadn't been terrified at all; just rip-roaringly drunk.

'I tell you what those waves are,' said Carlitos. 'It's the sea falling away from the land. When I go riding up in the hills, I find rocks which I'm sure were once in the sea. They've got marine fossils on them. It just shows that the sea is falling away from the land.'

He looked triumphantly at us, flaunting his disavowal of modern theory with immense pride. I subsequently met, in the north of Chile, two other people who subscribed to this theory for the same reasons. The land didn't rise from the sea – the sea fell from the land.

'Perhaps it's got to do with global warming,' I said. 'As the sun gets hotter, the sea evaporates.'

This drivel of mine was only partly mitigated by thorough drunkenness, since Armando had been pressing endless glasses of *chicha* on all and sundry for several hours by now.

'Have some *chicha*,' was his constant refrain. We drank so much of it that late in the afternoon Armando had to go and open up another keg in the storehouse.

'Come along, come along,' he said, beckoning me. We went, and I smelt the fermentation and heard the burps of the apple juice bursting against the floorboards.

'I don't drink anything but *chicha* and *mate*,' Armando confided in me. 'Mapuches never go thirsty, that's for sure!'

He laughed drunkenly.

'The *huincas* [the Mapuche word for Chileans] may try to starve us to death, but they can't take away our real petrol!'

He thought this uproariously funny, and I laughed with him back to the house. Before evening we all tried to doze off our drowsiness. Carlitos was the only one who was successful, since his thundering snores consigned sore headaches to the rest of us. With the night we talked more evenly and patiently. Armando advised me on the route I should take on the morrow. Then he prepared my bed, thrusting back the bedcovers with aplomb, and returning with a bowl for the night's *chicha* exhalations.

'Sleep well, *gringo amigo*,' he said. 'I'm sorry I haven't been a better host this evening. I've got to go out.'

He could not have treated me with more consideration, and yet still he felt guilty. He looked at me with a sudden wave of sadness.

'I'm not well,' he confided after a moment. 'I'm going to see the *machi*.'

He had laughed, along with Don Chilo and Carlitos, when they had tried to teach me some Mapudungu (the Mapuche language); now this man was going to see the community's shaman.

I left at dawn. After two hours, I came to the beach, and followed its murky line northwards. The day was deafening, the waves constantly crashing to shore, sometimes breaking several hundred metres out to sea. The water mixed permeably with the sky, dissolving into a colourless haze on the horizon, and the haze spread inland, beyond the sea, dragging the dangers and uncertainties of the ocean ashore like a shipwrecked sailor blighting virgin land with his first footfall; hanging loosely over the fields and forests, disguising habitations from my keen eyes. Occasionally the cliffs dissipated into a long beach, sprayed with clumps of grass, dappled by evanescent hoof-prints and the ripples of the waves. The immensity of the scene will always be with me: the bellows of the ocean, as eloquent and potent, subtle and soothing, poetic and lovestruck as a dictionary of all the world's languages drawn into one cultural epitaph; how flimsy, culture's coughing in the drowning echoes of the waves; and yet, despite the roars, the silence; the motionless sand and dunes; the apparently drab haze hanging everywhere; the unity of light and space which scorned all categories; the abandon which I felt, as I rode, cowed by the ferocity of the sea and the emptiness, beholden to my fate only, giving myself up absolutely to destiny.

There was no road here, just a succession of hoof-prints to follow through the sands. With evening nearing, I saw an ox cart lurching along a track inland, and I followed it. I had to buy fodder for Martillo, and find somewhere to camp, since the beach was only for the wild waters. I found a small farm, and asked the Mapuche lady where I could camp and find fodder.

'I'd like to let you stay here,' she said, 'but my husband is out. If I let you, he may beat me. That's life, isn't it?' she said matter-of-factly. 'The men get cross, and we get beaten.'

With the help of the primary school's head-teacher, I was recommended to the farm of Don Pablo, a community leader who could sell me oats. Don Pablo would be home shortly, but in the meantime he sent me with a letter of introduction to the farm.

I was met by his wife, María. Don Pablo's father, a toothless old man whose cheeks angled in perfect symmetry down to his chin, peered at me as she read the letter, his head hidden beneath a battered felt hat. Once she had read it, her face burst into a smile, open and warm now that her suspicions had been allayed. She told me to unsaddle, put Martillo into a field, and come into the kitchen and warm myself up by the fire.

The farm was desperately poor. Pigs squelched in the mud, grunting and tearing after anything that looked like extra food. The storehouse stank of chicken shit. They chopped wood for a fire with a small and irretrievably blunt axe, ate potatoes and bread, and occasionally slaughtered a chicken or pig. The children did their homework by the bare glow of a hurricane lamp.

Once I had finished unsaddling Martillo, I went and sat by the Aga. Don Pablo's mother was sitting next to María. She shuffled towards me as I entered. She was blind, and her face shook with the effort of bending over to greet this stranger lingering in the darkness.

'Where are you?' she said; slowly, for she rarely spoke Spanish.

María gave me a cup of sweet tea and some *sopaipillas*. I apologized for not being able to speak Mapudungu.

'That's all right,' María said. 'My children can't speak it either. Or at least, they understand it all OK, but when I speak to them in their language, they just reply to me in Spanish.'

'Yes, we're all becoming *huincas* now,' said her mother-in-law. 'No one wants to know about the Mapuches any more. We've lost all our customs, I don't know why. Everyone's Chileanized these days, not like before when no one spoke Chilean, we all spoke Mapudungu. Before, a woman had to learn how to sew and that was it. Now they all go off to school, and don't even know how to do that. These days, the only thing the girls can manage is marriage.'

'Some people say it's better, these days,' said María. Don Pablo's father nodded all the while. 'What do you think, *suegro*?' she yelled at him, and he smiled wryly.

'He's deaf,' the old woman said. 'He can't hear anything. Some people think it's better now, but I don't. We're forgetting the old ways, and the Lord will desert us soon. So much suffering has the Lord made me endure! I had so many children, and only two survived. This poverty that he designed for us, the Mapuches. We always prayed to the Lord, and at least we never starved. What do you think of that?' she asked me.

What could I say?

'With a journey like yours, you must believe in God,' she went on. '*Si Dios no te acompañe, quién te va a acompañar*? If God isn't with you, then who on earth is?'

Don Pablo arrived, and dinner was served. He had once worked in Santiago, but had returned to care for his ailing parents. As the evening wound into its sheath of darkness, we talked about the Mapuches. He told me that the potato – the staple crop of all these coastal communities – had fallen fourfold in price in the past year.

'It's all because of these economic agreements. Mercosur [the Economic Common Market for the south of South America]. Our president signed these agreements, and now Chile is flooded with potatoes from all over the place. Last year, a sack of potatoes went for 6000 pesos; now, it's going for 1500. They're worth nothing. We are praying daily that this resolves itself, for otherwise we will starve.'

They wouldn't be able to buy their basic necessities, and people would be forced to migrate to the cities.

'That will be a tragedy,' said Don Pablo. 'As long as people are

working in the countryside, they are near God. But then they go to the
city, and they forget themselves. Then they forget God.'

In the morning, Don Pablo gave me a huge bag of oats for Martillo.
When I tried to pay, he would have none of it:

'God will pay me,' he said.

It was a day's ride from this community to the small town of Puerto
Saavedra, a supply centre for the surrounding Mapuche communities.
The tracks continued in the same style as before. Near the town, the
way swooped down the cliffs to a shingle beach. The tide was high and
the furious seas broke almost at the foot of the rock, licking Martillo's
hooves. Martillo jumped and leapt up the shingle, frightened by the
foam – as I was too. We passed the danger, and when we were barely
three kilometres from the town, I heard a sound of tearing material.
Looking down, I saw that the saddlebags had ripped and fallen apart.

With my rapidly diminishing budget, I had chosen to ride with
only one horse in Chile. Instead of carrying unnecessary quantities of
clothes, books and medicines, I was only travelling with one change of
clothes, my tent and my sleeping bag. I had made myself up a new set
of saddlebags, known in Argentina as a *maleta*: a piece of strong
material with a slit in the middle, swung over the saddle beneath the
sheepskins, kept in place by my backside as I rode. It was this material
which had frayed and ripped, and I couldn't go anywhere without it.

In fact, with the *maleta* ripped, it was quite difficult to go anywhere
at all – even the distance between here and Saavedra was a struggle. I
tried carrying the bags and leading Martillo, but they were so cum-
bersome that the two things could not be done together, so I had to
ride Martillo, while trying to balance the *maleta* precariously on the
saddle. I had to trust him to find his own pace down the hill whilst
clinging to the flapping pieces of saddlebag that threatened to spill my
few belongings over the road. I came to the first houses, and saw that
a school bus was dropping children off. I asked them to take my
maleta and leave it at Saavedra's police station, and so was spared the
embarrassment of riding into town looking even more completely
ridiculous than I usually did.

The police directed me to a guest house, where I could stay while I
found a tailor to make up a new *maleta*. I led Martillo down the street,
stared at by everyone (as I always was). When I found the guest house,

I was greeted by Don Beto, a boarder. By this stage I was thoroughly frazzled, worn out by the problems with the *maleta*, and all I wanted was to find a place to lie down for a while. But Don Beto had other ideas. I asked him where I could unsaddle Martillo.

'Where have you come from with the horse?'

'Valdivia.'

'Valdivia,' he said, astounded. 'That's far! Five or six days. How many?'

'Six.'

'Six days' slog from Valdivia! That's far south.'

'I know.'

'You must be tired. Valdivia, Osorno, Puerto Montt. Then you've got Chiloé. Then Coyhaique, Punta Arenas, Tierra del Fuego, Antarctica . . . You're not from Punta Arenas, are you?'

'No, I'm English,' I said, too tired to change the conversation's tack. 'But I've come from Valdivia.'

'English. I learnt English at school. *Caballo* was . . . horse.'

'Yes.'

'*Oveja* – sheep. *Vaca* – was it cow?'

'Yes.'

'And what was *perro*?'

'Dog,' I said.

'Ha!' chuckled Don Beto delightedly. 'This man knows his stuff, he really does! What about *chien*? No, that's French. *Je parle français.*'

'Where can I unsaddle?' I asked again.

'Unsaddle? Are you staying here?'

You don't think I've been having this ridiculous conversation to amuse myself do you?

'I'd like to.'

'Oh, I don't know anything about that,' he said. 'You'll have to ask the landlady. Six days' slog from Valdivia . . .'

When I had settled myself, Don Beto offered to help me find fodder for Martillo.

'We'll go to see Cheque Castro,' he said.

As we went, we passed the local hospital. Don Beto was concerned about my health.

'You're not ill, are you?'

'No.'

'Flu?'

'No.'

'Headaches?'

'No.'

'Blood pressure? Cancer? Rabies? They can cure it all in there.'

'I'm fine.'

And so we went on, Don Beto talking in endless lists.

'Chile are playing football tomorrow. Who's it against?'

'I don't know.'

'Bolivia? Perú? Ecuador? Argentina? Or Panamá, Costa Rica, Guatemala, Mexico. The United States, Canada. Then you've got Greenland. Do Greenland play football, I wonder? ...'

'I don't know,' I said firmly, trying to shut him up. As we walked towards Cheque Castro's, I noticed that there were many fewer Mapuches here than in the rural areas.

'Why's that?' I asked Don Beto.

'Hee, hee! The country's got nothing but Mapuches, has it? *Puro Mapudungu.*'

And he started to reel off lists of Mapuche words; his madness tinged with sadness as he spoke the dying tongue.

When I told Martillo's breeder that I would ride to Concepción along the coast, he thought it was a good idea.

'Very beautiful,' he said, before frowning. 'The only problem you have is the Mapuches.'

'What's wrong with them?'

'They're terrible! Thieves! Drunkards! Sluggards!'

Among the wealthy classes of Chile, Mapuches have this reputation. Chileans in general have an antithetical perspective on the Mapuches, since most of them have some Mapuche blood and are proud of their ancestors having been the last undefeated indigenous tribe in the Americas; yet they also like to think of themselves as European, and so try to hide the Indian blood from the national psyche. The prevailing attitude often seems to be that since Chile has brought them medicine and schooling, the Mapuches should forget the iniquities of the past and embrace the developments of the present.

Mapuches see things differently. Schools generally teach in Spanish only, thus acting as a form of cultural destruction – this is why many children no longer speak Mapudungu at home. Mistrust of doctors and hospitals also runs deep among the older people, since they are seen as just another part of the baggage of cultural destruction which colonization has wrought. The gradual murder and assimilation of Mapuches by an invading culture is a distressing story. Alonso de Ercilla, the conquistador, told that when the Spanish first arrived they found crime and injustice absent from the Mapuches. In a flash of self-knowledge, he wrote that it was the Spanish, 'destroying everything that we touched',[1] who opened the way for these trends. Ever since the Spanish arrival, the Mapuches have been retreating: from Santiago to the Bío-Bío; and then, with Cornelio Saavedra's offensive in the 1860s, the final unconditional surrender of their lands to Chile.

The 1881 treaty declared all Mapuche lands Chilean national property. The Mapuches were given paltry parcels of land for their communities: they received 500,000 hectares from the government, while 5 million hectares were kept for Chile. Over the years that followed the communities were severely repressed. There are even stories of Mapuche children being imprisoned for trying to sell milk, since the authorities wanted them to have no part in the monetary economy. The combination of this and the miserly landholdings which they were given has been disastrous. Under the 1881 treaty, each Mapuche was given 6.1 hectares of land. However, families have grown faster than the Mapuche power to acquire new land, so the same amount of land has to feed more and more mouths, forcing migration and assimilation into Chilean society.

The process seems irreversible. I imagine that within two generations there will be hardly anyone speaking Mapudungu as their first language. Mapuche culture is dying – now. It is a prime example of a culture being consumed by the generality of globalization. Some Chileans might say of the Mapuches: it is a good thing to be rid of the lazy thieving drunkards; it will help our economy to grow.

Those who might say this, of course, will never have spent any time with the Mapuches. These are the people that say there is no poverty in Chile, yet they could not live for two minutes in a Mapuche community and maintain this view. I saw for myself that these stereotypes are desperately false. No one works harder than the impoverished Mapuches, slogging their guts out to keep their families alive whilst being unfailingly kind, humble, courteous, generous and noble. Today, when our culture has taught us so much about controlling the material world, I find it loathsome that we do not care to save people like the Mapuches from cultural extinction.

Some say that these emotive considerations are irrelevant and back-ward looking. What matters is prosperity and economic development, and if this involves cultural unification then so be it. Having seen the penury of these Mapuches communities, I am the last to extol it. Yet their loss in material comfort does have compensations. A Mapuche *campesino*, Victorio Pranao, writes: 'This life and work in the country is synonymous with a struggling existence, but at the same time it is very entertaining and worthwhile, since you can get to know the countryside at close hand: the hills, woods, animals in the woods, all the birds ... It is wrong to undervalue the life in the country.'[2] It is surely wrong to see urban life as full of rewards and no struggle, and rural life as full of struggle and no rewards. I have lived in large cities all my life, and I know the namelessness and dull struggles which exist there, as everywhere. Nonetheless, cultural and economic evolution and revolution swarm across the planet, tossing everything aside in their wake. Any culture which tries to avoid the tune of the generalizing concepts and theories of our anti-perspectival language is swept aside. Morality, as something more personal than the objective wonders of rationality, becomes a dirty word.

Language is the very lifeblood of culture. Language stores cultural traditions, language transmits information, language defines our cul-tural sense of ourselves; we communicate far better with others without words; language is not for communication of feelings. As language generalizes, so culture must shed diversity, and unify. This generality gives us the impression of control and command, for the theories are general and seem universal, becoming more vociferous with each new development – thus disguising the deceitfulness of their insidious untruth that we can grasp the universal.

I had to spend six days in Puerto Saavedra, since finding a tailor with strong enough material for my *maleta* was difficult. I fell in with other lonely men – three truckers who were on a five-week contract here, and a local butcher of English descent called William Fuller. On our third night of drunken companionship, Fuller invited us to an *asado*.

It had been several months since I had left carnivorous Argentina, and I was unprepared for what followed. We were going to eat a goat that Fuller had bought only the day before. I didn't like the idea of killing it, but soon Fuller appeared with a sharp knife and I was required to hold the kicking legs of the goat as one of the truckers – Pedro – slit its throat and the blood gushed out. Prior to the slaughter, I had been wondering why a bowl with parsley and coriander had been prepared and placed beneath the goat's neck to receive the blood.

Things were about to be made clear to me.

'Come on, Inglés,' said Fuller, 'come and drink some *Ñachi*.'

'What's that?'

'The fresh blood.'

Pedro carried the bowl inside, where he poured blood into a glass and handed it to me.

'No, no,' I said, deciding that they were pulling leg. 'After you.'

'Go on,' said Pedro.

'No, after you.'

'OK, then,' he said, and supped the blood back. I could see the congealed lumps of jelly and hear the sporadic thuds of the goat's twitches outside, but I had no option but to drink the fresh and warm blood.

'Ha, ha!' laughed Carlos, another trucker. 'When you go home, they're all going to think that you're a vampire.'

His lips were blood-red. I drank the blood, and when I came to the jellied bits I was close to vomiting. I recovered from this obscene aperitif by drinking copious quantities of wine, hoping that I would be able to sleep it off in peace the next day. But the fates were against me.

At about eight the following morning, I heard the querulous and quavering voice of Don Beto:

'*Pero, donde estará el dueño del caballo?* But, where do you think the horse's owner has got to?'

This sounded like bad news. The owner of the horse was in bed with his hangover. Suspecting that Martillo was restive for his morning feed,

I struggled downstairs, just in time to meet Don Beto hurrying outside. He was greatly excited.

'Come on, come on,' he said. 'The horse has escaped.'

'What!'

'He's broken out of the enclosure, and he trotted off that way.'

Don Beto pointed towards the plaza.

'But how did he break out?' I asked, beside myself. We ran to the plaza, where we found Martillo standing in the middle of the tidily mown lawn, grazing happily.

'Oh dear,' said Don Beto. 'The Council aren't going to like this.'

I went to catch Martillo, but he bounded off down a side street, and the whole town watched in high amusement as Don Beto and I charged after him. It was ridiculous, and we ran to the tune of many catcalls – for this was not the first time that Martillo had broken free and found his way to the plaza.

Since the guest house had no grass, I had taken to leaving Martillo grazing in the streets by day, on a long tether. On our second afternoon there I wandered down to see how he was doing, and discovered to my horror that he was gone. When I asked one of the neighbours, she said that she'd seen two men leading him away early in the morning. I ran back to Don Beto to ask if he had been involved, but he hadn't.

I ran to the police station, all in a tizzy, and reported the theft to the police. They rang all the stations in the area, and the hunt was on. I ran back to Don Beto to tell him the news, only to find him gone.

'He's found the horse,' Carlos told me. 'He's in the plaza.'

I discovered that Martillo had just gone for a walk to find better grazing. How he had freed himself was a mystery, but I was quickly learning about his intelligence. Another time, I took him for a ride a little way back towards Valdivia, just to maintain his fitness. Martillo broke into a tremendous gallop as we went, which was wholly uncharacteristic of him. When I turned him back towards Saavedra, I had a tremendous dispute about this change of course – and I realized that Martillo had thought that he was going home: he remembered the way perfectly.

I enjoyed my break at Saavedra. This journey was becoming a haze of faces and places, all blending into one another, and it was pleasant to find some continuity amid the changes. It is difficult to convey just how many people I was obliged to meet when travelling by horse. Every day I had to find someone with a field, someone who could sell me fodder and somewhere for my tent, and these necessities threw me together with up to twenty people in a day (sometimes more), each of whom I might get to know relatively well. I must have met several thousand people in this way during the year. Everyone was fascinated by this equine journey. They often saw tourists on bicycles, but almost always they said that this was the first time they'd seen someone going by horse. Children were particularly drawn to me, and they bombarded me with questions. I remember one child in particular, who was fascinated by the fact that horses farted just like people:

'He farted, he farted!' he yelled at me. 'Is your horse OK?'

'Of course.'

'Why did he fart?'

'Don't you fart sometimes?'

He seemed happy with this explanation, and asked me why I didn't go home instead of camping in the field of a complete stranger.

'I live a long way away,' I said.

'How far? It can't be that far. Why don't you just go?'

'It is far,' I said.

'What? As far as Santa Cruz?'

Santa Cruz, the local town, was about fifty kilometres away, well over ten thousand kilometres nearer than Britain.

So in Saavedra, as I made friends, I felt content. I was spoilt by Doña Ana, the landlady, and often gossiped in the kitchen with her and her sister. She was typically resolute, having set up the business after her husband had left her for a younger woman. She invited me along with Carlos to her daughter's seventeenth birthday party, showering us with wine and *asado*. Carlos, who was always polite and respectful, was her favourite of the truckers. He was sensitive and intelligent, with wide watery eyes that opened his soul as easily as a key turns a lock.

That night, we forged the sort of close friendship which can be sealed in a night that merges with morning. We talked until five thirty, when the accumulation of *pisco* and wine was too much and sent us to sleep. We talked about the state of Chile, about the Mapuches, and about the wholesale expropriation of natural resources, most often by multinational companies, which is being exercised in Chile in the name of development by the liberalism of the free market (although how the term 'free' can properly apply to a situation where the world's resources are carved up between a tiny group of conglomerates is beyond me).

Just to set the picture: even the government recognizes that Chile lost 83 per cent of its marine biomass in the 1980s; the world's largest cellulose factory is being planned by American and Japanese companies, near Valdivia, to process the vast tracts of the Chilean forest which are progressively being cut down; I saw only two patches of native Chilean forest (such as *Alerce*, *Pehuenche* or *Araucaria*) in the 1000 kilometres I rode between Valdivia and Valparaíso – all the forests are being replaced by pine and eucalyptus plantations, which grow more rapidly and give quicker profits; the soils are universally drier, since these trees are great drinkers, meaning that their fertility for agriculture is being progressively eroded; everyone agrees that the climate is changing rapidly, that it is much drier than before. In short, the trends of Uruguay and Argentina are no different in Chile.

Carlos was a realist about these things.

'These companies are just coming in,' he said, 'to make some quick dollars. Once they've cut the trees down, do you think they're going to reinvest in the country? Do you think they're going to care about us when they've made their millions?'

'The Japanese don't do business to help out the Chileans.'

'They're clever,' he said. 'They've got their heads screwed on, all right. Like the rich everywhere. It's the same in Chile.'

'The thing about Chile,' I said, 'is that the economy is too stuck in the past. There's plenty of money in the country, it's just that the rich don't want to spread it about.'

'The thing is,' he said, 'they want to be developed without paying the price. The price is that they have to give everyone opportunities to advance, not just themselves.'

'You can't have a situation like the Mapuches,' I concurred. 'How many of those kids ever get to secondary school? One in ten? And then university ...'

'That's just impossible. That's impossible for everyone in Chile but the rich.'

It was late, and we were both feeling impotent and irate at the injustices of the world, as only drunkards who start pontificating can.

'The thing is,' I said, 'the thing about this development business is this: development always comes at the cost of the environment. Everyone talks about sustainable development, but it's rubbish. Because development means that you have to exploit your natural resources. Money means production, and production means producing things from nature. People say that economies have to grow, but if they grow they eat up more and more resources as they produce more and more. Eventually there'll be nothing left, and it will have to collapse. It's got no other way to go.'

Carlos smiled at me.

'Of course,' he said. 'That's what's going on everywhere. That's why all these foreign companies are so desperate to come here now. They want to grab what they can before it all goes bang.'

He was silent for a moment.

'It's all rubbish,' he said. 'But I don't see that anyone's going to stop it.'

II

It was, however, exceedingly interesting to observe, how much more active and cheerful all appeared than could have been expected. It was remarked with much truth, that from the destruction being universal, no one individual was more humbled than another, or could suspect his friends of coldness.

Charles Darwin on the aftermath of the tidal wave at Talcahuano

As I travelled north up the coast towards Valparaíso, I was often a guest of the Chilean police. Southern Chile was a difficult area for camping with horses, with its relatively high density of population (compared to Uruguay and Argentina) and thick expanses of forest. The Chilean police frequently have horses, and they often let me camp at their stables. I soon discovered why some Chileans say that nothing is madder than a policeman's horse.

In one station they had two colts who were greener than grass. They were kept in a yard at the back of the station, separated from the town's main street by the sergeant's new car and two wooden bars slotted horizontally between the gateposts as a barrier. After camping for the night, I led Martillo onto the main road. As I was about to climb on, the two colts burst furiously onto the street, having somehow ducked beneath the bars in a bid for freedom, bucking and neighing and kicking each other as they went, unfortunately also smiting the sergeant's car with their frolics. The assembled crowd of policemen and townspeople gawped in horrified hilarity as the horses trampled through the street's flower garden and tugged at the recently mown grass, before galloping wildly off down a side street in a flurry of kicks and bantering bites. Then, as we were all wondering what on earth to do, the horses emerged at their unbroken gallop from around a corner. They careered like wildfire towards us and bounded past the car, under the bars and into their stables, almost before we had been able to comment on their absence.

Two weeks later, I stayed in a police station on the coast. The duty officer took me to see one of their horses, a hugely fat grey gelding. When I asked the man why he was so fat, he replied that none of the officers ever went near him – they simply filled in the reports as if they had ridden him, because of the grey's fun and games. This horse, it seemed, was stubborn as a mule, and never did what any of the officers wanted when it came to catching him and putting the tack on. However, once the jockey was aboard, the gelding suddenly calmed, becoming the most responsive of horses, trotting alert with his ears pricked, every inch the picture of a noble and intelligent animal. On reaching the beach, though, the gelding would show his true colours; the obedience had been a sham; for now, without warning, and regardless of whipping and rein-tugging, he would turn and gallop irrepressibly towards the sea, cantering far out into the waves and soaking his jockey from head to toe. Apparently, he did this every time someone climbed aboard – so now they just left him to grow fat on his oats.

Towards the end of my time in Chile I stayed at a rodeo club which was also home to Chile's school of border guards. I watched them learning how to ride in the arena. The lieutenant was a tough old sod who barked the way lieutenants are supposed to bark:

'Backs straight. STRAIGHT, Ramírez, not hunched! You look like an old crony!'

Laughter.

'Close the gap, Soto. CLOSE THE GAP! Are you deaf, Soto?'

Poor Soto was swearing like a compulsive gambler at his horse, but he was on a hopeless case here. The horses were enjoying prancing around with the novices, as clever horses do. They paid not a blind bit of attention to their jockeys.

'OK,' the lieutenant growled, 'now let's try a controlled gallop.'

This was always likely to be a mistake. Only the lead rider, who seemed alone in knowing his bridle from his stirrup, was able to carry on. Everywhere else lay in chaos. Half the horses careered wildly around the arena, while the others trotted in infuriating circles or came to a standstill. Into their midst came two mules, bolting and spreading their cargo of firewood haphazardly over the sand. The lieutenant was beside himself:

'A controlled gallop, I said,' he yelled. 'González, go clockwise. CLOCKWISE.'

'He doesn't want to, *mi teniente*,' trilled out a desperate González.

'Right, you're on stable duty for a week. Where did those bloody mules come from? Someone get them out of here! Cárdenas, why do you walk when I tell you to gallop and gallop when I tell you to walk...'

After an hour, their misery over, the men unsaddled. I stood apart, watching. One grey horse was trying to kick and bite the cowering cadet who wanted to wash him down. He looked desperately towards me.

'Excuse me, *Señor*,' he begged. 'The horse is a little wild. Could you help me?'

I looked at the huge horse, and saw two scornful eyes berating me for even thinking that I might wash him down. He was the complete opposite of my own favourite grey horse, Martillo, whose affability and tameness had made the journey much easier for me. Thinking over all I had learnt about horses in the year, I sympathized with the cadet.

Arriving at Talcahuano from Valdivia, Darwin found destruction everywhere: 'The whole coast being strewed over with timber and furniture as if a thousand ships had been wrecked. Besides chairs, tables, bookshelves &c., in great numbers, there were several roofs of cottages, which had been transported almost whole.' Compounding the earthquake, a tidal wave had destroyed virtually everything that had survived the tremor. The mayor of Quiriquina told Darwin of the severity of the quake in this region (which was nearer its epicentre than Valdivia): 'the first notice he received of it, was finding both the horse he rode and himself, rolling together on the ground. Rising up, he was again thrown down. He also told me that some cows which were standing on the steep side of the island were rolled into the sea.'

Wherever he walked Darwin discovered evidence for changes in the earth's geology. An islet in the harbour had developed scores of cracks nearly a metre wide; rocks were pulverized into tiny fragments; and – most significantly of all – the main beach at Concepción, and the islets of Santa María and Quiriquina, were raised about eight feet above their previous level. This last discovery was communicated to Charles Lyell, who was immensely pleased at this confirmation of recent land elevations. The earthquake, and its aftermath, catapulted Darwin towards a definitively Lyellian stance. Here was the evidence, before his eyes, that the composition of the land changed with time and with natural – not supernatural – forces. Wandering amid the ruined towns, he concluded that they 'presented the most awful yet interesting spectacle I ever beheld'.

In Concepción, the cathedral's façade had been swept aside, and Darwin wrote that 'It is quite impossible to convey the mingled feelings with which one beholds this spectacle. – Several officers visited it before me; but their strongest language failed to communicate a just idea of the desolation. – It is a bitter & humiliating thing to see works which have cost so much time & labour overthrown in one minute.' This was a quintessential reminder of human and geographical frailty. In Chile, this is something that is lived with every day. Serious earthquakes hit the country about once every ten years, and there are strong tremors every month or so. Many cities have been flattened by earthquakes; Valparaíso, Talca, Concepción and Chillán have all suffered this fate.

I remember one tremor clearly. I was outside, about to saddle up Martillo, when I noticed that the fence posts appeared to be shaking. Then I saw the infinite grains of sand on the corrugated iron roof of his stables falling to earth, spinning like a million tiny seeds as they went, and felt the ground shuddering beneath me, so that I could indeed imagine that the earth was nothing but a lattice of breakable dust which the slightest dislocation might cleave apart, leaving nothing but planetary fires.

It is no surprise that living amid earthquakes, volcanoes and such like, in a land where flash floods and landslides are also relatively commonplace, encourages a certain fatalism in Chileans. Perhaps this explains the resignation which Darwin remarked upon at Concepción, for Chileans live in the awareness that, sooner or later, a natural disaster is likely to hit them.

It took me ten days to ride from Puerto Saavedra to Concepción. Every day was an endless string of experience, bewitching my eyes then and even my memory now with the fullness of the journey. I remember the family stopping me and offering me *chicha* by the roadside; the drunk

Mapuche selling me oats, taking me through the fields to his home, sitting me around the fire with his family and grandmother, darkened by the dyeing hues of dusk; the schoolteacher inviting me to speak to the primary school about my journey; the farmer offering to buy Martillo, so much did he admire my horse; chatting to groups of neighbours about the way ahead; caught out in the winter rains, soaking myself silly, saved from a cold by a policeman's fire.

I feel content when these memories touch me, thinking of the continuity of experience which distinguishes the perceiver from what is perceived. The face of the farrier who shod Martillo swims past, laughing with his friends; the man was so drunk that, when trying to lift Martillo's hind leg, he several times pulled himself off his feet. I can now smell the sickening sweetness of the cellulose factory near Concepción, and see its scattered diffusion of smoke clouding the fields. Then, in the languorous evenings, I allow myself to watch the changing colours of the days; the mist rising with the drifting sheets of rain; the damp grass glittering in the sunshine; the scarlet buttering of the sunset's knife over the water, where the fishermen cast their nets far across the ocean, and sit, watching them bob out of sight along with all the melodies of the past, diminishing along with the clarity of their dreams. Then, inevitably, the countryside falls away, and so too, along with the rains and the mist and the wonder, do my memories.

Now I was nearing the industrial centres around Concepción, aware that I had another battle in store. In fact, I struggle to think how my arrival in Concepción could have been more different to Darwin's. I had followed the *Beagle* from Valdivia along the coast for three weeks, and Martillo and I were by now looking forward to a well-deserved rest. However, first of all there was the matter of a few flyovers and a dual carriageway to negotiate.

For nearly sixty kilometres south from Concepción the coast is clogged by industries and mines – this is one of the most industrialized areas of Chile outside Santiago. It is also one of the most dangerous. The coal mining town of Lota is known as the poorest city in Chile, and its neighbour – Coronel – is little better off. Both were bedrocks of support for Allende's Popular Unity government. The mines in Lota – perilous caverns several kilometres out to sea – had been closed down for good only two weeks before I rode past, after functioning for 150 years. The area was in turmoil, beset with violent protests. These people were paid a pittance, scrabbling the poor-quality coal away from beneath the ocean and dying prematurely because of the appalling working conditions. However, most of the miners had been born in Lota, and they were trained to do nothing else; the mine's closure held a miserable destiny for these families.

For several days before I reached the area, people had warned me to be careful around Lota. On the road between here and Concepción, groups known as the *perrerros* lie in wait. The *perrerros* wait for cargo trucks on the area's steep hills, and when the trucks pass they clamber on to divest them of as much of their loads as possible. I was told that they were bound to hassle me, and, sure enough, as I rode down the wide sweep of the road, past the misery of Lota, a group called out to me, demanding cigarettes and money. They were all wiry men with hungry faces. There were several of them, lining themselves along the road to be as threatening as possible.

This was to be the longest day's riding which Martillo and I did together, fifty-five kilometres past all the trouble-spots into the heart of Concepción. We had already been riding for three hours, and I did not want to try and out-gallop these men on the hard road. So I had bought a packet of cigarettes to throw the *perrerros* as I passed.

'Hey, *gringo*,' one of them yelled. 'Is that all? One packet isn't enough.'

They came after me down the road, and I spurred Martillo into a trot.

'¡Hey, *gringo*, concha de tu madre!'

I heard something whistle past me and clatter into the road: they were throwing stones. I had been warned that this happened, but I hadn't believed it until now. I couldn't worry any more about Martillo on the hard road, since he was in more danger from them if we stayed still, so I spurred him into a fast trot for several minutes until they were safely behind me. This was the only time all year that I felt physically threatened by people.

However, this was only the beginning of the fun and games. There were still another five hours of riding until I reached Concepción, and the road now became a dual carriageway. Martillo seemed completely unperturbed. Even when we had to wait in line with cars for the traffic lights, he didn't budge. Juggernauts came whistling within inches of us, but I just had to trust in my fate. I could not worry, since this situation was too ludicrous to be worrisome. We had to swing over a narrow flyover, cross the longest bridge in South America (over the Bío-Bío River) and pass two more flyovers, all the while heading along the inside lane of the dual carriageway.

With any other horse, I would probably not have made it, but Martillo was so wonderfully tame and trusting that we passed through the troubles unscathed. The police at the small town of Laraquete had telephoned ahead to the Mounted Police Division at Concepción, and they were expecting me when I arrived at dusk. I unsaddled, and fed Martillo plenty of food to make up for the hard and terrifying day's work. We had completed what proved to be the most difficult day's riding I would have all year. When I looked back at everything that we had passed, the day seemed to expand into a week; then it retracted, and condensed itself into a pinprick of fear at the bottom of my memory.

I had been riding continually for ten days, all day every day. As the autumn glided towards winter, the days shortened inexorably. Even when I woke at first light, I would not be away before eight thirty in the morning; and since night fell by six, I had to start looking for a place to sleep by four thirty. I would ride without stopping, almost every day, so that we did not have to risk the dangers of travelling by night. I had no watch, nor the money to buy one – the sun was my guide. Since I was following the Pacific, I could watch the star's graceful fall to the darkness of its sleep in the waves. I would follow it, hiding ethereally behind the clouds, or burning, or giggling noiselessly and flirtatiously as it was swept from sight by a storm – but always there, always speaking to me and telling me when to stop. The journey into Concepción had been the most stressful of all, since I had had to ride quickly all day, rising as early as possible, to ensure that I arrived before dark. This dual carriageway was no place to be at night. The police lieutenant told me that I could stay awhile, so I rested for the weekend and explored the area.

First, I went to Concepción: as ordered and banal a place as I had seen for many months, where the only interest of the day was the torrential downpour which had everyone groaning at the onset of winter. There was no residue of the fascination which Darwin found in the aftermath of the 1835 natural catastrophes. So in the afternoon,

I went to Talcahuano. I did not ride there, unlike Darwin – I had had enough of these dual carriageways. This is now one of the most polluted ports in the world, a green slush of bacteria in the sea mingling with the appalling stench of industrial waste. The port is divided into three: the naval warships, out of bounds for ordinary visitors; the merchant navy, next in size and importance; and the tiny motorized dugouts, piled high with crates of shellfish dredged up from the sea, sweeping up to the disorganized crowds on the quay. I joined the crowds, fascinated by the pot-pourri. I had never seen such a collection of shellfish: as well as mussels, sea urchins, king crabs, shrimps and abalones, there were several huge shells that I did not know. The fishermen, tired after their long and dangerous days at sea, argued with the buyers on the dock, who bought the crates for a song, sometimes a couple of dollars for fifty or sixty shellfish. The buyers were all fat and arrogant, while the fishermen were leaner and lither, looking likely to pack a punch in a knife fight; the two proving the eternal law that he who labours hardest is poorest. The throng watched disinterestedly: there were arguments; porters staggering past, teetering on the water's edge beneath the weight of a massive crate or three; old sea dogs snaffling a mollusc from a passing crate and swallowing it raw and whole; bleary eyes, sunken into the stubble-soaked faces of the fishermen; beggars, dwarfs and other members of the world's dispossessed laughing and chattering on the dock, hearing the recurrent rhapsody of the port jar their ears once again. I saw no thieves, but I sensed the brinkmanship, along with the feeling that the order could, in a glimmering second, spill over into chaos, stabbings, robbery, or possibly even a tidal wave, sweeping aside the palisades of poverty's capital punishment in a bloody deluge.

And the thieves and scavengers tumbling through the disorderly wake might indeed, as Darwin noted after the *maremoto*, have cried '*Misericordia!*', wondering at the wretchedness of the world.

The Mounted Police radioed ahead to several police stations further north, telling them that a mad Englishman would shortly be arriving on horseback. I carried with me a printed sheet from the lieutenant, which each duty officer filled in as I passed, lending my journey some official backing.

In rural Chile the *carabinero's* job is social as much as anything, for crime is minimal. I remember one station where there were five *carabineros* in charge of a hamlet with 300 inhabitants and two shops – the commander told me that they hadn't had anyone in their cell for over a year. The *carabineros* are sent from all over the country, for years at a time, to maintain order and health in the small communities. They keep horses to check up on all the small tracks and isolated settlements in their catchment, riding out in the wintry wet, often covering seventy kilometres or more in a day, returning to their station late at night.

In rural areas, *carabineros* are widely respected. Two days' ride from Concepción, I reached the village of Vegas de Itata. I was hoping to find a way to cross the Río Itata, but the river had swollen with the rains, and it was impassable at this peak flow. I had planned to tie Martillo to the back of a fishing boat, and find someone to paddle us across the river, but the *carabineros* told me that this would only be possible if the river's flow abated. I tied Martillo on his long tether in a grassy field, but as one of the officers was taking me on a drive we noticed that he had freed himself. The officer stopped his car next to a group of children waiting for the school bus. He called out to them by name, and then pointed to Martillo.

'Kids, will one of you tie up that horse. Or all of you go, if you want,' he added, noticing that they were all gawping at me. They ran off to do his bidding, as if he were a benign uncle.

I waited until morning, but the river was still flowing widely and rapidly, just like the day before. I changed my plans, and rode thirty kilometres inland to the bridge at Coelemu, crossed back to the other side of the Itata, and then continued northwards. North of the Bío-Bío, I was firmly leaving the Mapuche lands behind me. Instead of drinking themselves silly with *chicha*, the men drank red wine. Mexican *ranchero* music coughed its sadness over the fields. The land was better here, the horses sleeker and fitter, used instead of oxen by the farmers to plough their fields. As well as apple trees, there were peaches, pears, plums and cherries, all bristling in the orchards. One woman told me that, fifty years ago, you used to be able to buy someone's fruit tree for a day and eat all you could from it. This symbolizes the fertility of the soil in this part of Chile, for these trees burst with fruit, and I have several times seen what I judged to be many thousands of plums on a single tree.

I was following tracks along the beach, towards the towns of Cobquecura, Chanco and Constitución. In some areas, the road was being 'improved'. In practice, this meant that the routes were less passable for horses than before, since the earth was savaged by bulldozers, and the constant mechanic growls and shrill bleeps from reversing vehicles could frighten even Martillo. In one part of the 'new road', I came to a place where the route came to an abrupt end, in the shape of a ravine and a bog. I coaxed Martillo through the obstacles, and managed to disassemble enough of the fence on the far side to lead him through, only to discover that the route terminated even more finally a few hundred metres further on in an earthen cliff. I had to lead Martillo, who was most reluctant, through a eucalyptus plantation, and several patches of marsh which had us both floundering, before we broke out onto an alternative route.

Sometimes I rode in the wet, and felt miserable. I had to press on, with my time and money running low, since the longer I waited, the worse the rain and the winter might prove to be. When it was at its worst, the water would fall in straight seams, without a breath of wind to blow it one way or another. The rain dripped from the pine needles, dimpling the puddles and cascading in impromptu gutters along the track, washing the mud away from the banks and browning the rivers. When it rained like this, straight and strong, it was possible to believe that it would rain always, for, as in Chiloé, this land suited rain. At times I passed small hamlets, where young boys hammered metal into shape, and chickens clucked irrepressibly as they plucked maize from the mud – otherwise, I rode with my thoughts and the sea. Water had become the constant companion of my journey, and I did not feel alone. I could always hear the rush of the waves, or the patter of the rain.

I was no longer pained by my loneliness in the countryside. It was only when I reached urban areas that my solitude hurt me. Where there were crowds of people I felt alone, but where the population was smaller I felt calmer and more in contact with others. When I reached a place like Concepción, I would feel bored to tears. I wandered cities alone, eating and drinking alone, confronted everywhere by people yet knowing none of them, and able to know none. But in rural areas people stopped to talk to me, I hailed them and was hailed back, and when not passing the time with a new friend I was perfectly happy; exhausted by a day's ride and completely without comforts, sleeping in barns, among rats, in bales of straw, yet nonetheless radiantly happy at the calm here, at the humanity and companionship against all odds.

One Sunday, I reached Chanco. As I rode through the town, I was the cause of an unfortunate accident. A car swept past, and its driver was so amazed to see someone travelling by horse that he turned his head round 180 degrees to stare. I was used to this response by now, which was fairly standard. Predictably, the car in front of my new fan at this moment pulled unannounced to a standstill, with the result that the careless voyeur drove straight into its rear fender at a good speed. There was a crash and a shout, followed by much hilarity from the assembled *guasos* who happened to have taken a break from their drinking. Discretion being the better part of valour, I hurried myself away from the mess as quickly as possible.

By now, I was only two days from the Río Maule at Constitución, the river which marks the beginning of Chile's heartland. I began to notice changes in the land's composition. The spread of farms and wild beaches turned into endless plantations. There were pines and eucalyptus everywhere. The small *parcelas* [plots of land] had been sold for agroforestry twenty or thirty years ago, by *campesinos* who had been bowled over by an offer of so much money outright for their little patches of earth. They had migrated to the cities, to the mindless industrial poverty which is so much more soulless than the rural way of life, and had left the land to parch itself to a thirsty death. In the forty kilometres south of the Maule, I came across only one farm, owned by a bitter old man who fulminated against the changes. He was reluctant to let me stay, but the skies were skirmishing with the beginnings of a storm, so, after several minutes of nervous pleading on my part, I was allowed to sleep in the filth and straw in the barn. He invited me in for some bread and coffee.

'I know what you're going through,' he said. 'I've been out wandering in my time as well. I've worked in the mines in the Atacama. In Chuquicamata, even in Potosí. Tell me, young man – for I believe that honesty is the most important thing in life – why are you doing this?'

I talked about Darwin, and then admitted that I planned to write a book. This often encouraged garrulousness, and the old man was no different: he railed against the changes in the country, against modernization, spitting ire for half an hour or more. Before, he said, a *fundo* would have had twenty workers, whereas these plantations had only one guard. And now, of course, the harvests were deteriorating every year, as the pines drained the water from the earth and the crops were left to dry out along with the soil, contemplating those cracks that quickly developed in the earth, and the fires puffing beneath them.

'We used to grow hay,' he said, 'before all this cellulose rubbish. Now we have to get it from Rancagua. People say that cellulose brings jobs, but that's rubbish. It takes work away. Everyone goes to the cities. No one cultivates a thing. *Then* people complain that there's no food! No wonder everything's expensive, these days.'

He chuckled bitterly to himself, and the next day sent me out into the teeth of the storm.

'I'd like to let you stay on in the barn,' he said, 'but I'm worried that your horse will fight with my animals. Go on – it's only half an hour to Constitución.'

More than two hours later, I rode into the town, soaked from head to toe, thinking of nothing more but trying to find my first bed for several days; ruing my dampening experience at the hands of the old man's 'honesty'.

III

I must express my admiration at the natural politeness of almost every Chileno. In this instance, the contrast with the same class of men in most other countries is strongly marked.

Charles Darwin

Darwin made two important horseback excursions from Valparaíso. The first took him north to San Felipe and Los Andes via the valley of the Río Aconcagua, thence to Santiago past the gold mines at Yaquil. From Santiago he completed the circular route of his journey, travelling south to Cauquenes, and then following the Río Tingiririca to the coast at Navidad before returning to Valparaíso. The second journey took him over the *cordillera* via the Portillo pass, to the city of Mendoza, before he returned to Santiago via the Uspallata pass.

I had good reasons to be pessimistic about my chances of following either route. Darwin's rides through Chile's Central Valley have been rendered precarious – to say the least – by industrialization. His direct north–south route between San Felipe and Cauquenes via Santiago has transformed itself into the Pan-American Highway, while the valley of the Río Tingiririca has been flooded by a massive hydroelectric project at Rapel, and the whole valley is now a lake. Meanwhile, not only was it winter, so that the passes into Argentina were prone to being cut off by snow, but my previous experiences had shown me that horses and borders were unhappy bedfellows.

Crossing the Río Maule, I was now within a few days' ride of the Tingiririca. I had no intention of following Darwin along the Pan-American Highway, for that would have been utter suicide. I decided to make for the Tingiririca, and shadow its sides until I reached the coast. From Valparaíso I would head for the Río Aconcagua, and see if I couldn't make for Mendoza, *si Dios quiere* ('if God wills it' – a common phrase in Chile).

Persistent rainfall had swollen the Maule to such a degree that the ferries in Constitución weren't crossing. I had to make a detour to an old railway bridge across the river. It was a gorgeous day, swirling wisps of mist hung over the great brown river, shielding it from the growing golden light. The river itself was thick and glutinous with mud, and the early hour partially shaded the higher slopes of the valley from the dawn firing at the hilltops. It was on days like this that the peace of riding could not be tainted. Sometimes, of course, I came across problems – rivers to negotiate, tracks which vanished, the stone-throwing *perrerros* – but most of the time, by far, was spent calmly. I have tried not to convey the image that every day was filled with tremendous dangers, for that would be a lie. In fact, so peaceful and fascinating was this life that I became increasingly unsure how I was going to relinquish it.

North from Constitución, I reached the town of Putú, where I met Ignacio, a boyish *carabinero*. He was bored, and happy to see me.

'There's nothing to do,' he said. 'Look at the log!'

I leafed through the weighty book for that day. The first entry reported that the sergeant had gone to make a tour of duty on his motorbike; the second that he had returned *sin novedad* (nothing to report); the third that he had gone to make another tour of duty; the fourth – and this was the longest entry by far – that I had arrived on horse; but fifthly, that I had alas also arrived *sin novedad*. Later in the afternoon, Ignacio went to make a tour of duty, but he returned – sixthly – *sin novedad*.

So, with nothing to do, and the afternoon and evening before us, we chatted:

'I was born in Valparaíso, but when I was seven my parents abandoned me, and my grandmother brought me up ... Why?, why do you think they would have done that? ... I asked my grandmother, and she said that, when I was born, a great flock of birds had whistled past the window ... a sure sign that the witches put a spell on me...'

'I wonder if they didn't put a spell on my horse in Chiloé, as well. I have come almost to believe in witches. Do you believe in witches?'

'I was brought up because of witchcraft,' he said, 'because of my parents' foolishness in this matter. They could have gone to the *machi*, they could have put a counter-charm on the bad witch, but they didn't bother. They thought it was nonsense, that it made no rational sense, and yet still they *should* have gone, I would have gone if it had been my child...'

'Still, it's often like that,' I said, trying to sympathize. 'We are told so many lies and untruths that we cannot distinguish one opinion from another.'

'It's all lies, anyone who tells you they know the truth is a liar, because you can't *know* anything, not with your stupid little brain. Only with the witches, only when we embrace the irrational is there truth, in opposites...'

Everything, everything is twin; good and bad; life and death; mountains and valleys; black and white; we can only see things in terms of opposites.

'You see,' said Ignacio, '*amigo*, our prejudice, our eyes, our reality, whatever we really know, we have to knock it aside before we can see the truth. The *machis* know that, but my parents forgot. I think that my parents must have felt bad about the witches. But my grandmother did a good job for me at least, she always made sure that I ate, that I was as happy as possible.'

After we had talked for some time, we lapsed into silence. Nothing happened in the duty room, nothing except for the creeping advance of darkness over the town, lancing through the windows like time through a black hole. Ignacio made us cups of tea, and, after we had drunk them, time after time, I went and rinsed them out in the sink. The water spurted and coughed from the pipes, as if it was ill. After an hour of desultory silence, Ignacio spoke again.

'Perhaps I am scared by myself, *amigo*. I want to find myself a woman, because I want to have children. I'm quite happy to live in a place like this, with not much happening, so long as my children are happy.'

'So long as you are content, it doesn't matter much where you are.'

'Yes,' he agreed, 'although it's best not to remember the past. You can't do anything except cry when you remember what you don't have. I cry, often. That was why I began to write poetry.'

His eyes welled up with sadness, flickering transiently in the room like the flame burning on the stunted wick of the night.

'Even poetry has its problems,' I said. 'Nature gives us beauty, and we replace it with metaphors.'

*

I rode on into the Chile which Darwin would have known. Reading his account of this journey is enough to show up the differences between Chile and Argentina. Although he found the Chilenos agreeable, he found landowners less cordial than their counterparts in Argentina: 'A traveller does not here meet that unbounded hospitality which refuses all payment, but yet is so kindly offered that no scruples can be raised in accepting it. Almost every house in Chile will receive you for the night, but a trifle is expected to be given in the morning; even a rich man will accept two or three shillings.' Thus it was that Darwin, instead of staying at *postas* or with *estancieros* as he had done in Uruguay and Argentina, often used to hire a field and camp with his horses and guide, the *guaso* Mariano González.* Darwin writes of the rustic Chilean countryside in ways which make me visualize how little some parts of the country can have changed: he talks of the 'cottages ... surrounded by vines, and by orchards of apple, nectarine, and peach trees'; of the country being 'exceedingly pleasant: just such as poets would call pastoral; green open lawns, separated by small valleys and rivulets'. However, although he was an admirer of the beautiful Chilean countryside, he did not esteem the *guasos* as highly as the *gauchos*: 'The Guasos of Chile, who correspond to the Gauchos of the Pampas, are, however, a very different set of beings. Chile is the more civilised of the two countries, and the inhabitants, in consequence, have lost much individual character ... the chief pride of the Guaso lies in his spurs; which are absurdly large.'

As I rode through central Chile, I came to a series of old towns which still maintain the colonial style of architecture. The houses were aesthetically stunning. Their whitewashed walls, bleached and burnished by the sun, gave out into grey-tiled roofs sloping symmetrically to an apex from all sides, and sturdy pillars propped up the eaves over cobbled patios. Some of these settlements were small villages, where the workers all belonged to one immense *fundo*. In these areas, I could see the customs of ages at work. It was generally the poorer Chileans who were most open and friendly. The *campesinos*

---

* González accompanied Darwin through all his rides in Chile, and Darwin was saddened to have to say goodbye to him, finally, in Copiapó.

treated me tremendously well, but only twice was I invited to spend any time with wealthier men.

In Darwin's time, the feudal *inquilino* system was in operation: 'the labouring agriculturists ... live almost exclusively on beans. This poverty must be chiefly owing to the feudal-like system on which the land is tilled: the landowner gives a small plot of ground to the labourer, for building on and cultivating, and in return has his services (or those of a proxy) for every day of his life, without wages.' The *inquilino* system was finally dismantled by President Eduardo Frei Montalva in the 1960s, and each labourer was given his own plot of land by the government. But this process created its own problems, for the *inquilinos*, although they now had land, had no tools and no training with which to make their land viable. I was told by those who had been there at the time that the money had gone within a few years, and people had been forced to sell their *parcelas* and migrate to the cities. The development had merely led to their exchanging one sort of poverty for another, and was the precursor to the mushrooming shanty-towns which now surround Santiago on all sides.

Guasos and *inquilinos* are different. The *guaso* works exclusively with animals, like the Argentine *gaucho*, whereas the *inquilino* works with agriculture. Darwin's indifference to the *guasos* is not contradictory to his applause of Chilean politeness, since by far the majority of Chileans work in agriculture and not with animals. Often, *guasos* and *inquilinos* live together on the same farm; this was the case of the next place I reached after Putú.

Ignacio had told me that I could cross the Río Malaguito by a new bridge near its estuary, meaning that I would be able to cut along the coast. However, there was no bridge, so I had to follow the river twenty kilometres inland. As I rode, Martillo dropped one of his shoes, so I had to dismount and lead him to the nearest town, to avoid damaging his feet. Martillo became recalcitrant – he loathed being led – so I spent the afternoon heaving and cajoling him along. Our progress was sluggish, to say the least. Night hurried on rapidly and I realized that I wouldn't reach the town before dark, so I called in at the first large *fundo* that I saw. I led Martillo in, and met the caretaker, a descendant of the *inquilinos*, a stout old man whose voice seemed to sing even when its intonation was flat; silent melodies falling with his lyrics and calling along with the birdsong across dusk. He found the idea of this journey immensely funny:

'Valdivia,' he kept saying to himself. 'You've come from Valdivia?'

I never told people how far I had really come, because I feared that I wouldn't be taken seriously.

We talked in the gathering gloom. The farmyard was saturated with mud, and I squelched here and there as I unsaddled. I was unhurried. The man had told me that I could stay, even that there was a room where I could throw down my sleeping bags on the floor, sleeping on my saddlecloths and sheepskin as I always did. He shuffled over towards the small mud house where he lived with his wife and two daughters, all sleeping in the same room.

'Come over, after you've talked with the *guaso*,' he said.

The *guaso* had just finished for the day. He was riding an excitable rodeo horse into the yard as the other man spoke. The *guaso* had huge spurs, which seemed to spin and twirl of their own irrepressible accord as he rode. He was tall and thin, with a bare little moustache and a talent for laughing at everything. When I discussed the way I should take the next day, he launched into a long explanation of the forests, the turns in the track, and so on.

'I've got a map, we can look at that,' I said.

'Oh no, don't worry,' he laughed. 'I won't understand the map.'

His spurs were as Darwin described, and it is still true that, all over Chile, spurs are much more an integral part of horsemanship than they are in the Pampas. But this man was, nonetheless, a very warm person, not the 'vulgar, ordinary fellow' described by Darwin. He felt sorry for me, alone when he was going back to spend the evening with his family, alone and wistful as the first and last sparkle of the stars at dusk and dawn. He would have invited me back, he said, if the other man hadn't beaten him to it.

'But don't worry,' he said. 'I'll shoe your horse for you in the morning.'

The other man's house was desperately poor. The floor was earthen, and there was a fuzzy black and white television next to the door. The walls were bare as the earth that held them together. A splayed jet of steam spread from the Aga, and the man's wife was throwing some logs into the stove as I entered. She was barefoot. She moved away to wash her feet in an old tin bowl, peeling potatoes as her leathery feet, callused and wrinkled and heavy like the hands of a lumberjack, soaked their grime away.

We all wanted to talk, to soften the growling loneliness of winter to a whisper. Yet there was little to talk about. I asked the man about the state of farming in Chile, and he laughed it off as terrible: the values of livestock were plummeting with the Mercosur, the wood industry was taking over all the hills, even the values of the crops were diminishing. For five years, they had been stuck in the worst drought that anyone could remember.

We were eating what is known as *once* (Chilean high tea). His wife said nothing, but she kept on proffering me things to eat: milky coffee (which is Chile's equivalent to *mate* as the choice drink offered to a guest), bread and *dulce de leche*, scrambled eggs. This was typical of *onces* that I was offered in many parts of rural Chile. There was never any deleterious insistence on a conversation. We could be quiet if we wanted; eat our bread, drink our sweet coffee, slurping and chewing and sharing nonetheless; sharing furthermore the sallow candlelight, which breathed along with the changing currents of air laughing their way around the room.

On my journey, I was hailed and fed by so many different people: the owner of a sausage factory; a lumberjack whose pride and joy was his Italian air rifle; a hotelier who refused to charge me because I was out of season and no one would come instead of me. A thousand faces speak unheard to my memory, drowned out by more recent music, and they are so numerous that they are lost in the impossibility of untangling the past.

These parts of Chile are heartrendingly beautiful. Several times, I rode along tracks which climbed high up into the coastal *cordillera*, until from the same road you could hear the roar of the Pacific, and at the same time, looking distantly to the east, pick out the snowy peaks of the Andes. The folds of earth in between would fall into purple haze, a dark cloak to disguise the forests and fields from the majesty of the mountains. Where the mountains gave way to valleys, they were verdant. But mostly, the land was a giant furrowed knot, rising, crumpling, bunching, but never uniform. The tracks I followed would stick to the ridges, the folds, and somehow find their way to valley floors hidden from the haziness which hangs indistinctly above them.

*

Chile had been plagued by a severe drought for four years before my arrival, suffering as much as its Trans-Andean neighbours. On the fringes of the Atacama desert, it had not rained for seven years. In the transitional zone between the Atacama desert and the fertile Central Valley, many of the reservoirs were almost dry. In much of the country, councils were having to arrange emergency water supplies for outlying communities. As in Uruguay and Argentina, everyone I met told me how drastic the situation had become. Even in Punta Arenas and Chiloé, there had been dark mutterings that things were not right, that men were being punished by God for their greed; further north, as the land became drier still, the effects on people had been yet more pernicious. The whole country had been praying for rain – being British, I brought it with me.

Nearing Rapel, I reached the small town of Litueche. The police directed me to the vicarage, whose priest – Cristián – had a small plot of land at the back where Martillo could graze freely. It was pouring with rain as I arrived.

'Of course, *hombre*,' Cristián said, when I explained myself.

'Could I stay in one of the barns?'

'Don't be an idiot,' he laughed. 'You're going to stay with me. There's plenty of room inside.'

The vicarage was a bungalow, contorted into several disparate L-shapes looking out over the grey winter's day. Cristián lived with some of his extended family, and a friend from Litueche's school called – for some unfathomable reason – Berlin. We went inside, and Cristián sat me down in the kitchen.

'So,' he laughed – his eyes twinkling, as they often did – 'you're following the heretic, Darwin!'

But this wasn't meant as a challenge; only as a joke.

'I didn't know that Darwin came past here,' said Berlin.

'Yes, right this way,' said Cristián. 'He went to one of the forests near Navidad. What did he say about it, then?' he asked me.

'He was pretty ill when he came past. He caught a fever in Valparaíso and was in bed for a month.'

'You see,' said Cristián, 'only spiritual unease could be the cause of that. Darwin was an ill man all his life, isn't that right?'

'Yes. A lot of people think he caught Chagas disease* when he crossed the *cordillera* to Mendoza.'

'Nonsense,' said Cristián. 'If you catch Chagas, you die of it. But Darwin lived on another fifty years! It was his soul that was ill.'

He looked at me triumphantly, as if he had proved that Darwin was wrong. The rain was thudding down harder and harder, and its roar silenced us for a while. We were mesmerized by its lashing against the windows, by its incessant chaotic fury.

'We've needed rain for so long,' said Raúl, Cristián's uncle. 'And now it rains like this. This won't be any good. It'll wash off the soil.'

'It's going to rain a lot this year,' said Cristián, 'because of *El Niño*.'

'We need rain, we certainly need it,' said Raúl. 'But I tell you, this isn't going to be any use, not this rain.'

I had been praying for rain also. The drought in the north was so serious that continuing by horse had looked extremely problematic. But now that it was raining, the wells would fill, and there would be more forage.

It rained without respite for four days, and Chile switched from water shortage to water surplus in a week. This was the beginning of the catastrophic *El Niño* of 1997 and 1998. The storm was so devastating that in Copiapó it rained more in the space of ten days than it had done in the preceding thirty years. Scores of people died; the roads were washed away in some parts; the Rapel reservoir, fifteen kilometres from Litueche, nearly flooded itself completely, coming within metres of topping the bridge and washing it away. As I listened to the reports from around the country, it dawned on me that all the places through which I was planning to ride were the worst hit of all: the Aconcagua Valley and the regions around Limache and La Calera – north of Valparaíso – were disaster areas; the valley of La Ligua had flooded completely, and the roads north from Cabildo were washed away. Tragically, the driest areas had been the worst affected: the drought of several years in the north had made the soil so crusty that the sudden storms had simply swept it away, and huge landslides had made tens of thousands of people homeless.

---

* Chagas is a disease caused by the excrement of the vinchuga bugs of rural South America, for which there is no cure.

At first, I greeted the rain happily, since it should have made the journey easier. But as the scale of the disaster became more and more apparent, I realized that the rain was in fact making it far harder for me. Reports said that many of the forage stores for the winter had been washed out, and that farmers were relying on emergency rations supplied by the government.

'Poor old *gringo*,' said Cristián. 'You were praying for rain, but now it's rained too much.'

I spent several days in the vicarage. We played cards, and told each other jokes. Berlin turned out to be a great one for riddles and practical jokes, and I was a great one for falling for them.

'How do you draw a square with three lines?' he asked me, and I spent five minutes racking my brain, Berlin barely being capable of suppressing his mirth. Then he showed me: drawing a square, with three little lines squiggled inside it.

Cristián usually went around the remote parts of his parish during the week, giving services in the isolated communities, but now the roads were impassable so he stayed in the vicarage all day. It was impossible not to discuss the weather. Notwithstanding the storm, it was drier, everyone admitted that – there had been dry periods before, but they had never lasted so long. Cristián did not try to seek the explanation for this in biblical predictions of the Apocalypse, unlike many religious people in Chile. He tried to be rational, even though sometimes it was difficult.

'Every year,' he said, 'the farmers find it harder.'

'When I was growing up,' said Raúl, 'we used to harvest a hundred bushels of wheat per hectare, without fertilizer. Now they get forty bushels, if they're lucky, even with all this chemical nonsense they stuff the earth full of.'

'It's the plantations,' said Cristián. 'They make everything so dry.'

'We used to plant chickpeas here, but the soil's too dry. Crops fail all the time. That's why they're turning to pine trees. But it just makes it worse. Even drier.'

'But it's raining now,' I said.

'It always used to rain like this in wintertime!' said Raúl. 'The difference now is that people aren't used to it. They don't know this sort of rain, and when it comes they get frightened by it. There never used to be radio and television showing how terrible things were, people just got on with it.'

'Still,' I said, trying to be optimistic, 'it means that the drought's over.'

'No it doesn't,' said Raúl. 'That's the mistake. We get terribly dry weather for years, and then it rains and everyone thinks it's normal. But it used to rain every year. The desert's advancing, mark my words.'

I had been noticing the changes in the land for some days. The pastures were meagre, and what grass there was seemed wiry and shorn by sheep. This was an area of wide and undulating plains, the beginning of the Central Valley; buzzards arched over their fastness, and rattling winds jarred the tinder-dry branches of the thorn trees. For the first time I had seen cacti and prickly pear trees. For the first time, I could believe that the overbearing fertility of southern Chile was really going to dwindle into desert.

My fourth day in Litueche was a Sunday, and one of the local land-owners came to lunch with the priest. He invited me to his *fundo*, and, as I left, Cristián took me aside:

'Watch out,' he said. 'Watch out for Juan-Carlos, and his friend Antonio. *Los Diablos*. The Devils.

Juan-Carlos was an only child, son of a lawyer in Santiago. He managed his father's farm. His face was red from wine and *asado*, his lips were thick and his laugh vivid and ironic. He was a brash man in some ways, but also a sensitive one, feeling the deep wells of tragedy bubbling and frothing at the fringes of his eclectic memory.

'I'll tell you some history,' he said, as he drove carelessly. 'Just so that you can see what Chile used to be like. This whole valley, a hundred kilometres from Alcones to Navidad, used to be owned by one family. Our *fundo* was one of their three houses. Of course, Allende appropriated it all, and then my father bought a piece of the land in 1973, after the coup.'

He drove me up to the farm. The old part of the house was like a museum. The divans and armchairs were so lush and receptive that they seemed to sink to the floor when you sat in them, and beyond an ancient wireless still spat sound venerably around the room. Water-colours draped the walls, talking of a rural Chile which was long since gone – the sun gilding the image of a *guaso* fording a river in a valley full of beech trees – and beneath the pictures were centuries-old chests and mantelpieces, the wood shining in its glowing polish.

'I don't like coming in here,' said Juan-Carlos. 'It's so silent. It seems full of ghosts. Let's go and get something to drink.'

We drove to a nearby hamlet, and he bought a bottle of *pisco*. As we drove back, he told me that there were five bars in this hamlet – a fact which says a great deal about Chile, since I had not even seen five houses. We returned to his house, and we started to get drunk, before confiding in each other like old friends. Juan-Carlos told me about the loves of his life. He was racked with the guilt of a rich man who knows that his wealth is built on misery.

'When Pinochet came in, in '73,' he said, 'we were all so happy. Something had to be done! The country was in a mess. But then he stayed so long ... so long. You know, that bastard even burnt people. They sent people to the ovens in Lonquén, and just threw them in. But I'm the only farmer around here, the only one who recognizes the evil ... The others, they still love Pinochet. Like my friend Antonio ...'

Antonio arrived later in the evening, and we all continued to demolish the *pisco*.

'The thing about Pinochet,' he said, 'is that if it wasn't for the old man we still wouldn't have any metalled roads in this silly country of ours.'

We drank more and more *pisco*, drowning ourselves in silliness instead of rain. For the rain was unrelenting, battering the earth which for so long it had forsaken. It was just as unforgiving as the drought, for now it unleashed itself with such fury that we only wished that it would evaporate completely. It rained so much that, in the morning, the peon told us that a brook had burst its banks, flooded the land, and drowned ten sheep.

'Food,' chortled Juan-Carlos. It was his Saint's Day, and he was celebrating. Although he was still drunk from the night before, he drove off to the hamlet and bought wine: five litres of wine.

'They didn't have anything smaller,' he said apologetically when he returned with the carafe.

The peon had butchered several sheep, and was in the process of grilling four of them. The three of us sat around, befuddled by our hangovers and the vast quantity of meat. There was enough meat to feed the whole of Litueche. Juan-Carlos disappeared to the kitchen to cook himself a special Saint's Day breakfast of sheep's testicles. I began to moan to Antonio.

'How can I carry on?' I asked him. 'It just rains and rains, and I've got to get to Copiapó.'

'You can't *viejo*,' he said. 'Look at this rain. There won't be any forage. The roads will be washed away.'

'The thing is,' I said, 'travelling by horse means that I have to rely on people, finding a field and some fodder. It's not right to continue when the situation is like this. People have enough troubles without me.'

'I tell you what,' said Antonio. 'I'll buy your horse off you.'

'But I've got to ride.'

'You can't. Why don't you walk, or something, and then buy yourself a horse when the situation is less drastic?'

This was sound advice. I was loath to take Martillo much further north, since people had told me that no one used horses in Copiapó, and that I would have to sell him for horse meat. I could never have sold Martillo for meat. I loved him so much. Here the grass was still relatively green, and I knew Antonio – who was wealthy and a horse lover – would treat him well. I was sad to sell him, but it was better to part with him here, where I knew he would have a good life.

Juan-Carlos came back, and we got drunk again. I always seemed to be getting drunk with these two Devils, and perhaps this was because my situation was otherwise too absurd. At least when I was drunk, I did not have to try to see things clearly, and I was happy to allow my mind to wander. That evening, as I sat with the Devils and the tremors of drunkenness hit us, I recalled the earthquake which Darwin had seen. I also thought of those fissures that were so easily opened, seen by Darwin and sensed by myself and Martillo, as we travelled in his shadow.

I drank another shot of *pisco*; and another. And the more that I drank, the more uneasy I became. I was going funny with the drink, and I could not help thinking of the countless possible cracks which the plains might produce in the future. The cracks might even swallow up the stunted trees which covered them, like the stones on the sea floor. It was surely no coincidence that those trees stood nude upon the plains. The thorns which stuck to them seemed ready to stab me, and pierce any rational certainty which I might have had regarding those plains. Or so it seemed that evening, for I was certainly far too drunk to know anything at all.

We drank and drank. We even finished the *pisco*, and moved on to a vintage Chilean red wine. The problem was that, owing to our drunkenness, we did not leave the wine to air, and the taste was strangely dissatisfying, almost bitter, leaving me with no possible outlet to conceal my fear of the plains from a maddened imagination.

Of course, when I eventually awoke the following morning, it was easy for me to forget that I had been afraid of the indeterminacy of the plains. The sky had cleared, and it seemed as though the storm might be blown away once and for all. But my brain thumped with my hangover, and I felt sad. Nothing was certain. I was leaving Martillo behind. He was my loyal friend, and I hated the thought of never seeing him again – and I believe that, as the months passed, he came to share my sadness.

Some months after I returned to England, Berlin came from the *padre*'s bungalow in Litueche to London for two days on an exchange programme. He stayed with me. We did the fullest day-tour of London that I could devise, beginning at the Tate and the Houses of Parliament, before watching the changing of the Guard, going to Trafalgar Square, eating a curry near Covent Garden, taking in the British Museum, Portobello Road market, St Paul's and Tower Bridge.

Wherever he went, Berlin took photographs. They were the proof of his visit, which he needed to show to all his many friends and family in Chile, thereby giving them a taste of life in the *viejo continente*. Globetrotters are relatively uncommon in Chile, and so photographs from abroad are still eagerly awaited. On his return to Litueche, Berlin maintained his prodigious photographic production – at my request. He went to the farm belonging to Antonio, and managed to photograph Martillo, even though the horse was in a herd of twenty animals and all the others ignored the camera. But Martillo's ears were pricked, and he was staring at the camera with utmost attention, as if he knew for whom the photograph was meant.

This, at any rate, is what I should like to believe, and when I am thinking wistfully of this journey – which I know can never be repeated – and of Martillo, I like to think that my beautiful grey horse still remembers me, and thinks fondly of the times when we travelled across Chile, before I left him with the Devils, and the crumbling earth over the plains.

PART EIGHT

To the Flowering Desert

I

We spent the day on the summit, and I never enjoyed one more thoroughly. Chile, bounded by the Andes and the Pacific, was seen as in a map ... Who can avoid admiring the wonderful force which has upheaved these mountains?

Charles Darwin on the view from Cerro La Campana

It took me five days to walk to Valparaíso. The roads were hard and bit unrelentingly at my legs. I didn't have cushioned trainers, just the same battered pair of boots which I had been wearing constantly for several months. On the first day I walked over fifty kilometres, since one of Antonio's friends had offered to put me up in the resort town of Santo Domingo. His parents owned a disco, but the last thing I felt like doing was dancing. I only arrived late at night, having walked all day.

I was following Darwin and the coast from Navidad to Valparaíso. These areas were so urban that they would have been exceptionally dangerous to ride through. There was a thriving port or beach resort every few kilometres, hiding from its neighbours in the many coves of the coastline. The roads were full of trucks and local transport, and at the beginning it was incredibly difficult to continue while a steady stream of taxis and local buses swept past me. But I managed to carry on walking, and after the second day's foot-march it became easier.

Now that I was walking, the character of my days changed. People still stared, since they rarely saw a grubby *gringo* trudging along the coastal highway with a hole-ridden bag slung over his shoulder, but they did not stare as much as when I had passed on horseback. Sometimes, when I reached a town, people would look at me limping and feeling sorry for myself. Often, they sidled up to me and asked what on earth I was doing. I remember one man, in the small town of El Quisco:

'Where are you going, *amigo*?'

'North,' I said unhelpfully, and then added: 'By foot.'

'I can see that!' he laughed.

'How?'

'Look at yourself! No one limps like a dog unless they're walking. Why are you walking?'

'It's a long story.'

'That's OK. I've got time.'

So I told him, over a couple of beers, the story of the last year.

'. . . and then, these bloody floods came along. I was going to go on, but it seemed like it would be difficult with things like this.'

'Just a bit! You know that Viña del Mar is still flooded out. And it's even worse further north. We were lucky here, really.'

'Yes. So I sold my horse, and now I've just got my bag and myself.'

'Aren't you afraid of dying?'

'I can't imagine myself doing anything else just now. I've been wandering for so long, it seems normal. Nothing's happened to me yet, really.'

'Nothing!' he exclaimed, uproariously. 'You're funny. You started out with three horses and a girlfriend. Now you haven't got any horses and you haven't got your girlfriend. And you tell me that nothing's happened!'

He invited me to his house, so that I could pass a comfortable night. I was down to such little money by now that I only went to a hotel once every three weeks or so. I tried to find a quiet place for my tent, or else I begged for some floor-space in a restaurant. I had spent so much time alone that ordinary manners came slowly to me. I never ate properly (eating was a matter of stuffing some gooey mess into my mouth), I rarely washed in hot water (to be frank, I rarely washed), and I hadn't used deodorant for several months (but I was immune to the smell).

I stank. And as I walked on I stank more and more. Each day became a challenge. There were endless towns by the roadside, in each of which I was tempted to stop, buy a beer, relax. It was always difficult to find a place to sleep. As a last resort, I camped on a beach at Algarrobo. Then, as I neared Valparaíso, I twice ducked under fences and camped where I shouldn't have done. Without my horse, people no longer talked to me so much, and I was returning more and more to loneliness.

In many ways, my arrival at Valparaíso was similar in spirit to Darwin's. I was as dirty and unprepared for the bustle of a modern city as I could have been. Nonetheless, I loved the place. To my mind, Valparaíso is one of the world's great cities – as colourful as Buenos Aires, almost as dramatic as Rio, its architecture in places as varied and grand as that of London or Paris. The city is built on forty-six hills rising precipitately from the Pacific, and it is said that even a Porteño (someone from Valparaíso) can easily lose themselves in the baffling warren of alleys and pathways which criss-cross the hills. The houses are all brightly coloured, and the kaleidoscope hurts the eyes, the deep greens, yellows, reds and mauves all fighting with the rightly royal blue of the skies. Cobbled passageways swing tortuously between the steeply rising houses, disappearing into mystery. It is a city which was born to be a mythology, and every crevice reels with tales of ghosts, witches and miracles. The irrational flourishes here, where reason can finally lose itself in the drunken mazes of its experience.

The disarray of Valparaíso is difficult to describe. The commercial district is built on a level strip alongside the dock, and seems orderly. From here, a clutch of cable cars and funicular railways rise into the labyrinthine streets on the hills, where chaos allows the city to draw life, over and above the superficial order below. Alleys are filled with dumb dogs, who stare and bark curiously at everything and nothing, sucking their calluses and waiting with indefatigable canine patience for something to happen to them. There is, in fact, a disturbing quantity of dogs, running aimlessly hither and thither in filthy packs, their existence showing nature's wanton disregard for the city's sanity. But there is nothing sane here, which probably explains this detail. The streets plunge here and there, noise assaults from every angle, dogs yelp and rummage through the piles of rubbish left festering in some of the more abandoned alleys, music coughs from basements and from tall corrugated iron sheds – and then suddenly the disordered collage clears, and you are left with a view stretching across the city to the glittering resort of Viña del Mar, the sun burning golden in the bay, and then, peaking above the rim of the furthest hill, the highest mountain of the Americas – Aconcagua – stands to attention. This is Chile's great beauty, and a reminder of her frailty also, that from the coast you can see her border with Argentina quite clearly. From its beginnings, the icy end never hides itself.

Darwin's first visit to Valparaíso, in the winter of 1834, charmed him absolutely. He found the town very pretty, by far the most attractive metropolis he had visited since Rio, a 'sort of London or Paris, to any place we have been to.' One of Darwin's few complaints was that returning to civilized society obliged the *Beagle* company to shave and dress decently – a loathing which I now shared with him absolutely. He took up lodgings in the house of Richard Corfield, a schoolfellow from Shrewsbury, and delighted in meeting the many other English merchants who lived in the port. On returning from his journeys around the Rapel region, though, Darwin was struck down for six weeks by a mysterious illness, which he put down to drinking some bad wine. This was the first crisis in a life which was ultimately to be dogged by ill health.

However, the illness did not curb his adventurous instincts. He also found that one of the most pleasant things about Valparaíso was its stupendous views towards the *cordillera*. After the hardships of the south, the distant mountains kept Darwin rapt: 'After Tierra del Fuego, the climate felt quite delicious – the atmosphere so dry, and the heavens so clear and blue, with the sun shining brightly, that all nature seemed sparkling with life.' Darwin talks of viewing the Andes from Valparaíso, saying that 'viewed from this point they owe the greater part of their beauty to the atmosphere through which they are seen.' He thought that seeing the mountains through the wonderful light made a great difference to their appearance: 'How opposite are the sensations when viewing black mountains half enveloped in clouds, & seeing another range through the light blue haze of a fine day: the one for a time may be very sublime, the other is all gayety & happy life.' On his first visit, he was prevented from exploring the highest peaks because of the winter and then because of his illness. However, on returning north from Valdivia and Concepción, Darwin determined to journey over the mountains to Mendoza. The high peaks were irresistible. Their brilliant summits had been winking temptingly at him for almost a year by the time he finally set off for them in March 1835, and their geology was sure to be crucial in his developing thought. It was on this journey that he discovered a petrified forest on the Argentine side of the Uspallata pass, at a height of 7000 feet [just over 2000 metres]. This convinced him conclusively of the geological forces which could isolate continents from one another, create islands in oceans and play a major role in the evolution of life.

But almost as memorable as the *cordillera* to Darwin was his ascent of Cerro La Campana, ('the Bell Hill'), about forty kilometres north-east of Valparaíso. He climbed the hill on his way to the Aconcagua Valley, during his first excursion in central Chile. On reaching Santiago, he wrote to FitzRoy: 'The difficulty in ascending the Campagna is most absurdly exaggerated. We rode up 5/6ths of the height to a spring called the Agua de Guanaco & there bivouacked for two nights in a beautiful little arbor of bamboos ... I spent one whole day on the very summit ... I do not think I ever more enjoyed a day's rambling.'

I headed for the hill from Valparaíso. Gradually, it was becoming apparent that the worst of the floods were subsiding. This was a blessing, because my legs could barely take the pain of the hard roads any more. There was nothing to walk on but tarmac or concrete, and my rough boots had my knees aching more every day. I should have walked from Valparaíso to the hill, but my knees were such agony that I finally succumbed to the temptation of a little bus, and was in the small village of Granizos, at the foot of the hill, within two hours instead of eleven. The bus followed Darwin's route precisely, past Quinteros and thence to Limache. Limache, which had been badly hit by the floods, was still dotted with lakes of stagnant floodwater, which were slowly evaporating as the sun dried out the earth. Looking at the scene, it was easy to see what had happened: the river, which had been virtually dry for many years, had swollen and washed away the houses and many of the stores which had been built in the floodplain. As La Campana loomed ahead of me, my knees aching and the floodwaters ebbing, I decided to look for another horse after I had climbed the hill. People had told me that emergency forage had eased the situation, and I could carry on by horse. I would have to return to Litueche for my saddle, but I could then continue.

La Campana is the focal point for legend in this region of Chile. Wizened old *lugareños* say that long ago the summit sported a cone of gold and gems. The riches were bright as silver in the night, and so brilliant by day that they blinded those who looked directly at them. The legend of the gems spread, for the light burnt indefatigably, revealing the jewels clearly. A conquering army came to lay their hands on the jewels themselves, and the local witches, rather than let their own earth's riches – the gentle riches of clarity – be swallowed up by foreign greed, drew a thunderstorm from the skies. The cone was struck by lightning, and the jewels scattered across the neighbouring hills: the riches indistinguishable, now, from the dusty spreads of earth drifting towards the thin blue line of the ocean.

Others say that the cone was buried by a deluge of hailstones, and that riches are still to be unearthed on the summit. Yet a person who, mocking tradition, takes it upon himself to climb the hill and unearth the stones, must die mysteriously, sucked into the infinite rocky clefts of the hill by witches who lie in waiting. Today, as the sun abandons the valley of Olmué, it can strike a glittering element of light high up on the rock-face, burning and melting it until the light, blinding and mesmerising as the sun, dies, solitarily sparkling still, this last spot of magic vanishing into the dark.

I tried to ignore the legends as I climbed the Cerro; my legs now bruised as mushy apples, my mind clearing as I climbed. The path began low, in the valley, clinging to the comforting grandeur of forest on all sides. The trees shaded the path, as it climbed steeply through them – the whole valley was in shade. The mountain was so high and the slope so sharp that even the sun found it difficult to surmount such an obstacle. Yet the light was much more brilliant when it crested the ridge above, now dazzling the shadows with its ineffable light; much clearer, after the confused darkness of morning. Only in the contrast, the dialectic, could the brilliance unfold itself fully. I forded two wide and rushing rivers, and splashed through canyons buried in mud from the rains. My hands were sullied with the mud, but the grime would not come out here – I had passed the waters, and there was no cleansing spring until much higher up the mountain. Although it seemed that in the shadows should be silence, the valley was deafening. There was a roar from the river, licking the air with its force like the crackles of spreading wildfire, drowning both its valley and my thoughts, swallowing up every other sound in its own selfish plunge to the ocean. This river would suck itself free of water in a Dionysian burst of excess, and then die of thirst in the needy times to come. Only as I climbed did the roar recede, masked and dimmed by the forests covering the lower slopes of the mountainside. Higher up, the air seemed silent, and for the moment the river was lost. As I gained height, the hills around the valley gained definition. From below, they had been vast and oppressive, but now I could see where they began and ended, how they blended one into another and presented themselves peacefully to the skies.

In spite of the physical effort I smiled to myself as I climbed, for this peace had seemed impossible when I had been absorbed in the morass at the base of the hill. Higher still, and I began to see the unattainable white line of the *cordillera* creeping beyond the ridge of the Campana. The colours were more intense, sharpened and moulded by the brilliant light aching beyond the ridge. The climb was tiring, and took an age. But I revelled in the task, in the beauty that crept up on all sides of the journey.

As I climbed still higher, passing now the spring where Darwin bivouacked, I came to the rocky barrenness of the highest slopes. Little grew here. The rocks were jagged and tough, unforgiving in themselves, ready to send me tumbling back to the roaring shelter of the valley if I slipped. I passed an aged and faded plaque to Darwin, knowing that he had come this way. There was little to distract me but the climb now. I had no need of thoughts or distractions. My feet hurt, and I was breathless, but the snows of the Andes were peeking more and more prominently into my eyes, and I knew that the whole view would leave me, finally, speechless. The wind did not rise to whisper. The birdcalls and the reptiles rustling through the grasses were way down the valley. The path was steep as an abyss. Now I came to patches of snow, hidden from the melting sun by rocks. I slipped and stumbled my way up. But the snow helped me too – I grabbed fistfuls of it, and quenched my thirst. Behind and in front of me the mountains were rising, but still I had not reached the jewelled summit of legend, so still I could not see their entirety.

And then, almost without warning, the slope levelled, and I reached the summit. The view was staggering. To the east, the great wall of the Andes stretched fully 300 kilometres or more, separated from the Cerro by a pall of smoggy haze drifting over the valleys of central Chile. These valleys were clouded and impossible to distinguish one from another, but the Andes rose from them, as a phoenix, laughing maniacally at the ashes below. To the north and south, there were hundreds of ridges, diving towards each other and seeming to converge where the haze was thickest. Although I tried to see the precise point where they did meet in the golden whorls of light, I only managed to see their outlines, which became indistinct long before the beautiful ridges met one another. To the west lay the yawning untamed monster, the Pacific, which in its vast uniformity frightened me and turned me back towards the ridges. In these at least I could forget the rushing river below, and lose myself in their indeterminate beauty.

For I could never have reached the top of the Bell Hill without bridging the river, and, as I stood on the summit, alone in the heart of these mountains, I seemed to hear its soft roar from below. And I could not help feeling that, if I had stayed for any important length of time at that height, the river would eventually have swept me away, still as I stood there, dashing me against rocks which perhaps once even fell from this mountain. Without a doubt, had I stayed, that river far below would have come to displace me, flushing me out disdainfully into the seizing seething sea.

I had only a day in which to climb the Cerro, and the threat of the river receded as I descended the mountain, forded the water again, and emerged into the oppressive security at the base of the hill. I reached my campsite just before evening and, looking up at the Cerro's peak and the brilliant light which now engulfed it, it was easy to understand the legends spawned by this mountain.

I slept deeply that night, before leaving to visit Santiago. Darwin reached the city via the Aconcagua Valley and San Felipe, but before arriving I wanted to see where I might buy a horse, so I went to La Calera, just north of Quillota, a town well known for its horse market, and found out the date of the next sale. From here I took a bus to the capital, which now has about five million more inhabitants than it did in the 1830s – not a place for riding any more. I wanted to find out if I could cross the Andes to Mendoza, but it quickly became clear that this was not possible. The Portillo pass had been snowed under after the storms, trapping several hundred passengers at the customs post (they had only just been airlifted to safety), and conditions were still extremely unstable. The horse idea was definitely ruled out by the conditions and the paperwork, and it was feasible that I could be trapped if I went by road. Instead, I would follow the Maipó Valley for the beginning of the route which Darwin took over the *cordillera*, after revisiting all my old haunts from the time when I was an English teacher in the city.

Santiago is like all modern cities: bright, energetic and exhausting. It is a reminder of the ever-decreasing circles in which we all live. Shopping mall culture has wheedled its way into the conscience of the city, as have hamburger restaurants and takeaway pizzas. You can still find old-fashioned *peñas* where bands play the *cueca* – Chile's national dance – and waltzes, but most young people are into *el rock progresivo* or *la música tecno*. There are the same multinationals as everywhere else, the same skyscrapers glass-fronting the drive to do business which consumes the world with commodification. I could not help noticing how much more international Santiago was than it had been before. When I first arrived in the city in 1992, as a naive eighteen-year-old with several layers of puppy fat still to burn off, strange situations had abounded: a transvestite clown made a pass at me while doing his comedy act in the city's biggest park; I was nearly caught up in a Communist protest which was put down by the riot police; the secret police came up to me and two British friends to check on what we were doing. In those days, you knew that the city was on a different continent (McDonald's had only just opened) – but on my return, I saw the same businesses and shops and symbols that are everywhere, the same economic priorities falling from the street hoardings into the consciousness, based on the same premises as everywhere else.

An example might be the premise that a successful economy is a growing one, which has as its inescapable conclusion that economies must grow. But why must a successful economy grow? If it is to be truly successful in the long term, on the contrary, if available resources are contracting, then the economy must also contract to be successful – precisely the situation at the moment, and precisely the situation which the multinationals, with their colossal and frightening power, try to buy out of sight. In our soundbite culture, words define our arguments and discussions more than anything else, now generalizing our outlook on the world, and spreading its generality across cultures, so that soon there will be one mega-culture, one language of cultural understanding – and a bitter memory harrowed by the loss of a million other voices and languages, loss of a time when there was more than one way of listening to the world.

As I roamed the city, I imagined what it must have been like in the 1830s. On his arrival, Darwin stayed in an English hotel, and enjoyed the social whirl of balls and civilized society. He thought that the location could not have been more perfect, halfway between the Andes and the coastal *cordillera* – he loved to climb the Cerro Santa Lucía, on the edge of the city, and admire the view. Now, the view from the Cerro is usually obscured by smog (Santiago is one of the world's most polluted cities). Cerro Santa Lucía, far from being on the fringes, with fields and *fundos* separating it from the Andes, is in central Santiago, separated from the Andes by many kilometres of office blocks and luxury residential districts. When Pedro de Valdivia founded the city in 1541, it must have seemed a perfect location; he could never have imagined that the city would swell until it filled the valley completely.

Santiago had been my home before, and I was thrilled to see old friends after such a long time. But the city itself filled me with nothing but emptiness. I hadn't been in a place like this since Buenos Aires. I was used to peace and space, but here there were only distractions. I felt battered by Santiago's countless images. I thought of Darwin's theory that the sharpened senses of people like the Yámana were due to the increased problems which they had in surviving. I felt something completely different: that with so many sights and sounds and smells bombarding cities, we withdraw from our senses, forgetting the rudiments of feeling. I had spent so long in the country, retuning myself, that Santiago quickly exhausted me. Going anywhere was a great effort, since I could not ignore these bombardments which only wanted to withdraw me from peace.

I took refuge in the home of an old friend, Leslie. She lived with her mother and two sisters in the south of Santiago, twenty metres from one of the main transport arteries of the city. Leslie's grandparents had built the small house when they had first come to the city from the countryside, and the building had been so well constructed that it had withstood two earthquakes, mocking the more grandiloquent high-rises which had crumbled like mountains sliding back to the land. Whenever the front door opened, the dissonant hum of the city's tuneless orchestra entered into the sanctuary of the house, like an audience at the interval of a particularly moving performance.

Leslie's youngest sister, Cynthia, was only three years old, and her hyperactivity helped all of us to keep our spirits from flagging. She would run around the compact kitchen like a dervish, playing with any object which she could lay her hands on, screaming and ranting when no one would play with her. She raised our adult, catatonic frames from slumber, for we would all be worn out by the end of the day. After spending my days catching up with numerous old friends, I would return home shattered by the city and my journey, quite content to sit for hours at a time and do nothing, trying to recall how to relax. Leslie travelled for over an hour through the rush hour traffic to work on the other side of the city, as a manager at the switchboard of an international telephone exchange, and would only return home long after the rest of us. Leslie's mother and other sister, Susanna and Karen, struggled to look after Cynthia and the stall which they ran at the local flea market. If Cynthia had not been there with her ebullience and childish will to play, we might have been allowed to stumble into the inertia of televisual evenings and silent goodnights. But she giggled and laughed and joked with us, often until well past midnight, exhausting us all, but also keeping us alive, entranced, amused by her journey of discovery, only recently and loudly begun.

I spent a week with my friends. We did not do anything extraordinary, but passed our time sitting around the table, chatting over *once* long after the food and coffee had been consumed. Susanna and I would sip from our *mate* gourds, laughing at the others who turned up their noses at the distinctively bitter taste. The light in the sitting area was stark, and threw itself into the crevices of the room, passing the door of the bathroom which was attached to the wall by a thin steel catch, and penetrating into the gloom of the cramped kitchen and small store cupboards. I cannot remember a single thing which we talked about, for it is the fact of those days of shared exchanges and jokes which matters to me now, sticking to my memory as resolutely as the most beautiful natural experiences of my journey, as a moment which rescued my identity from solitude, and allowed me to remember what it was like to feel at home, among friends.

All too quickly the time came for me to leave, breaking this special time through my departure. When I heaved my luggage through the narrow door and out into the narrow alley in which they lived, we all had to hold back our tears, which surfaced in spite of the irritating rumble of the main road, growling from only a few steps away.

II

The Chilian miners are a peculiar race of men in their habits. Living for weeks together in the most desolate spots, when they descend to the villages on feast-days, there is no excess or extravagance into which they do not run.

Charles Darwin

When I left Santiago I made my way back to La Calera, where I spent a day at the horse market. Unfortunately all the horses were either as wild as those in a *jineteada* or distressingly thin, and I could not ride towards the Atacama desert on a horse whose ribs were as prominent as the bare frame of a ship's hull. On the advice of a *guaso*, I travelled to the small town of Cabildo. Here I made enquiries in a bar whose doors continually swung back and forth with the comings and goings of prostitutes and their admirers, and managed to buy a horse, whose previous owner was a gentle man who worked in Cabildo's gold mine for eight hours each day. I called my horse Apple, and shortly set out to follow Darwin towards Copiapó.

My relationship with Apple became very close almost at once. He neighed appreciatively whenever I brought him his forage, and always seemed enthusiastic to carry on. He pricked his ears and seemed to enjoy the beautiful scenery. As with my other horses, I came to love him in no time at all. We relied absolutely on one another. I depended on him for transport, he depended on me for food. It was an equal, loving relationship. Sometimes I sang to him, or asked him how he was. Speaking to a horse might seem like madness, but when you have spent so much time alone with one there is nothing that seems more sensible.

Darwin initially followed the coast north from Valparaíso, but the scenery quickly palled. He passed the districts of Quillota, La Calera and Conchalee, and, as they went, 'the country became more and more barren. In the valleys there was scarcely sufficient water for any irrigation; and the intermediate land was quite bare, not supporting even goats.'

Darwin was so thoroughly frustrated by the coast road that he struck inland for the mining district of Illapel, and then crossed to Ovalle via Los Hornos. From Ovalle, Darwin reached Coquimbo, where he rested for two weeks, and rode up into the interior of the Elqui Valley. With Apple, I planned to follow Darwin to Ovalle, and then cross directly over to the Elqui Valley, following him down to the industrial area around Coquimbo and La Serena.

Cabildo was surrounded by towering mountains on all sides, some of them rising 1000 metres and more into the bulges of the central *cordillera*. Just north of the town a tunnel bored through the mountain. I was loath to ride through the tunnel, since there was no light, it was single-lane (operating with traffic lights to allow one side through at a time) and this was no way to begin my relationship with Apple. Instead I asked around for the old track, which I could see climbing the mountain. I rode off on my first day with Apple in brilliant sunlight, fording the Río La Ligua, which had broken its banks after the floods. After about half an hour, I turned off the main road and rode up a path towards the old pass.

Gradually, the path became sodden. The mountain was so precipitous that the sun rarely had a chance to dry out the earth in winter. After twenty minutes, I came to a section where there had been a mudslide after the rains; the thick chute of rocks and mud could clearly be seen tumbling from top to bottom of the mountain. However, the mud on the path looked solid enough and Apple trotted contentedly into it, his ears pricked, looking happily about him at the beautiful landscape. He took three steps forward, and then floundered and flailed, sinking quickly up to his belly in the morass – completely immobile.

I hadn't even been riding my new horse for an hour, and he had become a stick-in-the-mud. He had sunk so far that I literally stepped off the saddle into the mud, praying that I wouldn't sink as well. But the mud held my weight; I was left standing a metre from a precipice, with my poor horse sunk up to his guts, his eyes popping out in fear as the mud pressed hard into his lower body. I took off the *maleta*, so that he had less to weigh him down; but the saddle was unrecoverable, since I couldn't get at the girth to unbuckle it. Apple was making desperate attempts to heave himself out of the mud, whinnying in terror, breathing as rapidly as if he was galloping. I tried to help him, fixing the lead rein to his head-collar and heaving him as he heaved himself. He managed to squeeze one leg out, and then lay squirming and squelching in the mud. We continued to struggle for ten minutes, me tugging him, Apple squeezing legs out, squirming, heaving himself again. He was panting so hard that I feared he might have a seizure and die. It was a horrible sight, but I was helpless, and there would be no one coming this way to help. All I could do was try to coax him out.

Eventually we made it. Apple shook himself free of mud, his nostrils flaring with the effort of it all, and we rested awhile until he had calmed down. Then I led him back down the track, since there was no way around the mudslide.

Riding through the tunnel would have been suicidal, so I waited at the entrance, hoping that some trucker would be willing to carry Apple through. After ten minutes, a gleaming red pick-up stopped. As we were working out how to proceed, the driver unfortunately trod in some fecund faeces which happened to be lying on the road.

'Shit!' he said.

I looked sympathetically at the brown mess on his shoe.

'I've trodden in some stools.'

There were no two ways about it.

'I don't believe it!' he said. 'Fresh shit on my new shoes!'

It was extremely unlucky that stopping to help me had done anything but leave him smelling of roses. However the man was cheerful, and he laughed it off. We tied Apple to the back of the pick-up, and I kept hold of the lead rein while he drove slowly through the tunnel, his headlights glaring so that no one came the other way. I held tight onto the lead rein, watching Apple trotting unwillingly through the tunnel, with his eyes starting and glowing surreally in the darkness, and his hoofs clattering like hammerheads against the road.

On the far side of the tunnel, I quickly left the main road to follow an old railway line towards Illapel.

My route was set through high Andean valleys. Generally, we climbed slowly for several hours, heading for a barrier of mountains, before tunnelling through the rock and emerging into another valley on the far side. The mountains blinked with barren beauty. Each valley was progressively drier; the mountains shedding vegetative skins, returning to their bare essential; the grass ballooning gigantically into cacti; the cacti shrinking with the rainfall and the passage from valley to valley; the colours harsher and more brilliant with the growing vastness and depopulation of the valleys. Traffic was virtually non-existent here, consisting of two or three vehicles a day. The first car that passed was driven by two *carabineros* patrolling the valley. Once I'd shown them my papers, they were all smiles. They would go and tell the nearest school to prepare me some lunch.

'No,' I protested. 'Don't worry.'

They refused to listen, and I rode on towards the sun and the tremendous mountains on all sides. I sang songs as they came to my lips, feeling light and happy as laughing gas. The sun was burning, and I shielded my face from the cruel rays with a sombrero given to me Juan-Carlos in Litueche. After two hours, I came to the local primary school, which dominated a hamlet of perhaps twenty households. There was a small church, whitewashed and gleaming, like the rest of the buildings in the coruscating valley.

I hitched Apple to a fence outside the school. The children stopped playing in the yard to watch me.

'Is there a teacher around?' I asked. A row of dark, ruddy, inquisitive faces stared at me from the other side of the fence. The teacher came beaming towards me after a minute:

'Welcome, welcome!' he cried. 'The cook's preparing your lunch. Will you just go and tell them a story?'

'Story?'

'Just tell them what you're doing. The *carabineros* said something about it.'

I found some water for Apple, and someone went to ask about forage. I walked into the main classroom, where forty children stared avidly at me.

'Now listen, everyone,' the teacher said. 'The gentleman has come a long way, and he's very good at telling stories.'

He winked at me and drifted away. I took off my sombrero, and felt my face – flushed, burnt. My brain was overheated, and I could not really think straight. The children clearly had no idea what to expect.

'Um ... I'm from England. Do you know where that is?'

Silence.

'From Europe.'

I looked around for a map or globe, but there was none.

'A long way away,' I finished lamely. 'I've come by horse, from Chiloé, and I'm going to Copiapó.'

'Why?' asked one of the older children.

'That's a good question,' I said, and, hot and bothered as I was, I could think of no easy answer. 'I'm following the route of an English scientist. Charles Darwin. Have any of you heard of Darwin?'

Silence.

'Well, anyway,' I went on, 'he came past here about 160 years ago, and I'm following his route.'

I could think of nothing else to say. How could I possibly explain a year of my life in a couple of sentences? I was not really living up to the teacher's boast about my storytelling abilities.

'That's what I'm doing,' I finished. 'Has anyone got any questions?'

'Where did you come from?' one of the children asked.

'Chiloé.'

'Where's that?' asked another. 'Is it further than La Ligua?'

'No, no. It's in the south,' I said.

But they had no idea. I asked who had been to Cabildo, Petorca or La Ligua – the main towns nearby – and, of the forty children, one had been to Cabildo and two had been to Petorca, but none had been to La Ligua. They were my opposites, knowing only the immediate world. I had come so far, forcing myself to see as much as possible, but these children had been born in the valley, would probably live and die here, and might visit Santiago only once or twice in their lives.

We looked at each other in mutual incomprehension for some time. Their faces were kindly, inquiring, humble, poor and destined to be poor for ever. They swam against the all-encompassing floods of *El Niño*, which still afflicted me as I remembered my time on the Cerro La Campana. They were going the other way from me, climbing strong and defiant to the safety of land, whence the river was only a desperate and depressing thing. I would have stopped and talked among them, yet my journey took me away. I could not stop here, and listen noiselessly to the valley, to the blue silence by day and the black silence by night. I could not stop, even though the more I looked at the children, the more

I felt that I desperately needed rest: for the world had been exhausting me in its profundity and endless questions and images, and I was almost beyond bearing it alone.

Slowly, the children began to ignore me, and they talked to one another as I stared on silently. They had learnt nothing from me, that was clear. Sometimes it seemed that the whole year had been an exercise in oblivion; at others, I felt that I must have learnt something. Yet learning can be empty and speechless. And as they talked on, their words murmuring through the thick air, above the floor covered with dust and cracks, I felt that only if I had stayed in that valley could I really have learnt anything, watching soundlessly and recovering my identity beneath the tremendous mountains on all sides.

My eyes looked vacantly around the room for some minutes, as the children chattered. My mind was numb. There was no embarrassment here, for we did not know each other. The teacher returned after some minutes, and led me to the kitchen. I ate a bowl of fish stew in silence, before returning to my thankless journey.

The sun's power was waning as I rode on towards the mountains. After two hours, I came to a small hamlet high up, only a short distance from a tunnel through to the next valley. I did not want to pass through the tunnel that night, because I wanted to savour this valley through the rioting colours of dusk. A boy was wheeling his bicycle along the track – he recognized me as I came.

'Well,' he said. 'Did you tell a story?'

'What?'

'At school. The teacher told us that you were going to tell a story. What was it about?'

'Oh, it wasn't a very good one.'

The boy was called Elvis. His aunt, Leonora, was listening to our conversation, and now she asked me what I was doing. I explained, and asked where I could camp around here.

'With us, of course,' she said.

A neighbour could sell me hay. I could put up my tent, even more humble than their two-roomed house and alfresco bathroom, and tether Apple to the fence a little way from the house. Leonora had married a miner, Nivaldo, and her daughter Juana had married Nivaldo's son David. Juana was earthy and garrulous, and flirted rashly with me in

front of David. I liked David, who was quiet and honest, with a face
that creased into a medley of smiles whenever someone made a joke –
I looked at him supportively whenever Juana lapsed into coquetry.
Leonora was as warm and talkative as her daughter, compact and with
a mane of flowing black hair; she smiled and laughed regularly. Nivaldo
was a quiet, round man, with a dusky face. Leonora and Juana dominated the conversation while their spouses laughed as and when
required.

I sat all evening in the kitchen, initially talking just with the women.
The room was bare, possessing only a table, two chairs and a gas stove
with two rings. The night became cold here, up high after the sun had
hidden itself away for the day.

'Have some bread and chillies,' said Leonora. 'You must be tired after
your journey.'

'Where have you come from?' asked Juana.

'A long way,' I said. 'From Uruguay.'

'Uruguay! By horse?'

'Well, a lot of it has been by horse.'

'Hee, hee,' cackled Leonora. 'I think of La Calera as a long way by
bus, and you're going by horse.'

Her face softened and saddened as she thought about it.

'But don't you get lonely?' she asked. 'Away from your family and
friends. So far away. How long have you been gone?'

'It's been ten months now.'

'Ten months!'

It was impossible to contemplate.

'All alone,' said Juana. 'Don't you miss people?'

'Of course I do, sometimes. I write letters every week. But a person
can get used to anything, and I am used to my own company now.'

'What will your family say to you when you get back? Your mother,'
said Leonora sadly. 'What will you say to them?'

'I don't know. It's been such a long time since I've spoken English
that I'll be out of practice.'

'English? Don't you speak Chilean in your country?'

'No, we speak English.'

'Really,' said Juana. 'You don't speak Chilean? So how do you say
lechuga?'

'Lettuce.'

They both burst into roars of laughter.

'Say that again,' said Leonora. '*What* did you say?'

'Lettuce.'

They found it incredibly funny. The room was rent with laughter, and Juana leant on her mother's shoulder, so funny did she find this absurd language. Nivaldo and David came in to see what all the laughter was about.

'Ask him how he says *lechuga* in his country,' the women said, barely able to speak articulately. This was the richest entertainment.

'Lettuce,' I said; although the men did not see the joke as they joined me with their women around the dim light.

'What about *cebolla*?'

'Onion.'

Roars of laughter.

'*Zanahoria*?'

'Carrot.'

The laughter abated after a while, and we talked of more serious things. The hamlet lived off a carbonate mine which had been opened by Nivaldo's grandfather. The old man had come from the nitrate fields in the Atacama desert, seen a streak of minerals in the mountains, and settled here. All the people in the hamlet were cousins, descendants of the same man. But after the rains, there had been a landslide which had covered the entrance to the mine with rubble, and they were all unemployed until they could get hold of a bulldozer to shift it.

We talked about many things: UFOs high in these mountain valleys, using them as their runways for take-off and landing; the old railway which the road had replaced, and the lawless days when the workers had killed one another to steal a dead man's share of the payroll; what it was to scratch a living from the mine, knowing that if the rocks were poor in minerals, the family would go hungry.

Then I went outside, preparing to sleep. The day had been so long and beautiful, I was still flushed with its exhilaration. The sky was cloudless, clear as lunar air, and the stars shone clearly and brilliantly, this milky galaxy of light. I did not see a finer night all year. Only high up this valley was the sky at all open to my vision.

But in the morning banks of cloud rolled in, concealing the sky once again. Even here, on the fringes of the desert.

The road north was laced with tunnels. I passed through four between Nivaldo's house and Illapel. The longest of them stretched on for about two kilometres, and took twenty minutes to pass through. One of them described a semicircle and was blacker than pitch in its centre, so that even Apple banged into the side walls – despite the common superstition that horses can see in the dark. Apple was so tame with me after only a few days that he carried on through the darkness, knowing that we would reach the other side without dramas if he continued walking.

The relaxation which I usually felt travelling through these mountains vanished in the tunnels. Once inside, the light at the far end would initially seem nearer than it was; but then it gradually drifted further and further away with every pace towards it, until it seemed that I could never reach the brilliant light. This was a tunnel of dark thoughts, propped up by all the dead workmen whose bones had disintegrated and were etched into the arid mountainsides, the forgotten epitaphs of their kind.

Reaching the far side, I would relax again, and continue the conversations which I enjoyed now, silently in my imagination, with myself and another, my technique for coping with my own company. In my eyes, there were two of us, saddled side by side, thrust with one another and forced to coexist if we could.

'Still following me, eh? I thought you'd have given up long ago.'

'Still here,' I said.

'I don't know why you bother. It's impossible to repeat any journey – mine more than most. Whoa!'

His shadowy horse started as we passed between boulders on the narrow track over the mountain.

'Nearly lost her,' he laughed. 'See, your horse didn't even move! Too tame these days. Not like when I was here.'

'A lot of things have changed since you were here. Haven't you seen?'

'Only on the surface, dear boy,' he said. 'Not around here. Look at these mountains! A few tremors may have thrust them a little higher, but most things are the same.'

He was an extremely affable person. So much time living among strangers had made him calm and accepting. We rode in silence for a while. We were passing the rough houses of the goatherds, leaning and crumbling in the drying earth sweeping down to the valley floor.

'The thing is,' he said, 'geological time is so massive that you can't expect any important physical changes since I was here. It's only been 160 years! A milli-milli-millisecond for geologists.'

'I'm not talking about geology, though. I'm talking about culture. Have you been to Rapel? That valley's been flooded out.'

'I know,' he said jocularly. 'I was swimming there only the other day.'

'The Mapuches are dying out. The Yámana are already gone. The wildlife in Patagonia is devastated. There are droughts everywhere. Our culture is destroying all these things that inspired you so much.'

'Yes,' he said slowly. 'It makes me immensely sad. I ride through these places, and watch their changes like a mother watching her children growing up and becoming adults: saddened because they will abandon me now. But children never do what their parents want. I never wanted my children to be dogmatic as my opponents were, and look at them now.'

We had passed Illapel, and the way was desolate. No one lived here, the track was narrow and winding through the drying mountainsides. The earth was an amazing mélange of colours, minerals painting the world with their gritty joy: the stones were purple, red, orange, bright white. The colours clawed back some hope from the lonely road. For three hours we had not passed any habitation, but now we saw a desperately poor hovel silhouetted against the barren skyline, a few rags billowing in the winds from a wire.

'I wonder who lives there,' I said.

'Miners,' he said. 'The man will have his own little hole somewhere, which he works and tries to feed his family from. Who can say what the wife and children do?'

'They are very poor.'

'Forgotten,' he said. 'No one knows that they live there. For all the changes in this culture, you see, at least there are fewer men living like that. You can't support a culture which indiscriminately allows poverty. You have to see the black and the white of everything.'

'Yes.'

Beyond the hovel, the mountain was coloured deep red, and a seam of minerals could be seen striping down through the rock. The mountainsides were brimming with cacti. The thorns were so sharp on these plants that even the slightest brush of cloth against them frayed the material completely.

'It's the survival of the fittest,' he said. 'At the moment we're destroying other species, but if we destroy too much, then we'll destroy ourselves. So we won't be the fittest.'

I ruminated about this as we rode. The path was sandy, and we swept over a pass marked by an iron cross, seeing nothing but mountains beyond. The highest peaks were streaked with snow.

'Hang on, that's just a catchphrase. What does it mean? I thought that one of the key elements of your theory was that it was because of better adaptation to local surroundings, competitiveness for local resources, that one individual survived instead of another.'

'Yes.'

'Well, in many cases we're not better adapted naturally, it's only our culture that is.'

'Culture is just a product of natural selection.'

'How do you know that? That's just a stipulation. You've no evidence for it.'

'No, I know. This is what my children say today, and sometimes they seem right. It makes sense, doesn't it? We've all been evolving for billions of years, and eventually we evolve a highly complicated brain which is capable of producing words and culture. We've never been able to find a locus for ourselves outside of our bodies, so that suggests the brain is the locus and it evolves through natural selection.'

He shrugged.

'But then I look around all these places, alone in nature again, and I'm not so sure.'

'Look at what your children say,' I said. 'Even your argument for natural selection depends on proving artificial cultural selection, and then making an analogy for natural selection. If they're saying that artificial selection depends on natural selection, their use of your argument is circular.'

I was becoming more absorbed in the convoluted discussion as we rode, forgetting the small dusty villages that came into view; the rocky gorges; the plunging river billowing at the bottom of this precipice; the mining tracks carved high into the mountains, choked and cloaked by the dust thrown up by stuttering trucks.

'Evidence never points in one way only,' I said. 'You know that. You've seen things. Symbols are always confused, and depend on their opposites to have any meaning. There is a dialectic to everything. The strength of your theory, for instance, depends on the apparent weakness in our culture's eyes of the idea of its opposite, divine creation. If there was no opposite to you, your theory would lose meaning.'

'Now that *is* nonsense. I agree with some of what you say, but now you're talking to me about the theory of the theory. Whatever happened to facts?'

'Your theory *is* a theory.'

'We have to have theories. You can't go telling me that theories are rubbish. Look at all the advances in technology that we've made because of science.'

'But isn't there a difference between practical science and theoretical science? When we observe that something works, like when we make an electronic reaction, then that's one thing. But when we start to theorize about *why* it works, then it's another.'

'So why have you been following me all this time? Why follow me when you think I'm wrong?'

'I admire you, it's some of your children I can't stand. And anyway, it's not a question of being wrong. You're a great man because you challenged the orthodoxy of your time. Our problem is that we see everything in terms of objective right and wrong, but there's no such thing. Everything is twin, even truth. You provided the twin to religious creationism, and now someone needs to provide the twin to you.'

Perhaps a condor was circling in the skies, painting the sky white and black with its self-resolving wings.

'Why?'

'Because thoroughgoing materialism today has become its own dogma. There's no debate, no questioning. We think there is only one answer to truth. And whenever we think that, we're in for a shock.'

'You're funny,' he said. 'You say all these things and yet you trust technology every day. You praise poverty . . .'

'I don't praise poverty.'

'You think we should all go back to the country. The noble savage! There's plenty wrong with our culture, but that idea is rubbish.'

'Often people are taken to even worse poverty when they're forced to migrate to cities,' I said.

'You don't know anything about rural struggle,' he said.

'Neither do you. How can either of us compare urban with rural struggle? OK, so I'm a hypocrite. I rationalize but I believe in anti-rationalism. I moan about language and then write about things. But I can't help being a hypocrite. We're all hypocrites in the end, aren't we? I mean, you show me one person who is completely consistent in their values and beliefs! That's the endless dialectic of our concepts. We see things in opposites, so our rationality and logic have to be double also. Our culture has become so incredibly complex that we can't be anything but hypocrites. And we can't do anything but write. We communicate with words now, that's the way it is. Soon we'll communicate in one language only. And we're all cultural beings. I am, too. I can only write, because that's what I've become.'

'That's what you've evolved into, you mean.'

'Now we're just talking about the meaning of words.'

'You seem to think we never do anything else. Don't you want to understand all these processes which you've watched this year?'

'We understand best when we're not thinking.'

'You're mad. You – you're the definition of lunacy.'

The valley of the Río Illapel was green after the rains, but the gorges further north were dry as dust. I rode for two and a half hours from Illapel, along a wide-bottomed valley dwarfed on all sides by mountains. The slopes were white with huge boulders, occasional tufts of grass skulking in their ponderous shadows. The boulders fought with forests of cacti for control of the mountains.

I was heading for the small mining centre of Combarbalá, home to the *Combarbalita*, a purplish mineral found only here. The track plunged into a deep gorge, with neither houses nor a breach in the mountains visible. I wondered if I could possibly be heading in the right direction, for the path seemed sure to peter out. All I could see were the immense mountains, the barren foretaste of death and demise plastering their sides, and the pure blue skies beyond the summits.

I rode on. After three hours more, I reached a mining town, Farellón Sánchez. But Sánchez, living with the will of the walls around it, was all but dead. There were scores of mud houses, boarded up and deserted, their roofs held down by boulders from the grasping gales. Huge complexes of buildings lay around in rubble, their shells pathetic shadows of themselves. Yet there were still a few families here. I saw plumes of smoke spiralling from one or two houses, and I was greeted by the inevitable desperate dogs, at whom I growled in kind until they slunk away with their tails between their legs.

For someone who had grown up eyeing even the tiniest, most snivelling, irritating little mutt as a potential Hound of the Baskervilles, I had become remarkably blasé around dogs. In fact, I discovered that riding a horse was the best course I could ever have taken in conquering my fear of dogs, for as I rode I gradually discovered the undeniable truth: as pack animals, dogs lack any individual leadership qualities and, if left to their own devices without any pack leader, are simply idiots. Since dogs are usually left to fend for themselves in South America, the result is often ridiculous.

Arriving in a deserted ghost town like Sánchez on my horse, I would be greeted by a posse of canine chumps tearing out at me. To begin with, I believed that they were just being friendly, and marking out their territory clearly. But gradually, I came to doubt that they were doing this. In fact, I doubt that the dogs knew what they were doing at all. They came to bark out of unmitigated confusion with their lot.

'What does a dog do?' I could see them all asking each other. 'Why are we here?' they went on, asking the eternal question (much more of an imponderable for dogs than for anything else).

And then, seeing this stranger trotting along the track, they tore out to ask me.

'Look, look, perhaps this kindly vagrant can tell us,' they shouted as they came. These snarls and barks were actually cries for help, poor things. But sometimes they didn't even make it beyond their initial salutary snarls. My conviction in the potential of dogs for sheer stupidity was cemented by one incident, two days' ride beyond Sánchez. A pack of five huskies tore out towards me, as usual. I heard the lead dog shouting to the others:

'Here he is, here he is, this man will tell us what to do with ourselves,' he said.

However, as the lead husky was about to launch the question, one of his companions, instead of bolstering the onslaught with his own salvo, turned to the lead dog and attacked him instead of me. As I continued on down the road, I watched in hysterics as the dogs ignored me and indulged in a mass brawl on the roadside.

'I want to ask him!'

'No, me!'

'Grrrr!'

'Look, look, he'll be off if we don't get after him!'

After a few whimpers, the huskies disentangled themselves and chased me again. The lead dog was a picture of eagerness and pleading. Sadly for him, just as he was about to ask the question, one of the followers couldn't bear the thought of his pal beating him to it.

The huskies forgot all about me, and began their brawl again on the roadside, angry and desperate at their apparently senseless fate.

These were the paradigmatic dogs of rural South America, left to trace their own path through the confused ashes of their world. It was small wonder that rabies was so prevalent. In a place like Sánchez, with moribund history dripping from the seams of the hillside, there was little for the dogs to do except go mad.

Once the few dogs of Sánchez had let me be, I was left to the silence of the immense mountains and valleys. Above the town was a smattering of buildings from the mine, and a grating sound from the ore crushers still at work. The sound echoed hollowly around the valley, like a ghost singing of its former resonance. It was only mid-afternoon, but the sun had already abandoned the precipitous hole of this valley, dug deep from the mountain heights.

I carried on through Sánchez, heading for the next hamlet, Matancillas. Shortly beyond the village was a ford. As I tried to coax Apple across, a purple jeep eased towards me the other way. The jeep was driven by Juan, the paramedic at Matancillas. I asked him how easy it would be to camp there, and he told me not to worry:

'You can stay with me,' he said. 'I know everyone there, and I'll find you forage.'

He suggested that I rest Apple and go with him to the mine. I was driven by the foreman along a track bordering the gorge. When we reached the mine, the truck was filled with ore carted towards the truck by wheelbarrows. The men were stripped to the waist, despite the icy wind that was rushing about in the prelude to nightfall. Looking at them, I found myself thinking back to the miners seen by Darwin, the *apires*: 'The average load [carried by these men] is considered as rather more than 200 pounds, and I have been assured that one of 300 pounds ... by way of a trial has been brought up from the deepest mine.' Take away the truck – and that was from the 1930s – and it was difficult to think that this area had changed at all. There was no electricity in Sánchez or Matancillas except in Juan's house, where there was a generator in case of nocturnal emergencies. There was no television. Until twenty years ago, the copper mine had been booming. There had been 800 people in Sánchez; now, there were about twenty. The men were paid by the amount of saleable copper that they produced, and if they had a bad month it was their bad luck.

'When I first came to Matancillas,' Juan said, 'I couldn't believe it. I wanted to get out! Before I came I imagined that it would be like the Central Valley – green and flat. Sometimes people come from high up in the mountains if there's an emergency, and I have to go and deal with it by horse. You've no idea how those people live. They've got no water (they bring it on mules from Illapel), they all live in the same room. Most of them die of Chagas disease in their forties or fifties – there are plenty of Vinchuga bugs around. The kids start to work when they're eleven or twelve, so they can never get out. None of them goes to a secondary school. They all marry each other: first cousins, second cousins, third cousins. Sometimes people come from the universities in the summer to help with a local project – building an extension to the school or something. They leave in shock. No one, not even in Illapel, knows the extent of the poverty in these communities.'

I had been told by people in the south of Chile that northerners were mean. But I found that the opposite was true. Every night, in the smallest, poorest villages – in the region which, along with the Mapuche lands, is the poorest in Chile – I met people of unending human warmth. Here in Matancillas, I met the community leader who insisted on stabling Apple and giving him fodder, and when I went to the school, all the children listened to me with invigorating freshness, and all shook my hand warmly, turning their faces away out of shyness when I left. In Combarbalá, a fireman and his family insisted that I sleep in their kitchen, even though they had not finished building the rest of their house and they slept in one room, a twin bunk and a single bed having to suffice for the parents and their three children. In Manquehua, the caretaker of the primary school refused to let me sleep in my tent outside, and opened his house to me. In Huampulla, the village leader gave me permission to sleep in the local village hall, beneath a thatched roof of old vines.

This part of Chile is not often seen. This is poor, isolated Chile, the Chile which many would rather forget lest it recall their consciences from their choking death in the Santiago smog, sensing how difficult it is to believe in the ideology of modern society when you are forced to confront the humanity and generosity of people who have nothing.

This is an area of hovels by the roadside, their windows eternally open, throwing light on a broken iron bar and a table laden with dust, nylon clasping the roof, biscuit wrappers flapping in the wind. Wafer-thin boys, swamped by jerseys hanging from them like tents, ride troops of mules over the broken hills, delving into the hillsides along with the brilliant colours, passing the mining huts where the men work and drink, and the women work and get beaten, and the boys and girls prepare to marry young and sing their parents' song: over and over again, the miners' song, redemptive and cathartic and painful. This land, the Andean heartland, gives birth to some of the world's most soulful music, the wrenching melodies of pan pipes and *djarangos*; for it is a land of soaring mountains and snows, creeping desert sweeping sand in your face full of thoughts, and thorn-bushes clinging to the plateaux, ready to pierce hard skins at any time.

I chattered with anyone I met along these empty tracks. Sometimes I reached a village, and men would press me to join them in drink. I came to one small hamlet on a Saturday and played in the football match. The routes were tough and harsh. Several times I had to cross passes of over 2000 metres. At one point I came to a place in the path where a boulder had all but blocked the way completely after the rains, and I had to dismount and forge a way for Apple through the debris. Occasionally I fell in with other travellers: a mule train carrying alfalfa high into the hills, or an old man out riding with his dog. They would often admire Apple, crooning over his smart gait, alert and rapid along the paths. He was perhaps the quickest of my horses to cover distance, and he was never overly tired by the end of the day. In these massive surroundings, we quickly became inseparable, used as we were to being with one another the whole time.

Two weeks after leaving Cabildo, I reached the Elqui Valley, and followed it down to the twin cities of Coquimbo and La Serena. I was on the verge of the last leg of Darwin's journey in Chile. I would stop, with Darwin, in Copiapó, and then travel to the Galápagos. The Elqui Valley was industrialized and relatively prosperous, a world away from the mining villages. The thought of Copiapó had been tantalizing me for months now. I was about to finish something which had become my life, and I should have been thrilled.

But I felt only sadness. I did not want to leave behind this life of endless discovery. I did not want to finally fulfil my desire, for I knew that all I would feel would be the emptiness of the desert.

III

*While travelling through these deserts one feels like a prisoner shut up
in a gloomy court, who longs to see something green and to smell a
moist atmosphere.*

Charles Darwin

In La Serena, Darwin and FitzRoy were guests of Dr George Edwards,
an English resident. Edwards' son, Agustín, became an illustrious indus-
trialist, founding some of Chile's best-known industries. Darwin's principal interest in the area lay in the step-terraces at nearby Coquimbo.
Here, he found shells of many existing species at a height of 250
feet [seventy-five metres] indicating, as in Concepción and over the
cordillera, the volatility of the earth's surface. He arrived in Coquimbo
on 14 May 1835, and it was with Dr Edwards that he set out up the
Elqui Valley on 21 May. Coquimbo itself was an excessively tranquil
place, and Darwin found that 'the town is remarkable for nothing but
its extreme quietness.'

He longed to return to England, but the potential geological interests
of his journey between Coquimbo and Copiapó drove him to make one
last horseback sally in South America. He was, however, thoroughly
bored with the rigours of an outdoor life: 'Excluding the interest arising
from geology such travelling would be downright martyrdom ... I am
tired of this eternal rambling, without any rest.' The urge to travel had
left him. He longed to return to his family in Shrewsbury. The nomadic
itch had been scratched out once and for all by the years of wandering
and discovery, his heartfelt experience of the terrific power and depth
of life. Like an immense, convoluted, rushing discussion, Darwin would
switch now from one extreme to another: from the wildness of his
journey, to a life of quiet marriage and study.

I understood his tiredness. He had experienced more in three and a
half years than most of us do in a lifetime. Unlike many people, he
himself made the first discoveries of many of the facts which he spent

the rest of his life writing about. This was the common denominator of the other two major proponents of natural selection as the *modus operandi* of evolution in Darwin's era, Alfred Russel Wallace and Joseph Hooker: all three had spent many years exploring. Although his years of reflection and experiment led Darwin to be more certain of the truth of his theory, he was never as completely dogmatic as many rhetoricians today. Darwin was so disturbed by the gaps in the fossil record that he believed they could be used in a serious counter-argument to his theory; and, although championed by reductionist scientists as the first person to hammer out a coherent and forceful path against religion, Darwin was not as dogmatic an atheist as many Darwinists today. His religious ideas were severely shaken by the death of his daughter Annie, aged ten, in 1851; nonetheless, three years before his death, he wrote: 'In my most extreme fluctuations I have never been an atheist in the sense of denying the existence of God. I think generally (and more and more as I grow older), but not always, that an Agnostic would be the more correct description of my state of mind.'

Darwin was always a reasonable man. He recognized that his theory depended on certain factual elements for which the evidence was incomplete (the fossil record, for instance). Perhaps, more deeply, having spent his life fighting religious dogma, he knew the dangers and short-sightedness that lay in *any* dogma. He knew how important it was to remain open, since it was by being open to new ideas that he had conceived his theory in the first place.

In intellectual terms, Darwin championed openness – yet his most dogmatic successors today are blind to any other force. Natural selection, it is said by some, is the only driving force in life, with culture its by-product. There is a digital genetic code which will explain everything about human composition and human traits. This digital code began with nothing more than the power of molecules to replicate themselves – and that is all there is to life. We can tell a story about all developments of characteristics through this selfish genetic code.

It is a good story, and parts of it seem true. Yet it is based on cultural assumptions. The assumption of selfishness, for instance, is a reflection of cultural experience, rather than any verifiable fact. I find it difficult now to generalize about human xenophobia and selfishness when during every day on my journey I was helped, fed and sometimes given clothes, by people who would never see me again, and who had no personal motive for helping me, living in hardship as they often did. If selfishness is supposed to be a metaphor, then it is an evil and inappropriate one.

The deepest assumption of all, though, is that any theory should be able to tell the whole truth. Our experience of the world is not of some ordered place where everything is rational and has coherent explanations. As people, we are all inconsistent and hypocritical. There is no reason why our theories should be any different. In fact, *prima facie*, it is more reasonable to suppose that they would share these characteristics with us. And yet, dogmatic as dogma can be, some say that natural selection is a theory which explains everything about life's development. The theory is closed to alternatives: anything which is non-materialistic is dismissed, according to the modern theory's own dogma, as non-verifiable superstition. It is claimed by scientific materialists that these theories are non-verifiable, but how many materialists have taken it upon themselves to see if other ways of understanding – for instance, the supernatural way in which a witch invokes a spirit – are false?

Natural selection does explain a part of our experience of life. It explains why, in a stable ecosystem, some species do better than others – the best-adapted species to an environment surviving ahead of the rest. But across the world people are surviving in places (such as Tierra del Fuego) in which they are not better naturally adapted than the local species and tribes which they hunt or which their industries kill off – it is only their cultural evolution which allows them to win the day. This cultural evolution has become its own force, far more potent and influential than anything else in the composition of the world today. Fascinatingly, Alfred Russel Wallace became a socialist at the end of his life, because he believed that wealth distorted the natural choice of marriage partners – he saw that an entirely different force was at work here. Yet these problems and questions, these challenges to the universality of the theory, are not recognized by the dogma.

Language has won the war, and generalized our conceptions of the world away from our perspectival natural beginnings. It continues to generalize, with a single global language a real possibility in the not-too-distant future of globalization. The generality encourages dogma, and leads us to scorn any other way of looking at the world – rather than conceiving that there could be many layers to the meaning and functioning of the world, as there are many layers to almost every sphere of our experience. The eradication of tribal societies across the world is not a phenomenon of natural selection's proving the greater strength of capitalist culture; it is far more insidious than that: it is the triumph of culture over nature, of the general over the particular. Language has generalized as it has developed, and given us theories, and theories have generalized our understanding of our place in the world.

All these generalizations are bastardizations. It is only when we relapse into our natural selves, when language and generality escape our minds, that we return towards our beginnings; and then the pain of our separation from these beginnings seems almost too much to bear.

I followed Darwin down the Elqui Valley to a police post on the fringes of La Serena. This city is known to maintain the most traditional colonial architecture left in Chile. Old photographs show that Santiago, too, used to have imposing arches, porticoes and patios in all its main streets – similar to the old buildings in Quito and Bogotá – until developers moved in and flattened them to make way for the great progress represented by skyscrapers. The city centre of La Serena is still filled with houses of great beauty and character, but now that it has become Chile's premier beach resort 'extreme quietness' is no longer as noticeable as it was in Darwin's day.

For the first time in seven years it had rained as far north as Copiapó, and everyone told me that I would see one of the great wonders of Chile – the desert in bloom. Whenever rain falls among the sands of the Atacama, the desert flowers in springtime. When the flowers die, they leave their seeds behind them, ready for the next rainfall to bring the world to life: to wheel life around its circle once again.

'You can't imagine how beautiful it is,' one girl told me in La Serena. 'Flowers as far as you can see, right up to the horizon.'

Even in death was life; in one thing, its opposite; in dullness, colour; in a unity of opposites, beauty and truth.

I set out with Apple, with no other possible route but the Pan-

American Highway before me. Although there was less traffic than in
the south, so that the riding was not too dangerous, the hard road took
its toll on Apple's legs. After I had travelled for three hours, I noticed
him beginning to limp. I dismounted, and saw that he had cut into his
fore heel with his hind leg. The gravel along the roadside had been
picked up by his hoof, and had spread into the cut and worsened it.
Although the cut was not too bad in itself and could be treated, continuing along the hard road would put pay to any sort of recovery which
he might make.

I couldn't believe it. I seemed to have worse luck riding horses than
I did betting on them – a cataclysmic state of affairs.

Apple was limping badly, and the cut was already full of pus. I loved
him, and his pain choked me. I stood by the roadside for ten minutes
or so, stroking his mane and just allowing my eyes and his to do the
talking. These were my only conversations now, speeches without
words. These were the exchanges I liked best.

I resolved to end the madness then and there. There were barely any
horses north of La Serena, this was the desert. Anyway, I had no money
left to buy a horse. I had spent everything on buying a ticket to the
Galápagos, leaving only a minimum to get me to Copiapó. Apple's
well-being was the most important thing now. I would lead him gently
to the next village, and find a home for him. Then I would walk to
Copiapó. Alone, finally alone, I would walk through the desert, hoping
to see it flower.

'Walk?' laughed a trucker, when I spoke to him about my problems
in the next village. 'I'll give you a lift, we can be there by dinner time.'

'I have to walk,' I said.

'Why? Look, why don't you stay here and get your end away with
the waitress? It'd only be a question of asking.'

He winked lewdly. We were sitting at a truck stop by the Pan-
American Highway, and I was trying to come to terms with the end
of my horseback journey. I explained my year, and then the man
understood.

'Oh,' he said. 'You have to walk. You can't finish it in a few hours.'

It was another 320 kilometres to Copiapó. I sold Apple to some
fishermen who knew a farmer in Vicuña who would buy him. Early
the next morning I set out, on my final leg. I had no horse; I left my

saddle here at Caleta Hornos. I took only my one smelly bag, my tent, sleeping bag, and one spare T-shirt.

I had nothing else worth taking.

Darwin's route from La Serena to Coquimbo cut over the coastal *cordillera* as far as the Huasco Valley, which he reached at Freirina. He followed the Huasco as far as the main settlement at Vallenar, before cutting over the *cordillera* to the valley of the Río Copiapó. Following the river past Tierra Amarilla and Paipote to the city of Copiapó, he met up with the *Beagle* in the port at the river's estuary. From here, the *Beagle* would make brief calls at Iquique and Callao, before heading for the Galápagos.

I had one map of this first section of the Atacama desert. Piecing together Darwin's journey to Freirina, during which he passed the settlements of Carrizal and crossed the dry river-bed of the Río Chañeral, it seemed possible to trace his route along the tracks through the desert that still exist; Carrizal was surely the modern village of Carrizalillo, and the Río Chañeral is still marked on maps. So I followed the Pan-American Highway past the small mining town of La Higuera until I reached the junction for the coast road to Carrizalillo. For the first day, the journey was pleasant enough. The road climbed a steep chain of hills and then fell into a beautiful valley, with a few shanties for the goatherds on either side, and tremendous mountains in all directions. Even though the road was still near the coast, the first snows of the *cordillera* could be seen. I reached La Higuera after six hours, and camped near the town.

The Pan-American was irredeemably straight for nearly twenty kilometres north of La Higuera, heading towards the great grey mass of desert mountains blocking off the end of the valley. There was still a smattering of grass left behind by the rains, and a chimera of green touched the desert. High on one of the hills was a splurge of tall trees, stripped bare and aloof like the telegraph poles in the desert, the only trees that could be seen in any direction. They were eucalyptus at the abandoned mine of El Tofo, surviving because of the *camachaca*, a coastal fog which often descends in these parts of Chile, giving moisture and life to a few hardy plants. The vast plains, stretching to the fringes of consciousness; the rugged mountains, building barriers on every side; the aridity, the stillness, the total absence of life – this place was a close cousin of Patagonia.

After three hours' walking, I turned off towards Carrizalillo. This track trundled through another immense valley, following the dry Río Los Choros. Tremendous rock walls sprung up vertically on either side, leaping into the lonely desert, and the valley floor was carpeted with cacti. There were no cars tearing past, nothing but the utter stillness of the desert reclaiming me. Sometimes I might stop, and hear nothing but the humming buzzing coughing shouting screaming repetitive silence.

The garrulous chatter bunged up my thoughts completely.

After another four hours, I crested a hill and walked down into the hamlet of Los Choros Bajos – a village of two streets and several bars. I was famished, and had to find something to eat. I walked into the first bar I saw, and put my sombrero down on a dusty table, passing my hand through my hair and wondering where I would go to next; where I could put my tent up; how many more days my journey had left in it. Three men were sitting next to the bar, several empty cartons of wine fallen like dead flies around them. They were about as sober as the worm in a tequila bottle.

'Come on,' cried the oldest man, Don Manuel. 'Come and have a glass of wine.'

His companions were Lucho – a peon from southern Chile whom everyone called *el Temucano* – and a fisherman called Ramón.

'Come on,' they cried. 'What's a young man like you doing walking on his own through the desert? You must be mad.'

Words stumbled slowly from me. They took my torpor for unease.

'Don't worry about us,' said Don Manuel. 'We're good men. With us, everything is *legal*.'

'*Legal!*' cried the others.

'Ask anyone you like in Choros Bajos about Don Manuel, and they'll all tell you – everything's *legal*!'

'Have a glass of wine,' chuckled Lucho. 'I'm a long way from home. I flew in with my private plane seven years ago, but it crashed and I've been repairing it ever since.'

I was so tired and worn out that I actually believed this. Then Don Manuel concocted an even more unlikely story.

'I only came to Los Choros in 1949,' he said. 'I came by plane. With a professional pilot's licence.'

'Ha, you're so drunk you're still flying!' laughed Ramón. They all laughed so much that they nearly fell off their stools. At this point, even more improbably, a car pulled up in a flurry of dust and three elegant women walked into the bar, sat down, and ordered a litre of wine.

My three companions were paralysed by this unprecedented occurrence. They were red-faced and their eyes were like saucers. They all tried to forget their winey whimsy.

'*Niñas, niñas,*' cried Don Manuel. 'Come and talk to an old man like me. There are plenty of women in Los Choros, but none of them are as beautiful as you!'

Everyone laughed, even the women, who were students from Viña del Mar. They were heading for Punta de Choros, the next village, where they hoped to hire a fishing boat and swim with the dolphins who lived in the bay.

'I'm going there now,' said Ramón. 'I'll guide you if you like.'

'Don't listen to him,' urged Don Manuel. 'My son has a fishing boat, I'll come with you in the car and introduce you.'

'We haven't got room,' they laughed apologetically.

'I know lots of people in Punta de Choros. I've got children, grand-children, great-grandchildren, all there,' said Don Manuel. 'Space is no problem. You should be like the *amigo* here. He came on foot. He wouldn't mind about a little thing like that.'

'Where are you from?' one of them asked me.

'*¡Él viene de Inglaterra!*' shouted Lucho, and all three men roared with laughter. But none of the girls believed me.

'Honestly,' I said. '*Yo soy Inglés.*'

But they just took me for a wanderer as drunk and mad as my three friends, and they left the place quickly.

'What a shame,' mused Ramón, when they'd gone.

'They were all angels,' said Don Manuel.

There was nothing to be done, though, and we returned to plying ourselves with the haziness of red wine. Ramón soon left, but I sat with Lucho and Don Manuel for many hours. The old man had been a fisherman, a muleteer, a philander and a wanderer. He should have been an old man of the sea, wise and content, but his endless rampaging dissolution had brought him nothing but pain. He had looked at the young women with the eyes and will of a twenty-year-old, unable to accept age as a fact of life. In the morning, he would belch and groan, double up in the searing aches of his bones and his hangover, bitten by the pain of ageing when he still wanted to be young. The wine flushed out his pain glass by glass, as we became fuzzier and fuzzier, as our words slurred and lost their round edges, as we talked the wisdom and nonsense of red wine. Lucho was full of pain also, and the two turned to each other after many hours, to prove the saying that there is a poet under every Chilean stone. Spontaneously, without any apparent effort, they began speaking in rhyming verse, the one following the other. Don Manuel had lent me his harmonica, and I played a ditty which I had invented a few months before, as they spoke in verse, accompanying my song with their own feelings, accompanying this senseless sweating song, this drunken song, our redemption.

'What's the song about?' they asked me, when we had finished.

I laughed.

'It's not about anything. It's just music.'

They smiled, happy at the beauty which can come with purposelessness.

Lucho invited me to stay the night with him. I intended to leave the next day, along the coast towards Carrizalillo, but I stayed for three days. Why would I have done a thing like that? I was so close to my goal, and I was just procrastinating, delaying life. We didn't do anything special. He lived in a tiny box built of mud and straw, with one bed and one stove and one table and one chair. Here in the valley there were several olive groves, and Lucho was the caretaker for one of them. He ploughed the earth with his donkey, helped harvest the crop of olives, arranged the irrigation – he did all these things, and yet he was never very busy. He worked for a few hours each day, but the rest of the time he looked for wine or food.

'My father ran a bar,' he told me. 'There were always so many people coming in and out, drinking. We were thirteen brothers and sisters, and our mother couldn't control us. We all used to steal a glass from the vat when no one was looking. I started when I was seven and have never stopped.'

He was an alcoholic. When he drank, he was suddenly vibrant and forthcoming. He called me *viejo lindo* ('lovely old boy') as we talked. His face reddened, his eyes beamed brightly and he seemed content; and then in the morning, he would be dull and downcast, and his face would stiffen and his soul would clamp itself shut. With the drink, he was happy, like a little boy – returning to himself – as we sneaked out to the shop to buy wine, walking quickly and furtively, Lucho hiding from public gaze for he did not want his *patrón* to see him drinking. Then we rushed back to the house with our drink, conspirators and naughty boys, chattering about ourselves with absurd self-importance.

'Yes, *viejo lindo*, everything must be for a reason, mustn't it? Nature does nothing by chance. Everything is arranged and structured in the world. We Chileans belong to our country for a reason, just like you English people belong to yours. And then if things are changing, there must also be a reason. I look at myself and I think the same. I haven't seen my daughter for seven years. I came here just to work for a while, to ease the pain of my divorce, and I've never been able to go back. But God has done it for a reason, of that I'm sure. All I ask of my God is that he give me my health. My daughter may be getting the love of another man ... That ... that upsets me ...'

He choked and sniffed his tears; they fell down his cheeks, scorching and soothing his skin with their burning pain and the moist touch of their humanity.

'... But ... *viejo lindo* ... we have to have faith, don't we? Without faith, we're nothing. Ay, I will stay with my health, and I have faith that God will answer my prayers.'

He was immensely poor. On my first day there he took me on a twenty-kilometre walk along the coast towards Carrizalillo, where a friend – Juan – worked, fishing the sea.

Juan had a single solitary line which he slung out into the profound sea, hoping to hook out some vestige of life to keep his wheel turning.

'If he's got fish, he'll give me some. I've worked with him for months at a time, and we always get on.'

The land between Los Choros and Juan's hovel was unmitigated desert. Opposite the hovel was an oasis of green, a *parcela* of olive groves living off some invisible lifeline in the arid waste. Lucho left the main track, and we walked along a path of loose sand to the shanty, a miserable little room of corrugated iron covered by a tarpaulin.

Veronica, Juan's wife, was the only person there. Lucho asked if she could give us fish.

'No,' she said. 'We've hardly caught a thing all week. I haven't even got enough money to buy bread.'

She did have three fish hanging up on a wire hook by her hovel, though.

'I'll swap you three fish for two kilos of bread,' she said.

'I haven't got any money,' said Lucho. 'You don't have a thousand pesos, do you, *viejo lindo*?'

I paid her for the fish, and we began to walk back towards Choros Bajos. Near her hovel was another, and she and Lucho went inside to have a look. There was no one there.

'Look, look,' cried Veronica. 'They've got a *merluza* [hake]. Let's take it. Then we can have a proper meal.'

So they stole the fish, and I hung around guiltily. Then we walked back through the desert. Veronica floundered, because she was immensely unfit and unused to walking. The village twinkled dully through the brown light and the brown earth, an impossible sight, so far away that it looked near. The fish swung loosely at my side, dangling from the hook that broke the skin of their mouths and locked their jaws rigid and apart in the dumb cry of death.

When we reached Lucho's house, Veronica cooked the meal. I sifted through the olives which were soaking in a bucket of brine. An oily smell soon seeped through the house. Lucho put on the radio, but the batteries were long dead, and only a dull and uninformative crackle cranked out of the plastic box.

It would crackle and buzz and crack out its fuzzy code for ever, unless someone recharged the exhausted batteries.

'Can I have the batteries?' asked Veronica.

'What for?' asked Lucho. 'They're useless. They've been like this for weeks.'

'Will you give them to me?'

'All right.'

She pocketed them greedily.

'You have to boil them for an hour in brine,' she said. 'Then they'll work again.'

She finished cooking, gobbled down some fish, gaping like a gulping fish herself, and then went to buy bread in the village; leaving me alone with Lucho.

By this stage, my body was shattered by every step that I had taken. For the three nights I stayed with Lucho, we slept with the night and woke with the dawn, but still I felt tired and unwilling to leave. For I knew that Lucho would be the last of these wise and forgotten rural figures that my journey would bring me. When he laughed, I saw the faces of the *gauchos* and *guasos*, the Mapuches and miners, fishermen and policemen, marines and farriers, lighthouse guards and drunk old men telling me about witches. They were all there, talking with Lucho, sighing with Lucho, laughing and crying and bidding me farewell, regretting my departure from their ways.

Floods from the past year were washing over me in my thoughts. By the time I reached Copiapó I would have ridden and walked almost 6000 kilometres. My mind was a constant picture which would never stay still. It took me to plains and glaciers and deserts, cliffs and beaches and the *cordillera*; I was talking to thousands of people, laughing with them, sighing and saddening my soul with the depth of suffering, lightening and shouting joyfully with the heady nobility of the spirit, with the goodness and generosity of all these wonderful wisps in my imagination; I was following every strand of every street and track diving off into the desert or the forest, keeping to every twist and turn and then losing the path, foundering, overcome by loneliness and despair.

And then I was singing my loneliness, my ears waving with the song's happy air.

I was laughing, laughing, my brain addled by the wine, my face red, my thoughts unclear, all lines of sight fuzzy, blending, indistinct. All objects were collapsing into each other's souls, carousing with each other, falling from the windowsill out into the starry night. Suddenly they seemed clear, as I focused on their last disappearance from my experience. For, strangely enough, just as the memories vanished into the irredeemably drunken night, I thought I understood what I had seen.

But by the time I woke in the morning, I had forgotten.

★

I had been planning to walk from Carrizalillo over the desert to Freirina, but when I reached the village this turned out to be impossible. There were no roads as such, nor hamlets nor people. There had once been mines high in this *cordillera* but now these were deserted. Old hands told me that I would be sure to lose myself, in the maze of winding tracks that flourished in the interminable desert. I had no beast of burden for my water and provisions now, I had only my one smelly bag. The route to the Huasco Valley was no longer through the mountains to Freirina, but to the east. It took me two days to retrace my steps to the Pan-American Highway and begin the long and lonely walk to Copiapó.

When I arrived, the numbers of cars passing accentuated my solitude. Had I been on my own in the desert, I would not have felt so strange. But as it was, steady streams of cars rushed past. It would take them three hours to get to Copiapó – it would take me six days. Every day I walked. I got up with the dawn, and walked for hours and hours and hours. For the first three days – 120 kilometres to Vallenar – the land was barren but at least not too desperately empty. There were truckers' stops and hamlets spaced out at intervals of three or four hours along the road. I arrived, hot and flushed, and ate bowls of broth in stolid silence. Then I continued on in the afternoons, the sun killing my stride and heating my heart, my thoughts slow and vanishing into the fatigue of the end of the day. I would reach another truckers' stop for nightfall, and eat an evening meal. Then I would climb into the tent, sleep and ready myself for the morning.

It was my routine. I barely exchanged more than a handful of sentences in a day. A few comments as I arrived for lunch, a few as I arrived for dinner.

'What are you doing?'

'Walking to Copiapó.'

'Oh.'

'Do you get many people walking past?'

'Sometimes. People like walking.'

And the rest of the day I had left to myself. Beyond Vallenar, the truckers' stops were sparse. There were four between Vallenar and Copiapó, the last two stretched out at an interval of over fifty kilometres. That was a complete day's walk, and I would go on through the vastness, trying to occupy myself. I lost myself in the desert. I loved

that place, despite the heartless uniformity, the sterility, the loneliness.
I felt as free as I had done in Patagonia.

What is it about the desert which can move us so? What is it that
led Hudson to write his most beautiful and meditative prose? Is it the
stillness so absolute that you can hear nothing but the buzzing of your
thoughts? The sudden joy when a sound of life breaks the void of
silence, the faraway call of a bird wheeling over the plains? The endless
space which is void of any object to clutter your picture of yourself?
The contrast between this space and the deafening dialogue of a city,
loud and incessant, the city which hides us from ourselves through
distractions whereas the desert confronts us with ourselves – there
being nothing to study in the desert but yourself? Is it the silence of
God, the peace of being finally alone and able to talk to a world that is
able to listen?

Questions, only questions. Why must there be one answer, when
there are so many questions?

My mind turns from one thought to another and believes that each
might touch the truth. Or perhaps all answers possess truth. Like a
great manual of discussion and argument, detailing every possible
thought and demonstrating why each might be true, perhaps we can be
empathetic with every answer and every question, see the merits in
one answer and then in another – like a promiscuous bee buzzing from
flower to flower, scenting the beautiful pollen of life, dropping our
offspring beneath us as we flit.

They had told me that the desert would be in flower, and in parts it
was. North of La Higuera, I came across several blooms stretched out
between the rocks. Their colours burnt even though the day was dull
with *camachaca*. The brilliance softened the drudgery of walking along
the road, being laughed at and dismissed as mad by many of the people
who passed. But the flowers had not bloomed as much as I had hoped,
nor as much as I had been told. Their beauty evaporated as I passed
Vallenar, and walked on along to Copiapó.

Here, the road was straight and vanished into the distance. The valley
was bare and arid, set between great walls of mountains on each side.
I walked as fast as I could because I could only just manage the fifty
kilometres in the interval between dawn and dusk. When evening
came, and I pitched my tent, a shivering wind would hustle across the

plains, and the valley would be enveloped by haze. Before I slept, the stars would already be twinkling and ready to glitter through the night.

This was the conversation, the endless conversation of the desert. Long after our culture's single language has reclaimed the comfort of silence and the earth, the desert will be there, talking without signs and without time, and waiting for flowers to burst forth anew.

The restaurants were all fly-ridden and squalid, but they were my only contacts with people. When I left in the mornings, at the back of my mind I feared that I might never speak again. Perhaps the sun would strike me down with heart failure, in the long walk between one restaurant and another. I talked myself out of irrational fear, but my thoughts kept wandering, completely uncontrolled, as nomadic and senseless as myself. At the restaurant seventy kilometres north of Vallenar, the staff told me that there were no more buildings until the outskirts of Copiapó. So the next day I walked hard. I had to carry all my water and a few buns, the only food I could eat that day.

I camped alone in the desert, and then finally, ten months after setting out from Lockhart's farm, I reached Copiapó. The road crested a pass, and wound down slowly through the desert. Copiapó was waiting for me, in a hollow surrounded by mountains. My legs were worn out, and I was able to go on no more. I had managed to save my knees from too much pain by keeping to the sand by the roadside, but they were still groaning when I arrived. Darwin had made a brief excursion into the hills around the city, but I was too exhausted to follow him.

'Copiapó, Copiapó,' I kept saying to myself as I walked towards the target. The word sounded musical, poetic, meaningful to my ears. I tried tiredly to grasp what it meant to me, but I could think nothing more. Words were gone. I was left only with images, nature talking to me because my ears were too tired to listen to culture just yet.

I saw my road, set tortuously between the pine forests, plunging and rising and winding and falling and bridging rivers, and vanishing into a tangle of trees beyond; emerging suddenly on a high and barren slope, the mountains multicoloured with minerals, the air pure, the atmosphere transparent; tumbling into a valley and rolling into one enormous and unending plain, where I imagined that I could gallop for ever, leaving behind me the pungent stench of this tawdry mining city, where women fought each other and men drank hollowly in the rusting bars around the city, callous and sad and joyful and generous and fascinating in their first leave of absence from their workplace for months.

And, as I walked into their workplace, reaching the city of which I had dreamt for so long, I was not surprised to be greeted by a carbuncle of fumes and noise and pollution, offspring of the mines high in the Andes. My mind cleared, and I found it easy to picture those mines, and the workers, stripped to the waist, burrowing and drilling and tearing the minerals from their home.

PART NINE

Journey's End: The Galápagos

The birds are strangers to man. So tame and unsuspecting were they,
that they did not even understand what was meant by stones being
thrown at them.

Charles Darwin on the Galápagos

The more I travelled, the more careless I became. I lost everything. By the time I reached the Galápagos, the only book I had left was about exotic diseases. These books must be the worst items to have in your luggage if, like me, you are travelling alone, and – like me – you are a total hypochondriac. Flicking through it in the Galápagos I managed to persuade myself that a dog which had bitten me two months before had certainly been rabid, and that I had only hours to avoid the peculiarly unpleasant onset of rabies described in graphic detail in this book.

Luckily, my carelessness sometimes stopped me from reading. Near Ovalle, I had trodden on my glasses during a night-time wander (I always kept them discreetly hidden in my shoe overnight), smashing one of the lenses. So I tucked them safely away in the pocket of my only shirt, to keep the frame and the other lens intact. Then, as I was trudging up the Pan-American, I dropped my shirt on the floor, trod absent-mindedly on it before bothering to pick it up, and so contrived to smash the other lens as well.

My vision became at best misty. I trudged up that road, seeming to have lost everything. I had lost my glasses. I had lost my Dictaphone and two compasses. I had lost my clocks, watches and all toiletries. I had lost my horse, my saddle, companionship and all possessions save my bag and the grime inside it. I have always been clumsy, but my chaotic fumblings reached their apogee at this moment in my life. None of these things mattered to me any more. I had spent so long in my own company that the only thing that mattered was my well-being. Glasses? They didn't matter. It can be interesting to see only vaguely for a while. It allows your imagination to paint the world for you. Horses, saddles? Irrelevant. I would talk to myself now. A radio or books? Something to keep me company? –

– What for? I kept myself company, and everything else was a distraction.

Perhaps surprisingly, when I reached the Galápagos I still had my sombrero left. This wasn't the hat which Juan-Carlos had given me (I had lost that as well), but another that I had bought to replace it. Some days after arriving on the archipelago, my hat caught on a lintel on board ship and was blown from my head. It wafted gently backwards away from the ship until it had settled in the wake.

The ship ploughed on through the waters, tossing the froth aside as it went, leaving the hat rising and falling gently, standing there serenely in the waters from which we were irreversibly drifting away. The hat rested there for a long time, still in view, betraying the sensation that I could return to it and reclaim it as my own – even though it was gone – and I would return to England with virtually nothing of material value.

Sometimes I still see that hat, receding gently as time itself until it is a dot on the horizon. I could stare enchanted for all the daylight hours that are left, watching it until the wake vanishes into the eternal blue haze of the sea. I love this hat, now obsolete and washed away to a deserted shore. I will watch it still, even when it has no place to breathe but my memory, my painful glorious good memory; I will look on, as watchful of the sea as a lighthouse.

Then I will see nothing but bubbling watery wrath, stretching away into nothingness until it is gone for good.

The Galápagos Islands have developed great mystique over the years as the birthplace of Darwin's theory of evolution. Yet, as has only been realized comparatively recently, there was no spurt of sudden enlightenment, no 'Eureka' moment à la Archimedes. Darwin did not land on the islands, make a few observations and find that his ideas coalesced into one impregnable super-theory. On the contrary, it was only long after he had visited the archipelago that the islands' importance became clear.

The *Beagle* spent only five weeks among the Galápagos before setting out across the Pacific towards Tahiti and New Zealand. During this comparatively brief visit, Darwin visited just four islands: Floreana (whose English name is Charles), Isabela (Albemarle), Santiago (James) and San Cristóbal (Chatham). Darwin rushed around quickly, collecting as many species as possible, but he was also indebted to the work of other collectors on board the ship. In fact, he derived virtually all his locality information for the Galápagos finches by borrowing, after his return to England, the carefully-labelled collections of three other *Beagle* shipmates.

It was by collating the combined information and specimens of all collectors on the *Beagle* that Darwin amassed his overview of Galápagos flora and fauna. The result was remarkably complete. He identified twenty-six species of land bird – whereas modern ornithologists classify twenty-nine – all of which were endemic to the archipelago, describing all thirteen species of finch. He recognized both the land and marine iguanas, although he failed to distinguish between the common terrestrial iguana in the Galápagos and the one which is exclusively endemic to Santa Fé Island (Barrington). As far as the famous Galápagos tortoises are concerned – whence the islands derive their name* – although Darwin himself only recognized three species, he later recalled that an English resident, Nicholas Lawson, had told him that the tortoises varied from island to island, and that Lawson himself could distinguish between fourteen different species across the archipelago.

This was typical of how Darwin recognized the islands' significance for his ideas. It was when the species were examined by experts in London that he began to see the significance of those lonely lumps of rock in the Pacific. Although he had long been enthusiastic about studying the archipelago, having written to William Fox that 'I look forward to the Galapagos with more interest than any other part of the voyage', when the time came Darwin was homesick and worn out with travelling. The sterility of the deserts of northern Chile had sapped his wanderlust from him once and for all. He would still have over a year more of the voyage before him on leaving the Galápagos, and this thought would surely have tortured Darwin had he known it at the time. As it was, he had been impatient with FitzRoy when they had

---

* Galápagos meaning 'Giant Tortoise' in Spanish.

made what he saw as an unnecessarily lengthy break at Lima. Increasingly, he found it difficult to relate to the captain. He itched to return to England and begin analyzing all the species that he had amassed, and when he was in the Galápagos his state of mind cannot have been too cheery.

When he finally reached England, Darwin was delighted. Dazzled by the greenery of his homeland above all the wonders that he had seen, he wrote to FitzRoy during his journey back to Shrewsbury that 'I am sure we should have thoroughly agreed that the wide world does not contain so happy a prospect as the rich cultivated land of England.' He was welcomed by an impressive array of British scientists, all eager to hear of his discoveries. Lyell wanted more information about the earthquake at Concepción. Darwin was invited to lecture at the Royal Geological Society. His species were analysed by leading men such as Richard Owen (who studied his fossils) and the zoologist John Gould. And it was now, as the results of the analysis appeared, that Darwin became increasingly excited. In March 1837, Gould told Darwin that not only were the species of Galápagos finch completely new, but that they varied from island to island. This was a catalyst in shifting Darwin towards his radical new ideas, and shortly afterwards he began his famous transmutation notebooks. But it was not until eight years later that his friend Joseph Hooker's analysis of the Galápagos flora showed Darwin that the geographical distribution of the islands' plants was as unique and varied as that of the wildlife. Now his memory of Lawson's story about the tortoises could take its rightful place in the growing picture of the archipelago's unique ecosystem.

The islands were volcanic and, geologically speaking, very young. As they were volcanic, the islands had never been connected to the South American mainland, and the species on each island were separated from one another by natural boundaries. Separated in this way, the species had the opportunity to develop differently, although perhaps sharing a common ancestor (for although the species were unique and endemic, they bore close relation to counterparts in South America). Somehow – either swimming or flying or on rafts of vegetation – the animals' ancestors had come to the islands, and as they had moved to inhabit different islands, so the species had begun to diverge until a situation could emerge where there were different species of tortoise or finch on islands which were all clearly visible one from another.

Thus the idea was born that species were not created perfectly by an omniscient and omnipotent creator, but adapted and changed according to the success which genetic changes met with in new environments.

The Galápagos would present a curious spectacle to Darwin, if he were able to revisit the islands today. On one hand, the wildlife has the same characteristics as in 1835 – the animals are as tame and unique as ever, still trapped in their prehistoric time warp. On the other hand, the archipelago has changed beyond recognition, now being Ecuador's prime tourist destination, with 97 per cent of the archipelago under the jurisdiction of the National Park. The bays are full of luxury yachts and motor boats, shuttling well-heeled North Americans and Europeans from one unique site to another, bringing in needed hard currency to Ecuador. Away from the inhabited islands of Santa Cruz, San Cristóbal, Isabela and Floreana, visitors are only allowed to land on official visitor sites, of which there are fifty.

I was apprehensive about visiting the islands. I had spent the whole year in such wild and little-frequented places that I wasn't sure how I would take to being thrust amid throngs of tourists and the tension that I anticipated. Although there are plenty of people with plenty of money in the Galápagos, most of the revenue goes into the hands of tour operators and hotels, many of which are owned by foreigners (a lot of the most profitable businesses are North American). Meanwhile, the debate about tourism's impact on the ecosystem of the islands rages: one camp says that the tourists bring money to the National Park, allowing the animals to be protected from poachers; another camp says that the tourists ruin the natural ecosystems of the animals and pollute the islands.

It seems misleading to me to claim that tourism has been a primary cause of the deterioration of Galápagos ecosystems. Most of the harm was done long before tourists came to the islands (the promotion of tourism only began as recently as the 1970s). In the early nineteenth century, the islands became a great whaling post, not least because of their famous tortoises. The tortoises live for up to 200 years, so it is still possible to see the same tortoise that Darwin might have seen. They are famous for being able to survive for months without food or water, so the whaling ships used to fill their holds with tortoises, thus having fresh meat during their prolonged voyages – the *Beagle* itself left the islands with thirty tortoises which were eaten during the homeward journey. The consumption of the tortoises is just a part of the history of ecological destruction in the Galápagos that has been brought about by people. The feral animals, particularly goats, which are plundering the islands' vegetation and threatening the habitats of a large number of endemic species, have probably abounded since the first European ship reached the islands, under the Bishop of Panamá in 1535. The people who lived and fished in the waters around the islands – the Galapagueños – brought animals with them, and themselves used to kill the endemic species for food.

In fact, Darwin noticed that there were large numbers of goats on Floreana when he visited the island, and also that large numbers of tortoises had already been killed there. The wholesale changes in one of the world's unique ecosystems were going on even in 1835 – tourism is just the end of the process. When he arrived on Santiago, there were so many land iguanas that he found it difficult to find a place to pitch a tent, but the quantities of such species have plunged since then. Even today, economic pressures have brought new threats to bear: the market for exotic foods such as sea cucumbers and lobsters has made them distressingly scarce among the islands. Lobster fishing is a key economic resource for the Galapagueños, and yet the lobster fishery is largely uncontrolled, many baby lobsters being fished out as well as mature crustaceans, meaning that the stock is getting no chance to replenish itself. I spoke to a fisherman who estimated that the stock has dropped tenfold in the past thirty years.

As the islanders are forced to extract increasing quantities of goods in order to keep pace with the competition, stocks in the Galápagos are exhausted. Tourism throws a measure of control into this situation, since if people did not subsidize the animals by coming to stare at them, they would doubtless – given the current global climate – be killed and used for some other economic end. The situation is far from ideal, but it is scarcely an isolated case across the world. Nowhere seems to be sacrosanct, not even the paradigmatic paradise on earth. Before people discovered the islands, the animals lived in comparative peace (they mostly have few natural predators). But now the value of these species has been reduced to that which can be studied and ana-lyzed and 'known'.

And so, as the tortoises are depleted, along with the iguanas and the multitudinous species of birds and plants which are found only here, teams of students, lecturers, professors, tourists, writers, photographers and journalists come to observe, and leave with that perverse sat-isfaction of having filed the Galápagos in the reams of knowledge which expand progressively with every year. Every one of us that visits must know the islands, just as Europe came to know America – poring liberally over untouched beauty.

Darwin's theory is perhaps the centrepiece of this great body of knowledge. Scientists from a wide range of disciplines are exploring its ramifications in an eclectic body of fields. Philosophers and historians are beginning to use Darwinism as a key to unlock elements of their disciplines. It is a theory whose consequence appears to be almost universal. Now that I had followed Darwin so far, and was exhausted, sated, by the demands of this journey, I began to see how his experience was embodied in his theory. For Darwin's life was full of struggles, ever after he set sail with the *Beagle*. The rigours of the voyage were unceasing; and his health deteriorated so badly in the many years following his return that he was unable to work for more than four hours in a day.

There is no doubt that, had Darwin chosen to settle into a country parsonage rather than travel around the world, his life would have been immeasurably easier. But without those struggles, his life would ultimately have been less complete, and the intellectual landscape of our times would have been emptier. It is a commonplace obser-vation that many of the world's great discoveries and ideas have been wrought from struggles, and this fits very well with Darwinism and Darwin's own life. This is the theory which says that all existence is a struggle to survive and, were it not for the struggles, there would not be 'winners' and 'losers' in the battlefield of ideas. Those with radical new ideas must fight to overcome the prevailing conservatism which always springs from a ruling system. Darwin's theory is, in this sense, the perfect embodiment of itself, triumphant in the struggle.

Like Darwin, I had been struggling through my whole journey. I was washed out, and had no sense that I might soon feel the irrepressible wanderlust which had brought me here. I was all too happy at the thought that, by returning to Britain, I might be removing myself from the immediacy of these struggles. For through my experiences, I had become aware that the technological revolution has removed the real struggle from much of everyday life. Of course, in the poor countries of the world people still struggle to live day by day. But there is a sense in which 'struggles' have been redefined in industrialized countries, with the physical struggles that underpinned life in previous centuries largely being replaced by mental ones, so much so that mental health problems are threatening to constitute the next health epidemic. There is no longer a struggle to *live*: the comfort of technology, combined with the pillage of the world's poorest countries by the richest ones, have erased this in the corporate flab of post-modernity.

But as the struggle to live has ebbed away, so have the conditions for a rival orthodoxy to challenge that in existence. Perhaps never before has the struggle for independent thought been so crucial. Nowadays, the necessity of debate is belittled by neo-liberal 'certainties' and a political arena which is shaped by unquestionable economic mantras: the 'free' market, 'growth' and 'competition'. Along with the political one-way traffic has come cultural Unitarianism, while the press has lost all capacity to challenge accepted beliefs, and instead seems increasingly to be concentrating on opinion and not the reporting of news.

And so, as I pondered returning to the old life, away from the fictive wanderings of my mind and the chaos of my journey, irony refused to hide from me. Darwin's ideas – the spirit of struggle – would have troubled him even more than they did had he been born today. For with the growing encroachment of industrialization on the ecosystems which shaped his thoughts, even the sharp insights born during his travels might have struggled to emerge. Here on the Galápagos, the tortoise population – which was so crucial to him – has been decimated, and he would have been unable to visit all the relevant sites because of the control exerted by the 'mechanisms' of the free market. In fact, if Darwin had made the same journey today, he might well have been unable to reach the revolutionary conclusions which he avowed in *The Origin of Species*.

Only then, perhaps, could our great body of knowledge have been returned to the islands, untouched.

I hitched back from Copiapó to Santiago, said farewell to my friends in the city, and then caught a direct bus from Santiago to Guayaquil in Ecuador. Darwin had sailed almost directly from Copiapó to the archipelago, and the bus would be my *Beagle*. I had little time left, and there was no way I was going to try to ride across the Atacama desert when Darwin had gone by boat. The bus journey took four days, briefly passing Iquique and Lima in any case, and I then spent three days in Guayaquil waiting for my flight out to the Galápagos.

I arrived at Puerto Ayora, the main tourist centre on the islands, which was much as I'd feared. The place was full of Galapagueños overcharging and people with wads of cash complaining about being overcharged. The islanders felt overrun by tourists (it was August and this was the peak season), and the relationship was tense. The main bay was beautiful, its waters clear as an Andean stream, dotted with storks and frigate birds, the black volcanic rock beyond rising into thick vegetation. The bay was freckled with cruise ships, which twinkled like a small city by night.

I booked myself quickly on the cheapest cruise I could find around the islands, to see the famous Galápagos wildlife. I found myself on a boat that was so slow that it made the tortoises seem like motor boats. While the slick catamarans and luxury yachts motored tranquilly from one visitor site to another, our boat growled and chuntered leaden-footed in their wakes. It was a small boat and there were only four other passengers, three Germans and an Israeli. The captain was a wonderful cook, and what we missed out on through speed and comfort was made up for by his cuisine.

We visited many islands, and it was a very pleasant experience – exactly what these things are supposed to be like, but nothing at all like my experience of the rest of the year. I wasn't used to chatting in English, being waited on for my three meals a day, and I certainly wasn't used to having a guide, which is required by law on all ships touring the islands. We swam with the sea lions – who are so tame that they come and play with you in the waters – stared at the birds and the animals, and then relaxed in sun-soaked satiety in the afternoon and around mealtimes. Forget adventure tourism – this was decadence.

Getting to the islands no longer being a matter of turning up and looking around, as it was in 1835, I knew that I would be limited in what I could see of the archipelago. During my stay I visited Isabela, Floreana and San Cristóbal – of the islands which Darwin explored – as well as Española (Hood), Santa Fé and Plaza Sur. The animals were entrancing and unique: the blue- and red-footed boobies, with their bizarre courtship rituals and garish feet; the waved albatrosses on Española, with their enormous wingspans and their ponderous, sweeping, wandering flight when they launched themselves from a cliff; the angel and parrot fish near Devil's Crown off Floreana, twinkling luminously down under the seas, hiding in the shadow of coral; the huge and cautious iguanas on Plaza and Santa Fé, prehistoric enough to make you certain that dinosaurs once existed; the unique marine iguanas, the only sea-going iguanas in the world. The wildlife was very special, but there are countless natural history books written about the Galápagos by people far better qualified than me, so I shall not expatiate for long. Two of the animals, though, fascinated me particularly.

The waved albatrosses are extraordinary for nesting virtually exclusively on Española Island. Other than a very few nesting pairs on the Islas de la Plata in Ecuador, these birds are to be found on no other piece of land in the world. Their wings are brown, their heads a creamy yellow colour. Their eyes are hollow and frightening as a whale's, the great jellied mass of inquisitiveness staring at you circumspectly as you watch them. What I found intriguing about these birds – about all albatrosses, in fact – is that they mate for life and then, when one partner dies, the other follows into oblivion.

'Out of grief,' explained my guide.

The marine iguanas were my other favourites, or at least one particular brood of them: the marine iguanas on Floreana, Española and San Cristóbal. The Galápagos marine iguanas are all a charcoal black colour except for those on these three islands, which are streaked with splashes of deep red. All the iguanas live by eating seaweed, and it is thought that the red colouring in these iguanas is due to a type of plankton found only in the Humboldt current, which washes the shores of these three southern islands. The total interdependence of species in a very localized ecosystem is perfectly exemplified by these marine iguanas.

The trip was thoroughly enjoyable, and yet I felt that I wanted to do something more adventurous on the Galápagos. The end of this expedition should not have been about sitting on a tour and staring at animals. For, after all, this is not what Darwin did. If I had been clambering over the islands and discovering the wildlife for myself, that would have been fine. But you can't do that any more. I was stuck with the boat and the special walkways created for visitors.

There had to be a more fitting way of finishing my journey. When I returned to Puerto Ayora, I visited the Charles Darwin Research Station, responsible, together with the National Park authorities, for the monitoring and protection of species on the Galápagos. In the grounds of the Research Station were four fully grown tortoises who had once been pets of islanders. Since it was not known from which islands they had originally come, they were in a special rocky arena which you could enter, approaching to within centimetres of them.

I longed to see the tortoises in the wild, at least to be able to achieve this, as Darwin had. Yet their numbers have been completely decimated. Of the fourteen species referred to by Lawson, three are extinct, there is only one member of another ('Lonesome George', as he is known, from Pinta Island) and five are endangered; only five species are considered safe. Before I saw the tortoises in their enclosure, I had been reading about the prospects of the wild tortoises that are left. The largest congregation were on Isabela's Alcedo volcano, yet even these were under threat from the feral goats of the region, which were eating through Isabela's scanty vegetation at an alarming rate.

Seeing the tortoises here at Puerto Ayora, and reading of this threat, I decided to go to Isabela and try to find some of the last wild specimens that are left. There was a small town, Puerto Villamil, on the island, and a boat was leaving the next day. Instead of setting out across the South Seas for Tahiti, like Darwin, this was the end of my journey. I would return to Guayaquil, take a bus to Colombia, and return from Bogotá to London ten days after leaving the islands.

But before I did this, I would have one last effort at reliving Darwin's journey. He had set foot on Isabela, and now I would follow him there.

II

I should think it would be difficult to find in any other part of the world, an island situated within the tropics, and of such considerable size (namely 75 miles long), so sterile and incapable of supporting life.

Charles Darwin on Isabela

From the swell out to sea, I saw Puerto Villamil. A line of weather-beaten palms and mangroves protected the town from ululating winds, but the place itself looked uninspiring – just a film of concrete scrabbling away at the sands on the shore.

It was a peaceful place.

The town was green and tropical. You could hack coconuts off palms in the streets and suck out the sweet juice. No one cared, since the coconuts were ubiquitous. Gaudy blooms hung on houses and in the town square. The outskirts were verdant, as the town elapsed into a succession of farms which headed into the highlands in the interior.

Villamil was the sort of town where you saw the same faces every day. You probably never said more than 'Hello' to them, but this was enough to make them your friends. And sometimes, people would even stop you in the street and ask you where you were from. That was how I met Juan.

I was strolling through the town on my first day there, wondering how I could reach Alcedo and see the tortoises. The only recognized tour guide had told me that it was impossible to reach Alcedo, that the only accessible volcano was Sierra Negra. But I was determined to give it a try, and as I walked through a dusty street I bumped into Juan.

'Whoa!' he shouted when he saw me. 'A *gringo*! What's a *gringo* doing in Puerto Villamil? Most of them stay over on Santa Cruz.'

'Well,' I said, 'I've come over here on a mission.'

'A mission,' he nodded, wisely, as if understanding me completely. He was a lean man, and took irrepressible delight in life. He found it impossible to take anything seriously – except the most serious things of all – and invariably, after we had been talking for a while, he would collapse into chuckles.

I told him that I wanted to walk to Alcedo.

'Alcedo,' he said, and laughed. 'Hee, hee. *Éste* Tobías! That's a long way, *amigo*.'

'Is it possible?'

'Oh, we can walk there,' he said. 'It's just that it'll take us a while.'

'How long?'

'Six days, perhaps. There and back.'

'That's OK,' I said.

'The only problem will be the water. There's nowhere to find water, so we'll have to carry enough for six days.'

'Right.'

'And all our food,' he said.

'Right.'

'Perhaps we can get a donkey.'

Juan went to ask a man about a donkey; but the man was unhappy.

'He says that the land's too rough for the donkey, that he'll injure himself.'

'What's so rough about it?' I asked.

'Well, there's a lot of lava.'

That didn't sound too bad. I had dealt with bogs and deserts and the Andes, so surely lava would be feasible.

'Is it difficult to walk across the lava?' I asked him.

'No,' he said reassuringly. 'The lava won't be a problem. What I'm really worried about is the vegetation on the other side of Sierra Negra. I'm going to borrow a couple of machetes to hack our way through it.'

And so we spent two days preparing our journey towards the tortoises. Juan kept on telling me how beautiful they were, and convincing me that we would be able to reach them. I spent my time talking with him, and wandering through the lower slopes of Sierra Negra. They were incredibly lush, just how I'd imagined the Galápagos to be. The farms sprouted an incredible variety of fruits: avocados, papayas, bananas, oranges, pineapples, limes, mangoes, guavas – almost every tropical fruit you can imagine was there, bursting through the foliage of Isabela's highlands.

At last we were ready. We took a bus to the foot of the Sierra Negra crater, and then rode horses along a track towards the volcano. A thick *garúa* (mist) was hanging damply over the mountain, pressing moisture against our skins and shielding the island from view. It would have been wonderful to have been able to see the island stretching in golden magnificence to the sea, the shadows of other islands looming across the straits, and the small fleck of Villamil spreading along the shore, this tiny toehold of civilization across the vast island; but perhaps it was more special to see just the clinging mist, the grey glare of the imagination spreading through my mind, picturing greenery where there was barrenness, seeing abundance where there was absence – seeing what I wanted to see, and not what was there.

So we cantered through the gloom for an hour until we reached a rocky path where the horses' hooves could hammer no more. Now our own feet would beat down the brush and erode a path through to the volcanoes.

We had wanted to ride for as long as possible, to give ourselves the impression that the horses were doing the work, and not ourselves. Yet now that we dismounted we were still breathing heavily and the way had only just begun. There was much more still to hammer out.

We filled the water bottles from a spring, and tried to pack them into our bags. Yet once they were loaded, it was almost impossible to walk. We were carrying forty kilograms, what with the twenty litres of water each and the food, stove, tent and sleeping bags. The weight was so heavy on my shoulders that within minutes the straps of my rucksack had cut right through my shirt and were lacerating my shoulders. Juan's bags weren't big enough meanwhile, and so he had one rucksack on his back and carried the other on his neck. How we managed to walk at all was difficult to explain.

And yet we struggled on, stumbling over the rocks, almost buckling beneath the weight on our shoulders, this weight which was with us whether we felt it or not. We had to climb Sierra Negra because it was an obstacle in our way – surely the ground would be easier once we had passed it.

As we walked, Juan sang:

'¡Hay vida, hay vida en Jesús! ¡Hay vida, hay vida en Jesús!'

The song spurred on our legs. Perhaps we could soon be sprinting, if Juan and his singing had any say in the matter.

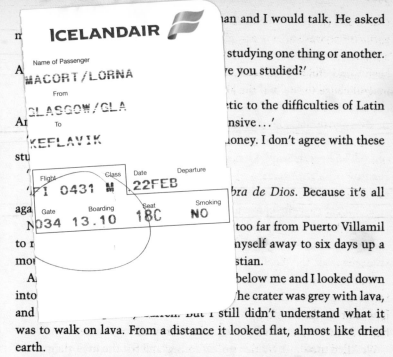

…an and I would talk. He asked

…studying one thing or another.

…e you studied?'

…tic to the difficulties of Latin

…nsive…'

…oney. I don't agree with these

…*bra de Dios*. Because it's all

…too far from Puerto Villamil

…nyself away to six days up a

…stian.

…below me and I looked down

…he crater was grey with lava,

…still didn't understand what it was to walk on lava. From a distance it looked flat, almost like dried earth.

'*Mira*, Tobías. It's the second oldest crater in the world after the Ngorongoro in Tanzania.'

There are five main volcanoes on Isabela: Ecuador, Wolff, Darwin, Alcedo and Sierra Negra. Volcán Ecuador is furthest north, Sierra Negra furthest south. And like a great map of age and wisdom, the age of the volcanoes is geographically determined, Sierra Negra being the oldest and Ecuador being the youngest. Like an imbecilic young man fighting with his grandfather's tremendous learning and wisdom, so Ecuador fights with Sierra Negra, scoffing from a distance, steaming with resentment that the greatest wisdom and wonder is always further south, that when the mass of civilization comes to an end, land becomes Patagonia, and then the wisdom crosses the South Seas to the last unclaimed mass on earth, Antarctica, further south still, unconquered, the last bastion of life.

So says Sierra Negra: Once we have conquered Antarctica we will be on the verge of the cataclysm, for in the south is wisdom.

Ecuador: What do you mean in the south lies wisdom? I see you in the south, and I do not see wisdom. Push on, that we can conquer every last shred of earth.

Sierra Negra: You do not see or hear wisdom, but that is because you are blind and deaf. I tell you, in the south lies wisdom.

Ecuador: Why take the word of an old man of the island like you? You are on the verge of death already.

And Sierra Negra laughs, coughs and splutters his steam; only quickly finds that he cannot continue, that the will is gone, that all he sees is cloud. So be it, he says, I have lived my life, and if they would die – so be it.

We walked past the crater and came to a giant spreading lemon tree, the last tree before the lava fields. For a few hundred metres still we passed through vestiges of life: brush and guava trees, a few lizards lying in wait for the sun. But the sun would not be penetrating the *garúa* today.

The vegetation gave way to cacti and prickly pear trees clinging to the lava; and then, within 200 metres, these too were gone. We walked slowly onto a barren bed of fragmented lava, and could see no plants in front of us at all. There was no *garúa* lower down the mountain, and I could see the island all the way to the great bulk of Alcedo, perhaps fifty kilometres away. I was looking out for the vegetation of which Juan had warned me, but all I saw was lava. Lava as far as I could see.

Juan led me to the active crater of Volcán Chico, and then we surveyed the route towards Alcedo. Our plan had been to cross down the other side of the island to the bay, and then follow the coastline as far as Alcedo, which we would then ascend. But there was nothing but lava. The lava was barren as a desert, grey as the mist, dangerous as death itself. On the inside of the crater, there were some ferns still clinging precariously to life, but the future beyond the ferns was lifeless. I could not even see three cacti between here and Alcedo.

'But don't worry about the lava,' I heard Juan saying in my mind. 'It's the vegetation that I'm worrying about.'

He sat high on a promontory above the crater of Volcán Chico, looking out over the barren plains.

'I'm thinking,' he told me. 'I have to reflect, or else it will be dangerous.'

'Dangerous?'

'Yes, there's a lot of fragile pumice stone down there. There are many air holes beneath the smooth lava, which can easily shatter with a man's weight.'

'Right,' I said.

Vegetation would have been a friend compared to the lifelessness before us. The abundance and glorious exuberance among the farms below was only a distant thought now. Yet it had only been hours before that we had been cantering between the guava trees towards the volcano. How quickly things had changed: how quickly the sterility had crept up on us, in devilish greedy silence, ready to claim as much of the island as it could. I had not even seen it until I realized that my next step would throw me in among it. Of course, we could have turned back, yet I had set out my stall to cross the lava, and my foolish pride would not see me turn back until I had at least tried to reach the tortoises.

'OK,' said Juan. 'Let's have a go.'

Below the crater of Volcán Chico was a scree slope, which we slid down until we had reached the lava bed. As well as the pumice stone full of air bubbles there was a second type of lava, a bed of red rocks constituted of lava exploded by the sheer heat of the last volcanic activity. The rocks were so sharp that the slightest touch of skin against them caused a deep cut; it was as if every pore in them contained an acid pincer. My shoes gave me no protection above the anklebone against the rocks, so my ankles received a fearful mauling. Meanwhile, with our ridiculously heavy packs, we could easily have overbalanced and mangled ourselves completely with the fall.

So I preferred the smoother pumice stone, although this was even more dangerous. The surface had been warped and smoothed into thick grey ridges and apparently clean sheets of rock. But this surface was so thin that people had been killed walking across it.

'The holes are sometimes fifteen metres deep.'

'What?'

'Oh yes,' he said. 'There was an Ecuadorian army expedition about fifteen years ago that tried to cross the Perry Isthmus [the narrowest part of Isabela]. About 400 of them set out but it was a disaster. Twenty of them died.'

'Died?'

'Yes. The red lava ripped their army boots to shreds, and then some of them couldn't walk on. Of those that did go on, many of them fell through the pumice stone. They had to send in a helicopter to rescue them.'

I later had this story confirmed by another friend in the islands. So Juan was trying to take me to Alcedo with forty kilograms of extra weight, across a section of the island which was notorious for being lethally dangerous. At this moment, the enterprise began to seem a little foolish.

'So,' I said, 'do you have much experience of walking across this pumice stone?'

'Yes,' he said. 'You can generally tell the safer places to tread by the colour of the rock. Step exactly where I do, or you'll be in trouble.'

'Is it all dangerous?'

'Some of it is and some of it isn't. Right now, we're in danger.'

This did not inspire confidence. We were on a piece of pumice stone that creaked as you crossed it. Sometimes Juan would stamp at a piece of weak lava until it splintered and revealed a yawning hole beneath. We performed tortuous zigzags to avoid danger areas, but it was still a perilous performance. Then we came to some more pumice stone and I put my foot through an air hole that was over a metre deep.

'Whoa,' said Juan. 'You were lucky there. That could have been much deeper!'

'I could have broken my ankle.'

'Yep.'

He looked out towards Alcedo, and a haze came over his eyes.

'Lava, lava, lava,' he said. 'It's going to be like this all the way to Alcedo.'

We couldn't go on this way. It was suicide. Even if neither of us slipped up, the going was so tremendously slow over the torturing terrain that we would run out of water long before we made it there and back.

This was my last chance: a year later Alcedo erupted, perhaps the final blow to these giant tortoises in this lethal terrain. There was no way I could see them on this route, no way to reach the last fortification of life on this barren land-mass. Even though it would have killed us, we were upset not to be able to make this journey. For death in this crypt would have been most fitting.

So we began to retrace our way leadenly back up through the lava. We had to find a clear patch of land where we could pitch a tent.

'Juan,' I said, as we went. 'You've lived with a lot of tourists.'

'Yes.'

'Am I very disorganized?'

'Yes,' he said; and then after a pause: 'Disorganized, and *very* dirty.'

We both roared with laughter, since neither of us cared.

After a while more, we found our way to a spread of fragmented flint which was smooth enough for camping. We slung our huge weights down, and lay exhausted in the desert, not speaking for a while. A late afternoon sun had fallen belatedly across the lava fields, but it had not cleared the *garúa* higher up. The sky glared dark, then lightened. The light danced over the surreal emptiness of the lava, freezing it still, lunar, absurd; like a photograph of living death.

'I'm not sure that your family will recognize you when you return,' he said.

'I don't know. It will be very difficult for me to be the same person there as I am here,' I said. 'I change my character with my language; I think we all do that.'

'Perhaps. But the language can't take your spirit away. That's what will count.'

'Life is very different there,' I said.

'God is life. There is a prophet for the modern age, and he tells the truth: William Marrion Branham. Do you know him, Tobías?'

'No.'

'He says that there are many religious sects in the world today, but that they all hide the word of God. God is there, but hidden. There are very many intelligent, erudite men, but they have failed to grasp the word of God. Do you see that?'

'I don't know.'

'Darwin. He was a very intelligent man. He said that this was such an animal, this other was another type of animal, he defined things, well, he said all sorts of things. But was he a wise man, Tobías?'

'An intelligent man, but not a wise one?'

'Perhaps. He thought he could think his way to understanding. But how can something finite understand something infinite? How could the mind ever understand the beauty of God? What do you think, Tobías?'

'I don't know.'

'It is better to say that. It is better. Only God can know.'

He was either a very wise man, or a very foolish one. We had walked into the lava beds, and that had been foolishness; and he spoke of God in the same, half-crazed, manic way in which we had walked into the lava. Sometimes we would plunge into silence for an hour or more, and then Juan would stop and speak of God. He would let his packs rest against his legs, his brow gleaming with beads of sweat, his eyebrows framed convex, his face speaking earnestness – then he would talk, and talk.

'Come on,' I said to him as he talked to me now. 'Why don't we try to make it back up to Volcán Chico? It's more sheltered for us there.'

So we heaved on our packs and struggled up the lava again. The volcanoes were scarred in brilliant colours with the flashes of the evening sun lighting up their minerals. There was a lot of sulphur, and some of the rocks were bright yellow. As we walked up the steepest slope of all, which culminated in a plunge into one of the most cavernous craters I had seen, a rainbow began to form, colours spirited from the grey nothingness of the mists by the magic of the Galápagos: a perfect, complete rainbow, curving in a complete arc from the highest crater down to the lava fields.

'Look,' I said to Juan, and gestured at the dallying film of light.

'Oh yes,' said Juan. 'That's the most beautiful rainbow I've ever seen. It's very special. A sign from God. Scientists will say that it's caused by light refracting through the water, by this that and the other – but it's a sign from God, Tobías.'

I didn't know what to think any more.

I spent two more days with Juan. We got on incredibly well. We were both very clumsy. I would stumble and flounder my way over the lava fields as we tried (and failed) to find another route down to the coast. Juan would drop things, leave things behind and sing irrepressibly. On our third night he tinkered with the petrol stove, and it promptly exploded when we tried to cook dinner, nearly setting our tent alight.

'Now that *would* have been a disaster,' Juan joked, as we tried to clear up the mess and find something that we could eat without cooking.

The sterility of Isabela will live with me for a long time. I would never have imagined that such a huge island, whose northern end passes through the equator, could be so utterly lifeless. The only sign of life I came across on the lava fields was the dried-out skeleton of a lizard, perfectly preserved, its bones bleached virginal white, clearly untouched since death. The island itself was the same – dead and untouched. Distance was a hazy phenomenon. You could see several of the other islands, and they seemed near; yet they rose from haze, and so you could only imagine what they were really like.

The imagination could have fun on Isabela: you could paint a picture in which you would like to live. The lava fields were as dead and featureless as the deserts in northern Chile, and yet they were within walking distance of lush vegetation and one of the most important ecosystems on the planet. Life and sterility were together at last, dressing as past and future, bride and bridesmaid, eternity and time; moving from one to another, like north to south and life to death, as the seconds expired with our wheezing breaths.

Now this journey is dying as I climb back to Volcán Chico, ready to look over the immense barren plains one last time.

And I am talking to Juan, and he is telling me about God and prayer. As I am thinking of the past, my memories are kindly killing me. For as they foreshorten my life so do they also sweeten it, as I remember what it was like to travel through these thousand lives, and live by stories and the luck of legends, and the will of fate protecting me against the threat of inertia. And I am wondering about the future, wondering where I can go but down to those same lava fields, where I played dead and dreamt of life one last time.

I would go back, but this journey must end. In the end will be the beginning, and the circle closing around my memories of a time when the death of the lava fields was beaten back by the humanity of Juan and me talking and laughing and singing among the lifelessness.

Now, I am thinking about that journey, and its progression appears to me in all the true indeterminacy of perception, so much so that I can believe that it was something which I underwent. It marches leadenly through my mind, the greatest symphony of them all, a symphony which we helped to compose and which extemporizes for us even in the depths of sleep, and death. Even in death, even amid the lava fields, the beauty of the journey blinks its stark truth at me, and my heart collapses into the withering folds of its arms.

And I am listening to my journey's song: nothing true is known. I hear the music, again and again, in the vivid pictures of this dream which will always be able to reclaim me. The dream of my journey is sound, and light. And in its lambent reflection, resting tantalizingly in my mind's eye whenever the present falls apart, I see Juan staring at me with fervour and passionate religious love, begging me to listen to the music one last time.

I am looking at the bag that Juan has taken out of his rucksack, the bag in which he keeps the petrol for his stove. It is one of those colourful bags made high in the Andes, that can be bought all over the world now that culture is global. I follow each of the innumerable strands that have been woven with such intricate and timeless care. Each one is bright and beautiful, and each bends in infinite directions. I try to follow one, and then another, but each time my eyes fail and the strands mesh with one another and become indistinguishable.

The bag is so beautiful; the colours so perfect from a distance, and such an immense contrast with the lifeless lava fields. I will try again, and this time I will follow one particular thin thread through its inestimable turns and corners and dangers, as it touches the other strands but never quite merges with them. This strand is unique, and yet could not exist were it not for the others.

I follow the colours again and again, and each time I seem to see the origin of the beauty of Juan's bag, but then my eyes tire and I realize that I cannot. My mind is frayed with the bewildering complexity of the threads, a labyrinth of their own. For they all seem beautiful in themselves, and yet I can see none of them in their entirety. They become lost in a frightening haze of their own, a haze which defines reality.

Then, my eyes swimming in the haze, I see them more clearly. The colours are brighter, now that they do not need to be analysed and stripped to their stripes and known absolutely. Being brighter, they are even more beautiful. Transcendental, almost. Forgetting about the particular strands, it is in the generality that I wonder.

So then perhaps I should step back and take a general look, without staring too hard at any of the details. Then I may be able to see the beauty of the colours, and have no need to follow any of the strands, nor worry about the individual threads of the fabric, since it is the fabric itself which is beautiful.

Yes, I tell myself, as I walk on with Juan, singing and laughing and playing the music of my dream, walking away from the volcano, back from the volcano, returning to the lush vegetation below: some time, I must look at that bag again.

ACKNOWLEDGEMENTS

This journey would have been impossible without the help of thousands of people. I would especially like to thank the following:

In the UK: my parents and my sister; my main sponsors Heineken (for making it all possible), the North Face, Damart, Supreme Plastics, Crooke's Healthcare, Peter Oakley, Sir Robert and Lady Felicity Waley-Cohen, the Hyde Park School of Riding, Nigel and Shane Winser, Jeffrey Frost, Jorge Tagle, Rosie Swale and John Labouchère.

In Uruguay: Mac and Lucía Herrera (for unbounded hospitality), María Ieuwdiukov de Nín, Dr Gonzalo Chiarino, Laura Chiarino, Dr Guillermo Lockhart, Carlos Lopez, Val Isaacs, Juan Amorín, Roberto Piríz, the Laggiard family.

In Argentina: Don Felipe-Juan Ballester (for two horses), Carlos Dowdall, Oneto Miguens, Roberto Mentana, Shami Calles, Angeles Ballester, Fernando Micuguy, the Colombi family, Jorge Sánchez, Marcos and Malala Oliva Day, Tino Peralta and the navy in Puerto Deseado.

In the Falkland (Malvinas) Islands: Kay McCallum, John Smith, Mel Lloyd and the army at MPA.

In Chile: my friend Leslie Solíz, her mother Susana, and her sisters Karen and Cynthia (for their enduring hospitality and emotional support); the Carabineros de Chile at the following police posts – Tirúa, Cañete, the *sub-comisaría montada* at Lomas Verde (Concepción), Dichato, Vegas de Itata, Cobquecura, Putú, Vichuquén, Pichasca, Río Hurtado, Vicuña, El Molle, the *tenencía carreterra* Elqui and La Higuera; *teniente* Carlos Dietert, the captain and crew of the PSG *Micalvi*, Gonzalo, Maco, Cristián, Don Gastón, little Macarena, Sandra, Gloría, Jorge, Gonzalo Maza and Alfredo Sepúlveda, the Trujillo family in Punta Arenas, the *padre*, Berlin and everyone in Litueche, and *los diablos* Juan-Carlos and Antonio.

When it came to the exhaustive process of writing, I was very fortunate with readers. Mike Dewey, Emily Fowke, Charlotte and Christopher Green, Tom Ground, Janak Jani, Marcos Oliva Day and Helen

Parr all made many suggestions which made this book easier to read. I must also thank my agent, Simon Trewin, whose confidence was critical in getting the project off the ground, and my editor, Cassia Joll, without whose shrewd suggestions this book would be infinitely less enjoyable.

I am also grateful to the following publishers for permission to reprint extracts from books to which they hold the rights:

As reproduced by permission of Hodder & Stoughton Ltd., extracts from E. Lucas Bridges' book, *Uttermost Part of the Earth*.

Penguin, for permission to quote from R.C. Lewontin's *The Doctrine of DNA: Biology as Ideology*.

W.W. Norton, for permission to quote from Stephen Jay Gould's *The Mismeasure of Man*.

Küme Dungu, for permission to quote in translation from *El Conocimiento de Los Mapuches*.

While every effort has been made to trace copyright holders, in two cases this has proved impossible. Omissions drawn to the author's attention will be rectified in any future edition.

Finally, a few notes about the text. Since it is difficult for a European man in rural South America to achieve any real friendship with women, I hope that female readers will forgive me for the greater number of men than women that appear in this book as a result. I have translated all conversations from Spanish into English – 99 per cent were in Spanish – except where a phrase is particularly idiomatic; in these cases I have put the Spanish first, and then an English translation.

Wherever I went I felt that people would look out for me. I hope that their unpretentious and natural goodwill permeates this book, and my own behaviour in years to come.

This book is dedicated to Emily.

NOTES

ONE: *Urban Latin America: Rio and Montevideo*
pp. 1–34

None.

TWO: *Across Uruguay*
pp. 35–70

1 As Hudson suggested in *The Naturalist in La Plata* (Dover Publications, 1988), Darwin may have been a little credulous here. The first answer sounds more like a joke than anything else; and the second could be the result of the *gaucho*'s laconic nature. Hudson suggests his meaning to have been that his horse was stolen, and that he could not afford another.
2 Quoted in *Our Benevolent Feudalism*, W.J. Ghent (London, Macmillan 1902).
3 Stephen Jay Gould, *The Mismeasure of Man* (revised and expanded edn, New York, Norton 1996), p. 54.

THREE: *Buenos Aires and the Pampas*
pp. 71–112

1 W.H. Hudson, *The Naturalist in La Plata* (Dover Publications, 1988).
2 Ibid.
3 W.H. Hudson, *Idle Days in Patagonia* (London, Dent, 1984), p. 4.

FOUR: *Hotfoot in Patagonia*
pp. 113–154

1 Ernst Mayr, *The Growth of Biological Thought* (Cambridge, Mass, Belknap Press, 1982).
2 Richard Dawkins, *The Selfish Gene* (Oxford, OUP, 1978).
3 R.C. Lewontin, *The Doctrine of DNA: Biology as Ideology* (Harmondsworth, Penguin 1993).

4 Ibid, p. 87.
5 Ibid, p. 103.
6 W.H. Hudson, *Idle Days in Patagonia*, op. cit., pp. 199–200.
7 Ibid, p. 213.

FIVE: *In the Bowels of the Earth*
pp. 155–207

1 Official Report 1239, 3 April 1982, cc. 650, 667.
2 W.H. Hudson, *Idle Days in Patagonia* (London, Dent, 1984), p. 193.
3 E. Lucas Bridges, *Uttermost Part of the Earth* (London, Century, 1987), p. 135.
4 Ibid. p. 34. The Bridges family knew the Yámana not as Fuegians but Yahgans.
5 Ibid, p. 63.
6 Ibid, p. 35.
7 Ibid, p. 35.
8 Thomas Bridges, *Yámana–English: A Dictionary of the Speech of Tierra del Fuego* (Mödling, Austria, 1933).

SIX: *Chiloé and the Chonos Archipelago*
pp. 209–234

1 The story of a Chilote – an inhabitant of Chiloé – translated by the author from *Folklore, Mitas y Leyendas del Archipielago de Chiloé*, by Isabel Vidal Miranda (SCL, 1979), pp. 55–56.
2 This story can be found in *Casos de Brujos de Chiloé* by Umiliana Cárdenas Saldivia (SCL, 1989), pp. 75–76; Cárdenas is a teacher who collects her stories from all corners of the archipelago.
3 From *Casos de Brujos de Chiloé*, op. cit., pp. 46–47.

SEVEN: *The Southern Chilean Coast*
pp. 235–282

1 Alonso de Ercilla y Zuñiga, *La Araucana*, Canto XXXII (Madrid, Isaias Lerner, 1993).
2 Quoted in *Pu Mapuche Tañi Kimün/El Conocimiento de los Mapuches*, Pedro Aguilera Milla et al. (Temuco, Küme Dungu, 1987), p. 3.

EIGHT: *To the Flowering Desert*
pp. 283–330

None.

NINE: *Journey's End: The Galápagos*
pp. 331–355

None.

BIBLIOGRAPHY

The abbreviation SCL stands for Santiago de Chile.

Abeijón, Asencio, *Memorias de un Carrero Patagónico*, Buenos Aires, Galerna, 1973.
— *Recuerdos de Mi Primer Arreo*, Buenos Aires, Galerna, 1975.
— *Caminos y Rastrilladas Borrosas*, Buenos Aires, Galerna, 1983.
Aguilera Milla, Pedro, et al., *Pu Mapuche Tañi Kimün/El Conocimiento de Los Mapuches*, Temuco, Küme Dungu, 1987.
Aldunate del Solar, Carlos, *Cultura Mapuche*, SCL, Departamento de Extensión Cultural del Ministerio de Educación, 1978.
Armstrong, Patrick, *Darwin's Desolate Islands: A Naturalist in the Falklands, 1833–1834*, Chippenham, Picton, 1992.
Aúza, Néstor, *La Patagonia Mágica*, Buenos Aires, Ediciones Marymar, 1977.
Barbarovic, Ivo, et al., *Campenisado Mapuche y Procesos Socio-Económicos Regionales*, SCL, Academia de Humanismo Cristiano, 1987.
Barlow, Nora (ed.), *Charles Darwin and the Voyage of the Beagle*, London, Pilot Press, 1945.
— *The Autobiography of Charles Darwin, 1809–1882*, London, Collins, 1958.
Bengoa, José and Valenzuela, Eduardo, *Economía Mapuche*, SCL, PAS, 198?.
Berry, R.J. (ed.), *Evolution in the Galápagos Islands*, London, Academic Press for the Linnaean Society of London, 1984.
Bilton, Michael and Kosminsky, Peter, *Speaking Out*, London, Deutsch, 1987.
Bowlby, John, *Charles Darwin*, London, Hutchinson, 1990.
Bowler, Peter, *Charles Darwin*, Oxford, Blackwell, 1990.
Brent, Peter, *Charles Darwin*, London, Heinemann, 1981.
Bridges, E. Lucas, *Uttermost Part of the Earth*, London, Century, 1987. First published 1948.
Bridges, Thomas, *Yámana–English: A Dictionary of the Speech of Tierra Del Fuego*, Mödling, Austria, 1933. Privately printed.
Browne, Janet, *Charles Darwin: Voyaging*, London, Random House, 1995.
Burkhardt, F. and Smith, S., et al. (eds), *The Correspondence of Charles Darwin, Vols 1–9 (1821–61)*, Cambridge, Cambridge University Press, 1983–94.
Campbell, John, *In Darwin's Wake*, Shrewsbury, Waterline, 1997.
Caplan, Arthur J. and Jennings, Bruce, *Darwin, Marx and Freud: Their Influence on Moral Theory*, New York and London, Plenum, 197?.

Cárdenas, Renato and Hall, Catherine G., *Chiloé, Manual del Pensamiento Mágico y la Creencia Popular*, Valdivia, El Kultrún, 1989.

Cárdenas Saldivia, Umiliana, *Casos de Brujos de Chiloé*, SCL, Editorial Universitaria, 1989.

Chatwin, Bruce, *In Patagonia*, London, Cape, 1977.

Chatwin, Bruce and Theroux, Paul, *Patagonia Revisited*, London, Cape, 1985.

Chávez, Fermín, *Testamentos de San Martín y Rosas y la Protesta de Rosas*, Buenos Aires, Theoría, 1975.

Clissold, Stephen, *Chilean Scrapbook*, London, The Cresset Press, 1952.

Coña, Pascual, *Memorias de un Cacique Mapuche*, SCL, 1930.

Constable, Pamela and Valenzuela, Arturo, *Chile: A Nation of Enemies*, New York and London, Norton, 1991.

Danchev, Alex (ed.), *International Perspectives on the Falklands Conflict*, Basingstoke, Macmillan, 1992.

Darwin, Charles, *The Voyage of the Beagle*, Harmondsworth, Penguin, 1989. First published 1845.

— *The Origin of Species*, London, Senate, 1994. First published 1859.

— *The Descent of Man*, Princeton, NJ, Princeton University Press, 1981. First published 1872.

Davis, J., *The Falklands War*, Andover, 1982. Privately printed.

Dawkins, Richard, *The Selfish Gene*, Oxford, Oxford University Press, 1978.

— *The Blind Watchmaker*, Harmondsworth, Penguin, 1986.

— *River Out of Eden*, London, Weidenfeld & Nicolson, 1995.

— *Climbing Mount Improbable*, Harmondsworth, Penguin, 1996.

Del Carril, Bonifacio, *El Gaucho: Su Origen*, Buenos Aires, Emecé, 1993.

Desmond, Adrian and Moore, James, *Darwin*, Harmondsworth, Penguin, 1992.

Domeyko, Ignacio, *Excursión a las Cordillerras de Copiapó*, SCL, 1845.

Ercilla y Zuñiga, Alonso de, *La Araucana*, Madrid, Isaias Lerner, 1993. First published 1597.

Espinoza Vivar, Oswaldo, *Las Islas Malvinas son Argentinas*, Huancayo, Peru, Impr, 1984.

FitzRoy, Robert, *Narrative of the Surveying Voyages of His Majesty's Ships Adventure and Beagle Between the Years 1826 and 1836, Describing Their Exploration of the Southern Shores of South America, and the Beagle's Circumnavigation of the Globe*, Vol. II, London, Henry Colburn, 1839.

Freedman, Lawrence and Gamba-Stonehouse, Virginia, *Signals of War*, London, Faber & Faber, 1990.

Ghent, W.J., *Our Benevolent Feudalism*, London, Macmillan, 1902.

Gould, Stephen Jay, *Ever Since Darwin*, Harmondsworth, Penguin, 1980.

— *The Mismeasure of Man*, New York and London, Norton, 1996 – revised and expanded ed. first published 1981.

— *Hen's Teeth and Horse's Toes*, Harmondsworth, Penguin, 1984.

— *The Flamingo's Smile*, New York and London, Norton, 1985.

— *Wonderful Life*, Harmondsworth, Penguin, 1991.

— *Bully for Brontosaurus*, Harmondsworth, Penguin, 1992.

— *Eight Little Piggies*, Harmondsworth, Penguin, 1994.

— *Dinosaur in a Haystack*, London, Jonathan Cape, 1996.

— *Life's Grandeur*, London, Jonathan Cape, 1996.

Grupo Lumbre, *Poetas de Valparaíso*, Barcelona, Ediciones Rondas, 1979.

Hernández, José, *El Gaucho Martín Fierro*, Madrid, Castalia, 1995. First published 1874.

Holmberg, Adolfo, *Cree Ud. Que Los Ingleses Nos Devolverán Las Malvinas? Yo No*, Buenos Aires, Editorial Grandes Temas Argentinas, 1977.

Hudson, W.H., *The Naturalist in La Plata*, New York, Dover Publications, 1988. First published 1892.

— *Idle Days in Patagonia*, London, Dent, 1984. First published 1893.

Keynes, Richard Darwin (ed.), *Charles Darwin's Beagle Diary*, Cambridge, Cambridge University Press, 1988.

Kon, Daniel, *Los Chicos de la Guerra*, Buenos Aires, Galerna, 1982.

Knox-Johnston, Robin, *Cape Horn: A Maritime History*, London, Hodder & Stoughton, 1994.

Larrahona Kasten, Alfonso, *Cien Leyendas de Valparaíso*, Valparaíso, Ediciones Correo de la Poesía, 1986.

Lemée, Carlos, *Reflexiones Sobre la Vida del Campo*, Buenos Aires, 1887.

Lewontin, R.C., *The Doctrine of DNA: Biology as Ideology*, Harmondsworth, Penguin, 1993.

Løvtrup, Søren, *Darwinism: The Refutation of a Myth*, London, Croom Helm, 1987.

Lynch, John, *Argentine Dictator: Juan Manuel de Rosas 1829–1852*, Oxford, Clarendon, 1981.

MacCann, William, *Two Thousand Miles Ride Through the Argentine Provinces*, 2 vols, London, 1853.

Madsen, Andreas, *La Patagonia Vieja*, Buenos Aires, Galerna, 1975.

Manzilla, José A., *Malvinas: Hambre y Coraje*, Buenos Aires, Abril, 1987.

Markham, C.R. (ed. and trans.), *Narratives of the Voyages of Pedro Sarmiento de Gamboa to the Straits of Magellan*, London, 1895.

Mayr, Ernst, *The Growth of Biological Thought*, Cambridge, Mass. and London, Belknap Press, 1982.

Meehan, John, *With Darwin in Chile*, London, Muller, 1967.

Mellersh, H.E.L., *FitzRoy of the Beagle*, London, Rupert Hart-Davis, 1968.

Montecino, Sonia, *Historias de Vida de Mujeres Mapuche*, SCL, Centro de Estudios de la Mujer, 1985.

Moorehead, Alan, *Darwin and the Beagle*, Harmondsworth, Penguin, 1971.

Perry, R., *Key Environments: Galápagos*, Oxford, Pergamon, 1984.

Quesada, E., *La Época de Rosas*, Montevideo, Tall. Graz. Percinulle, 1923.

Rodríguez Molas, Ricardo, *Historia Social del Gaucho*, Buenos Aires, Centro Editor de América Latina, 1982.

Swale, Rosie, *Back to Cape Horn*, London, Collins, 1986.

Theroux, Paul, *The Old Patagonian Express*, London, Hamish Hamilton, 1979.

Tschiffely, A.F., *Southern Cross to Pole Star, Tschiffely's Ride*, London, Century, 1982. First published 1932.

Vidal Miranda, Isabel, *Folklore, Mitas y Leyendas del Archipielago de Chiloé*, SCL, 1979.

Wheeler, Sara, *Travels in a Thin Country*, London, Little, Brown, 1994.

Williamson, Edwin, *The Penguin History of Latin America*, Harmondsworth, Penguin, 1992.

Wilson, E. O., *Sociobiology: The New Synthesis*, Cambridge, Mass., Belknap Press, 1975.

Wittmer, Margret, *Floreana*, London, Michael Joseph, 1961.